STEVE HILTON is co-founder and CEO of Crowdpac, a Silicon Valley political tech start-up, and a visiting professor at Stanford University. He was formerly senior adviser to Prime Minister David Cameron and played a leading role in the modernisation of the Conservative Party and in the implementation of its government reform programme. Steve graduated from Oxford University in 1990 and now lives in California with his wife and young family.

SCOTT BADE is a researcher at the Freeman Spogli Institute of International Studies at Stanford University. He graduated from Stanford and lives in California.

JASON BADE lectures on social problem solving at Stanford Law School and is active in the impact investing space. He graduated from Stanford University and lives in California.

MORE HUMAN

DESIGNING A WORLD WHERE PEOPLE COME FIRST

STEVE HILTON

WITH SCOTT BADE AND JASON BADE

3 5 7 9 10 8 6 4 2

WH Allen, an imprint of Ebury Publishing,
20 Vauxhall Bridge Road,
London SW1V 2SA

WH Allen is part of the Penguin Random House group of companies
whose addresses can be found at global.penguinrandomhouse.com

Penguin
Random House
UK

First published by WH Allen in 2015

www.eburypublishing.co.uk

A CIP catalogue record for this book is available
from the British Library

HB ISBN 9780753556788
TPB ISBN 9780753557112

Designed by K Design, Winscombe, Somerset;
typeset by e-type, Aintree, Liverpool
Printed and bound in Great Britain by Clays Ltd, St Ives PLC

MIX
Paper from
responsible sources
FSC® C018179

Penguin Random House is committed to a sustainable future for our
business, our readers and our planet. This book is made from Forest
Stewardship Council® certified paper.

To Rohan

Roop!

CONTENTS

INTRODUCTION

On 9 June 2014, Jennifer Devereaux boarded a jetBlue flight from New York to Boston. She was travelling with her two young daughters. Everything seemed normal: the passengers found their seats, the announcements were made, the plane left the gate and moved towards the runway for take-off. But then it all started to go wrong. The captain announced that there had been a delay and the aircraft would have to wait on the tarmac for around forty-five minutes. Jennifer's three-year-old daughter announced that she needed to use the bathroom. Since they were just waiting around on the tarmac, Jennifer thought it would be fine to get up and take her daughter to the toilet – they were sitting just a few rows away.

Big mistake. As soon as she started getting up, a jetBlue cabin crew member zoomed up and yelled, with that special kind of rudeness we all know and love:

'Ma'am, you're going to have to sit down.'

'But I'm just taking my little girl to the restroom.'

'You need to sit down right now, the captain has the seat-belt sign switched on.'

'Please can you let us go? She's a three-year-old and she can't wait.'

'Ma'am, I'm ordering you to sit down and fasten your seat belts. You need to comply with my instruction.'

That was just the start.

After another half-hour or so, the poor little girl couldn't hold it any longer, and wet herself in her seat. Jennifer, upset and wanting to do anything to reduce her daughter's discomfort, called a crew member and asked if she could have something to mop up the mess – a cloth, some napkins, anything. The flight attendant walked off – and didn't come back. After a few minutes of waiting, Jennifer couldn't bear it any longer. She remembered she had a sweater in the overhead bin, and thought she could use that to dry her daughter's seat a little. So she stood up to open the bin and – you've guessed it – a crew member raced down the aisle and screamed at her to sit down. Jennifer explained that since no one from jetBlue had brought her anything she was just trying to get her sweater so she could mop things up and surely since they weren't even moving it would be OK to—

'It doesn't matter what it is, the seat-belt sign is on and you have to sit down right now!'

In disbelief – remember the plane was just sitting on the tarmac – Jennifer kept going, reaching for her sweater.

'That's enough, ma'am. Sit down now!'

Defeated, Jennifer did as she was told. You can imagine how she felt. And worse, how her poor little girl felt.

Then the captain's voice came over the intercom.

'Ladies and gentlemen, I'm afraid that we have a non-compliant passenger on board and we're going to have to return to the gate to remove them from the aircraft.'

That 'non-compliant' passenger was Jennifer, trying to look after her three-year-old daughter who needed to use the bathroom.

Rude, aggressive, lacking in compassion – even though, thanks to the last minute intervention of an off-duty pilot seated nearby, the flight crew finally relented and allowed Jennifer and her family to remain on board, jetBlue's behaviour towards that family was inhuman. Talking about it after the event, Jennifer said: 'Why can't we just treat each other with kindness and decency, like human beings?'[1]

It's a good question and one this book will try to answer. You could look at that story and say: well, that's just the way some of these airline employees behave. You see that kind of thing all over the place with officious bureaucratic-minded people. That's just life.

But it's not just life. Being inhuman is not the natural order of things. People don't instinctively behave that way: they're made to by the circumstances they're in and by the *structure* of the world around them. And being inhuman is not just about bad behaviour – it's actually a big part of our deepest problems. Economic problems: our efforts to end poverty; to deal with rising inequality; to make sure everyone has the chance to get a decent, well-paid job. Social problems: how our children grow up and are educated; how we organise the places we live and the health care we receive. Political problems too: the way we're governed and the way we make policy. We are designing and building a *world* that is inhuman. Government, business, the lives we lead, the food we eat, the way our children are brought up, the way we relate to the natural world around us ... it's all become too big and distant and impersonal. Inhuman.

In governments the world over, political leaders who mean well (and who are, if anything, under-appreciated for the good they do) preside, frustrated and impotent, over vast bureaucratic systems that routinely disappoint and leave citizens enraged that they can't control what affects their lives. The schools we send our children to; the hospitals that care for us when we're sick; the very food we eat – we've allowed these intimate things, that matter so much, to be provided by anonymous, distant, industrialised machines. Business, such an awesome vehicle for human ingenuity and interaction, has become dominated by a detached and unaccountable global elite who think that the solution to the social and environmental problems *they cause* is to fly to Davos and pontificate on 'panels' and in 'plenaries'. Technology, with its incredible power to liberate and educate, has become unhealthily fetishised as an end in itself while those who dare question its remorseless rise are dismissed as mad – or worse still, old-fashioned. Nature? Who cares, let's conquer another planet.

We're told: things are getting better, GDP is up! Big Government is on your side, along with Big Business and Big Energy and Big Food and Big Tech and Big Media, all giving us Big Savings! Big Value! But the problem is, we're not Big. We are quite small, actually. We tend to be happiest when we can relate to each other in a human way. We do best when things are organised on a human scale.

But size is not all that matters. 'Big' doesn't capture the whole story: it's false to say that big is always bad, or that small is always beautiful. Just look at a company like Airbnb, the website that allows people to rent out spare rooms, flats, or entire homes. It has enabled previously unimaginable new personal connections, showing that big is not always inhuman and that technology does not necessarily dehumanise. In fact technology can help us to be more human – think how the washing machine and other labour-saving devices allowed families to spend more time together. There's an even more significant point about technology. The information revolution is giving us untold power; people talk warily about 'Big Data', but the truth is that big data is flowing into our own hands, giving us the chance to make decisions and choices as never before.

For all these reasons – the problems and the opportunities – it's time for a real shake-up. We need to make the world *more human*.

This aim of this book is to kick-start the debate. I don't have all the answers, but at least let's ask the right questions. The book offers an argument, not a prescription, and it is not a comprehensive survey of every problem under the sun. I've focused on areas where I have the greatest knowledge and experience, and frankly, on the things I care about most. I know there are important things left out. Chapter 1 looks at government and politics and the need to change priorities – and systems of measurement – so that government focuses more on real people than abstract numbers. We need to change the way policy is made so those who make it understand the lives of those who experience it; change the structure and organisation of government so that it's closer to people; and change our politics so as to revitalise civic life.

Next I take aim at our schools, where industrialised processes for cramming knowledge into children's heads are churning out young people equipped for the last century, not the current one (and making them miserable in the process). In Chapter 3, I argue that the care has been ripped out of health care by bureaucracy and an obsession with 'efficiency' that undermines one of our most human instincts – looking after other people when they're not well. But we should also look after ourselves, an aim made more difficult by the mighty culinary-industrial complex: our taxpayer-subsidised factory food system, which I'll investigate in Chapter 4.

Corporate bureaucracy is a common theme in this book, and I address it directly in Chapter 5, looking at the hotly contested arguments over business and the role of capitalism in society. In Chapters 6 and 7 I take on the urgent topics of poverty and inequality and show how a more human way of looking at these problems – with a particular focus on families – could move us further forward than the somewhat sterile debates we've seen so far.

Children are humans too: that's Chapter 8. One of the most

profound disappointments from my time in government was seeing how the needs of children are undervalued. This may seem strange in an age when family life is celebrated, parenting websites abound, and the imperatives of 'child protection' trump all other concerns. But as I will argue, we're getting it completely wrong. We are blasé about the impact of technology on children's lives, and at the same time are undermining one of the most natural, human, and above all, developmentally important aspects of children's lives: play. Chapters 9 and 10 examine the world around us: the spaces we design for ourselves, and the way we relate to nature.

Throughout, we'll meet people who in their own way are making the world more human – extraordinary people you may not have heard of yet. Nadine Burke Harris is a San Francisco paediatrician in the vanguard of reshaping how we see the effect of adverse childhood experiences on children's life chances. Jamie Heywood is an engineer who has used his brother's tragic death to change the way we see medicine. Paul Willis has made pig farming ethical at large scale, and Jason Pittman is creating the classroom of the twenty-first century. We'll engage with some of the world's brightest minds who are helping lead the way to a more human future, like E. O. Wilson, perhaps our greatest living thinker on ecology, and Dieter Helm (my Oxford tutor) who is in the forefront of the movement to make our national accounting systems make sense. I'll also introduce some of the people I've been lucky enough to work with, both in California – like Sarah Stein Greenberg who taught me 'design thinking' at Stanford – and in the UK – like Rohan Silva, my closest friend and former colleague in government, now creating the world's most innovative creative work spaces; or Louise Casey, an amazing civil servant leading the charge in helping to turn around the lives of Britain's most troubled families.

Some people might say: 'What are you writing a book about this for? You had the chance to actually change things when you were in government in the UK.' That is true. For two years, I worked in Number 10 Downing Street as Senior Adviser to Prime Minister David Cameron and had the incredible privilege of being in a position to help implement policies and reforms that could tackle many of the problems addressed in this book – and you will find some of the lessons reflected in these pages. For the five years before that, I was part of the team that oversaw the development of the Conservative Party's political strategy and policy programme. And before that, with my firm Good Business, I spent years working on social and environmental issues from a business perspective.

So is this book, as some will suspect, basically just a list of all the 'crazy' things I wanted to do in government but they wouldn't let me? Well, yes, partly. But a much bigger part of *More Human* is based on the thinking I've done since leaving government, and reflecting on what I got wrong as well as what went right. In particular, the book conveys what I've learned as part of the incredible, entrepreneurial community at Stanford University in California, especially its renowned Institute of Design, or 'd.school'. At the d.school, students are taught to solve problems by starting with people: what they need, how they think, how they feel. Learning to teach there has been a transformational experience, and it has profoundly affected my point of view on almost everything. In Chapter 1, I look at how we might apply the d.school approach in government, but its principles of human-centred design are present in every chapter.

There's another important point to bear in mind, which makes the idea at the heart of this book more relevant and urgent than ever. In the last few decades, great advances in science have given us new insights about who we are as humans – how we think, feel and behave; and why. Neuroscience, social psychology, behavioural economics: work in these fields means we can now base our judgements about how to organise things much more soundly on what we scientifically know. These human insights don't just tell us more about humanity; they tell us that to make things more human is itself natural.

For example, evolutionary biology shows that in the course of human history, we have become ever more empathetic. Scientific and economic progress has in part been accompanied by an expanded consciousness of the experiences of fellow human beings. We have in some ways become more human, even as the world we have built for ourselves pushes in the other direction. The expansion of our capacity to communicate and collaborate with each other has enhanced our capacity to understand each other's realities. As we've got to know one another better, we've extended basic protections and rights to ever-wider swathes of humanity.[2]

While our capacity for empathy has evolved, it has always been one of our defining traits as humans. And there are other human values that define us and for which we should strive. Not everything can be quantified by data or measured by chemical responses. There are certain things that we simply accept make life worth living: good health, happiness, beauty, fulfilment, passion, laughter, love, joy. These are the things that dignify our lives and which every individual deserves the chance to experience. Another key part of our humanity lies in our differences. Fulfilment in life will come through different things for different people – whether it's faith, literature, work, friendship, music, children … even baking a perfect loaf of bread. The burden of society – specifically of government – is to provide the greatest chance for us to find what life means and then live it to the full.

Society has another burden, though: to protect us from and help us to overcome our inherent flaws, the troubling aspects of our nature. For all the good of humanity there are plenty of impulses that are harmful: traits like avarice, malice, and intolerance. There is evil, and terrible cruelty. These too are human, and while we shouldn't forget that, we should do all we can to help people avoid the worst of their demons, especially when their weaknesses hurt others.

We are both individual and social creatures. We work better, as I will argue throughout this book, in communities, families and social networks, and on small-scale levels. So how then, if human nature is naturally inclined to be human, have so many of the institutions that shape our lives become so big, and distant, and removed from the human scale?

Think of it in historical terms. (Spoiler alert: for those of you familiar with the speeches of David Cameron – especially the 'early, funny ones' as Woody Allen might have described them – this is an argument you will recognise.) Before the Industrial Revolution, politics, government, and business were almost entirely local – because they had to be. Rulers simply did not have the information and reach to make decisions about individual people's lives or run centralised bureaucracies. Local governors or feudal lords were delegated almost all sovereign power, answering only nominally to the far-off capital. Bureaucracies existed, but even the most sophisticated ones in China and the Ottoman Empire relied heavily on provincial officials. Corporations were limited to the most complex of businesses like banks, even then often in quasi-official roles. Companies like the East India Company or the Rothschild banking empire delegated wide autonomy to local officials; superiors at the centre had only the most limited strategic control. This period we could call the pre-bureaucratic age.

As with many things, war, commerce, and technology changed the dynamic. With larger armies and more sophisticated warfare, the conflicts of the French Revolutionary and Napoleonic eras saw full-scale mobilisations that could only be managed through hierarchical and complex bureaucracies. At the same time, Napoleon applied these principles to the civilian part of his growing empire and created the first modern law code, the *Code Napoléon*, and an administrative state to implement it.[3] Meanwhile, economic trends led to similar developments in America. The invention of the cotton gin in 1793 spurred a revolution in the American cotton industry, but it required scale to really be revolutionary – especially in the form of railroads to connect distant farms and merchants. Unlike maritime trading companies, the railroad companies upon which the American cotton industry relied needed centralised management to ensure safety and efficiency (sharing track and sharing the seas are two very different matters). Bureaucracy was the only way to accomplish the logistical feat of connecting entire continents with one system.

Just like the cotton producers, railroad companies also had to consolidate, as building rail infrastructure was (by definition) large scale and expensive. Only big firms could manage the undertaking, and as the demand for capital correspondingly increased, a new, centralised banking system sprang up to finance it all. Bureaucracy was a cycle that built itself, feeding back into its own further expansion and centralisation. The new interconnected systems that enabled military and industrial growth soon spread to other aspects of daily life. Centralised governments were now able to build bureaucracies to run things on behalf of citizens, and consequently government evolved into an accretion of massive hierarchies. Over the course of the twentieth century this model grew into the form of government that we have today. It was – and is – the bureaucratic age.[4]

Bureaucratic modernisation brought a whole range of benefits, from universal schooling to a professional civil service, from health care to the rule of law. For Britain it built a national infrastructure and a global empire. These same, centralising mechanisms that enabled growth in the public sector eventually conquered the rest of the economy. With efficient transport and technology, unprecedented quantities of raw materials flowed to factories that, powered by steam-engine technology, could now produce and distribute manufactured goods. Firms adopted the administrative apparatus of the bureaucratic railways, and the modern corporation was born. As commercial empires emerged, a cult of management science, whereby businesses (and eventually government departments) were run by those at the top applying principles of 'engineering' to the workers below, soon dominated. It was all about mass production, mass management, mass distribution – and as the Second World War mobilised the American and British economies on national scales, the large corporation became a fait accompli. Coupled with automation and other improvements in technology, the process continued unabated; vast conglomerates were commonplace by the 1960s. The age of the independent local business wasn't over, but it was dealt a huge blow.

The inexorable growth of big business throughout the last century and a half has brought great benefits; in many respects, someone on an average income in the UK, Europe, or America today has a higher standard of living than even the very richest a century or so ago. But the mostly national corporations of the mid-twentieth century that had at least some sense of connection to and responsibility for their local communities have given way to rootless global entities – private-sector bureaucracies – many of which have lost all sense of community, of perspective. The never-ending trajectory of mergers, consolidation and growth has a cost – and not just a financial one (repeated studies have shown that corporate mergers generally destroy value for the shareholders of acquiring firms).[5] We are no longer driven by a human economy; we don't know where our products come from or how they are created; too many of our corporate bosses have no conception of their workers' or customers' experiences. We live in an age when the consequences of our decisions seem less and less important, because we don't really know what they are. We 'love a bargain' but don't see the appalling conditions endured by the people who produce a product that can be sold so cheaply. We troop to the supermarket but don't see the small businesses and farmers whose livelihoods are wrecked by 'everyday low prices'. The human consequences of our decisions are felt by people separated from us by time, space, and class.

In government too, we continue to live with a system that is a relic of the past. It did work once but we're no longer in the age of either sail or steamship, so why are we still governed as if we were? Empire is no longer relevant, and many of the services that centralised government provides – education, health care, social services, welfare – are well established and no longer require a centralised bureaucratic system to run them. Simply put, the raisons d'être of centralised government no longer justify it. But its costs remain.

You can see it in the way that twentieth-century factory-style approaches – standardisation, automation, mechanisation – still infect intrinsically human areas like education, health care, food, and housing. We used to think factories equalled progress. They were sanitary, standardised, and quality-controlled. They took urchins off the street while providing the middle and working classes with once only dreamt-of luxuries. Having tens of thousands of cows or chickens on a single farm seemed like the modern thing to do. But that vision is now out of date.

It's not just the arc of history, bureaucratic momentum, or mass standardisation that has led us to this point. We need to apply a critical eye to our unrelenting quest for progress, and how some of our leaders – in government, politics, business and society – define it for us. Where I live now, in Silicon Valley, the goal is to be bigger, faster, cheaper. Does that equate with better? Much of the time, it does. But too often the 'progress' we are offered is not an improvement, it's just more 'efficient' – and worse, more efficient for the producer, not the user. Astronauts consume Tang, a powdered orange drink, because it is compact and nutritious (a requirement on space missions). But should we substitute it for actual orange juice? Or oranges? Just because something is more 'efficient' doesn't mean it's better.

The misguided quest for efficiency has led to negative side effects that are only now being understood. As technology critic Evgeny Morozov points out in his book *To Save Everything, Click Here*, efficiency can undermine much of what makes us human. 'Imperfection, ambiguity, opacity, disorder, and the opportunity to err, to sin, to do the wrong thing: all of these are constitutive of human freedom, and any concentrated attempt to root them out will root out that freedom as well.'[6] I would add that a world programmed to perfection is no longer a human world: without problems to solve and imperfection to inspire us, we would become complacent. We would lose our ability to innovate and be creative, but worse, our world would become sterile. If we never get lost, we will never go to unexpected new places. If we never have to repair things, we will cease to tinker and make anew. Without the spontaneous discoveries (and mistakes) that so enrich us, humanity stagnates. Mother Nature is often 'inefficient' – providing us with two kidneys, for example, where one is enough. This is not to say that efficiency is always bad; of course not. But we need the cultural confidence to say no, sometimes to reject efficiency for human priorities that matter more.

As you will see this book calls for dramatic changes in how we do things. Some might ask whether that is really necessary. They could point to the UK's economic growth, political stability and social safety net; the falling crime; the strength of our culture; the growing vibrancy of our cities and say: 'Things are pretty good. Sure, they can always be improved but take it easy … we just need a touch on the tiller, not a change of course.'

Really? Have you noticed that it tends to be the wealthiest and most powerful who say things like that? Life is certainly good for them. But look around: life isn't great for most people, and in many ways is getting worse. With years of stagnating wages, people don't feel as though they're getting ahead.[7] They're living in smaller homes (Chapter 9). They aren't gaining the skills they need (Chapter 7). They're more unhealthy because the cost of the weekly shop goes up faster than other goods and nutritious food is not only more expensive than heavily processed, toxic junk (Chapter 4), but becoming so at an increasing rate.[8]

But the inhumanity of much of modern life – in schools, in hospitals, in urban planning – is no concern for the elites because they (we) don't have to experience it. Our children go to private schools; we supplement our NHS care with private insurance; and we eat our organic food from Waitrose or the farmers' market. When life gets rough, we go on exotic holidays or to our homes in the country; when things get busy, we employ nannies, housekeepers, and delivery people to buy ourselves more time.

For most people, though, the current system simply isn't working. Incremental change isn't working. This is true in America, where I live now; and it's true in the UK. But there is hope: small signs that things can be different; examples of the kind of change we need. I have seen them and learned from them over the last few years I've spent in California, and some of those signs of hope are profiled in this book. That is, of course, not to say that everything on the West Coast of the USA is perfect. America has its problems, just the same as – in many cases far worse than – the UK. In both countries, when most people haven't seen a rise in living standards for over a decade, and many have seen a fall; when daily life is such a hassle for so many; when people's quality of life is way below what they see in other countries; when there is a massive underclass persistently poor in every way for decade after decade – I think that calls for a sense of urgency. It's a crisis, and it demands a big shake-up, not steady-as-she-goes. Our debates feel small, stunted, fiddling around the edges – and this fuels the dissatisfaction with politics and the political system, increasingly expressed in support for fringe parties and politics.

For all these reasons, I think we need a revolution, not evolution.

I want to show you in this book that it's possible. That we can move to something better: a post-bureaucratic age. An age when we take back power over the things that matter to us from the anonymous, distant bureaucrats in government and business. An age when things work on a comprehensible and controllable scale. An age that is more human. This book is an argument for change. Apart from any specific changes, however small, that might happen as a result of the people, stories and ideas that follow, I also hope that they collectively help you to see the world a little differently. A little more humanly. And who knows where that might lead?

The modern world is a fantastic place full of excitement and ingenuity. But as we continue to invent and innovate and move forward, we should remember what makes us human: people, relationships, spontaneity, emotions. As we create and spread wealth and opportunity, build a world of technological wonder, remake our institutions, and push the boundaries of knowledge, we should try to do so in line with these essential human truths.

CHAPTER I

GOVERNMENT

I once wrote a book called *Good Business – Your World Needs You* which was based on a simple argument: Business runs the world. The world needs changing. Let's use business to change the world.

Looking back, with the benefit of my experience since then – working with some of the world's biggest companies to try to solve social and environmental problems, and then working in politics and government to do the same, I can see that I was – how shall I put this – wrong.

Business does not run the world. In the end, government sets the rules by which business – and everyone else – operates, and it's quite right that it does. Government is (at least notionally) accountable to people in a way that businesses are not. Businesses clearly make a huge contribution to society (both positive and negative), and they should try to improve it. But if we really want to change the world – if we want to make it more human – then we must start with the people who call the shots. That means government. It means changing government: changing the priorities of those within it, changing the way they make policy, changing the way the whole thing is structured.

More human priorities for government

Sir John Cowperthwaite was the Financial Secretary of Hong Kong in the 1960s and the man widely credited with creating the conditions for its phenomenal economic success. When asked what advice he would give to a poor country trying to get richer, he said: 'They should abolish the Office of National Statistics.' Cowperthwaite believed that the collection of data simply encouraged governments and bureaucrats to interfere in the economy in damaging ways. His refusal to collect economic statistics in Hong Kong infuriated his masters in London. When they sent a delegation to persuade him to change his approach, Cowperthwaite literally sent them straight back on the next plane.[9] I love that story for its wonderfully British rebelliousness. But that rather eccentric episode from the 1960s also highlights the big problem with government today: its prioritisation of numbers over people. Of course it sounds obvious, trite even, to argue that government should put people first. And yet it doesn't happen. Look at what government's priorities are; what people working in the system spend their time on; the things that drive all the big decisions. It's actually about numbers, about economics.

The political world's focus on economics was most famously captured by Bill Clinton's 1992 election campaign strategist James Carville when he scrawled: 'The economy, stupid' on the office walls of Clinton's headquarters. But it goes far beyond election campaigns. In government, money reigns supreme, and I don't just mean lobbying and political donations. The most prestigious posts are the economic ones: in Britain, it's the Chancellor of the Exchequer. All the top civil servants want to work at the Treasury; moving to work anywhere else in government is seen as a demotion. The political calendar is dominated by economic events: GDP figures, unemployment figures, inflation, interest rates, what's happening in the stock market. In government, it really *is* the economy, stupid.

Economics first? So far, so Marxist. You can understand why. Generally speaking, the more the economy grows, the better it is for everyone. Economic growth pays for progress in other areas – the human things that really matter. On an individual or family level, the more money you have the better life tends to be. Money doesn't buy happiness, but it can certainly eliminate many of the things that make us unhappy. Money provides opportunity. It is often those who have never experienced what it's like to have little or no money who say that it doesn't matter. Try telling that to the mother of three who's working two jobs to feed her children and still can't afford to buy nappies.

So I don't have any problem with the idea that the political system should concern itself with how to improve economic circumstances – whether for a family, a community, a country or indeed the whole world. Of course there's more to life than money – much more – but political leaders could have many worse aims than making their people more prosperous. Prosperity generally has brought us longer, healthier lives, with better education, more art and leisure, greater civic and political participation: all good things. Economic growth has been a decent enough proxy for these important, human outcomes.

My argument is different. It is not about challenging the value of economic growth. My argument is about the *way* our system of government goes about it. We've made numbers – economic indicators – the priority while forgetting that 'the economy' represents something deeper, more important, and that is our society, our actual lives as they are lived. Basing everything on numbers pushes government policy towards mechanical, bureaucratic systems rather than more organic approaches that put people first. Take a so-called 'economic issue' like jobs. It's just as much – if not more – a social, human issue. Of course you can literally change the way statistics are collected, and that will change unemployment rates. More seriously, you can fiddle around with interest rates and taxes and that will have an effect on the overall economy. But the effects are far less certain or predictable than economic policymakers let on. The wiser and more self-aware of them know that there is very little they can do to 'improve the economy' or 'create jobs' in a general sense. If you want to see more jobs created and more people able to take them, the things that really work are specific, human things.

Help people get the skills they need. Help them gain the confidence and support to become entrepreneurs. Help make sure children are brought up in a way that gives them the character and the capacity to learn, to train, to hold down a job. None of the social policies required to bring about these ends are captured in the job figures or the GDP figures. But they are critical to achieving the economic results we seek. Economic issues on the surface are human issues at their heart. Another way to think about it? Social policy *is* economic policy, just more effective.

In 2013's *Evangelii Gaudium*, Pope Francis points out exactly how disjointed our priorities are: 'How can it be that it is not a news item when an elderly homeless person dies of exposure, but it is news when the stock market loses two points?'[10] When we talk about numbers and not the people behind them, we end up with the wrong priorities.

We know from the latest developments in neuroscience and evidence from long-term research studies that the conditions in which a child grows up – especially in the first few years of life – have a crucial impact on the rest of their life: whether they will be in work or on welfare, a contributor to society or a cost. But government doesn't prioritise spending on the causes of social problems; it wastes money on the symptoms. This flaw in our system of government is systemic. It's not because the politicians and civil servants are stupid or useless or malevolent; quite the opposite – they are mostly highly intelligent, dedicated and public-spirited. The problem is the system itself; how it forces every decision into a framework that is literally inhuman, putting numbers before people. It's one of the reasons that people feel so little of any real substance seems to change, whoever is in power.

That's why the first step in designing a more human world is to change the priorities of government. My argument is that we have to start from the notion that certain things *must* be in place for people to lead a decent life, and that government's overarching priority should be to ensure that they are. Government should lay the infrastructure (in its broadest sense) that will allow people to live happy, healthy and flourishing lives. That doesn't mean ignoring economics, or pretending there's no need to balance the books. But it does mean defining economics in human terms, making sure that the books we're trying to balance truly reflect our human priorities, not just the arcane and somewhat random accidents of economic history as is the case today.

Much of the debate on this issue has concentrated on our obsession with Gross Domestic Product. GDP, when used as a benchmark for an economy's – or a country's – success, focuses attention not on human problems and solutions but on numbers that can be measured. GDP has a central design flaw: it fails to consider much of what ought to be counted, while at the same time counting things that we as a society and as individuals aspire *not* to produce. Consider a car crash: someone hits you from behind, wrecking your car and sending you to hospital. The whole episode boosts GDP.

The surgery, the car repairs, the back-and-forth with insurance companies – it all adds to economic growth. Economists credit a world war with restoring America's economy after the Depression. Of course, it never goes as far as the government promoting car crashes or wars as some kind of twisted economic stimulus package … but GDP couldn't tell the difference. It is not human.

GDP only concerns itself with what can be produced and purchased in the marketplace. The time people spend on human things – from parenting to friendship to the care of elderly or sick relatives – all comes at the expense of formal market interaction and is implicitly negative. Balancing work hours with time spent on personal relationships, engaging in hobbies, connecting with nature, just resting or thinking – all this is what makes for a richer society. But not if you look to GDP.

Moreover, GDP disregards society's 'balance sheet'. A low-income household with above-average wealth is viewed the same as a low-income household with no wealth at all. Savers, who help make the economy more stable, don't contribute to GDP while spenders and borrowers, who can over-leverage and push the economy towards collapse, do. This is ridiculous, but when GDP governs economic decisions, it is how the world appears. What follows is the neglect and degradation of environmental, social, and human capital stocks for short-term gain.

Ironically, the economist who created GDP warned against over-reliance on his measure. Simon Kuznets worked for the US government after the Great Depression and developed GDP for President Franklin Roosevelt, who needed proof that the economy had shrunk in order to justify deficit spending and his Keynesian approach to stimulating the economy.[11] Kuznets understood GDP's limitations better than anyone and urged that it exclude things which detract from human well-being such as advertising, guns, and dangerous speculative finance.[12] He argued that just because you could simplify much of the breadth and complexity of the world into a single number didn't mean that you should.

As its flaws have become apparent, over the years countless studies and commissions have aimed to reform, supplement, or even replace GDP with improved metrics. The United Nations has used the Human Development Index (HDI), which mixes education and life expectancy with income, since 1990. Bhutan famously promoted the notion of Gross National Happiness. In 2008, French President Nicolas Sarkozy convened three of the world's leading economists[13] to undertake a multi-year study of a GDP alternative. Risking predictable mockery, we tried something similar in the UK, with Prime Minister David Cameron asking the Office of National Statistics to develop a measure of 'subjective well-being' in 2010 (the first actual measures being published in 2012). All of this leaves out the many other 'unofficial' studies and projects taken on by academics and concerned economists around the world. They all point to the same conclusion: GDP doesn't really work, but it's still important, so let's either have a dashboard of alternative measures to go alongside GDP, or let's aggregate them all into a single score, some kind of 'GDP-plus'.

The trouble is that none of this has made the slightest difference. In fact, the whole argument misses the point. In the end, the debate about GDP is a bit of a sideshow: it's not about finding better numbers; it's about the system within which the numbers are considered – the structure of our national accounts. For all its weaknesses GDP is just the tip of the iceberg, a symbol of this much larger problem, which prevents government from prioritising real, human objectives. The things that really matter to us, the things that fundamentally enable us to lead decent, happy, healthy, productive, flourishing lives: think of this as infrastructure. Of course infrastructure includes what we normally imagine when we hear that term: roads and railways, energy grids and utilities. But humans need more than that to flourish: education and health services; early childhood education; mental health, relationship and family support could usefully be included. Infrastructure poses a problem, however: it is expensive and tends to need significant upfront expenditure before the benefits flow. As a society, we already make a certain commitment to this idea – we subsidise our children's education, for instance, because we know it will enable productive lives later on; we think of school not as a cost but as an investment.

Now we need to adopt that same mindset across the board. This isn't new; the Victorians thought like this 150 years ago. As economist Diane Coyle points out, 'Victorian values' aren't just prudish or conservative, they 'also speak of hard work, self-improvement, and above all self-sacrifice for the future'.[14] The Victorians had the forethought to build tangible investments in their communities like railways, canals, sewers, roads, town halls, libraries, schools, concert halls, monuments, and modern hospitals. Meanwhile, they created new ways for people to contribute to society through the police, trade unions, mutual insurers, learned societies, the profession of nursing, and building societies. This 'sense of stewardship', as Coyle calls it, is what can fundamentally define success or failure for a society. Today, we have shirked our duties as stewards. We have chosen instant gratification and the tyranny of a narrow economic calculus over the long-term future for our children and our country.

Instead of putting people first, our current system of government insists on a dogmatic adherence to accounting practices which, much like GDP, are accidents of history and make no real sense if seriously examined. But they never are, because they are just 'there' – a fact of life, a way of organising numbers that 'can't' be challenged. GDP, as Robert Kennedy said, includes 'everything in short, except that which makes life worthwhile',[15] and our system of national accounts is similarly distorted. It forces politicians to operate on time horizons no further than the next parliamentary term or election cycle.

This leads to decisions and policies that are flawed in two fundamental ways: they focus too much on the short term, and on the symptoms of problems instead of their causes. That is why government massively under-invests in the long-term infrastructure needed to make the economy work properly and to help people flourish – because in the government's accounts, spending on infrastructure is treated as a cost with no benefits. That is why most of the energy in government is applied to the symptoms of social problems (welfare, crime etc.) rather than their causes (for example, what happens in early childhood). Long-term human needs come second to the short-term imperative of the numbers; sensible, long-term policies are rejected because their dividends come down the road. We have budget-based priorities instead of priorities-based budgets. So the real priority for reform should not be GDP but creating a whole new system of national accounts.

One way to think about it, as Oxford economist Dieter Helm suggests, is to distinguish in our national accounts between spending money on assets and spending money on liabilities.[16] Infrastructure is an asset – yes, it costs money initially, but we can predict (and later record) its 'dividends' – the economic activity a new fibre network produces, or the money an early childhood intervention saves later on. That money goes in the 'plus' side of the ledger and in any sensible accounting system (like the one used by businesses) can be offset against the spending. As with business investments, the point of infrastructure spending is that over the years it pays for itself many times over. But in government, spending on infrastructure is counted the same as any other spending. Tackling unemployment by building a high-speed broadband network that would in the long term lead to new jobs is counted as no different from handing out the same amount of money in welfare payments. Tackling crime through parenting programmes that could prevent crime in the first place is counted in the same ledger as keeping criminals in jail. As a result of this short-term thinking, policies and projects that would greatly improve people's lives never see the light of day. The numbers rule – in a totally irrational way.

I wanted to open the book with this question of government priorities because it's a good example of something we will see over and over again. To really change things, we need to understand the underlying causes of problems. In this case, it's easy to say (and people have been saying for many years): 'Why don't we have amazing modern infrastructure like the Chinese do?' or 'Why don't we have fantastic services for families and children like Nordic countries do?' The reason we have such short-term thinking in government – whoever is in power – is not because politicians, or civil servants, or even voters are choosing the wrong priorities. The reason is systemic. The system of our national accounts forces the wrong priorities. If we want government to have more human priorities – and put people first, not numbers – we will have to change that system.

A more human way to design policy

In 2000, Tony Blair floated a new idea to clean up antisocial behaviour on British streets. He proposed that offenders be made to pay an on-the-spot fine of £100; if they didn't have the money, they'd be taken to a cashpoint machine to withdraw it. The policy was never implemented. One of the main reasons was because it turned out that the 'yobs' targeted by this policy did not usually have £100 in cash 'on the spot', or a bank account to withdraw it from; often they did not even have £100 to their names.[17]

Why did Blair make incorrect assumptions about those committing street crime? Come to think of it, how did anyone in any government anywhere conceive 'that stupid new tax', 'that waste-of-money anti-poverty programme', 'that white-elephant urban regeneration plan', and so on? It's easy to blame 'useless politicians', 'jumped-up aides', and 'incompetent civil servants'. But that's too simplistic: we need to go deeper. One reason for the failure of so many government policies over the years is the fact that the people the policies are designed to help are too often an afterthought. The lives of the average person – especially the poor or those interacting with social services – are simply unknown to the policymakers. Blair and his advisers' daily reality was so far removed from that of the people who made trouble on the streets that no matter how right the theory, the policy could never work in practice.

It's not that politicians don't care about people or the effects of their policies – they do, most of them, sincerely and deeply. It's just that by the time politicians are in their government offices, trying to find slots in their overfilled diaries to actually think about policy and its implementation, they're unable to think about it on a human scale, in a human way.

It's not just the design of policies. It's the delivery too. Consider the New Enterprise Allowance (NEA), another well-intentioned idea, aimed at helping people off benefits. It was from the government that I worked for; in fact it was a policy I helped create and fought hard to introduce. The idea was that some unemployed people might want to start their own businesses; if we could get each of them a loan and some advice from a mentor, they'd be on their way. The NEA loan would be administered through Jobcentre Plus offices, which were already in most communities. When the programme was launched, the initial uptake was disappointing and the Treasury officials in charge of its funding wanted to cancel the whole thing. Rohan Silva (my friend and colleague in government who you will meet a lot in these pages) was curious about why the programme, loosely based on a similar one that had been extremely successful in the 1980s, wasn't working. On a hunch that perhaps it wasn't being pitched in the right way, he asked the officials running the policy what the staff at Jobcentre Plus offices were trained to say to potential candidates, and what their reasons would be for granting or turning down a loan if the conversation got that far. The officials had no idea. No thought had gone into that aspect of the policy at all. It was just assumed that since the opportunity was available, anyone who wanted it would sign up. If sign-ups were low, that meant the policy was defective. The government was about to cancel a potentially effective programme without any sense of how it was being implemented where it really mattered: the human point of contact between two people.

The d.school at Stanford

In 2012, I came to Stanford University where I taught a number of courses including some at its renowned design institute, or 'd.school'. Teaching at Stanford required me to reflect on how we did things in government: what we did well, what we did badly, and what we could have done differently. That reflection has been profound. I now realise why so many policies fail; why so much money is wasted; why so many promises are never delivered; why this happened in our government – in every government. It's not the ideologies of the leaders or the circumstances of the times, although obviously both are important. It's to do with a mindset, an attitude, an approach. An approach in which policymaking is much more about theory than practice; where the people making the policy, and the people implementing it, make no real effort to understand – in detail – the lives of the people for whom they're making or implementing the policy. I have no hesitation in saying to my students that the single biggest improvement we could bring to policy making in government is to make it more human: to put people at the centre of the process. That may sound platitudinous. But I mean it in a very precise way, based on what I learned at Stanford about the process of human-centred design – or, as it is known at the d.school, 'design thinking'.

Formally established in 2004 as the Hasso Plattner Institute for Design at Stanford, the d.school is the academic home of design thinking. In the late 1980s, the software usability engineer Donald Norman put forward his vision of user-centred design, and by the late 1990s and early 2000s, designers at the Silicon Valley design firm IDEO (the company responsible for Apple's first mouse), started to realise that they could apply user- (or human-) centred design (by now also called design thinking) not just to objects, products and software but much more broadly. In the 2000s, design thinking had been applied to entire business models, not to mention consumer experiences. By the time the d.school was founded, it was clear that since innovators in almost any discipline are creating new things – whether business ideas, health-care interventions, education policies, or consumer services – and that the act of creating is an act of design, graduate students from any university programme would benefit from a design-thinking education. Stanford's d.school was established to give them that opportunity. It's now run by Sarah Stein Greenberg, my brilliant co-teacher and the person who more than anyone else has helped me understand what design thinking is all about and how it could help improve policy making and implementation.

At the d.school, students are guided through a process that, though inevitably messier in practice, can be explained in a handful of straightforward steps:

1. Empathise with the user
2. Define the problem
3. Generate ideas
4. Prototype solutions
5. Test the prototypes
   … keep testing and adapting until you get it right.

Empathy is not a word you hear very much in government. But to understand a problem and imagine a solution requires an understanding of the people affected. This is an act of empathy, and human-centred designers put themselves in the shoes of those they are designing for. Empathy requires close, highly detailed observation of people, in the context in which they'll be using the product or service in question. This borrows from the anthropological practice of ethnography, which assumes that observations and open-ended interviews reveal more about a person's beliefs, needs, emotions, and desires than surveys and market research ever could. In the design-thinking process taught at the d.school, this means talking to users before doing anything else, which really means listening to users. Politicians will say they listen to their constituents all the time, either directly or through opinion polls and focus groups. But this is different. The kind of empathy work required for design thinking is about deeply understanding the life of the person you're designing for; forcing yourself to be open-minded rather than selling your own ideas. The first stage of the designers' process includes observing users in their day-to-day routines and immersing themselves in the user's environment for days, even weeks on end.

The acclaimed urban theorist and writer Jane Jacobs captures precisely the same sentiment in her 1961 masterpiece, *The Death and Life of Great American Cities,* in which she lays out all the essential components of a flourishing neighbourhood based entirely on her first-hand, street-level observations in cities around the United States. She writes that the only corrective to ineffective, top-down city planning (generally by 'visionary', egotistical architects and politicians) is to base policy on 'true descriptions of reality drawn not from how it ought to be, but from how it is'.[18]

These true descriptions of reality are the basis for step two: defining the problem. This might seem straightforward, but it's surprising how frequently policymakers can be found solving the wrong problem – a superficial one, a symptom rather than a cause – or a problem perceived in one way by the outside world but totally differently by those actually experiencing it. A great example comes from a student project that began at the d.school as part of a course called Entrepreneurial Design for Extreme Affordability. In 'Extreme' (as the course is popularly known), teams of Stanford graduate students come together for over six months to work on different problems facing the world's poor. Each group, which might include students from any field – law, medicine, business, history, computer science – is paired with a non-governmental organisation in the developing world to solve a specific problem in an extremely affordable way.

One team, which would turn into a business, was tasked with developing a lower-cost baby incubator to be piloted in rural Nepal; nearly 1 million children die each year globally from complications due to premature birth.[19] The team of four first met in January 2007 when the course began. They spent two and a half months researching incubators, as well as infant mortality and the medical requirements of premature babies. It is customary with Extreme for one or two of the students on each team to visit their partners on the ground. For the incubator team, Linus Liang, a computer-science student, travelled 7,000 miles to Nepal along with two other student groups working on similar health-related problems.

'We were very ambitious – we landed, got to the hotel, and went to the hospital that day,' Linus recalls. 'We did exactly what design thinking instructs – lots of interviews, observations, etc. We talked to at least twenty doctors and then went to the neonatal intensive care unit and observed all the different doctors and nurses, the amount of noise – everything.'

Linus discovered one odd thing. There were incubators everywhere, but with no babies in them. 'They had all these donated incubators. Some [of the instruction labels] were in Japanese, some were in German – there were all these different languages. And all of them were pretty damn good. There's this hospital with nothing, no resources – there's mould growing on the walls – with high-end incubators, and they were all basically brand new.' So Linus asked the next question: since Nepal had all these incubators, why did it have such a high infant mortality problem? It turned out that many of the country's premature births happened in rural villages, far away from the hospital where Linus stood and from the life-saving incubators that sat empty. The babies were dead on arrival.

It was clear that the d.school team needed to go deeper to understand the problem. So they got on a bus and went to a village outside Kathmandu. 'It was kind of horrible what they had out there. There was no infrastructure.' In the village he visited, it became quickly apparent that the team's initial idea – a cheaper incubator for hospitals – wasn't going to get them anywhere. There was no running water, no local hospitals – just shacks with barely trained 'doctors' who did their best to serve the villagers' medical needs. The incubators they used were simple wooden boxes with light bulbs in them, most of which were burnt out anyway, some for as long as four years. They told Linus that they had no money to buy new bulbs, but in any case there was nowhere to buy them, and no electricity to power them.

'You slowly learn all the constraints. And then we started designing for that when we came back,' Linus explains. 'That's when we really understood the need.' Back at Stanford, the team used its findings to develop a new point of view. They were no longer looking to design a cheaper, simpler incubator for local hospitals: 'We wanted to design for the mothers who have no actual health-care system, no water, no electricity, no transport, no money.' The team redefined the problem they were trying to solve based on the empathy they had gained. And it is at this point that they could start to generate ideas for what a solution might look like.

This might sound familiar – who hasn't sat through a 'brainstorming' session to come up with something clever or creative? But this step in the design-thinking process, like the others, is usually given short shrift by politicians and policymakers, many of whom already have solutions in mind that they're trying to advance, based often on ideology rather than empathy with the people they're trying to help. One of my favourite teaching moments at the d.school is our demonstration of a bad brainstorm versus a good brainstorm. Take it from me – most of the ones you see in government are bad. The cardinal rule for getting good results? Defer judgement. Whether you're alone or with a group of colleagues, the best way to kill potentially good ideas is to point out their flaws at the moment you're trying to come up with them. One of the most stupid things said in the context of brainstorming is that 'there's no such thing as a bad idea'. Of course there is – but the time for evaluating which ideas are bad and which are good is not when you're trying to generate them.

For me, the part of the design-thinking process that offers the greatest contrast with how things are done in government is the final stage: prototyping and testing an idea. The key is to embrace experimentation, testing a concept with cheap and rough prototypes before investing more in its development. This is a world away from how government does things. Yes, there are pilot programmes – but these typically cost many millions of pounds and are launched with great fanfare. The incentive is to prove that they work, not to find out whether they do. Prototype testing is not piloting. For example, rather than building a website (still a costly exercise), you could literally sketch it out on pieces of paper, put it in front of people, and get feedback on how they would use it based simply on asking them to point at boxes they would 'click' on and why. The methodology of rapid and low-cost prototyping and testing that was developed and refined at the d.school is now the basic modus operandi for every tech firm in Silicon Valley, from the biggest names to the smallest start-ups.

And that's exactly what the d.school team working on the incubator problem in Nepal did next. Based on insights gained from immersing themselves in the reality of Nepal's health system, they shifted their focus from the hospital and the clinician to the village and the mother. The team reframed the problem from 'building a cheaper incubator' to 'keeping premature babies warm'. The result was a wrap like a sleeping bag, warmed by a special heated insert, all costing about 1 per cent of the price of an incubator. When the course was finished, the team set themselves up as a company (called Embrace) and moved to India, determined to bring their concept to a stage at which it could actually be deployed. They continued testing new versions, each time gaining fresh insight from the mothers whom they watched using the prototypes. Small tweaks came from observation: a plastic window over the chest, allowing doctors to see at a glance if the baby was breathing; or a simple OK/Not OK indicator in place of the previous numerical temperature gauge that wasn't trusted by the mothers (digital displays tend to malfunction so often that there's an automatic suspicion of them). From its humble origins as a student project, Embrace has now expanded its operations to eleven countries across Asia, Latin America, and Africa and has gone on to save 50,000 lives (and counting).[20]

Designing policy for who we are, not for who we ought to be

It's amazing what you can discover when you listen to people. But a more human approach to policymaking doesn't just mean paying attention to details on the ground. It's about understanding behaviour too. Over the last thirty years psychologists, neuroscientists and economists have systematically catalogued ways in which we consistently fail to live up to traditional expectations of how humans 'ought' to behave. This means that we now have a rigorous body of work, rather than just our hunches, that we can use to enhance the effectiveness of public policy.

For example, economics assumes that we value money objectively – that a pound gained causes as much pleasure as the pain from a pound that's lost. But in the late 1970s, psychologists discovered that we tend to be much more averse to a loss than we are keen to have the equivalent gain. This work was so disruptive to traditional economics that its discovery by Daniel Kahneman and Amos Tversky earned the Nobel Prize in 2002.[21] An interesting application of the principle was an experiment in a Chicago school district. For many years, school administrators around the world have tried to incentivise better teacher performance through bonuses awarded at the end of the year if certain targets are met. In Chicago Heights, a group of University of Chicago academics tried an approach based on this behavioural concept of loss aversion. They gave the teachers their bonus at the beginning of the year and told them that at the end of the year, all or parts of it would be taken away if they didn't meet specified goals. Two control groups were also established: one in which teachers were given no performance incentive and one involving a traditional end-of-year bonus. The results were spectacular: the performance of the students taught by teachers in the two control groups was about the same, suggesting that the traditional performance bonus doesn't really make much difference. But in the group where the teachers were given an upfront bonus with a threat that it would be lost, the students' results improved two to three times more than the traditional bonus group.[22]

More human policy design would also recognise that we often neglect to do things that are in our own best interest (and that we even say we want to do), like put money in our pensions, take exercise, and remember to go to doctors' appointments. But government policy has been designed and implemented for decades based on the assumption that people will behave as the economic models predict they will, with perfect foresight and self-control. Consider government's approach to fighting poverty: programmes of the Left traditionally consist of giving money, jobs, food, and other resources to alleviate material deprivation; while programmes of the Right traditionally try to improve economic incentives so that poor people can 'lift themselves up by the bootstraps'. Both approaches, as the social policy commentator David Brooks has pointed out, errantly 'treat individuals as if they were abstractions ... shaped by economic structures alone, and not by character and behavior'.[23] The simple truth is that our actions don't always match our intentions. Human things like forgetfulness get in the way.

Human-centred policy design also recognises that people tend to do what they think other people are doing. One of my favourite examples comes from an experiment that psychologist

Robert Cialdini carried out in Arizona's Petrified Forest National Park. He posted signs drawing attention to the high incidence of looting pieces of ancient wood. They backfired: letting people know that theft was frequent – that it was a normal thing to do – actually increased the incidence of thievery.[24] Traditional efforts by governments to change people's behaviour so often make this classic mistake, highlighting the negative behaviour they want to *dis*courage rather than promoting as a social norm the positive behaviour they want to *en*courage.

If the key to a more human approach to policy design is to start with people, a shortcut is to find those who have already solved their own problems. One particular expression of this idea holds great potential: the power of positive deviance.

In 1990, Jerry and Monique Sternin, workers for the charity Save the Children, moved to Vietnam to set up a programme to fight child malnutrition in poor rural villages. While conducting surveys to understand the scope of the issue, they grew curious about the handful of children who, despite coming from families as poor as all the others, were perfectly healthy – the positive deviants. What were these families doing differently? If they could discover behaviours that enabled even the most materially deprived parents to raise healthy children, the implications would be tremendous. They found that all the parents of the positive deviants for some reason collected tiny pieces of shell from crabs, snails, and shrimp from rice paddy fields and added them to their children's diet, along with the greens from sweet potato tops. None of the other families did. Both these ingredients, though free and available to anyone for the taking, were commonly considered to be inappropriate if not dangerous for children, and so were generally excluded from their diets.

This finding enabled aid workers to set up 'home-grown' educational programmes that passed on the lessons to other parents. The beauty is that the solution required no more resources than the villagers already had. The answers to the problem were right there in the community.[25] Imagine if we designed our domestic policy programmes with a 'positive deviance' approach. Imagine if policymakers went to the very populations they were trying to help – to find not just problems but solutions too.

Near where I live, in Oakland, California, a project called the Family Independence Initiative (FII) is doing just that. Part of the problem of poverty, according to FII's founder Mauricio Lim Miller, is that government defines poor people by their problems, neglecting – even inhibiting – what they're already doing well. So at FII, staff are explicitly forbidden to advise families or give them ideas. For 'helpful' people (as social workers tend to be), it is very difficult (sometimes impossible) to control this impulse – Lim Miller has had to fire staff from time to time. But stepping back is essential, since it creates a vacuum that families fill with their own ideas. 'The best and most culturally relevant solutions are embedded in community,' Lim Miller explains, 'and people build and strengthen their social networks when they look to friends and neighbors who have successfully faced similar challenges.'[26] FII provides income support on the condition that its clients record and make steps towards achieving basic goals (on issues like income, debt, health, education and relationships), and that families meet once monthly to discuss them. Staff are allowed only to ask open-ended questions like: 'What do you think should be done?' and 'Do you know of anyone that successfully did what you want to do? Can you ask them for help?'

According to Lim Miller: 'When we respect families to lead their own change and give them access to resources the way middle- and upper-class people access them, they begin to transform their lives.' It hasn't been easy: families, used to the traditional give and take of welfare programmes, were looking for direction from FII staff. Sometimes it was clear that they were on their way to making a mistake. Only when they received no direction did they start to share goals, then ideas.

Jorge and Maria-Elena were a recent immigrant couple, refugees from El Salvador's civil war. After seven months of meetings, in which they had mostly talked about their health and their children's education, they declared they were going to buy a home. A Spanish-speaking real-estate broker had persuaded them they could buy a house in their neighbourhood, and friends would help them meet the down-payment. It took all the self-control Lim Miller and his staff could muster to stop themselves 'saving' the couple from what was (obviously to them) not going to be a rosy situation. Rather than intervene, Lim Miller told his staff to track them and simply accept that people had to make their own mistakes. The house was purchased; the broker made his commission – but Jorge and Maria-Elena were now saddled with a mortgage that was 65 per cent of their income. Losing the house seemed all but inevitable. Lim Miller felt bad, and his staff were upset that they had let this happen.

But that's when the couple surprised them. 'We had assumed the family was clueless,' Lim Miller recalls, 'but at some point they had recognized that they were in over their heads. They had included a refinance clause in their mortgage.' With the help of their friends, they renovated it, increasing its value so they could refinance the house and bring the mortgage down to 40 per cent of their income. 'From that point on,' says Lim Miller, 'I promised myself that I would try to avoid underestimating people's ability to solve their own problems.' (The couple still own their home, by the way.)

What makes this story interesting is the ripple effect that an organic, human success story has on others in the community. Now Jorge and Maria-Elena's friends knew what to do (and not to do) to buy a house, and two months after the refinancing, everyone started saving more so they could follow suit. Within eighteen months, the four other families in their FII cohort had purchased homes – but without using the predatory broker. By helping families find other families who succeed in overcoming problems associated with poverty, Lim Miller is building a self-perpetuating platform from which the working poor walk away not just with lessons learned but also with inspiration.

The results are clear: household incomes of the initial twenty-five families increased by nearly a third after two years. Moreover, 40 per cent had bought new homes within three years.[27] A year after the programme's payments ceased, household income continued to increase (now 40 per cent higher than baseline).[28] After the programme had been extended to San Francisco, the numbers continued to impress: amongst families there, in two years, household income increased by an average of 20 per cent, half the school-age children showed improvements at school, and three of five households reduced their debts.[29] The initiative has since expanded to Hawaii and Boston, where within one year of its operations, incomes increased 13 per cent. 'When you come into a community that is vulnerable with professionals with power and preset ideas, it is overpowering to families and it can hold them back,' says Lim Miller. 'But the focus on need undermines our ability to see their strengths – and their ability to see their own strengths.'[30]

Awash with data

This type of human approach acts as an important antidote to the increasing overreliance of policymakers on data, which seems only to bolster their confidence in being able to solve problems from afar. I'm not against data or evidence or statistics as tools in policymaking: they can be helpful in understanding the extent of a problem's existence, scope, and distribution – as well as its trend over time. Data can help us see if existing policies are having the desired effect or if concepts that worked well in one place are effective in others. Perhaps data's most crucial function is helping us understand what has *generally* worked or failed before. But when it comes to the design of specific policy interventions, it's dangerous to make assumptions based on data, as if people were all the same. Here's David Brooks again, on efforts to combat teenage pregnancy: 'A pregnancy … isn't just a piece of data in a set. It came about after a unique blend of longings and experiences. Maybe a young woman just wanted to feel like an adult; maybe she had some desire for arduous love, maybe she was just absent-minded, or loved danger, or couldn't resist her boyfriend, or saw no possible upside for her future anyway. In each case the ingredients will be different. Only careful case-by-case storytelling can uncover and respect the delirious iconoclasm of how life is actually lived.'[31]

At the height of the crack-cocaine epidemic in the 1990s, New York City Police Commissioner Bill Bratton instituted a programme called CompStat in an effort to radically realign the department around a clear principle of accountability for crime reduction. Police officials were required to attend weekly meetings at which they discussed the key data of the week, with statistical trends analysed across departments and over time. While it was largely credited with reducing the specific measured crimes (muggings, murders, etc.), the programme precluded tactics that might have been more effective in the long term but were less amenable to measurement, such as trust-building in communities. Events like the 2014 riots (and over-militarised police response) in Ferguson,

Missouri, or the brutal chokehold arrest and subsequent death of an unarmed petty criminal in New York are partly the result of such a targets-driven culture. Bratton, who advocates CompStat around the world, himself acknowledges that too much attention has been placed on 'the numbers of stops, summonses and arrests' and not enough on 'collaborative problem-solving with the community'.[32] Jim Bueermann, another US police chief, admits: 'If you ask a traffic officer how many tickets he wrote today, their emphasis is on writing tickets to meet a number, as opposed to a desired outcome, which is safer streets.'[33]

This data obsession is how we've ended up in the UK with the loss of public trust in the police. When the issuing of a fixed penalty notice was defined for statistical purposes as a 'cleared-up crime', it's no surprise that police forces went on a rampage of aggressively hassling basically law-abiding people for the most minor (often traffic-related) offences. It's much easier to do that than clear up an actual crime, involving actual criminals – and if they're both counted the same way in the crime figures who wouldn't take the easier option?

In the end, numbers are just not that helpful in designing policy. Knowing if a family is above or below the poverty line tells us nothing about *why* that's the case. And if we don't know why a family is in poverty, we can't know how to design policies to help that family out. No statistics or set of data can substitute for the intimate, nuanced knowledge that a policymaker should internalise by going out and experiencing the complexity of the world where the policy will have its effect. This point seems so obvious that it should hardly be worth mentioning. And yet it's nearly always overlooked.

'Go out into the real world'

In government, we tried to move things forward. In 2008, while we were still in opposition, Rohan ordered ten copies of *Nudge* by Dick Thaler and Cass Sunstein, a book which sets out the case, in theory and with practical examples, for using behavioural economics to improve people's ability to make decisions. The book promotes a sort of 'libertarian paternalism': steer people in the desired direction without outright compulsion. David Cameron picked up a copy from the pile on Rohan's desk and shortly thereafter started referring to it eagerly. Within weeks of becoming prime minister, Cameron gave the go-ahead to set up a 'nudge' unit of our own. Under the direction of social psychologist and Cabinet Office veteran David Halpern, the Behavioural Insights Team worked with government departments to help improve policy design. Consider this 'nudge' aimed at getting more job seekers to turn up at the Jobcentre. First, they sent one group the following text message:

> 8 new Picker Packer jobs are now available at Pro FS. Come to Bedford Jobcentre on Monday 10 June between 10am and 4pm and ask for Sarah to find out more.

The response rate was 10.5 per cent – an improvement over normal responses but not that impressive. Then they added the claimant's name (we'll call her Kate):

> *Hi Kate,* 8 new Picker Packer jobs are now available at Pro FS. Come to Bedford Jobcentre on Monday 10 June between 10am and 4pm and ask for Sarah to find out more.

That bumped the response rate up to 14.8 per cent. Then they added the adviser's name (we'll call him Michael), so it looked like this:

> Hi Kate, 8 new Picker Packer jobs are now available at Pro FS. Come to Bedford Jobcentre on Monday 10 June between 10am and 4pm and ask for Sarah to find out more. *Michael*

The response rate went up again, to 17.4 per cent. Already impressed that these minor tweaks could make such a difference (imagine how many thousands more people this would affect), they tried one more thing. They got the person who sent the message to wish the claimant luck:

> Hi Kate, 8 new Picker Packer jobs are now available at Pro FS. Come to Bedford Jobcentre on Monday 10 June between 10am and 4pm and ask for Sarah to find out more. *I've booked you a place. Good luck,* Michael

Response: 26.8 per cent. With ten simple words, David's team was able to nearly treble response rates ... a pretty high return on investment.[34]

Another success has come from applying human insights to pension participation. For decades, enrolment in any sort of retirement savings plan has been a fraction of what it could be, leading to a chronic savings shortage. (In one study looking at twenty-five defined benefit plans – those where the benefits accrue without any employee contribution – still only 51 per cent of eligible employees signed up. As *Nudge* authors Thaler and Sunstein put it, it's 'equivalent to not bothering to cash your paycheck'.)[35] So, through an adaptation of an experiment by Thaler and fellow economist Shlomo Benartzi, the government asked employers to test an auto-enrolment plan for new employees that took advantage of a behavioural phenomenon called default bias.[36] Simply put, we're inclined to accept choices that have already been made for us (think of the ringtone on your phone or privacy settings on your computer). Of course, any worker still retained the right to opt out, but many more have chosen to remain enrolled. So far it's worked well: in the first six months of widespread roll-out among large UK firms, pension participation rose from 61 to 83 per cent. That's 400,000 people. By 2018, auto-enrolment will cover all workers across the country.[37]

Design thinking, too, has started to make inroads in government. After Rohan's experience of the New Enterprise Allowance brought home to him how detached officials were from the actual people who government policies were trying to help, he decided that something had to be done to bring the users of government policies back into the way programmes were designed and run. 'I was so frustrated by the officials' answers to these basic questions about the way this policy was presented to the people who might benefit from it. What is the script? What posters are up? What materials do people get if they're interested?' he recounts. 'Just imagine the individual lives that could have been changed, the amazing businesses started, the jobs created, if there had just been this small change, if there had just been a moment's thought given to the actual human interaction. Why is there such a dislocation between policymakers and reality? And this is just a small policy in the overall scheme of things. Think about all the policies right across government and how much more effective they could be.'[38]

Rohan initiated a process to bring design thinking into the heart of government. He met with experts at the Royal College of Art – Jeremy Myerson and Anthony Dunne – as well as Tom Hulme from the UK office of design firm IDEO. From that came the idea to run a design-thinking course for top civil servants. 'I wanted to devise a systemic response to this systemic problem,' Rohan says. So, in November 2012, he convened a group of a couple of hundred of the UK's top civil servants at Number 10 for a design-thinking workshop. The venue – the State Dining Room – emphasised the importance of the enterprise: 'I chose that room very specifically because it's the grandest room at Number 10,' Rohan recalls. 'Civil servants are a pretty cautious bunch, and Whitehall is not a particularly amenable place to new ideas, so I wanted them to understand that this was serious.' Professors from the Royal College of Art's new Service Design programme, who led the day-long crash course, made good use of the space, covering it in Post-its (the global medium of design thinking, I've discovered since teaching at the d.school). Cabinet Office minister Francis Maude kicked it off; Cabinet Secretary Jeremy Heywood and head of the Civil Service Bob Kerslake weighed in to make closing remarks. 'The day was bookended by the people in charge,' Rohan explains. 'I did everything I could to frame this as legitimate and mainstream.'[39]

There are now signs that design thinking is entering the bloodstream of the civil service. The recently established Open Policy Making Team was a product of that day's events. It works with departments across the civil service to bring more of a human-centred mindset, and an approach involving rapid prototyping and testing of ideas, to their policy efforts; now it's helping to make design thinking part of the core training programme for all Whitehall civil servants. The Ministry of Justice (MinJ) and the Government Digital Service have been particularly enthusiastic. MinJ has embraced an 'agile' design approach to both their digital and offline interactions with those who use its services. Of course all this – the jargon, the Post-it notes, the brainstorming – is easy to mock, or portray as the latest management fad. In fact it's much more than that. It's a fundamental re-orientation of policymaking, from a focus on bureaucratic needs and priorities to the real lives of the real people government is supposed to serve.

***

But let's not get carried away. Although there have been steps forward (for example, Prime Minister David Cameron commissioned intensive 'mystery shopping' research so he could learn how policies were actually being implemented in the real world), the vast majority of government policymaking and implementation is still mired in a bureaucratic mindset. The number of politicians, policymakers, and other public officials who have even heard of human-centred design or behavioural economics, let alone experienced it, is minuscule. While having specialist units – like the UK's Open Policy Making Team – is a promising start, the big benefits, in terms of a much higher hit rate of policies and programmes that actually work, will most quickly be realised if the principles of design thinking are integrated into the everyday habits of every member of the public sector. That is not some outlandish aspiration: after all, we're simply talking about a way of working that puts people first.

That means government officials regularly spending time with their 'users' – i.e. citizens. Of course ministers and officials are busy, but it's really just a question of priorities. Instead of spending half their time in meetings being briefed on policy problems, they need to go out and actually experience them. In a small way, before I went to Stanford and really understood all this systematically, it's what I tried to do while I was working in government myself. Before designing a new parenting programme, I went along to parenting classes and talked to the parents about their experiences. Before implementing one of the government's biggest and most ambitious domestic policy initiatives – National Citizen Service, a personal development and community service programme for teenagers – we spent years prototyping and testing the model, even in opposition, using precious resources that would normally have been devoted to purely political activity.

From the highest levels of decision making to the front line of service delivery, we cannot just assume we know the nature of people's problems and what solutions would be best for them. Development expert Robert Chambers, who has campaigned for decades for a more human-centred approach to global poverty alleviation, complains of the pervasive 'we know what needs to be done' problem among experts. He calls for 'immersions' – for officials and policymakers to join the poor communities they're serving: staying in a home overnight, helping with daily tasks, participating in life. To him, this is the only way to avoid missing key insights hidden in the nuance of life on the ground. Unless they do this, poverty experts get stuck in a 'self-referential trap' of workshops, conferences, meetings, articles, and reports, all from air-conditioned offices in capital cities.[40] All the more credit to Jeremy Hunt who, as Health Secretary, spent one day a week actually working in the NHS.

The point of human-centred policy design is literally what its name suggests – to put humans at the centre. Before they begin, before they even know what problem they're solving, our politicians should seek out and gain a thorough understanding of the human relationships, human dynamics, and human realities of the lives they're trying to change. Any policymaker about to approve a policy or programme without having done this should stop, put on their coat, go out into the real world and talk to the people who their policy will affect.

But there's still a problem: scale. How can policymakers (most of whom are holed up in London or other administrative centres) possibly achieve such a nuanced awareness of people in communities around the country? Even regular visits and 'immersions' are no substitute for the local knowledge embedded in those who live, work, and play; who struggle, strive, and cope in their own towns and neighbourhoods. Not to mention the fact that capturing such a rich understanding of each region and town, and then tailoring policy and programmes accordingly, would be impossible to deliver from central government. Unless government were closer to home – closer to people ...

A more human way of organising government

Saint-Céneri-le-Gérei (population 140) is a fairly unremarkable village in French Normandy. But for nineteen years between 1995 and 2014, it was remarkable for its mayor: Ken Tatham, an Englishman from Leeds.

Tatham's path to the mayor's office started when he decided to forgo university in Britain, instead travelling around Europe. In Spain, he met the Frenchwoman who would become his wife. Her father had a second home in Saint-Céneri-le-Gérei, where they married. They lived in Paris for a while but ultimately returned in 1969 to raise a family in the village which, he says, is 'one of the most beautiful in France'. Tatham's wife was a village councillor and he was constantly telling her: 'You should do this and that' and she got a little annoyed and said: 'Why don't you get involved yourself?' Tatham, who by then was a dual citizen, was eligible to run for office. So in 1995 he ran for the council, won, and became mayor. At first people were a bit sceptical. 'A lot of the villagers didn't take too kindly to having an Englishman as mayor,' he recalls, 'especially as the English had demolished the village castle at the end of the Hundred Years' War,' but 'they forgot that very swiftly … it used to come back as more of a joke in the end.' Tatham found that local government in France was quite different from local government in England. In France, mayors form a central part of civic life: 'If somebody has a problem, it becomes yours,' he says. 'You're like a social assistant in a way. Your door is always open to people and their problems no matter what they are.'[41]

There are nearly 37,000 mayors in France, one for every commune, village, town, and city. Unlike local government in the UK, French mayors have real, autonomous power.[42] But the French get more than powerful, accountable public figures in their mayors: they also get a personal representative in government. Tatham was intimately involved in the lives of his citizens. 'If anything goes wrong or if there's any sort of problem they come and see me.'[43] He remembers getting a call one Christmas Eve. 'We were eating the Christmas meal and suddenly the telephone rang. Somebody told us that an enormous wall to the castle had fallen on the main road,' which in the village was fairly narrow. Being Christmas, the normal road and municipal workers weren't around, 'so we all trundled off there,' Tatham recalls, 'and picked up the stones to make a small passage for at least one car to get by.' Even though this fell outside his 'official' duties, Tatham happily helped out. Life might sometimes be difficult for *Monsieur le maire*, but the advantage of the French system is that if something goes wrong, there's someone down the road who, if not directly responsible, is at least there to help. Residents have a human connection with the state: 'They know someone's listening,' Tatham says.

Big government disasters

We've seen how government tends to be focused on the wrong priorities – numbers rather than people – and we've seen how government tends to go about things the wrong way, failing to put people at the centre of the policymaking process. These are deep and important flaws. But there's something deeper still. A flaw that can't be corrected by a change of focus or a new approach. A flaw that is structural.

The biggest problem with government today is that the people making the decisions are too far from the people affected by them. Government is too big, too distant. The UK has one of the most centralised governments in the world: to an absurd and counterproductive degree, things are run from the centre. Britons have no Ken Tatham at the local level (or any level for that matter). While in France the average size of the population in the lowest tier of executive government is 1,500,[44] in the UK it is 150,000.[45] As a result, our connection with the state is inhuman: bossy letters; demands for payment of taxes; maddening bureaucracy if you want to do the simplest thing. Who can name their councillor? Or the leader of their council? Or their MP? Or pretty much anyone in government apart from the famous faces at the very top?

As a result, accountability is fuzzy – lying with endless obscure bits of government and bureaucracies with multiple overlapping responsibilities that are not clearly defined, least of all to the people who matter most: citizens. Decisions about – and crucially, funding for – local services are determined in London as ministers and officials in central government, rather than local leaders, dictate city, town, village, even neighbourhood-level policies.

Here is a comically bizarre example of the British state's staggering centralisation. Tony Blair's government had the perfectly reasonable aim of wanting people in hospital to eat better food. So they hired television celebrity Loyd Grossman, former presenter of the BBC's *MasterChef*, to advise on menus. Amongst other things, Grossman asked the Secretary of State for Health to require that henceforth, all macaroni cheese served in the National Health Service should be 'four-cheese macaroni cheese'. I am prepared to believe that four-cheese macaroni cheese is better than the single-cheese variety; but I am not prepared to accept that the number of cheeses in every pasta dish in every hospital in the country should be decided by a minister in London.

When decisions are made by those out of touch with the reality on the ground, the outcomes are worse: policy aims are not met, money is wasted, and people feel increasingly disconnected from, frustrated with, and unable to have a say in, their government. (Just one in five British voters thinks government acts in their best interests.)[46] Big, centralised government – a relic of the bureaucratic age – is one of the main reasons for the growing distrust of and dissatisfaction with politics. Ministers pretend they can solve every problem and never do; on the occasions when things go right, it's often just luck. Bloodless bureaucrats puff up ministerial egos with unrealistic assurances of impact and effectiveness that typically turn to dust – but only after a reshuffle has moved the minister on and the same civil servants can agree with the new boss how ridiculous it all was in the first place. Systems designed in the pre-telephone age, never mind the pre-Internet age, creak and crumble with the strain of keeping up with the expectations of citizens who want to be in control, not controlled from on high. The whole centralised farce, played out year after year, parliament after parliament, government after government: Labour, Conservative, coalition – people see little difference whoever is notionally in charge because little underneath, in the structure of government, actually changes.

But there is one thing that has changed: our ability to do something about it. Thanks to the information revolution, technology and innovation, we really can take power out of the hands of centralised, bureaucratic government and place it where it belongs – in the hands of the people. If we are going to see any transformational improvement in the way we live, in our economy, in our society, then power must be dispersed.

***

The hubris of big, centralised government has grown to the point where its self-inflicted catastrophes are now clearly undermining the rationale for centralisation. It used to be said that centralised government is more efficient. Occasionally, yes. There are obviously certain public policy objectives that are best handled at the national level. Localising our foreign policy doesn't make much sense. But many problems that beset government arise precisely because they are handled on a national scale. This is most obviously the case when it comes to the contracting out of enormous parts of the state to external organisations, often in the private sector – the biggest change in the structure of government we've seen in the last few decades. But the problem is not the contracting out: it's the size of the contracts.

In *The End of Big*, Nicco Mele identifies 'Nerd Disease', in which technical experts make things needlessly complicated in order to justify their own maintenance services. He describes consulting for a business that had an online staff in one building and another team that worked in a warehouse across the street, shipping orders. The company wanted to integrate the computer systems for the two sides of the business and the technical staff were advising the CEO to spend $1 million on a contract with an external supplier. Instead Mele suggested something different: simply have someone walk between the buildings twice a day with the orders.[47]

As expensive as nerd disease is when things go according to plan, it is even worse when they go wrong. The ramifications tend to be massive. Instead of a small, local failure, it's national and affects everyone in the system, often all at once. And because, for political reasons, bureaucrats and contractors are reluctant to inform superiors of problems, they only become apparent when it's too late. Consequently, big government contracts often end up mired in waste, failure, fraud, and abuse.[48]

In Britain, we had a potent example with the NHS National Programme for IT. Tony Blair wanted to reform the NHS, and among his perfectly admirable goals was to make it more patient focused, with best practice spread around the system. Blair decided in 2002 to build a single electronic network that would store patients' records centrally and make them accessible to doctors and hospitals across the NHS. Conceptually, that's an important idea. As we will see, electronic patient records are a crucial step in delivering a more human approach to health care. But the attempt to implement this idea through a big national contract? Problems soon arose.

It all started with nerd disease. The Department of Health was ill-equipped for such an ambitious project, so it hired a number of consultants, one of whom, Richard Granger, formerly of Deloitte, took over completely. The first mistake was to nationalise the project; the NHS would manage it centrally. This would be overseen by Granger through a new agency called Connecting for Health (CFH). But building the project became too difficult. Over five years, the project's cost estimates ballooned from an initial £2.3 billion contract to £6.2 billion to £12.4 billion.[49] In a 2006 interview with the *Financial Times*, Lord Warner, the health minister in charge of the project, admitted that the costs could reach as high as £20 billion.[50] Meanwhile, despite delays, the withdrawal of major contractor Accenture from the project and significant technical problems when the system was delivered, Granger, the politicians, and other bureaucrats involved maintained their support for CFH. Political scientists Anthony King and Ivor Crewe observe in *The Blunders of Our Governments* that Granger 'was keen not only on succeeding but on being seen to succeed'. Contractors didn't want to incur penalties, and politicians didn't want to lose the political capital they had invested in the scheme.[51]

By 2007 Granger was out, but it would take another four years before CFH was put out of its misery. Even after the project was shut down the costs kept mounting, and the latest estimate of its lifetime costs was £9.8 billion, after years of wasted effort and multiple failures.[52] What a terrible waste of money. Regardless of Granger's competence, the true problem was the sheer scale of the project. The Blair government expected the NHS to build one of the most ambitious IT systems anywhere, without trials or pilot projects, without significant feedback from doctors and health-care workers, and with little technical capacity.[53] While the project succumbed to a combination of all of these difficulties, the scale of the failure can be singularly attributed to needless centralisation. The bigger the project, the harder the fall. The trouble with bureaucracy running amok in this way is that it has the unfortunate tendency to keep running amok. During the twentieth century, as we turned to the state to provide and organise vast new areas of activity – education, health, welfare – we tolerated bureaucracy in order to achieve scale and efficiency. But once the ball started rolling, bureaucracy begat more bureaucracy; government grew larger and more distant. This is not just bad for citizens: it's bad for government workers too. Most are well-intentioned, intelligent, and hard-working professionals; yet centralisation robs them of discretion, of the chance to use their experience and wisdom. Centralisation inevitably generates the endless targets and rules and systems and procedures for teachers, police officers, nurses, judges … restrictions which entirely disregard our public servants' common sense and expertise.

But there are people who benefit from centralisation – and they're the ones helping to prop the system up. The concentration of power in London or Washington or Brussels leads directly to the work of the special interest groups and lobbyists that descend there. Centralisation makes it easy for large firms to lock out smaller ones, resulting in the biggest interests making the rules without the small ones having a seat at the table. Big, centralised government attracts the flies of corporate lobbying. Decentralise power, and you make it much harder for the lobbyists to twist it to their ends.

A powerful mayor in every town

To democratise the levers of power and restore faith in politics and government, we need a total transformation of our political system into one that operates on a human scale. Margaret Thatcher's government is perhaps the sole example in recent British political life of such a radical structural shift. Believing that state control of industry was holding the country's economy back, she privatised (amongst others) British Gas, Jaguar, British Telecom, British Aerospace, British Steel, British Airways and BP, and deregulated many other industries, including finance and energy. She wanted to 'give power back to the people', she said. Whether you support or oppose her agenda, she clearly effected a major transformation in the role of the state. But while she may have decentralised economic power through policies like the promotion of home and share ownership, she was not exactly radical when it came to dispersing political power. Indeed, the Conservative governments of the 1980s and 1990s have been accused of exactly the opposite: of centralising power by taking policy discretion and funding away from local councils and giving central government increased control over local budgets, rules, and development. So while Thatcher demonstrated that radical change is possible, she also symbolised the work that still needs to be done.

We need to make government and public services more accountable, more transparent, and more effective by applying the techniques and innovations that have transformed many consumer markets in recent years, with higher and higher levels of user control and service quality. Government needs to be small, nimble, and above all more local. Some policy areas – monetary policy, the armed forces, foreign affairs – are by necessity a national endeavour. But the vast majority – welfare, education, health care, social services, planning, conservation, policing, economic development – can and should be delivered locally. We need to devolve to the human scale.

The most human possible scale is that of individual people and their families. Alan Milburn, the former Labour Health Secretary, remembers at nine years old coming home one day to his council flat and finding the door painted yellow; in the morning it had been red. 'The colour wasn't chosen by my mum. Nor by my granddad. It was chosen by the council – but they didn't live in that house, and we did.'[54] This story shows that the best possible decentralisation is directly to people themselves, so they can make as many of the decisions that affect their lives as possible. That is typically how the richest and most powerful members of society live, and we should want those same freedoms for everybody.

Where individual control is not possible, where collective provision and decision making are required, we need government. And the first step towards a less centralised, more human structure for government starts right where we began this section: with mayors. A directly elected local leader is recognisable, accountable, and responsive. Whoever put faith in a committee? Mayoral government is more human. It is also more pragmatic; often non-partisan, mayors are doers. They might nominally identify with one party but their typical concerns are fixing street lights, not bloviating about political controversies. They focus on getting things done because they literally have to live with the results. Making the buses punctual, the parks clean and the city centre thrive might not inspire intellectual debate in newspaper opinion pages but they're the stuff of everyday life: they are what matter to most people.

Of course, it's not enough simply to have a mayor. Mayors must have real power. Somewhat ironically (given that in our over-centralised country pretty much everything is decided in London), the capital city does have a mayor. But the Mayor of London has comparatively little power to wield or budget to deploy. It's better than nothing, and it's encouraging to see more power being devolved to Manchester (with a mayor for the metropolitan region and more control over health, social care and business taxes), but most cities and towns in the UK don't have directly elected executive mayors at all. You might say that some of England's largest cities had the chance to move to a mayoral system of local government, and they said no in referendums held in 2012.[55] Of course people said no. They were not offered the kind of strong mayors seen in other developed countries, an institution with real power to drive change and manage policy effectively at the local level.

America's system is a great example. Mayor Michael Bloomberg of New York implemented a radical school reform programme, made aggressive fiscal reforms to balance the budget, and took bold steps for public health like banning smoking in public areas and trans fats in restaurants. He was a prodigious policy innovator – whether in developing new ideas for tackling poverty, greening the city, or encouraging volunteerism and philanthropy. While Bloomberg certainly had policy misses, he was able to use his influence as a single accountable figure to take the courageous but unpopular decisions an anonymous council would never make, like confronting teachers' unions or challenging religious bigotry.[56]

It's not just in America. Mayor Bertrand Delanoë of Paris saw the success of Lyon's bike-sharing programme and started Paris Vélib', now the second largest such system in the world. And it goes beyond big cities, too. In France 80 per cent of mayors are responsible for fewer than 1,000 residents each,[57] but they still have local policy discretion.

Even in Britain, this is not a new or foreign idea. It's the more recent centralisation that's out of place. In 1417 the first street lamps in Britain appeared on London streets thanks to Sir Henry Barton, the mayor. Strong civic leaders appear throughout the histories of Britain's greatest cities. Joseph Chamberlain, a nineteenth-century mayor of Birmingham, perhaps represents the pinnacle of British localism. He provided the big, simple things local people needed – like clean water, natural gas, and education (he campaigned for universal schooling). But he also knew that it took more than that to truly nourish a community, and actively sought to provide access to art through museums, and learning through the foundation of the University of Birmingham. In Victorian Liverpool, Sir Archibald Salvidge, chairman of the local Conservative Party, was known as the 'King of Liverpool'. He used his influence to build the Mersey Tunnel, connecting the city with Birkenhead, in the hope of revitalising its port. Salvidge worked to find the funding for the project, which became a symbol of the feats cities could accomplish on their own. Liverpool under Salvidge (like Birmingham under Chamberlain) benefited from investing in public assets, public transport, and electric and gas companies. Salvidge knew that these investments paid for themselves, and the Liverpool Corporation, buttressed by the strong local government led by Salvidge and others, was able to pay for a revitalisation of the city, including comprehensive public housing for 140,000 people (15 per cent of the population) and a transport system that connected the city to the suburbs.[58]

Decentralising power is not just about the principle of control or the practice of pragmatism. It is also the best way to generate and test new ideas. In the United States, experimentalism is seen as a critical part of localism. Governors at state level and mayors at municipal level pioneer fresh approaches and policies that get adopted elsewhere in America and sometimes the world over. Former San Francisco Mayor Gavin Newsom is a great example. In 2004, he used his local executive power to preside over the first gay marriage in America. It prompted years of public debate, referenda and legal wrangling – but the result is one of the biggest social changes in history, with the legalisation of gay marriage sweeping across the United States and the world. That incredible, liberating revolution began in earnest with the conviction of an assertive mayor. President Obama's health-care plan was based on the reforms of Mitt Romney, Massachusetts' former governor. The mayor of Providence, Rhode Island, Angel Taveras, won the Mayor's Challenge (a prize established by Mike Bloomberg to encourage local civic innovation) for his initiative Providence Talks, which helps poor children, who hear millions fewer words during childhood than their more affluent peers, hampering cognitive development – to close the 'word gap'. Providence Talks is a groundbreaking early-childhood intervention programme in which parents wear devices that record how many words they say on a daily basis and receive regular advice on how better to talk to their children. The idea is to establish a model that other places can follow. In America, in areas as diverse as civil rights, education, the legalisation of medical and recreational marijuana, environmental protection, assisted suicide, food safety, even the regulation of drones ... change often starts at the bottom and trickles upwards. It's even true in Japan, where the most recent advance in gay rights has come from a district in central Tokyo, Shibuya Ward, which announced in February 2015 that it would give same-sex couples the same legal rights as married heterosexual couples – a major step forward in a country that while tolerant of homosexuality, grants gay couples relatively few rights.[59]

Can anyone in the UK name a single modern-day policy or innovation that began at the local level? For all the problems of US government and politics, America has at least one thing right: for the best results, policy innovation cannot happen in a vacuum, and it cannot all come from the top. This role of local jurisdictions as 'laboratories of democracy', articulated by Supreme Court Justice Louis Brandeis and based on the Tenth Amendment of the US Constitution, might be an American creation but its applicability is universal. We should bring it to the UK.

MVG – Minimum Viable Government

Strong mayors are just the beginning. In Silicon Valley, there is an overused cliché about when to launch your start-up that nevertheless contains an element of wisdom. The term is Minimum Viable Product, or 'MVP'. It means that you should get your business out in front of real customers (or 'users') as quickly as possible. If you wait until your product is perfect before you launch it, you're too late. Hence, MVP – the smallest, simplest version of your idea that might possibly work. When it comes to politics, our rule should be MVG – Minimum Viable Government.

Power – and budgets – should be devolved to a level just high enough to be practical. This would vary for different areas of policy: it is of course impractical, indeed impossible to decentralise everything. The key to dispersing power effectively is the rather wonkish term subsidiarity, which means devolving power to the lowest possible level. It is supposed to be the operating principle of the EU – a claim that is rightly met with hollow laughter in most quarters. But it makes sense in theory and is a good guide for Minimum Viable Government. For example, when it comes to the regulation of ozone-depleting chemicals, arms control, or (as we'll see later) meaningful animal-welfare rules, MVG is the international level. For policy areas like immigration, or product safety standards, it's the national level. For urban transport and economic development, it's the city (or metropolitan region). And throughout any decentralised system, there will need to be some kind of fair redistribution of resources. But in a wide range of policy areas – especially social policy – we can decentralise power much further than anything we've seen in recent political history.

There is a clue in evolutionary biology. British anthropologist Robin Dunbar found that based on the size of our neocortex, humans can only have around 150 meaningful relationships at once, and that villages and hunter-gatherer societies worked best at a median population of this size.[60] This has been extrapolated by others to include work settings and other groups. In Sweden, for example, the heads of the tax authority are using the idea of 'Dunbar's Number' to restructure the organisation, reasoning that if you can't know more than 150 people, you can't work well with more than that number either.[61] W. L. Gore & Associates, the innovative materials company, builds a new office each time an existing one is about to exceed 150 people.[62] I'm not proposing that we carve up the world into governing units of 150 people. But I mention Dunbar's number because it shows how low we can go if we really want to understand 'human scale'.

When it comes to government, the closest viable unit to this scale – the level at which people can realistically know and interact with their leaders and decision makers on a direct human basis – is the neighbourhood. This might not comprise as few as 150 people, but it's certainly not as many as 150,000 (the average number living in the lowest tier of executive government in the UK today).[63] The neighbourhood is a vivid expression of the concept of Minimum Viable Government, and more policy could be run at that level than you might think. Parks – obviously. Schools? Certainly –

especially if we make our school system more human, along the lines set out in the next chapter. How about social services? Or welfare? Some aspects of these services, unlikely as it may sound, are actually ideal candidates for devolution to the neighbourhood level. They are intensely personal, human services, absolutely demanding the kind of empathetic approach described earlier in this chapter. Neighbourhood governance goes with the grain of human history, traditions and behaviour. It's our neighbourhoods and our villages that we identify as our communities. And in the future, technology could help make neighbourhood governance more realistic, with services like Nextdoor – a kind of Facebook for your neighbourhood – offering new and convenient ways to bring people together in a community at the local level.

Localism will face inevitable challenges. People talk about the dangers of a 'postcode lottery' – as if everything was uniform (and uniformly good) under centralisation. There's a postcode lottery *now*. At least with proper decentralisation (of power and budgets) local people would be in control: instead of a postcode lottery, postcode power. Others point to local government scandals like the sex-abuse case in Rotherham and say: 'See – look what happens when power becomes entrenched and unaccountable in a local one-party state.' Yes, but that's like saying we should condemn cars because there are car accidents; it's actually an argument for dispersing power more, not less.

It seems that everyone in government is in favour of devolution as far as their level, but no further. (If you're at the top, that's not very far.) But radical localism is an essential step towards a more human system of government. If more power is devolved, those in control will be members of the community, not far-off rulers. No more faceless committees: local politicians will actually know their constituents (like Mayor Ken Tatham in Saint-Céneri-le-Gérei) and therefore, as the writer Nassim Taleb has argued, be less likely to be wasteful or corrupt. It's harder to betray your community's interests if you have to live with the consequences, right there amongst the residents. Instead of decisions being made in distant Whitehall or even the council chamber, which can often feel just as distant, decisions for communities will be made *by* communities *in* communities. Not only would this improve the quality of policymaking, make government more responsive, and help citizens feel better represented – it would be harder for special interests to game the system, for lobbyists to buy the outcomes they want, and for mistakes to have such devastating consequences.

Pedants might say: 'How are you going to implement all the ideas in your book – including the decentralisation of power – without a strong central government to push it all through? It's contradictory.' No, it isn't. It's just a question of sequencing. Of course it's true that it would require bold central government action to bring about the decentralisation that Britain needs. Just as it's true that many recommendations in this book would require strong central government leadership or enforcement, even after decentralisation of many political powers had taken place. The principle of Minimum Viable Government doesn't mean everything should be decentralised, but spurious arguments like these are often thrown up as distractions by those who basically think nothing should be decentralised. It's always easiest to stick to the status quo and conjure fears of the 'chaos' that radical change would bring. But only radical change is enough to deal with the deep problems our democracy now faces.

Our opportunity to initiate the kind of big change we need is right before us, with the commitment of all parties to the decentralisation of power following 2014's Scottish independence referendum. If we don't use this chance to dismantle our antiquated, sclerotic, bureaucratic-age state and put something more human in its place, we will pay a heavy price: the guarantee of still more years of government underperformance and political discontent.

More human politics

More human government needs one more thing: everyone's engagement. In most democracies, trust in politics is falling, and one of the main reasons is people's belief that their vote doesn't really matter. Think about the difference in participation if we made the process itself more human.

You can see one version of this every four years at the start of the US Presidential election. In the Iowa caucuses, voters gather in small groups in homes, school gyms and community centres and hear from proxies for each candidate. The participants debate, ask questions, engage with each other. Then, caucus-goers 'vote' by standing in a group next to the proxy of the candidate they support. Candidates without enough backing are eliminated and their supporters move to someone else in the next round, until only those candidates with a certain threshold of support remain. At that point, the precinct's votes are divided proportionally between the various candidates.[64] The voters have spent an evening engaging as democratic citizens, learning about the issues and candidates, but doing so in a human way, face to face.

It's fashionable to decry how poorly informed voters are today. This might be true of the voter who feels detached and unimportant, but because the caucus-goers can see the impact of their role, they are better informed: while fewer voters attend caucuses than vote in primaries, those who do are more aware and involved than voters elsewhere.[65] Rather than leading to campaigns fought in the media, as most elections increasingly are, caucuses favour 'grassroots campaigning' in which voters have to 'be more attentive', but candidates have to be 'better ... face to face'.[66] It is a recipe for more civic-minded elections that engage the population.

We should introduce caucuses in the UK – perhaps trying them first for local elections. Combined with other ideas, like shifting voting to weekends, or making polling day a public holiday – a true, community-based day of civic participation – this could really galvanise a new spirit of engagement in democracy. But even that wouldn't be enough. Civic participation shouldn't just happen once every five years.

Civic service

The Park Slope Food Co-op is a neighbourhood grocery store in Brooklyn, New York. I was first taken there by my friend Chloe Wasserman around fifteen years ago, and I fell in love with it instantly. Each of its 16,000 members contributes to the community by working in the shop once every four weeks for a total of two hours and forty-five minutes in a squad which almost always works together as a close team. Every member must contribute equally in time but can participate in a variety of tasks. All co-op members are entitled to play a role in the store's governance. Not only is it a close-knit community, but by saving on labour costs, the co-op can provide its members with high-quality organic, local food at a 20 to 40 per cent discount.

What can a grocery store teach us about civic participation? It shows us that if you humanise the process, members of a community are happy to give their time to that community, working alongside others. And they get something concrete out of it – lower prices for their shopping. But when it comes to engaging with your community through the political system, it's a completely dehumanised process. An anonymous trip to the polling station once every few years, and the payment of local taxes. That's it. No wonder people are disengaging from politics.

We could change that. We could strengthen a neighbourhood's social fabric by actively bringing residents into the civic sphere through the concept of civic service. This would be a bit like jury service, except more predictable and regular. Let's identify roles in the local community currently provided by taxpayer-funded government employees that could be provided by local residents, and then invite (or even require) residents to give two or three hours' service a month, just like the members of the Park Slope Food Co-op. It would cut costs, help people connect with their neighbours and lead to an increased sense of belonging and social responsibility. Perhaps most significantly, it would enable a big reduction in people's council tax bills – an added incentive to participate. Civic service is a natural, human complement to neighbourhood government. The aim should be to make local service a social norm; make it easier to do by specifying the time, the place and the people to do it with, and offer a tangible incentive in the form of lower local taxes. Even with a compulsory version of civic service (which might seem extreme), if the benefits are clear and the social connections strong, people will love it, appreciating being of service and the engagement with their community.

By making politics more human we can make people more engaged and better informed. For a system of government that has increasingly lost the trust of its own people, it would be a small step towards rehabilitation.

CHAPTER 2

SCHOOLS

South Korea's education record is the envy of reformers around the world, with its students consistently topping international league tables. Korean students do well in tests, because preparing for tests is all they do. The competitive culture of Korean schools, in which all the students in a given class are ranked against one another, and the culture of Korean families, which equates academic success with family honour, means that when a student falls behind in class rankings families pull out the stops to ensure success. They might hire tutors or nag them to study. Or they might just send them to a *hagwon*. *Hagwon*s are, according to Korean journalist and academic Se-Woong Koo, 'soulless facilities, with room after room divided by thin walls, lit by long fluorescent bulbs, and stuffed with students memorizing English vocabulary, Korean grammar rules, and math formulas. Students typically stay after regular school hours until 10 p.m. or later.'[67] According to Koo, who taught at one of these schools for a time, Korean students might succeed in the tests, but they suffer elsewhere. Koo remembers how his students lost clumps of hair, hardly slept, and were even suicidal (like half of Korean teenagers).[68] Suicide is in fact the leading cause of death for South Koreans aged fifteen to twenty-four.[69] This is what, it seems, we are striving for.

'The kids didn't want to leave'

Jason Pittman didn't begin his professional life as a teacher – he started his own tech company. But when he found himself rushing home from work to get to his volunteer teaching gig, he realised it was time for a career switch. So he went to graduate school and soon afterwards took a position teaching fifth graders at a public [state] elementary school in Alexandria, Virginia, a suburb of Washington DC. 'I had such a wide variety of student need,' Pittman recalls. 'More than half our families lived below the poverty line. But we also had quite a few that were fairly well-to-do. We had first-generation immigrant families that were just getting started in the United States, and we had parents who were lobbyists on Capitol Hill.

'I had a little girl from El Salvador … no English-language support at home. But she was reading out of a college geology textbook! She was so in love with understanding the earth better. I had another who was ten years old. He had left Somalia and was in a refugee camp in Kenya. He came into my classroom not having spent a day in school in his life. According to the school district I was supposed to be teaching him American history, fractions, reading comprehension … but none of it made any sense to him.' What frustrated Pittman was the curriculum's absurd rigidity. 'If I taught the fifth-grade lesson that was in the state's standardised curriculum, it was, no matter how hard I tried, the right lesson for absolutely nobody. I could make it an average lesson, but I could never really make it valuable to even one student in my class. There was such a wide variety.'

One day, he tried something different. 'I pretty much threw up my hands and told the class: "I'm so sick of disappointing you every day, what would you like to do? What would be something fun we could just do together?" A couple of kids wanted to build a robot, so we got some NXC chips [NXC is a programming language used with Lego robotics] and put them on robotics parts. We had a couple of kids who were into gardening, so we got them in the garden. The girl from El Salvador who was into geology – she ended up lecturing the class on types of rocks and how they were formed. All of a sudden it was fantastic – my students were doing well by every way I could assess them, even on standardised tests, and I didn't even teach to the test!'

Pittman then started to run a programme aimed at preparing children for a science-orientated magnet school in the area. On a weekly basis, he would teach science, maths, and technology to all 700 students in his school, from pre-kindergarten to sixth grade. From the start, Pittman diverged quickly from how science is typically taught.

'The traditional science-lesson format starts with the teacher giving a concept, then explaining how it all works. You give a bunch of step-by-steps to prove that what I told you at the beginning of the lesson is true, and then I ask you to write a conclusion verifying what I told you at the beginning. There's no science in that at all, obviously. So I dropped the cookbook-recipe science format. I just said: "Look, let's just rip out all the procedure pages from these lessons." I even ripped out most of the upfront concept explanations as well. I was happy to provide all the same materials that we were going to use in that lesson, but I basically said: "Let's just play with this a while – let's tinker with it." And we used the question to actually get to the answer.'

Pittman's lab quickly became a sanctuary for bored students across the school. 'I left the lab open every day so they could come in and work on their projects,' he remembers. 'They could come down and work in the garden, work in the lab, and build their robot or their rocket or whatever it was they were excited about.'

Once again, it worked. Pittman's low-income students were closing the gap with their better-off peers.[70] He was so successful that he's since won multiple national teacher-of-the-year awards; First Lady Michelle Obama visited his 13,000 square-foot educational garden; and he was twice selected as an 'educator-at-sea' for *National Geographic*, joining oceanographic explorer Dr Robert Ballard (discoverer of the *Titanic*) on board his vessel E/V *Nautilus* to conduct lessons from maritime expeditions.

But then, out of the blue, Pittman's programme was cut from the school's budget. Eliminated entirely. 'It was so frustrating. I felt like I'd proven that we have a better way here, and we can actually serve kids and not serve tests.' But that's not what the school was interested in. His methods couldn't be tested or quantified or regulated, so when the budget tightened it was his programme that was cut. Thankfully, the community disagreed with the school district. A group of local business owners and parents got together and started a charity specifically to raise money for his programme. It was an imperfect solution, though, because it turned Pittman from a teacher into a perpetual fund-raiser. 'Every year I had to be a part of the advocacy, making speeches at fund-raisers, raising my own salary. And I was still getting the same pressure to help kids practise multiple-choice tests.'

So here was a teacher, recognised on a national level and achieving incredible results for low-income students, being forced to spend his free time raising the money to pay his own wages (which were in any case being systematically cut). He'd had enough. During an appearance on the popular American public radio show *This American Life*, he described how he went to the Pentagon to receive a science-teaching award, and then got back to find another pay cut. 'My frustration sort of hit a peak,' he recalls. After talking to the host Ira Glass about what was going on, he announced, on air, that he couldn't do it any more. 'As it turned out, making yourself available in front of two million people is not a bad way to find something else!'

A couple of months later, the phone rang. It was Sal Khan, the brilliant hedge-fund analyst turned social entrepreneur who founded Khan Academy, one of the world's most popular online learning platforms. 'I had been using Khan Academy in my classroom, so I thought it might be a joke.' It wasn't. Sal wanted to start a school – a prototype for the school of the future, one that could literally help every school in the world teach children in a more human – and more effective – way. And Pittman would be just the right person to run it.

Khan Lab School is that prototype. Launched in September 2014 with a handful of children whose parents shared Sal's vision, it's a year-round, mixed-age, mixed-gender 'one-room-schoolhouse'. It is 'mastery-based', free of grade levels and grade assessments, meaning that each child moves at a pace that's right for them. They aren't advanced just because the calendar says so. As Pittman explains: 'We're trying to get kids to practise a certain skill until they can demonstrate it a proficient level.'

At Khan, 'traditional' learning – that is, adherence to standards and curriculum – manifests itself in lessons by the Khan teachers (sometimes one-on-one; sometimes in small- to medium-sized groups) as well as computer-based tutorials from Khan Academy and Udacity (whose founder we'll meet in Chapter 7) which mix videos and exercises that students work through at their own pace. The benefit of using self-directed tutorials is that they create data in real time about student performance (and any roadblocks) that a teacher can view from day to day. 'I can literally see where they're struggling as they're working through their content independently, and then I can organise a lesson around that,' Pittman explains.

The students always seem to be building things. Like a giant ribcage made out of cardboard, paper, and papier mâché. They could have learned about a ribcage with a diagram or passing around a plastic model, but Pittman's students learned by building one – big enough for them to stand inside. The project started out with students thinking about ways in which they were similar to one another. They used an online course from Udacity to learn about the human genome, discovering that our organs and internal systems are largely the same, which led them to zero in on the ribcage.

Pittman's philosophy as a teacher is that his students should be 'makers' as well as learners. 'There's a basic human desire to create things,' he says. 'If we can let that sit in the driver's seat it will be much easier to get kids investing in their own education.' At Khan Lab School, the afternoon is creation time. 'There's a high level of engagement because you're building these projects with groups of friends.' Contributing to their own learning in this way also 'eliminates the "When will I ever use this?" question,' says Pittman. '"Well, you'll use it this afternoon in the giant ribcage project," I tell them.' It's not just a free-for-all, of course: 'We curate the content behind the afternoon projects in the morning. There's knowledge acquisition, direct instruction and practice in the morning, and then you're putting those skills to work in the afternoon.' For instance, to build the giant ribcage, his students applied the geometry they had been learning during morning lessons.

Self-directed projects like this aren't just a better way to engage students from hour to hour. They teach a broader set of skills that are essential to being a better learner overall, regardless of the subject. Traditional content areas – maths, writing, reading, communication, art, music, and physical activity are all important at Khan. 'But the most important skills to us are the skills that allow you to acquire that content most efficiently,' says Pittman.

It's not just about the skills that enable children to acquire content. It's about developing in them the intrinsic desire and motivation to do so. For over a century, there has been a pervasive belief in education that you have to make children learn content in blocks of time, or 'lessons', as we know them. Forty-five minutes of maths, then English for forty-five minutes, and so on. The philosophy at Khan is to turn this on its head – to replace the traditional 'extrinsically motivated' approach with a sense of independence and responsibility in the students themselves, with the freedom to choose what they work on when, what projects they choose to do, where to set things up, and so on.

The school is also available to students all day. 'We go from eight-thirty to six p.m. every day,' Jason explains. 'It's not mandatory for students to stay that long, but most want to. And there's no homework after that, so if you want to execute that project you're really into, you can stay. What it also does is preserve home time as family time. But I love when parents come to pick up the kids at three-thirty or four, and they negotiate with them to stay until six. They don't want to leave. They're really invested in themselves and what they can do here.'

Pittman admits they make mistakes (he glances over at some of the messy work areas as he says this), but they're all part of the process. 'It's actually very helpful for them to come here in the morning and need to get back to work on a project and have the room so disorganised that they can't work in there. For me to remind them to clean up or any of the common 'sit down, stand up, raise your hand, yes, you can go to the bathroom, no, you can't go over here, look this way, don't look this way' – all of that stuff is exhausting as a teacher to manage. And if I did that, I would always have to manage their behaviour. They won't really learn it. If it's me saying it over and over again, it's the teacher that holds that value – the value never passes on to the students. You're just a snooze button they hit.' Ultimately, by letting his students see the value in these qualities themselves, it becomes much more powerful. They develop personal responsibility.

While some students at first weren't used to having so much ownership over what happens next or to having so much attention paid to things like 'perseverance', 'cooperation', and 'entrepreneurialism' alongside maths and science, they bought into it pretty quickly. 'Students have so much responsibility in everything – from setting up the furniture, setting up lunch every day, cleaning up … scheduling their own lessons if they think they need instruction from me. They coordinate with me and other students that might need that instruction, and we put that on a shared calendar. They're organising around what the learning tool should be. And it's wonderful,' says Pittman, with a smile that betrays a very proud teacher.

He is spot on. I know this first hand. One of those kids he's talking about? He's my son Ben.

Factory schools

The terrible truth about our education system today is that it is more like South Korea's – children with hair falling out from stress and the highest youth suicide rate in the world – than the Khan Lab School, whose children negotiate with their parents to stay on at the end of the school day. We have dehumanised our children's education. Schools treat students like statistics, mandating lesson plans across regions – even countries – to hit specified test results. We obsess over how our children rank compared to their peers (at home and abroad); if they aren't 'falling behind' the Chinese or the Singaporeans, they are falling behind each other or even themselves. This is a disastrous way to prepare children for their lives. Measuring their success based on how well they do in an academic test is superficial. It ignores the deeper learning that will actually help them thrive. Our current approach takes the creativity and individuality out of learning, forcing children into a common style instead of letting them evolve intellectually into independent-minded people. It's time for more human schools.

'Public schools are trying to go in this direction,' Jason Pittman explains. 'But there are so many non-negotiables in the mainstream system.' He tells the story of when he was back in his classroom in Washington DC and starting to experiment with such 'radical' techniques. 'There was a day we were working on a math project, along with another classroom remotely. The kids were trying to build this "monster", so they were describing its parts with mathematical arrays – projecting the designs they had set up, cutting them out, sticking pieces onto the monitor. It was one of the greatest math lessons I had ever seen. It was really practical. You really had to understand multiplication in order to create your piece of the puzzle. Then all of a sudden this little girl runs in and says: "The principal's coming! Everyone look like you're doing math!" So they got out books, sat there for a moment when he came in, and then got back to it when he left.'

The regimented, top-down approach not only turns children off learning by treating them all the same; it also discourages teachers, the very people best positioned to respond to each child's learning needs. Industrialised, mechanised, centralised; applying outdated and ineffective methods:[71] our children are mass-produced in schools that are literally designed to resemble factories. We need to leave behind the nineteenth-century mindset.

The culture of tests is a big part of the problem. Education policymakers' obsession with test scores (particularly maths) is in part motivated by their own desire – need – to 'prove' the success of their policies. It's also a way of evaluating teachers. But the price paid by children is a relentless drilling and testing culture and the neglect of unquantifiable skills that are actually – and increasingly – more important. Worse, if you examine the tests forensically, they fail even on their own terms.

Consider PISA, the OECD's Programme for International Student Assessment. This has become the totemic indicator for every education policymaker around the world. Every time the PISA rankings are announced, politicians jump all over themselves trying to prove some point or other about whether their country has 'fallen behind' or 'moved ahead' (depending on whether they're in office or not). It's the yardstick everyone uses.

This might make some kind of sense if it were an effective yardstick. But it isn't. Politicians trumpet PISA scores as if they were a key factor in economic success, yet Germany and the US, two leading global economies, have terrible PISA scores. It is assumed by many that the PISA rankings are based on rigorous, statistical analysis of educational data from around the world. They're not. The scores are based on a one-off test taken by a tiny sample of children in each country. And the test itself is hopelessly flawed. It is long (two hours), and many students simply don't finish.[72] Not all students are assigned all the questions or even all the sections – so sometimes they are given a reading or maths score without having answered a single reading or maths question.[73] Considering its international scope, the test obviously faces cultural challenges, but it totally fails to address them: questions in different languages create inconsistencies across countries; some countries (particularly in Asia) teach directly to the PISA test, while other countries treat it as simply something that is done casually once a year alongside whatever they're doing anyway. Some questions are used in some countries while the same questions are thrown out in others. The test also fails to take into account disparities within a country.

Perhaps its biggest flaw is the 'headline factor'. No matter the nuance PISA notes within its reports, it is the league tables that get all the attention and drive headlines – and thus put pressure on policymakers. This is the GDP of the education world, the metric that drives all yet includes just a fraction of what matters. Yes, maths is important. But because of PISA, we focus on maths at the peril of other, more pressing subjects. Children need to learn to be creative and collaborative to succeed in the twenty-first century economy; drilling them for tests fosters no skill except memorisation; no character trait but individual ambition. Obsessing over maths will not nurture children who are adaptable and entrepreneurial but 'worker bots' that are readily replaceable by technology.

The culture of tests is a fitting symbol for schools as factories, complete with bells, separate facilities, batches of children. Students, like factory workers, labour at a single output measured by a single metric. Our education system today is rooted in the industrialised system of the past, ignoring different learning styles, intelligences, strengths, or weaknesses. A certain kind of thinking is rewarded while those with other strengths are told to suppress them and conform – or face failure. Factory schools produce stale thinking. Yes, the basics of literacy, numeracy, history and science – subjects taught and tested in factory schools – are important, but they are more effectively taught in the non-factory model, as we'll see later. We also need to focus on developing the skills that will enable our children to succeed in a globalised, knowledge-based, rapidly changing world. Success is no longer just learning facts; it's about more human skills like empathy, self-regulation, conscientiousness, grit, teamwork, resilience, problem-solving, innovation and critical thinking, skills which will give children a platform to build a successful, happy life.

These 'twenty-first-century skills' build on themselves. Teamwork has been shown not just to improve output, communication and planning but also – through increased engagement with others' ideas – to lead to even more learning and skills enhancement than going it alone.[74] Self-discipline has been shown to be more important than IQ in predicting academic performance.[75] Yet have you ever seen traits like perseverance or altruism on a test? If the increasing number of workers who code, create, analyse, and solve problems for a living don't know how to be creative, how can they hope to innovate? (Creativity, by the way, is considered the most important leadership trait by global CEOs.)[76] A test-taking culture that shames failure kills the impulse towards entrepreneurship and risk taking that we should most want to encourage.

Our current education system is designed to ignore these vital skills. Creativity is consigned to art class. We say we're teaching critical thinking, but we test it with box-ticking exercises that have 'correct' answers, regardless of how thoughtful they are. We tell ourselves that students are allowed to plot their own intellectual journey, but really that just means choosing between chemistry and physics. And while we stress individual achievement, we forget the power of collaboration for success; humanity's most celebrated individuals almost all rely on (sometimes lesser-known) partners to achieve greatness.[77]

It's not as if there's no opportunity for children to learn these skills today: it's just that it's only there for a fraction, and then mostly not in school. Middle-class parents provide their children with the enrichment opportunities they need outside school to gain the skills and experience that increasingly matter. But the children who need them most – those from socially and economically disadvantaged backgrounds – never have that chance. So they grow up learning how to take tests but never develop their character. Much of this can be addressed with early-childhood interventions as Nobel-prize winning economist James Heckman has shown (and as we'll see in Chapter 6), but so much more could be done in schools as well.[78] As the social policy commentator Jenni Russell has observed about British schools, the obsession with tests crowds out the teaching of character, with disastrous results:

> On my son's first day in a state school reception class, skinny, pale Madison tugged at her mother's arm to ask a question and was told to f*** off. At the end of the day, four-year-old Wayne was left crying in

the classroom as his mother, a Caribbean woman with a mysterious job, a council flat and a brand new 4x4, set the pattern for his school life by failing to pick him up.

The school had no interest in dealing with these children's emotional states so they never flourished, despite sitting through hundreds of literacy and numeracy hours. They fought, swore, cried, failed to read and fell further behind with every passing year. By the time they were 14, both were truanting most of the time. Madison ended up with a couple of GCSEs and Wayne, who had joined a gang, with none. A dozen years of public investment in these children's education had been so badly focused that it had created two truculent, ignorant, helpless people.[79]

As Russell points out, this is no surprise if we look at what is considered 'success' by the system today. Schools have no incentive to think about social and emotional learning, character, or twenty-first-century skills unless they serve the very instrumental function of improving test scores. No student is graded on grit; no teacher evaluated on how entrepreneurial their students are. A study undertaken by psychologists collaborating across Oxford, Cambridge, and Exeter Universities shows that mindfulness, a calming technique based in Buddhism, reduces mental-health problems, improves well-being, and makes children better students.[80] Many Silicon Valley entrepreneurs consider failure to be an essential experience for ultimate success; indeed as we saw in Chapter 1, design thinking, one of the best problem-solving techniques there is, only works because design thinkers constantly fail, try again, and make improvements, learning all along. How does learning how to fail and iterate, or being mindful, meet a benchmark or mesh with PISA scores? It doesn't. As long as our education system ignores human factors, focuses on test scores and teaches only those things that can be quantified and ranked, our children will not be prepared for the reality of the world they are entering. They will be entering the twenty-first-century world with twentieth-century skills. And those are the children who succeed in our current system. If they fail, as Jenni Russell saw Wayne and Madison do, they'll have no chance. Instead of treating our children like the factory workers we once trained them to be, let's treat them like the knowledge workers we hope they will become.

***

'Factory schools' is not some pejorative term plucked out of thin air. Our education system today is rooted in the Industrial Revolution. Charles Dickens captured the essence of the industrialised-education mindset in the form of Thomas Gradgrind, the headmaster in his novel *Hard Times*. Gradgrind is determined to suppress his students' imagination with facts, seeing children's transformation into machines as the ultimate educational virtue. William T. Harris, the United States Commissioner of Education at the end of the nineteenth century, praised the direction schools were taking at the time. That a 'modern' school had the 'appearance of a machine' was the very quality that proved its worth. Machine schools, he found, fostered 'punctuality, silence, and conformity to order'.[81] Perhaps Harris is excused by the context of his times: obedient factory workers were needed in abundance, as those with 'semi-mechanical virtues' (his words) were both more productive and less accident prone. But since the world and its workforce have evolved, why haven't our schools? Though it's hard to say which came first, factory schools are perfectly intertwined with the centralisation we discussed in the last chapter. Centralisation, after all, is an industrial factory's distinguishing feature. Mass manufacturing extended to the people who made the products: a standardised workforce required schools to work in concert, each producing the same type of student. A diverse schooling system would be complete anathema.

But since outputting uniform workers is no longer society's goal, we need to move on. Just as we saw with bureaucracy in the previous chapter, centralisation distorts and deforms, costing a fortune while giving unnecessary power to those far away at the top but conferring almost no advantage on those who should come first – our children. There is absolutely no reason why education should be centralised. Schooling, by its nature, can be a local, intimate process. We're so used to the status quo that most of us never stop to acknowledge the fact that parents and teachers don't need standardised tests to know which children are performing well and which need more attention. We accept tests as the best way to monitor our students' learning, when really they're just the only tool distant administrators have at their disposal. We 'need' them, because *they* need them.

Of course, we do need a centralised education authority for a few specific things: the fair distribution of funding across regions and towns; an accreditation process to ensure that not just anyone can claim to run a proper school. But I can't imagine what other functions need to be carried out at a central level. The quality of education would be much higher if power over it were decentralised as far as possible. As we saw in the previous chapter, that means neighbourhoods. To see how successful this model can be, look no further than Finland, home of one of the most successful – and decentralised – education systems in the world.

Trusting teachers

The Finnish school system is a perfect example of subsidiarity. Schools are 'small-scale democracies' according to Finnish education scholar, Pasi Sahlberg, with the only centralised aspects relating to professional requirements for teacher training and standards regarding learning outcomes (not teaching methods or test results). Teachers and school-level principals are given tremendous leeway in developing their own curricula, with the understanding that they know their own students and local conditions best.

Perhaps in many circumstances, policymakers would be concerned at placing such tremendous trust in education providers at a local level. Finnish officials solved this dilemma by putting only the very best people there to begin with. Good people don't need authoritarian bureaucratic diktats to do what's right; they do what's right because responsibility lies with them, and because they're good – and Finland is a land of unequivocally great teachers. Year after year, Finland attracts all its new primary-teacher students from among the best graduates. To teach in Finland is so competitive that only one in every ten applicants is accepted for preparation (there are only eight accredited academies). All Finnish teachers must earn a master's level degree that includes theories of pedagogy and is research based. The expectation is that all teachers learn not just to teach but to learn – and innovate and share what they find out – for the remainder of their careers. Teaching in Finland is a highly respected professional career, akin to being a medical doctor, lawyer, or architect (one poll even ranked teaching ahead of these three as being a 'dream profession'[82]).

It's not just that having good teachers enables policymakers to trust teachers without testing their students to death; not having the tests is what attracts and keeps the best teachers in the first place. It's a 'culture of mutual trust', explains Sahlberg.[83] 'Although the pursuit of transparency and accountability provides parents and politicians with more information, it also builds suspicion, low morale, and professional cynicism.'[84] By the time they enter upper-secondary school, Finnish students, therefore, will have *no* experience of taking high-stakes tests, progress instead being judged differentially by their teachers against students' respective characteristics and abilities.

So what happens when you let highly trained and respected teachers on the loose with no standardised tests to hold them accountable? You get a fantastic education system. Though most Finnish educators think PISA exams measure only a narrow band of what's important (one of the reasons they prefer no standardised testing is that it allows more time to be spent on 'non-core' subjects like art and music), the country scores exceedingly well on them – often placing first or second among other countries in maths, science, and reading since the early 2000s.

Yet Finnish fifteen-year-olds spend less time on homework (about thirty minutes per day) and in class than peers anywhere else.[85] And teachers spend almost 500 fewer hours in the classroom per year than their American counterparts.[86] They understand that if quality is high and circumstances right, less teaching can mean *more* learning, since most students can only absorb so much in a passive lecture format anyway. They have to be out exploring, investigating, arguing with their peers. (Standard practice in Finland is to send children out after every forty-five minutes or so for an unstructured fifteen-minute break, when they can refresh, and practise socialising and exploration.)[87] Perhaps that's why only 10 per cent of Finnish students feel anxious tackling maths tasks at home, compared with over half of their French and Japanese peers.[88]

And what do teachers do with their 'free' time? They develop and refine their curricula, engage in student welfare support, collaborate with parents, work with other teachers and staff on school-wide improvements, and design and conduct locally appropriate assessments. And they keep learning how to teach better. Remember, Finnish teachers are also, by training, educational researchers – so they never stop experimenting and learning from each other, not to mention looking to other countries as well as industry to see what new thinking they can bring in and try out. There is a collective sense of collaboration and friendly rivalry – everyone wants to do a better job, and then have pride in knowing they've raised the bar of the system.

There are some who discount what we can import from the decentralised Finnish education model on the grounds that Finland is somehow special – that a system like this can be run because of the country's small size and 'Nordic' attitude, etc. This is frankly ridiculous. Less than fifty years ago Finland was a mostly impoverished, illiterate, agrarian state. Other social reforms (many of which are closely tied to education) have certainly played their part, but I wouldn't suggest changing Britain's schools without addressing these issues either (see Chapters 6 and 7). Moreover, Finland's population is slightly less than 5.5 million people – that's the same size or larger than thirty US states, all but two provinces in Canada, all but five of Germany's sixteen Länder, and twenty-four of the twenty-six French regions – all units of government to which school administration powers have already, largely, been devolved. In fact, one of America's largest school systems shows what radical decentralisation of education can achieve.

New York City's education system used to be characterised by huge public schools with a capacity of up to 3,000 each. They were disproportionately attended by poor and minority students, who had graduation rates as low as 40 per cent.[89] When Mayor Michael Bloomberg came into office he set out to close these 'dropout factories'. He closed large failing high schools and replaced them with small specialised ones. Called Small Schools of Choice (SSCs), they follow a localised, competitive model: they were created independently by community groups featuring year groups no larger than 100 students, organised around different themes, with personalised learning. These new, small schools are holistic; given that most of the students are at risk of dropping out, they offer community and social-service support. In these new small schools, 71.6 per cent of students graduate, as opposed to 62.2 per cent in normal schools; among black male students, an especially vulnerable demographic, 42.3 per cent enrol in college compared to 31 per cent at conventional schools.[90] All this at a lower cost per student, because fewer students now need an extra year to finish. New York is showing that moving to smaller, locally controlled schools – just like in Finland – can make a big difference.

These examples and others show us that there are now robust, tested alternatives to the century-old, one-size-fits-all school. These modern alternatives offer new and effective ways of educating our children, but the dominance of factory schools remains a structural barrier to a more human education system. Until, like Mayor Bloomberg, we actively close them down, the vision of educating most children in fresh, innovative and more human ways will remain just that.

Some in the UK point to academy schools as the answer to removing this structural barrier. Academies are independent schools within the local state system: they're not private or fee paying, but they can avoid the systems, rules and curricula forced on mainstream schools. They have a long heritage; similar to charter schools in the US, they were first introduced as grant-maintained schools by Education Secretary Kenneth Baker under Margaret Thatcher in 1988, and later championed by John Major. Labour at first opposed them (in 1998, Tony Blair's government abolished them), but later reintroduced them in 2000 under a different name – academies. Labour's academies were meant to replace *failing* schools, but when David Cameron came to power, Michael Gove, his Education Secretary, dramatically accelerated the programme, allowing all schools (not just struggling ones) to convert to academy status. There are some great charter schools, just as there are great academies.

But there's a problem. The academy programme – massive advance though it is – still doesn't address the underlying structural issue: that there are simply not enough fresh, innovative and more human schools on offer. Achieving that diversity is ever more vital as we see a new threat of standardisation and centralisation coming over the horizon. Media companies like News Corporation, Pearson, Disney, McGraw-Hill and Houghton-Mifflin Harcourt (some of which already own school textbook publishers) are pushing into education technology systems as a new sales and marketing strategy: a way to get as many eyeballs as possible on their products.[91]

Instead of repudiating the old factory model of standardised tests and all the depressing bureaucracy that surrounds them, these so-called 'reformers' want more. In a Pearson report ominously titled 'Preparing for a Renaissance in Assessment', authors Peter Hill and Michael Barber – in a shockingly blunt embrace of the worst aspects of the factory-schools model – argue against teacher autonomy and in favour of top-down testing to put them in their place: 'Without such a systematic, data-driven approach to instruction, teaching remains an imprecise and somewhat idiosyncratic process that is too dependent on the personal intuition and competence of individual teachers.'[92]

This desire – mania, really – to produce endless data, fed by tests, is pure centralisation. Uber-centralisation; where tests are the solution and teachers are the problem; where testing is a 'solution' not to the pedagogic challenge of educating children but to the management challenge of running a school. This is not the answer. To get to the heart of how things need to change, we must turn our attention to the school system's most human element.

Michael Gove talks often about how the most powerful factor influencing the quality of education is the human part: the teacher. We have amazing people who enter the education world to share their gifts, and yet we shackle them, limiting their ability to do what they know is right, particularly through testing: 'Exams are like limits for the teachers,' says Sergio Juárez Correa, a somewhat rebellious (and, as a result, extraordinarily successful) state-school teacher in Mexico. 'They test what you know, not what you can do, and I am more interested in what my students can do.'[93]

We need people in education who are true entrepreneurs and innovators, not corporate stooges. In fact, we need people exactly like Juárez Correa. He is a teacher at the José Urbina López Primary School in Matamoros, Mexico. A border city of half a million, it's a grim place, at the crossroads of an interminable drug war. The school is built next to a rubbish dump and has been nicknamed '*un lugar de castigo*' – 'a place of punishment'. Here, children are lucky to survive childhood, let alone dream of careers and success.

As you'd expect, Juárez Correa's students were disengaged from the official curriculum (which bored even him), and their test scores were correspondingly low. He was desperate to try something different. According to Josh Davis, who profiled him and his students in the magazine *Wired*, he voraciously read educational materials online, trying to find something to stimulate both him and his students. It was on one of these searches that he discovered the work of Sugata Mitra, an educational theorist in Britain who experimented with giving computers to children in poor countries and letting them direct their own learning experiences through online material and lectures. Mitra's work, rooted in the methods of educational reformers like Maria Montessori and Jean Piaget, took hold of Juárez Correa; he resolved to try it in his classroom. Perhaps, he thought, this was what would shake him and his students from their stupor?

On 21 August 2011, Juárez Correa walked into class on the first day of the school year. He told the children that they had potential and that 'from now on, we're going to use that potential to make you the best students in the world'. His approach would be completely radical; he didn't have computers, but he could pose open-ended questions and give his students as much autonomy as possible to work out the answers. For instance, instead of explaining fractions he wrote on the whiteboard '1 = 1.00' and then wrote '½ = ?' and '¼ = ?'. While his training would suggest explaining the concepts of fractions, using Mitra's methods he stayed silent and let his students stew it over. He brought various coins in to help them work it out; the students noticed that two half-peso pieces were the same as four quarter-peso pieces, prompting a debate on the nature of what one-half meant. One student, Paloma Noyola Bueno, quickly understood and helped convince the other students how fractions worked, counting out the centavos for each side of the pile.

This streak of brilliance in Paloma, it would turn out, was not a fluke. One of the great tragedies in the world is the inequality of opportunity for the multitude of bright children who never get a chance of an education. It's not just tragic for them personally but for all of us: society will never gain from the gifts they have to offer. Whether through class barriers, infant mortality, or poverty, many don't get the opportunity even to go to school. The students in Juárez Correa's class had it better than most: they were at least there. And he was curious about Paloma: she excelled at relatively simple tasks like the basic fractions exercise and then others way beyond that. One day he raised the bar to a seemingly impossible height. He told the story of Carl Friedrich Gauss, an eighteenth-century German mathematician. As a student, Gauss had famously answered an extremely difficult question in just a minute: Juárez Correa thought he'd try the same question, not expecting anyone – even Paloma – to solve it. So he asked the class: what is the sum of every number between 1 and 100? Within a couple of minutes, Paloma raised her hand: 'The answer is 5,050. There are 50 pairs of 101.' It was so simple, so elegant, but so advanced for a child of Paloma's age. Juárez Correa, awed, asked Paloma (who had until then showed no real love for maths) why she hadn't engaged before. 'Because no one made it this interesting,' she told him.

When national testing rolled around in June, Juárez Correa was anything but enthusiastic, but it had to be done. It was a good sign at least that his students breezed through it. While Correa didn't put much stock in the results, even he was excited when he learned what they were a few months later. Scores were high: the previous year, 45 per cent had failed maths and 31 per cent had failed Spanish. Those numbers had now dropped to 7 per cent and 3.5 per cent respectively. But it was the highest-achieving students who proved a real shock. Three placed in the 99.99th per centile for Spanish, ten at the same level for maths. Paloma had the highest score in the school: 921. When the school's assistant principal showed Juárez Correa the results, imagine his surprise when he moved the cursor over the high score for the region: it was 921. Then he moved it to the high score for the country. Paloma was the top maths student in Mexico.

Without the experimentation of Juárez Correa, his students would not have succeeded; instead of being feted in Mexico City and in articles read around the world, Paloma Bueno might still be languishing next to a rubbish dump. All teachers should be creative and daring like Juárez Correa, and we should encourage and support them. We need to draw our most creative thinkers and doers from the rest of society into teaching as if it were the latest tech start-up. We need our superstars to be teachers; our teachers to be superstars (even if fame is not the result).

In many fields, it's taken for granted that only the best can join, and teaching should be one of them. We need to elevate its position in our society. We should pay teachers more, hold them in high regard, and then hold them to the high standards they deserve. We need to trust them, treat them like professionals. As we'll see in the next chapter, doctors and nurses are distracted from caring for their patients when bureaucracy becomes too burdensome. The same is true for teachers who are subject to a huge number of regulatory and reporting requirements. If we respect our teachers, then instead of being a recalcitrant trade union, the National Union of Teachers could be an arbiter of professional quality like its counterparts in medicine, law, and engineering. As leading educational reformer Sir Anthony Seldon puts it: 'If teachers are to have the status of [these] other professions, they need to have a serious professional body at their head.'[94]

But how do we actually do this? If we're to empower teachers and close the factory schools, what should rise in their stead? Can we really have an education system designed to meet the modern world's dynamism and interconnectivity? Rather than a lumpen, monolithic travesty designed for the needs of the 'average' child, couldn't we teach all our children in a way that puts each of them first, as humans?

Real school choice

Yes. But first we must dispense once and for all with the idea that the right way to run education is for the state to provide 'a good local school' in every neighbourhood. The lazy philosophy of 'one school per neighbourhood' is exactly what has led to the outdated model that we need to get away from. Even if the central authorities give 'autonomy' to a local school; even if the local school is run as an academy, or independent of local authority control; the problem is that there is one local school. As in other areas of life, it's the fact of the monopoly that does the damage, that enables – indeed requires – the standardisation.

Yes, you can point to individual examples – remarkable teachers like Sergio Juárez Correa who despite their confines have achieved tremendous breakthroughs. Granted, there are some wonderful, creative, innovative schools out there within the local monopoly system. Lucky you if you happen to live near one. But these are the exceptions. Why shouldn't every child, everywhere, have the right to be educated in a more human way? We need systemic, structural change to bring the benefits of innovation to every child, everywhere. That means ending the local school monopoly. Progress comes from innovation, innovation comes from competition, and competition comes from choice.

Of course 'school choice' has been a political slogan for decades. But the kind that proponents of this idea usually argue for is barely choice at all. It's the illusion of choice – between one dominant school in an area and one alternative. Or maybe in larger towns and cities, between the closest big school and four or five others within a reasonable distance. It's no surprise that critics of school choice have found a receptive audience for their argument that this 'isn't parents choosing schools, but schools choosing parents'. I agree. Nothing that has been proposed or implemented anywhere comes close to the kind of diversity I'm talking about.

To get to a more human education system, one that gives every child the chance to go to a school that is individually perfect – whether that's something like the extreme entrepreneurial innovation of the Khan Lab School in California, or the more mainstream version in Finland; whether it's a traditional school or a progressive one; an academic curriculum or one focused on character – whatever it is, whatever is perfect for every child, knowing that no two children are the same: the only way to achieve this is something wildly, fantastically more radical than anything we've seen or talked about up till now.

Not just the odd boutique school here and there, not just two or three, or four or five, or even eight or ten schools in every area. I mean twenty, thirty schools for parents to choose between; schools that are smaller (a reasonable aim for a human-scale school would be, perhaps, 150–300 students); schools that offer whatever approaches they think might work for the children in that neighbourhood. Each child is unique; so is each teacher. In order to thrive, they need to be able to find the school that fits them – that fits their uniqueness. This is what a more human education means.

This is not some outlandish fantasy. The demand is there, the ideas are there. Pioneers have already done it. Students around the world, right now, are experiencing the benefits of human-scale schools. It doesn't even have to cost more. The assumption that a new school is more expensive is often just the result of lazy, old-fashioned thinking, or worse, the efforts of local bureaucracies to cling onto their monopolies. They define a school as exactly what it is today – a big factory – insisting on unnecessary and often byzantine requirements about building size, parking spaces, land use, traffic access … you name it. This is how the vested interests in local (and central) government managed to block expansion in the number of Michael Gove's new 'free' schools, even though the demand from parents was there. The idea that we can't have a school in a converted office or high-street retail space, for example, has nothing to do with what would benefit our children, and everything to do with the established monopoly providers fearing they would be shown up by any competition. New schools with more human ways of educating children are there if we want them. There are many models, all with advantages and disadvantages – we shouldn't pick one from on high. But their popularity points the way to what our school system might one day become – a place where teachers and students are treated as people.

Nothing puts this in clearer perspective than seeing it through the eyes of your own children. When it was time for us to put our oldest son, Ben, in preschool, the thought of sending him to a school where they force academic study on children at too early an age; where his childhood curiosities would be squashed; and where his propensity to ask, to explore, and to create would be stifled in the name of 'proper behaviour', was terrifying. Thankfully, we found Mr T.

Mr T is Jeff Thomas, who, with his wife Rachael, runs the most wonderful preschool we could ever have imagined. Jeff remembers the exact moment his previous classroom became a factory. He loved his job as a teacher in a public [state] school in Redwood City, California. He loved teaching his children new skills, facilitating their play, seeing the satisfaction they got when they learned something new. But one year at the start of term, he was given a package detailing the curriculum and the lesson plans he needed to teach. It came, literally, in a box. Worse was the test that came with it, which left his children struggling with question after question about material that the district had never required be taught before. The children simply had no idea what they were looking at. Jeff sat watching them, frustrated and disheartened, wondering all along what the point was. It was then he realised he could no longer be part of a system that dehumanised both him and his students.

Jeff left that school soon afterwards, but thankfully he didn't leave education. Instead he and Rachael, also a teacher, decided to innovate and create their own school, geared for four- and five-year-olds. Little Man School House ('little man' is the name of a doodle Jeff has drawn since childhood), the small school Jeff and Rachael created in their back garden, is a paradise for children like Ben. When you walk up the drive, you see a huge rope swing on an enormous tree. Some children are playing on the drive in small go-karts; others are creating stuff with paint. They spend time indoors, on actual lessons, but also explore the expansive garden, where they do everything from growing vegetables to damming a tiny stream. The key is that Jeff and Rachael have created a safe space, free from rigidity, where children can challenge themselves on their own terms.

Central to their method is combining lessons with practical experience. For instance, in the garden are several large planter boxes, where they grow vegetables. One morning, Jeff shows the children how to dig a small hole, put in a seed, cover it and water it using the planter's drip irrigation. He then gives each pupil a few seeds, and they take turns planting them. Once they're all done, they turn their attention to the planter next to them, which has small turnips peeping out of the soil. Each turnip is labelled by the pupil who planted it, and they take turns examining their growth (or lack of it). One is ready to eat, so Jeff picks it up, washes it off under a tap, and breaks off a piece for a student to try. Liberated from the constraints of a factory school, Jeff and Rachael can take liberties in their lesson plans. On the morning the children planted their seeds, Jeff had read them a relevant book, helping them understand that what transforms a seed into a plant isn't magic, just nature. But to the children, the process remained magical. Those liberties also allow them to make spontaneous connections that might present themselves on a random day. One winter morning, they noticed frost on the window so used it as an opportunity to explain the basics of cold, temperature, and weather. Jeff treats the children like people, not outputs.[95]

The Little Man School House was limited to a small number of students aged four and five: a one-year programme only. Ben needed a new school. The Khan Lab School had not yet opened its doors, so we chose the Waldorf School of the Peninsula. Waldorf schools (better known as Steiner schools in the UK) are based on the educational philosophy of Rudolf Steiner, a visionary education theorist of the early twentieth century. The Steiner approach emphasises building up students as individuals instead of trying to teach *at* them; it values more than just intellectual development but human development too. Pupils are encouraged to connect emotionally, physically, and morally and to learn practical skills like woodworking and knitting. And they are taught to build each other up. Because Steiner schools don't use standardised tests and focus on cooperation instead of individual performance, the children aren't just more social, but are actually more responsible and determined according to a German study; the responsibility given to them makes them more enthusiastic learners.[96]

One of the most striking things about the educational philosophy pioneered by Rudolf Steiner in Central Europe nearly a century ago is that the intuitive insights and beliefs he had about how best to educate children have, in subsequent decades – and especially with advances in neuroscience more recently – been validated by evidence that simply was not imaginable, never mind available, a hundred years ago.

Take, for example, the Steiner approach to reading and writing. In Steiner schools, children aren't taught to read or write until they're at least six or seven – sometimes later. Contrast this with factory schools' insistence that children should read and write by four or five – or even earlier. It's easy to dismiss this as lacking in rigour (even though it's the norm in European countries like Finland and Germany[97] where children perform better in school and are happier than in the UK).[98] But there is developmental science on the side of this approach: we now know that learning to read, write, and compute requires more than academic knowledge; it requires the ability to control your body. Proprioception (the sensing of our body parts in relation to each other) is one of the most important functions we develop – and it's vital in the classroom. The brain uses information from proprioception (along with information from the vestibular system, which tells us about the world physically around us by giving us a sense of movement and balance) to physically control our bodies and perform complex tasks like walking with our eyes closed, or skipping.

The creation of proprioceptive pathways in the brain is a normal part of growth, but forcing children to learn how to write and read letters before that process is mature can actually inhibit their development. A child without proprioceptive control over their body will have trouble learning letters, not out of any kind of intellectual deficit but because they are unable to perceive their body without moving around.[99] Children without a fully developed proprioceptive system are unable to perceive their bodies in three dimensions; this makes drawing shapes difficult if not impossible. In fact, drawings of people by children are good signs of their development. A child under two should be expected to simply scribble, while toddlers can draw stick figures with circles for heads; they don't perceive digits, but they perceive limbs. By the age of seven, a neck and more detailed clothing appear. Until they are fully proprioceptively developed, children have to exert immense mental and physical effort to perform basic actions like keeping their eyes tracking the words on a page, even to stay sitting upright. They simply don't have brainpower to focus on other tasks and so will be easily tired and stressed and have difficulties in social situations. A more human approach to education needs to recognise this.[100]

Learning to read is a complex neurological task that requires children to recognise letters and patterns while also forming mental pictures, concepts and scenes. It takes time to develop the skills involved.[101] When learning to read, children need to connect the words in a story with the letters on the page and the story in their minds. That's one of the reasons Steiner schools teach children to read and write later. If they start the reading process before they are fully proprioceptively developed, they will use the right side of their brain (the first side to develop) on the taxing task of recognising letters. Yet the right frontal area of the brain 'has a much more important task than trying to figure out words by sight', according to behavioural paediatrician Dr Susan Johnson. 'Children need the frontal area of their right brains (and eventually the frontal area of their left brains) to create and analyse mental pictures when they are listening to stories or reading books for themselves. If children have to use the frontal area of their right brains to recognise words by sight, this area of the brain is not free to create inner mental pictures and scenes associated with the words they are hearing or reading.'[102] So while it's possible to teach children to read and write before they are ready, that doesn't mean it's good for them (or that waiting is harmful).[103] This is especially true for learning English, which some linguists consider one of the most irregularly spelled languages.[104] One study found that English-speaking children need three years to master reading and writing compared to a year or less for their European peers.[105] Moreover, starting formal education early is dangerous, according to a group of over 100 prominent educators, especially for reading and writing. Not only does it make no discernible impact on literacy, but it can actually damage children's development by prematurely ending nursery education, which 'provides their only opportunity for the active, creative and outdoor play which is recognised by psychologists as vital for physical, social, emotional and cognitive development'.[106] Steiner schools' philosophy – allowing children to learn and develop at a more human pace – is surely the obvious and sensible one. Yet today in the UK it is considered unconventional.

If you want to see an educational approach that's really radical, you should go – as Rohan and I did in 2012 – to the Acton Academy in Austin, Texas. We were intrigued by this new school we had heard about and wanted to see what lessons it might hold for school reform in Britain. It makes Steiner schools look conventional. But before making any snap judgements, bear in mind that the Acton Academy was started in 2009 by Jeff Sandefer, a Texas oil and gas tycoon who later went on to found one of the top business schools in America.

Acton Academy, a school for five- to sixteen-year-olds, focuses on teaching character, not content. Acton uses the Socratic Method; its teachers are 'guides' who facilitate 'journeys' and 'quests' for the students, who work with each other to learn organically. For the same reasons as Jason Pittman and Sergio Juárez Correa,

Sandefer rejects the idea that students should be *taught* anything, reasoning that only a few teachers can be the best at teaching a particular subject anyway. In order to 'learn to know', Sandefer uses games, activities, and technology to inspire children to seek out information for themselves, in the process holding themselves accountable for their own learning.

His curriculum also emphasises 'learning to do'. Students take part in activities that build skills and give them real world experience. In one instance, rather than read a story book or hear a lesson on the American Revolution, students dressed up in eighteenth-century colonial costumes and simulated for three days the situation in the run-up to the War of Independence. By putting themselves in the place of the American revolutionaries, they didn't just learn history but also how to solve problems, negotiate, and empathise with others. Such character traits are central to the third part of the curriculum, 'learning to be'. Students take part in long 'hero's journeys' that have many steps on the way to an end goal, for instance finding 'the world's greatest treasure' stolen by an 'evil sphinx'. Each week, the students have to overcome a new challenge to get closer to their goal. Along the way, they act, perform role play and practise public speaking, creative thinking, problem solving, decision making and time management. These tasks inculcate honesty, patience and gratitude.[107]

Jeff Sandefer's ultimate vision is for a school with no teachers at all, where the students run the place entirely, the older ones taking responsibility for the younger ones and all children collectively taking responsibility for the entire running of its community life. Much of this has already been implemented at Acton: for example, the students meet weekly to make collective decisions about disciplinary matters, and punishments meted out by the collective student group to any individual child are publicly displayed to foster a sense of social responsibility. And remember, it really is children we're talking about here. The level of responsibility and empowerment given to Acton students is far greater than in any university I have ever heard of; yet they are six, seven, eight years old, and as Rohan and I saw when we visited, thriving in this extraordinarily bold, innovative school regime. We looked on as a plan was being developed for the next school year: the ideas and themes that the students would be exposed to.

They included Karl Popper on the scientific method and Nassim Taleb on 'antifragility'. Anyone who thinks that a more human, progressive, innovative style of education lacks intellectual rigour had better think again.

We need diversity and innovation and that means educating our children in ways that are more tailored and personal and human. We have to experiment with places like Khan Lab School, Little Man School House, Waldorf-Steiner Schools and Acton Academy. None of them is perfect, but the successes of these small-scale innovations demonstrate that we need to escape the rigidity of the current system. We need to create the space for many more new schools, more human schools. And the only way to do that is to close down the factories. We have to shut them down altogether so that an array of new schools can take their place and the place of their monopoly.

There's one more reform we need, one more vital step on the road to a more human education system. We need a truly fair, egalitarian system that doesn't discriminate against different types of schools run along different lines. State schools, charity schools, non-profit social enterprises, for-profit schools ... as long as they are all funded on a fair basis and are free, rather than fee-paying, true educational diversity means all of these being given an equal chance to offer children a great education. It's particularly important that we should allow organisations that make a profit to run schools. Companies that think for the long term are more willing and able to invest in setting up new schools, because they can make their money back later. (Although as we've already seen, the capital costs of starting a school are often inflated by the predatory tactics of local bureaucrats and their stooges in central government, desperate to cling onto their monopoly power even if it means a worse education for children.) If we want to see many more – and many more types of – schools on offer at the local level, we need to open it up to all. The current discrimination against 'profit-making schools' is particularly random and bizarre, given that huge chunks of state-school operations – the textbooks, the buildings, the testing (!),[108] supply teachers, the teachers' pensions – are provided by companies for profit. As is this book. Or your phone. Or the newspaper you read. I'm not quite clear why the idea of making profits is OK for all those activities but not for running schools. In fact, one of the most inspiring examples of social justice, emancipation of the poorest, and the transformative power of education that I've ever seen was a visit to a profit-making school. It happened to be in one of the world's worst slums, in Lagos, Nigeria.

James Tooley is a Professor of Education at Newcastle University. He has helped establish and champion a thrilling phenomenon in some of the poorest parts of the world: private, for-profit schools in developing countries that are transformationally better than the failing state schools so depressingly propped up by corrupt local bureaucrats, the United Nations, international aid, and the whole panoply of sanctimonious, ignorant, hypocritical hand-wringers who argue that the evil 'profit motive' mustn't violate the noble innocence of education. (Oh, wait, apart from the private schools and private tutors used by the policy makers and pundits who peddle those views.)

Private schools for the poor show what rubbish that is, and also that you don't need a massive national education bureaucracy to have good schools. When we were accompanying the Prime Minister on a 2011 visit to Africa, Rohan and I asked to see one of James Tooley's schools – Linda Whetstone (my wife Rachel's mother) had told me about one in Lagos. At first, the local British officials refused to take us, saying it was too dangerous. We kept on about it and in the end they gave in, and we went. While the UK-government-backed state school in the city was a disaster, the Tooley-backed for-profit school was a sensation: eager children, in pristine uniforms, learning literacy, maths, science – even a solar-powered computer. This is in the middle of a slum. Literally. To get there, Rohan and I had to pick our way through stinking, festering garbage, open sewers, ramshackle structures that could and would be washed away by the next rains. To arrive at that school, peep over the makeshift wall and see rows and rows of eager pupils happily studying in the midst of utter chaos and squalor was completely astonishing; incomparably inspiring.

Let me repeat: this is a for-profit school. The parents – all of whom live in the slum, the poorest people in the world, part of that economic category lightly bandied around as 'living on less than a dollar a day' – these parents are paying to send their children to the Tooley-backed school. The UK-government-backed school, run by the state and financed, via the Department for International Development (DfID), by the British taxpayer, is completely free. DfID refused to fund even the tiny amount of capital the school needed to open a second location, because it was not run by the centralised bureaucracy. And yet the parents – who earn less money in a year than a liberal commentator who rails against 'profits in schools' would spend on a good lunch – choose the for-profit school over the free state alternative. Why? Because it's better. And surely that's all we should care about – the quality of the education, not the organisational form?

Some might say that the argument I've set out here is mad: there's no way we can get rid of the local school monopoly; that the kinds of educational approaches I've described go way too far for most people, and that even if they had a much greater choice of school, parents have neither the time nor the inclination to evaluate schools and choose between them. In the innocuous but devastatingly destructive cliché, 'parents just want a good local school'.

Think of the parents in Nigeria, who actively sought out James Tooley's school. They live in one of the world's poorest slums and fight every day for access to clean water, shelter and enough food to eat, yet take the initiative to find the best education for their children. If they, with everything stacked against them, can take an active role in education, of course we can in Britain. I believe that the majority of parents are perfectly capable of looking out for their children's best interests and knowing which school – of many options – is the best fit. Who are we to say they can't? Yes, there are some dysfunctional families that would struggle. But why should everyone else be denied the choice of a more human education just because of a problem few?

Critics of decentralisation and choice ask how parents can decide on schools without a metric. But the premise of the question is intrinsically flawed: why should parents decide anything as important as a school on the basis of something as superficial and narrow as a test or a quantitative metric? How do you choose a neighbourhood to live in? You might want to know a few statistics, but you base your decision on what it feels like when you walk down the street, the character of the area, your sense of whether it's a decent place to live.

You can't discern a student's character from a test score; you can't determine how creative he is or how well she works in a team. The skills our children need to learn are not measured on standardised tests, so using those scores as a means to judge a school, a teacher, or a child's performance is hopelessly outdated. We tried to rank our children by number because we thought that was the best we could do. But now we know better. Parents and students know what a good school is without looking at statistics. They get a feel for the building, the environment, the culture. I wrote earlier about the importance of trusting teachers and students. If we trust students and their parents, we can empower them to fuel a revolution in education.

Critics might also point to Little Man School House, Khan Lab School, the Waldorf-Steiner schools, or Acton Academy and say they are elite because they are private and fee-paying. Yes, they are. These schools represent the best innovations in education – so why shouldn't we make them available to everyone? Universities, secondary schools, even teaching basic literacy once seemed elite until we decided it was for everyone. The same applies here: why should the best in education be a luxury for the few?

As long as schools are factories, our children will suffer. They will continue to be treated like outputs, like commodities, like cogs in a machine. Children are not products. They are our future and they deserve to be treated like individuals. It isn't about ideology, it's about the values of our society. Surely we want to live in a world that prizes creativity, rewards ingenuity and fosters brilliance? Our school system today is designed to crush these things. Let's create a system that encourages and inspires all our children. Let's close the factory schools and make our schools more human.

CHAPTER 3

HEALTH

Jane Locke, a forty-six-year-old woman, was being treated for cancer at Stafford Hospital. Cancer didn't kill her, though. She died after contracting three superbugs, *C. difficile*, MRSA and a streptococcal infection, during her stay. 'They left her in sheets that had faeces on,' said her mother, June. Around the same time, John Moore-Robinson ruptured his spleen in a cycling crash. In their rush, doctors at Stafford Hospital failed to notice the severity of the twenty-year-old's condition, gave him painkillers, and sent him home, where he died. Gillian Astbury, a sixty-six-year-old diabetic woman, died after Stafford NHS nurses failed to provide her with the routine insulin she needed to stay alive: they didn't notice her high blood sugar, so she lapsed into a coma from which she never emerged. Ellen Linstead's body was so infected with the *C. difficile* that killed her that she had to be buried in a sealed bag. Her daughter, Deb Hazeldine, complained that faeces was so often on her mother's hands that she regularly would wash them off herself. Reports have suggested that in the years up to the scandal breaking, there were between 400 and 1,200 deaths that never should have happened in a hospital of Stafford's expected quality.[109] Elsewhere in the NHS, at Walsall Manor Hospital, eighty-six-year-old Frederick Thomas died – but not of the hip replacement for which he was admitted (that operation was a success). In twelve days, not a single doctor or nurse noticed that he was both malnourished and dehydrated, an error that could have been corrected simply by hooking him up to a saline drip.

It's too easy to think of the disgusting treatment of those patients as isolated cases. It's much worse than that. These NHS horror stories reflect a deeper, structural problem.[110]

We are rightly proud of the idea of the NHS. What a wonderful thing that anyone can receive health care for free, based on their medical need and not their ability to pay. The guarantee of affordable health care is a hallmark of a decent society – and one which few countries are able to boast. But we tend to conflate two things that are not related at all: the idea of state-supported health care and the institution that provides it. It's a brilliant idea that anyone can get medical attention without worrying about cost. What's not brilliant is the behemoth institution that has emerged to deliver this promise. Having one centrally controlled organisation with over a million employees is perhaps the best way to take something that should have been the epitome of humanity (what could be more human than to care for others?) and send it down a path of industrialisation, mechanisation and dehumanisation.

Furthermore, by consolidating medical operations in large centralised hospitals, distant from local communities, we have created a clinical environment that actively fights intimacy and personalised care. 'Efficiencies of scale' have become enemies of effectiveness, allowing decisions to be made far from patients, and responsibility to be avoided. NHS hospitals have been described as 'conveyor belts' that 'churn' out their patients whom they treat like 'parcels'.[111] The scandals in Mid-Staffs and elsewhere are symptoms of a larger truth: that in our health system today, patients have become outputs; their health outcomes, products; our hospitals, factories. It's not the fault of those who work in the NHS. As in so many other areas, it's the structure that's to blame.

Factory hospitals

Stanford medical professor Abraham Verghese thinks about health care in a more human way. He argues that touch is an incredibly helpful diagnostic tool: one study found that one in four physical examinations resulted in a novel finding.[112] And those findings can be crucial. Even when a doctor might not technically need to touch the patient, human contact is part of an important ritual. Verghese found that beyond reassuring the patient, the ritual of contact helped him bond with his patients and greatly enhanced his ability to treat them. And yet in hospitals today, touch is too often not used:

When we lean towards ordering tests instead of talking to and examining the patient, we not only overlook simple diagnoses that can be diagnosed at a treatable, early stage, but we're losing much more than that. We're losing a ritual. We're losing a ritual that I believe is transformative, transcendent, and is at the heart of the patient–physician relationship.[113]

At Stanford, he takes his students on his rounds to show how person-to-person contact makes for better medical outcomes. It also makes for more human outcomes. Sometimes the doctor's role is not just to cure, but to comfort, to connect, to be there in a patient's worst moments. That's what care means.

It's hard to care in a factory hospital, though. Go to a hospital today and it's an ordeal: navigating the large car park, walking what feels like miles through corridors, travelling in giant lifts before finally reaching a soulless waiting room where you have to wait endlessly to be called. Need a test? Walk through another mile of corridors to another soulless room where you receive your test. Then wait hours or days for the results. This only describes the experience of people who are in and out. For those who are admitted, it gets worse. Patients eat factory food (how else to serve it in such an institution?) and stay in a sterile, depressing place. But the worst part is that they are seen as outputs: treatments are commodified, tests done without doctors ever entering the room, medicine performed on and around the patient but seldom *with* the patient. According to Jocelyn Cornwell of the Point of Care programme, 'today's hospitals are vast, time is at a premium and in these busy medical factories care of the person can unfortunately get squeezed out'.[114] Joyce Robins, the patient advocate who described the NHS as a 'conveyor belt', elaborates further: 'Patients are sent into hospital and then rushed out before they are ready.'[115] Those at the top see this problem too: more often than not, hospital stays are a 'series of brief encounters', as Jeremy Hunt, the Health Secretary, put it – and the lack of continuity in care means that patients and their families don't know who's in charge to ask questions of or make requests to.[116] Sometimes, the medical staff don't even really know their patients. That 'failure to see the person in the patient' as a report by the King's Fund on point of care puts it, dehumanises the patient and can lead to serious problems. In the report, one woman describes the distress caused to her eighty-seven-year-old mother:

> … *the ambulance crew were the only people in the entire seven weeks who formally introduced themselves and asked what she would like to be called. Thereafter, for the first six weeks of her admission, she was called Elizabeth, which is her first name, which she has never been called in her life, ever. She's only ever been called by her middle name. But the NHS IT system records your name. All her labels were wrong. In spite of the fact that on a daily basis all of us told the people caring for her that her name is Margaret, and that is what she likes to be called if they want to call her by her first name, all of them called her Elizabeth. And that became very significant when she became confused.*[117]

In a bureaucracy, paperwork reigns supreme, and patients, like at Mid-Staffs, can end up ignored, sometimes with horrific consequences. Our factory hospitals are designed for everyone *but* patients and their families. We can design physical spaces that are palliative and soothing – just having plants and using natural light over stark fluorescents would be a start. But I want to ask a more fundamental question. If everyone – from patients, to relatives, to doctors, to investigators, to patient advocates, to the Health Secretary – agrees[118] that our current system dehumanises patients and inhibits the kind of care we want to see, why do we persist with this way of doing things?

iPatient, or real patient?

The argument for the status quo is that big hospitals are 'efficient': they bring together the expertise, technology and facilities needed for specialist procedures, operations, and complex treatments. Efficiency, of course, is the argument for many things these days, including the role of technology in health care. Used well, technology can be positively transformative in health care (as we shall see) just as in other fields. But it can also hinder care by putting efficiency ahead of the patient. Dr Verghese's evangelism for the physical exam stems in part from his experience with technology in the exam room. 'I joke, but I only half-joke, that if you come to one of our hospitals missing a limb, no one will believe you till they get a CAT scan, MRI or orthopedic consult.' Technological tests can be invaluable, but not when doctors rely on them too much or even forsake actually examining the patient. 'I've gotten into some trouble in Silicon Valley,' Verghese says, 'for saying that the patient in the bed has almost become an icon for the real patient who's in the computer. I've actually coined a term for that entity … I call it the iPatient. The iPatient is getting wonderful care all across America. The real patient often wonders, where is everyone? When are they going to come by and explain things to me? Who's in charge? There's a real disjunction between the patient's perception and our own perceptions as physicians of the best medical care.'[119] When doctors need not enter a room, it means that medicine becomes theoretical for them. But for their patients, it's very real indeed and when they feel technology takes the caregiver's place, they feel neglected.

If technology replaces human contact when healing is what's called for, it makes health care less human. But interestingly, when it replaces the bureaucracy of health care, technology can make it more human. When used right, technological advances can make more space for doctors to interact with their patients. And as technology gets cheaper and smaller, going to a big factory hospital will be less and less necessary. Instead, local doctors will be able to use devices like GE's Vscan. Vscan is a handheld ultrasound machine that replaces the huge ones otherwise used. Doctors can thus administer ultrasounds personally in the exam room or even in a patient's home and get instant results; the patient need never go into the cold, dark, testing room again.[120]

Telemedicine, once a pipe dream, is increasingly a reality that frees patients from the burden of cumbersome tests and lengthy doctor visits. In Estonia, digital monitoring is such that doctors often have no need to see their patients for routine tests, which according to President Toomas Ilves, 'isn't necessarily a good thing' in the first place. 'The term health care has to be revised in a digital age,' he says. 'Most of what we've called health care since the era of Hippocrates is sick care. You go see the doctor when you're sick … The less I see my doctor, the better I am.' Estonia, like other European countries, faces a demographic pyramid, with the population of senior citizens expected to increase greatly. The key to providing care to the ageing and elderly, according to Ilves, is to prevent them from getting sick in the first place. That's why Estonia is looking into telemedicine to monitor people who are especially at risk, like the ill and elderly.[121] President Ilves predicts that 'in the future, we'll be monitoring people constantly, certainly older people, so that before you get really sick you go see a doctor'.[122]

That future is increasingly a reality. Estonia has already revolutionised health information through its Electronic Health Record. Started in 2008, the EHR does not centralise medical records but rather integrates them into a standard format readily available for both the patients and their doctors. Most powerfully, Estonians, through their national ID system, have digital access to their records and those of their children and can control which doctors can see which parts of their records. And while the government can compile statistical data or track disease outbreaks, that data is anonymised and never outside a patient's control.

While Britain, wary of national ID cards, is far from a system like Estonia's, British entrepreneurs are making strides in electronic medicine. Ali Parsa's start-up Babylon is seeking to create a virtual health service by solving several problems at once. First is the simple fact that most people in the world have little or no access to health care – and technology can get it to them. But like the Estonians, he also sees a future where medicine becomes preventive instead of reactive. He compares medicine to the sensors and indicators in our cars; we know exactly how long we have until something fails or runs out. Mobile technology is now allowing us to do that in medicine. Parsa believes 'we are entering a completely new era of diagnosis, where we can continuously diagnose by monitoring symptoms with mobile devices.'[123]

Babylon doesn't pre-empt the traditional doctor yet – there is still a need for in-person procedures and examinations. Increasingly though, much of medicine can be performed remotely. And that, Parsa, believes, is actually more human. His patients prefer to have a video conference on a phone or tablet rather than visiting the doctor's office or the hospital. 'They find doctors on the other side of a video call more intimate than going to see them,' Parsa reports. First, he believes, patients appreciate 'not leaving the comforts of their own home to spend on average three hours to get to a doctor's surgery. My mother, for instance – every time she gets her blood pressure taken at her doctor's surgery, it's high, while every time she has it done at home, it's not. We all know it's because of the stress of getting to the surgery at her age and meeting the doctor too.' With telemedicine, 'patients use the same medium to talk to their doctor that they use to talk to their friends and family. It's a much friendlier experience.' Increasingly, too, patients can take medicine into their own hands. While Parsa concedes that sometimes you need to go in for a test, why bother if it's something that can be done at home? For instance, if a patient needs a run-of-the-mill blood test, Babylon sends a courier to deliver a simple prick-your-finger test that the patient can do at home and then send back by courier to get the results within the day.

Social networks are another way that technology is helping to make health care more human. When Stephen Heywood, an architect and builder from near Boston, Massachusetts, learned he had ALS, the neurodegenerative disease also known as Lou Gehrig's Disease, he was fortunate to have a wonderful support network of his parents, two brothers and soon-to-be wife. They came together to make sure he could live the fullest life possible in the few years he had remaining, including a wedding, trips to Europe, and the birth of a son. But (as much as anyone can have 'luck' with a deadly disease), Stephen was lucky that his brothers and father were all MIT engineers, and in addition to helping him design solutions to the daily physical obstacles that ALS imposes, they set about developing a treatment for the disease itself. His wife and brother Jamie started the ALS Therapy Development Institute, the world's first biotech charity and largest ALS research centre in the world, researching the latest treatments in a desperate race to save Stephen and bring attention to this 'orphan disease' – as it is known because it isn't prevalent enough for drug companies to seriously invest in a treatment. Through the foundation's work, the award-winning documentary 'So Much So Fast' and the book *His Brother's Keeper: A Story from the Edge of Medicine* (both of which profile Stephen), Jamie and ALS TDI have been passionate and effective champions. Stephen sadly lost his battle with ALS in 2006, but his legacy lives on, both through the research institute and in an even bigger way through the company that Jamie then founded, PatientsLikeMe.

Stephen had a support network that created a charity to save him, but that is clearly not the reality for most people. In fact, Jamie recalls, his brother's experience showed him that 'the system is profoundly broken when you get really sick'. He had an epiphany: 'No one [in medicine] systematically learns from bad experiences. I didn't want anyone else to go through what Stephen went through for themselves.' He realised that while modern medicine is good at generating, testing and implementing new ideas, there is little room for feedback from patients to go back to the doctors and medical professionals who treat them. 'We have a system where doctors are paid for doing procedures,' Heywood says, 'but there are not checks as to whether or not they did any good; it's just assumed.'[124] But 'technology gives us an opportunity to find out where things go well or poorly'. PatientsLikeMe is a social network that connects patients suffering from the same diseases with each other and with their doctors, creating 'feedback loops' whereby health-care providers can quickly learn how patients respond to their treatments. 'The faster the feedback loop, the more responsive it is to humans' – so PatientsLikeMe harnesses human connectivity to increase responsiveness.

PatientsLikeMe is based in part on experiments in Sweden's health-care system. In the 1970s, a group of Swedish hip surgeons realised they had no way of knowing which procedures worked best. Their solution: work out what patients wanted as 'outcomes' and then do their best to measure them. At their annual conference each year, they published a table to show which doctors – and techniques – had the best outcomes. As a result, they 'visit each other to try to learn, so [there is] a continuous cycle of improvement', says Stefan Larsson, a Swedish health-care consultant. 'For many years, Swedish hip surgeons had the best results in the world, at least for those who actually were measuring.'[125] Similarly, PatientsLikeMe has designed its system 'to discover if interventions have impact in the real world', but goes a step further by actually empowering the patients to make that determination and to do so holistically. It is designed to work globally: 'Great systems learn across boundaries,' Heywood says, and he is exactly right. If medicine is to get better, its practitioners and their results can't be walled off from one another.

That's why PatientsLikeMe is so revolutionary: it is 'inherently democratic'. And it is intrinsically human. Patients log on and document their outcomes and experiences, giving doctors, drug companies, and everyone concerned a real-time social network to understand their practices better, while giving patients for the first time a role as true partners able to learn from and bolster each other in bad times. 'Patients contribute research ideas, they are involved in the design of trials and experiments, and they keep doctors honest. They interact around the data themselves, so if there's something not quite right with it, they will dive right into that.' Ultimately, Heywood hopes to reinvent the health-care system: 'imagine a world where everyone else's experience can help improve your own.'

Health care that makes you sick

This would not just improve care within the existing system, it could disrupt it altogether. The current medical system is geared to deliver one type of health care (typically a procedure or pill of some sort). But in the face of some conditions or diseases, certain behaviours and exercises or nutritional and lifestyle adjustments might be more effective. The factory health system is built (decades ago, before today's exponentially greater knowledge about human health) to produce a particular set of medical interventions. It is not designed to prescribe something non-medical or innovative (or if it does, it's only after a battery of tests and exams to confirm that a more complicated procedure didn't work).

This is not to say that we should stay away from doctors when we're seriously ill. Obviously, there are many conditions and diseases that are best treated by medical procedures or drugs. But health is not just a function of medicine. More than just optimising the effectiveness of a particular procedure, a more human health-care system would optimise individual health and well-being. As Jamie Heywood saw, today's medical system is based on how well a particular action was executed – 'Was the hip successfully replaced? All right then, success!' – rather than its actual, ultimate effect on the patient – 'Can you walk without pain since the procedure we did last year, Mrs Smith?' As a result, the system needlessly precludes non-medical interventions, not to mention the path almost never taken – non-intervention – from its repertoire of solutions.

Having feedback systems in place based on ultimate health outcomes will also help us see where treatments make us worse. Nassim Taleb talks at length about the danger of this phenomenon, iatrogenesis – the harm caused by treatment – that results from our deeply rooted desire to intervene, or, as he puts it, 'this need to do *something*'.[126] The problem with this approach is that interventions aren't costless. There is no drug in the world without an adverse side effect. There is no surgery without risk of greater injury or death. There are certainly many conditions for which we absolutely need the medical system. The tragedies of trauma and disease are made far less blunt by tools which doctors and nurses can now use to treat them. And I'm certainly not suggesting you attempt to treat cancer with herbal remedies (Steve Jobs famously tried to treat his pancreatic cancer with fasting and juice diets, later regretting his decision to forsake conventional treatment).[127] But without fully understanding the full, long-term costs and benefits of any one regimen, including less invasive treatment or non-intervention altogether (knowledge that a rigorous feedback system would give us), we take tremendous risks prescribing otherwise healthy people with powerful treatments.

Our bodies are exceptionally complex, and attempts to oversimplify the interactions that happen within them in an attempt to mechanise them courts unintended consequences. Doctors almost automatically prescribe proton pump inhibitors (e.g. Prilosec, Nexium, Prevacid) to people experiencing heartburn or stress (45 million in the UK per year)[128] – but more than six in ten are inappropriate according to the *BMJ*, a British medical journal.[129] The drug works by reducing acid levels in the stomach. This certainly eliminates heartburn, but it increases the risk of infection (acid kills germs in the things we eat) as well as vitamin deficiency (acid is also necessary to break our food down). Considering that for many people, simple changes in diet or behaviour (like eating an evening meal earlier) can eliminate acid reflux disease altogether, altering the chemistry of our bodies so casually for so many people seems haphazard at best. The same can be said for much of the advice around nutrition (which seems to change every other year, anyway): attempts to isolate what's causing one thing or another in the midst of our body's complex chemistry can lead us on wild goose chases that do more harm than good. Bingeing on pills of fish oil or antioxidants is more often than not a total waste of time, even though these nutrients are good for us when we eat them in the foods of which they're a natural part. A 2014 meta-study published in the *Annals of Internal Medicine* found that supplements like vitamin E and beta-carotene – both essential nutrients – are useless and sometimes harmful when taken in isolation.[130] It's their dispensation in such a mechanistic way that's the issue; as public-health scholar Marion Nestle notes: 'It takes the nutrient out of the context of the food, the food out of the context of the diet, and the diet out of the context of the lifestyle.'[131]

Now, Nassim Taleb explains, pharmaceutical companies find themselves 'scraping the bottom of the barrel, looking for disease among healthier and healthier people, lobbying for reclassification of conditions'.[132] Perhaps 'restless leg syndrome' ('RLS') really is a medical condition, but does it require prescription of ropinirole (usually used to treat those with Parkinson's)? GlaxoSmithKline thought so, and ran an aggressive marketing campaign to that effect. They also lobbied doctors directly to 'educate' them about the disease.[133] Doctors accuse the company of 'disease mongering'.[134]

Restless leg syndrome isn't the only disorder with a 'modern cure'. In the decade leading up to 2013, prescriptions to treat ADHD have more than trebled in England to now over one million per year.[135] Even greater excess can be found in the United States, which spent an incredible $7.9 billion to treat the condition in 2011.[136] Dr Michael Anderson, a paediatrician near Atlanta, Georgia, and an outspoken critic of the overtreatment of ADHD, still finds himself prescribing pills to the low-income elementary-aged patients he treats who are having trouble in school. 'I don't have a whole lot of choice,' he says. 'We've decided as a society that it's too expensive to modify the kid's environment. So we have to modify the kid.'[137] Our factory health system puts the needs of the children's factory-school system over the needs of children themselves. There's no question that drugs like Adderall and Ritalin help stimulated children pay attention in class and prevent them from acting out, especially those whose families can't afford tutoring and counselling. But we're taking children with very normal child behaviour – being energetic – and categorising them as ill and in need of treatment for the convenience of the adult world that serves them. It's a completely inhuman 'chemical straightjacket', says Dr Nancy Rappaport, a child psychiatrist who works with low-income children.[138]

Such 'straightjackets' aren't costless. One family with four of its children in Dr Anderson's care has a shelf lined up in the kitchen with all their medications: Adderall for the twelve- and nine-year-olds, Risperdal (an antipsychotic mood stabiliser) for the two eleven-year-olds, and – to top it all off – Clonidine, a sleep aid for all four of them to counteract the other drugs. When one of the children started to go through puberty, the Adderall he was on caused him to begin hearing voices and imagining people around him (a recognised side effect of the drug). Having become suicidal at one point, he even spent a week in a psychiatric hospital and was consequently switched to Risperdal, another ADHD drug). This is surely madness; cruel madness.[139]

But dehumanised, factory health care is not just limited to pharmaceuticals. Back pain is one of the most overtreated conditions there is. The best cure for chronic back pain is usually pretty basic: over-the-counter pain relievers, ice and heat, gentle exercise. Yet the trend of overtesting, overdiagnosis, and overtreatment continues to grow. The US spends $86 billion a year on back pain – much of it on unnecessary MRI and CT scans, prescription pain narcotics, and injections or surgery. People with routine back pain are eight times more likely to have surgery when they've been referred to have an MRI scan.[140]

It's all a product of the factory health-care system we have built: big hospitals operated by big bureaucracies working with big pharmaceutical companies. Patients – people – take a back seat to the imperatives of the system itself. None of this is to say that it is irretrievably broken, or cannot claim great results. We are healthier and longer lived as a species than we ever have been, and much of that is to do with our state-of-the-art abilities to cure disease and treat traumatic emergencies. Doctors are among the cleverest and most caring people anywhere: it takes a very special type of person to become one. But they're often caught up in a system that cares more about doing something – anything – than doing what they know to be best, which is often nothing at all.

Slow medicine

There is an alternative taking hold. In the food world, there is a growing movement called Slow Food, a direct response to 'fast food'. We will learn more about it in the next chapter, but the philosophical tenets behind it have inspired doctors as well. Proponents of 'slow medicine' argue that in making medicine 'reductive' and 'mechanical' we forget that human bodies are complex organisms that can often heal themselves.

Dr Victoria Sweet, who was a doctor at Laguna Honda Hospital in San Francisco, America's last almshouse (which has since closed), is one of those proponents. Laguna Honda Hospital was unique. 'It looked like a medieval monastery,' Sweet recalls. 'It had cream-coloured walls and a red-tiled roof and a bell tower and turrets. The hospital was huge, on 62 acres of land in the middle of San Francisco and it had 1,178 patients. [There was] the chapel, which looked more like a small church with polished wooden pews and real stained glass, and then we went outside and [there was the] greenhouse, the aviary, and the barnyard.'[141]

Sweet was both a doctor and a historian of medicine. Her subject was the medieval abbess Hildegard of Bingen, who among her many talents as a composer, writer and polymath also wrote on medicine. Hildegard believed that the human body was like a plant, and accordingly 'took a gardener's approach to the body. She did not focus down on the cellular level of the body; instead she stood back from her patient and looked around,' describes Sweet. 'She manipulated and rebalanced the environment inside of and outside her patient. She did so slowly, like a gardener … then she waited to see what would happen. Which is to say that she followed the patient's body; she did not lead.'[142] Hildegard believed in the body's *viriditas*, or vitality, and that given the right conditions, it was perfectly able to heal itself.

Sweet didn't really understand this concept until she treated her patient Terry Becker, who was homeless and an addict. Becker, Sweet recalls, had woken up one day paralysed from the neck down. She was diagnosed with a very rare viral disease, but since it has no treatment and tends to get better with time, she was admitted to Laguna Honda and became Sweet's patient. Terry had a bad influence: her boyfriend, also a homeless addict, who would pull her onto the streets for months at a time. In a one-year period after she had left Laguna Honda, she was sent to hospital twenty-two times. Medically, her biggest problem was that by sitting in a wheelchair, she had acquired an enormous bedsore. Doctors had tried skin grafts three times, but the bedsore had become too large to operate on and Terry was sent back to Sweet and Laguna Honda.

'When I saw that bedsore for the first time, I was absolutely shocked,' Sweet recalls. 'It went from the middle of Terry's back to her tailbone. It was so deep that I could see the bone at the base of Terry's spine. It was filled with all this decayed tissue from the failed grafts. It would have to heal on its own. I couldn't imagine how Terry would survive all the infections she would get.'[143]

Despairing over what to do, thinking that this bedsore was 'probably the end of Terry Becker', Sweet looked at a plant in her office and asked herself: what would Hildegard do? 'Maybe Hildegard would just remove what was in the way of Terry healing. So what was in the way? All the dead tissue was in the way and had to be moved. Anything that was uncomfortable, like wrinkled bed clothes or a hard mattress or any medication that she didn't absolutely need. Fear, uncertainty, hopelessness. Then I thought, Hildegard would fortify Terry's *viriditas* with the basics: good food, fresh air, deep sleep, sunlight. So that's what I did. And it was amazing to see how fast Hildegard's prescription began to work.'

At Laguna Honda, patients weren't treated mechanically, but organically … humanly. 'Medicine is personal, face to face. And when it's personal, it works,' Sweet says. At the almshouse, nothing was rushed, paperwork was kept to a minimum, and doctors aimed not to get patients out as quickly as possible ('efficiently'), but to let them heal. Sweet concedes that modern medicine completely explains how Terry Becker got better. This is not a call to arms for medieval necromancy. But in our rush to offer an immediate prescription, a mechanical 'fix', we often forget that time and care can be the most natural – and effective – treatments of all. This is what she calls 'the efficiency of inefficiency'. She is fond of a quote from Dr Francis Peabody, a noted professor at Harvard

Medical School in the early twentieth century: 'The secret of the care of the patient is caring for the patient.'[144] Often what would otherwise be seen as inefficient is actually most efficient. When we put bureaucracy ahead of patients, 'in the interest of efficiency, we became less efficient', she says. 'In the interest of putting the patient first, we put the real patient last.' Sweet's one recommendation for fixing health care: 'Put inefficiency, that is unassigned free time, back into health care because it's that free time that gives us the space to be personal and that is the most efficient health care of all.'[145]

Geriatrician Dr Dennis McCullough understands that the elderly are much better treated with this 'slow medicine' approach. Often the most important part of their health care is the community around them, building a family support system and a trusted medical team. This is one part of the 'slow' method. But the other is recognising how what might be inconsequential tests or procedures for younger people can actually cause great harm for the elderly. McCullough writes:

> For instance, aggressive screening and treatment for prostate cancer and even breast cancer for those over eighty may actually cause more problems than they solve. Early detection of very small cancers of uncertain danger often leads to more testing for confirmation, which imposes risks, discomfort, and cost without clear benefit. A simple physical exam of the breast or prostate in the office and home-testing cards for blood in the stool are perfectly appropriate low-tech alternatives for detection of cancers that would make a difference in health in elders over eighty.[146]

Dr McCullough's diagnosis is exactly right. If there's one aspect of health care guilty of an inhuman approach, it's how we care for those at the ends of their lives.

Death and dignity

Sheila Marsh was dying. Stricken with cancer, the seventy-seven-year-old had one wish: to say goodbye to her favourite horse, Bronwen, for whom she had cared for twenty-five years. So the staff at the Royal Albert Edward Infirmary in Wigan arranged for Bronwen and another of Marsh's horses to come and visit, wheeling her outside to greet and be nuzzled by them. Though unable to speak due to the ravages of her disease, she 'gently called to Bronwen and the horse bent down tenderly and kissed her on the cheek as they said their last goodbyes', according to Gail Taylor, one of the nurses. Sheila died soon afterwards, but her medical staff had helped end her life in quiet dignity, fulfilling her final wishes to bid farewell to the horses that had meant so much to her.[147]

That Sheila had such a dignified death in hospital is extraordinary, really. Because death in Britain (and indeed much of the developed world) is a horrendous experience. Most people, of course, want to die a quiet death at home surrounded by their loved ones. But instead many die in hospital, hooked up to ventilators and IV drips, surrounded by beeping monitors, lying in a sterile room devoid of life and soul.

We suffer tremendous indignity in the last years of our lives. Our bodies fail us, but doctors, obliged to preserve life at just about any cost, work to prop up our dying organs, our weakening limbs, our tenuous grip on reality. We lose the ability to do simple tasks by ourselves, like use the toilet, shower, even eat. It is humiliating, painful, frightening, torturous; it is inhuman. And we make things worse by letting people die exactly where they don't want to end their lives. A majority of people prefer to die at home,[148] and yet only 21 per cent do; 53 per cent die in hospitals.[149] The sad part is that of those who die in hospitals, some 40 per cent have no medical reason for being there.[150]

It is deeply inhuman that most people's final moments are not as they'd like them to be. And factory hospitals are inappropriate places for the elderly, as Dennis McCullough points out:

Large 'industrial-scale' environments like hospitals focus on disease and tend to lose sight of the complexity of an older person. Speed is at a premium and slower-moving, slower-responding elders don't fit well with the pressured environment of fast medical care.[151]

But hospitalising elders is also, from a public-policy perspective, a bad idea for the rest of us. End-of-life care costs the NHS about a fifth of its annual budget (or about £20 billion), with an expected rise to £25 billion by 2030.[152] Some 20 per cent of hospital beds were occupied by those who were dying and who often had no medical reason to be in hospital.[153] So if no one wants to die in hospital and it is so costly to the system for people to do so, how can we give people a more dignified and more human end-of-life experience?

We can invest in better hospice care and end-of-life community services. One report estimates that an investment of £500 million – just 2.5 per cent of the total the NHS spends annually on end-of-life care – in community services, hospice care and family-care capacity would allow up to 50 per cent of people to die at or close to home rather than in hospital.[154] And we can help people work out what they want. One of the great tragedies of end-of-life care is that we simply don't know what most people want. Erring on the side of the medical principle 'to do no harm', doctors continue to intervene to prolong life, even when we might not want them to do so. That's where living wills, also called 'advance directives', come in. Living wills help relatives and loved ones know what to do in case of medical dilemmas in which patients are incapacitated and can't make decisions for themselves. The vast majority of people don't have them – only 30 per cent in the United States[155] and fewer than 10 per cent in the UK.[156] But communities like the town of La Crosse, Wisconsin, are leading the way in demonstrating how we can change the norm.

Bud Hammes is a medical ethicist at Gundersen Health System, a local hospital in La Crosse. He found that without living wills, most of his patients' families had no idea what to do when patients were in a coma or on life-support machines. Despite years of illness, no one had thought to have the conversation. Consequently, 'the moral distress that these families were suffering was palpable. You could feel it in the room,' he says. Hammes resolved to help families solve the problem in advance, and started a programme to train nurses to ask people if they wanted to fill out an advance directive. The idea caught on, and now it is the norm in La Crosse to have a living will; in fact 96 per cent of those who die in the town have documentation for their end-of-life wishes and it is normal for neighbours to gossip about who doesn't have one. And while this wasn't the goal, medical costs at Gundersen Health System have declined as patients make clear they don't want to be kept on dehumanising (and expensive) life support.[157] By helping patients make their wishes known, Hammes has made death in La Crosse more dignified.

A pie is in the oven, vintage tracks are playing, and half a dozen women are gathered around the kitchen counter at Pathstone Living, a nursing home in Minnesota specially tailored for those suffering from memory impairment. It's a typical afternoon there, with staff offering a wide range of activities for the senior citizens in their care. Staying busy, it turns out, can relieve the agitation that's common among those suffering from Alzheimer's or dementia. At another nursing home, such agitation would be managed with anti-psychotic medicines (which are approved to treat serious illness, like bipolar disease and schizophrenia): 300,000 nursing-home residents are prescribed them annually in the United States. But anti-psychotics increase the risk of death for those with dementia.[158]

Beatrice DeLeon experienced over-medication first hand. An Alzheimer's patient, DeLeon was sent to a care facility not for her memory, but because she had had multiple falls. Even though over-prescription of antipsychotics – a 'chemical restraint' – is banned by law, 'they just kept giving her more and more', says DeLeon's husband, Manuel. 'And I noticed when I used to go see her, she'd just kind of mumble, like she was lost.' Beatrice was administered two very strong drugs (approved to treat bipolar disorder and schizophrenia), drugs that effectively made her a mumbling pile of flesh, writes Ina Jaffe, the reporter who visited her. According to Bradley Williams, a professor of pharmacology and gerontology at the University of Southern California, such drugs are usually unnecessary, especially given their significant side effects. 'They blunt behaviours,' he says. 'They can cause sedation. It increases [seniors'] risk for falls.'[159] And doctors prescribe them like sweets; a 2011 US government study found that 88 per cent of Medicare[160] claims for antipsychotics were for dementia or other conditions for which these drugs were not intended.[161]

While enforcement against nursing homes that over-prescribe antipsychotics is weak,[162] Dr Tracy Tomac hopes Pathstone will provide a realistic alternative. Pathstone's new, 'anti-antipsychotic' approach came after Tomac, a psychiatrist and medical consultant there, decided with a colleague to see if they could reduce the drug's use. They tried it at one of the smaller nursing homes run by the same charity, Ecumen. By six months in, they were successful – everyone was off antipsychotics. So Ecumen decided to scale the approach to all of its nursing homes across the state – about a dozen in total. Their initial goal? Reduce their use by 20 per cent. After the first year? Down 97 per cent. Now at Pathstone, only 5 to 7 per cent of patients are prescribed antipsychotics at all. Shelley Matthes, who's in charge of quality assurance for Ecumen, says that the numbers were not the only thing that changed: 'They started interacting … people who hadn't been speaking were speaking. They came alive and awakened.'

The programme, which actually came to be known as 'Awakenings', derives much of its success from training staff simply to pay attention to people. While individualised dementia care is not an original concept (the nursing staff borrowed from techniques demonstrated elsewhere), attending closely to patients in a human way eliminates the need to medicate them for the behavioural problems dementia can create. Maria Reyes, the person in charge of Awakenings, explains that if any staff member notices a patient misbehaving, they need to dig into that action's root cause. Knowing what each patient likes and dislikes and what their life story was outside the nursing home can help nip issues in the bud. It's less risky, less costly – and more human.[163]

Decentralised health care

Now here's the critical question. How are we going to bring the benefits of all these thoughtful innovations and others like them – others that haven't been invented yet; all these ways of making health care more human – and get them working in a big way in the UK? In the NHS?

The answer is, we won't. Not unless we make some really big changes. Because the truth is, the very structure of our system – the very structure of the NHS – is designed to stop things like Jamie Heywood's PatientsLikeMe, Victoria Sweet's Laguna Honda, or the amazing Awakenings programme. The system is designed to perpetuate one particular, rigid, centralised and frankly outdated approach to health care: the factory approach where everyone is treated the same, and where the operational priority puts rules and processes and targets first.

Many would dispute that claim. With its system of locally controlled trusts, the NHS is, they say, already fairly decentralised. It's a question not of geographic centralisation, however, but of centralised decision-making. The tremendous power the NHS wields overs its trusts through mandates, contracts, regulations, standards and incentives creates a centralising force of bureaucracy that is the impetus for some of the system's worst problems. We have to free the NHS of these bureaucratic bonds so we can allow more personalised, more human providers of health care into the system. None of the people we've just discussed have any place in the current NHS model. The local health monopolies leave no room for innovation or a different approach – including from those within the system today.

In the name of setting and enforcing minimum standards (where have we heard that before?) the NHS has developed onerous reporting requirements that take doctors and nurses away from patients. According to the Cavendish Review, an independent report commissioned by the British government into the state of nursing and the quality of care after the Mid-Staffs scandal, nurses consider paperwork to be one of the major impediments to delivering good care.[164] 'There's an intolerable amount of it,' Camilla Cavendish (the report's author) said. 'I had a friend, who was an off-duty doctor at a different hospital, who walked onto a ward in Mid-Staffs and found only one nurse on duty, buzzers going off everywhere, but the nurse was writing care plans. She told my friend she had been told that they must come first.'[165] The top-down 'endless requests' result in medical professionals worrying more about collecting the perfect data set than helping the patient.

The diktats of the NHS bureaucracy come from the centre, but they also cause trusts to regulate themselves, with disastrous results. Reforms in 2002 allowed 'high-performing' hospitals to become autonomous Foundation Trusts with more independence from the centre.[166] While the original idea – that local, independent providers are better than centralised ones – is a good one, the implementation has gone awry, with wrong incentives all over the place. Instead of putting care first, trusts prioritise financial targets in order to achieve foundation status, and since they only reach that status through ticking certain boxes, those became the end goals. Numbers, not people, are the priority.

It led directly to the horror of Mid-Staffs. The Mid-Staffs Trust was trying to become a foundation trust and had to show that its finances were in order. When it cut funding for nurses and medical assistants in order to meet budget targets, conditions in the hospital suffered. While the NHS didn't force the trust to operate that way, the system it designed tilted local administrators to seek foundation status. As a result, the trust put a bureaucratic goal ahead of its patients, and consequently, patients died.[167] No one wanted that outcome, but when the system makes those running the trusts forget about the people they are meant to serve, such an outcome is inevitable.

Another way that centralisation gets in the way of human care is through extensive contracting out of services like cleaning, meals and laundry. This separates the people carrying out those services from caregivers like nurses, and by not integrating the workforce into a cohesive team, everyone is liable to tend their own patch rather than working collaboratively. Without such cooperation, messages are lost, problems overlooked, and patients left in deplorable conditions because no one takes responsibility. It is the epitome of a factory approach.

Spending less time with patients is another consequence of a culture that overworks doctors and nurses and keeps them away from their charges. In her report, Cavendish writes of the 'false economy' in which authorities pay care workers by the minute rather than by the well-being of the people being cared for. While this is more problematic for social-care workers, who must travel from home to home and fit in as many visits as possible in a day (which along with low wages and a failure to compensate for travel time leads to high burnout),[168] it also rings true for treatment in hospitals; when doctors and nurses have to rush through appointments because they are over-scheduled and overburdened, they provide insufficient attention to their patients, missing crucial points and failing to provide reassurance.

In the current NHS structure, problems can easily be put down to other units (i.e. the ward isn't clean because it's not the nurse's responsibility, but an unseen night-time cleaning crew contracted from London). When individuals at the local level are empowered to exercise responsibility over their small bit of the system, not only do they rise to the challenge more than in a large bureaucracy, but they are in fact more efficient. And because decisions are being made by those literally walking the hospital halls every day, the nurses and doctors in charge are able to notice weak signals – those small, unmeasured observations that are unimportant in isolation but over time, in aggregate, can highlight opportunities as well as warn of potential failures. The ward matrons of old would never wait for a cleaning crew to ensure their wards remained in good condition.

So what should we do to fix things? We need to bring the NHS back to a human scale, so the people who work for the NHS can emphasise care. It's not that doctors and nurses are uncaring, it's that in a factory-hospital system, bureaucracy gets in the way. Health Secretary Jeremy Hunt had to actually sign a directive that the names of attending physicians be written over the beds of their patients because too many mistakes were being made. I'm not attacking Mr Hunt; he understood the problem and moved to fix it. But how dehumanised has the NHS become when doctors have to be forced to remember who their patients are? We need smaller, more local facilities. Of course it's true that there aren't enough – and there isn't enough demand for – specialist doctors to be spread around every community. But equally, there is no need to warehouse them in huge buildings; giant, Kafkaesque labyrinths that impose themselves on sick, frightened and vulnerable people. If we transform hospitals into places of care, we can take the first step towards setting a tone that puts people first, not a bureaucratic, top-down version of 'efficiency'.

We also need more patient control. Doctors are traditionally seen as 'priests' of medicine, interpreting results and pronouncing what is to be done to patients and their families. We know that this makes patients feel ignored, misunderstood and out of control. So instead, we should advocate for medicine in which instead of doctors telling their patients what to do, they ask their patients what their goals are and give them realistic options to help reach them. In the end, it should be up to patients, not their doctors. And, while some degree of doctor-knows-best can be helpful, doctors and patients need to meet in the middle: we need to trust individuals to control their own fates. Patients are people, not products, and shouldn't be treated as such.

We can borrow from models that work. Sweden has succeeded with decentralised, regional health providers that are known for their expertise in using patient feedback to constantly adjust procedures and practices. Estonia, as we've seen, has worked out how to feasibly put health records in people's hands (unlike the British fiasco described in Chapter 1). And, thinking for the next generation, we can look to Singapore's national medical savings account. Singapore's medical system is universal, but depending on income level, individuals are subsidised different amounts, ranging from almost everything for the poorest to very little for the wealthiest. In order to prevent over-treatment and wasteful testing, every patient pays some amount, however small, for every procedure, no matter how much he or she is subsidised. And Singaporeans can save and spend health-care money as family units. These funds are heritable, so people have an incentive to not over-treat themselves – unnecessary spending depletes the pot that's there for the family. This is especially relevant at the end of life; if you know how expensive different treatments might be, you can choose what to prioritise, giving you power over your own health and your own life.

The problems we have in our system are not the fault of any one doctor, nurse or administrator: it's the system. As it stands today it will continue to foster and incentivise the inhuman behaviour and practices we've seen. What it really needs is a transformative reboot, to undo the cumbersome apparatus that, while built in the name of efficiency, now serves as a barrier to better care. To bring the human touch back to medicine, we need a system devolved to the smallest efficient unit. Yes, very particular specialists will still have to be centralised, but for the vast majority of our health needs, a highly localised system is ideal (even to the point of your mobile device). By working not in large hospitals, but small ones, doctors can establish a more personal relationship with their patients. We need a system built around humans, their needs, and what really works for them – not the medical establishment. No more enormous bureaucracy that takes doctors away from their patients. No more byzantine rules that get in the way of treating patients. No more national contracts imposed across service providers with no thought to local circumstances.

Just as with schools, the only way to bring about the transformation we need is to understand that the problem is structural. We need to decentralise the structure so that smaller, more innovative, more human providers of health care can operate within the NHS system: state providers, private providers, mutual organisations owned by their workers ... This is why it's so important to distinguish between the idea of the NHS and the institution of the NHS. The idea of the NHS is and always will be profoundly human. The institution? Not so much. For a good part of the last century, there's no doubt that large-scale factory hospitals enabled health outcomes never before experienced. But we're in a new century now; science and technology have evolved to make this model out of date. With no more excuses to prop up the big, centralised health system, it's time we moved on – because a country that ignores the human side of health care really misses the point.

CHAPTER 4

FOOD

What has happened to us that we think it's all right to throw live chicks into a mincing machine just because they're male; that piglets' tails are chopped off and their front teeth broken to prevent 'stress-induced cannibalism' and chunks of their ears cut out for identification, all without painkillers; that cows are milked to breaking point so they live out just a third of their natural lives? This is how you get your food. This is how I get my food. This is where pretty much all of us get our food, because what we typically eat today has been farmed in factories and manufactured in factories.

It's the 'farmed' part that's truly indefensible. The fake food concocted from artificial ingredients by vast industrial machines, food production that's just another branch of chemistry – well, it may be disgusting and make you unhealthy, but in the end it's a question of taste. (Although as we'll see, it's not quite as simple as a question of consumer choice.) The way we treat animals though? That's a question of ethics. Farmer and poet Wendell Berry describes eating as 'farming by proxy'. In the case of eating factory-farmed animals it's cruelty by proxy. If we don't care about the sickening things I've just described, we've lost one of the qualities that is essential to human beings: the capacity to be empathetic. More animal cruelty equals less human.

Of course none of us is deliberately choosing to torture a pig when we buy a hot dog. Any more than the jetBlue employee went to work the morning of the flight described at the start of this book planning to treat a mother and her young daughter in an inhuman way. But as we've seen in other contexts, people are often made to behave in inhuman ways by the systems and structures around them. When it comes to factory food and cruelty to animals, our shopping and eating habits make us complicit in horrific acts. But it's simplistic just to blame ourselves; to blame consumerism. That lets the real culprits off the hook: the politicians, regulators and business executives of the culinary-industrial complex, whose grotesque practices are encouraged through subsidy and permissiveness. The resulting pervasiveness of factory food in our society makes it hard for even the most conscious consumer to avoid propping up this rotten, inhuman system. It is a structural problem. That's why, if we're going to do anything about it, we need to go deeper than campaigns to shop differently or support animal-welfare charities. We need to dismantle and reconstruct the entire food industry.

Factory farms

Most summers when I was young, we would visit my family in Hungary. My grandmother grew most of her fruit and vegetables in the garden, and there were chickens running around the place. On the other side of town, with the other side of the family, it was pigs: my family owned a small salami factory. My cousin and I would help out, and that included killing pigs. And I mean really killing them – by hand. Lots of blood. But I was pretty young then and anyway over there they were … you know, Communist. A bit backward. Actually, as I now know, the way we treated and killed pigs in our small local meat-processing business was much more humane than the horrors taking place in the big, industrialised plants in the more 'advanced' UK where we lived.

For most of my life (I suspect like most people) I never gave much thought to the origins of my food. I began to develop a greater understanding while working on these issues with some of our clients (including McDonald's) during my time running Good Business, the corporate responsibility firm I started with Giles Gibbons in 1997. (And I'm so proud that in 2009 Giles started the Sustainable Restaurant Association which has had a hugely positive impact on our food culture.) But then, in 2013, at Rohan's suggestion, I read Jonathan Safran Foer's *Eating Animals*. I know there are other books like it; people and organisations that have been campaigning on animal welfare for years. But that's the book that I read, and it influenced me hugely, opening my eyes to the sickening world of filth, pollution and abuse that is responsible for the food we consume.

Factory farms are disgusting places. A quick YouTube search for one of the many undercover activist videos shot at chicken, egg, beef, milk, veal, or pork factories will suppress even the most robust appetite. But the point is this: it took reading a book for me to understand the unconscionable origins of much of the food I ate and prepared for family and friends. Reading a food label in the supermarket would have been useless. When I buy a burger for my children at the zoo café or eat in a restaurant, there isn't a label. Or even a company website I can check. The vast majority of fast-food places are not McDonald's or Burger King with a valuable brand to protect and an incentive to respond – at least on some level – to campaigners' animal-welfare concerns. Most of the time, we're getting fast food from outlets with no clue as to what kind of horrific treatment was endured by the animals who died to make our snacks. I'd love to know how many of the 'conservationists' at London Zoo, for example, who prattle on with tediously gushing self-righteousness about Asiatic lions or Philippine seahorses or whatever, have the first idea about the lives of the chickens, pigs and cows they serve up for lunch?

No one has the first idea: not the people at the zoo, not the shelf stacker at your supermarket, not the waiter in your restaurant. Of course that's just how the big food industry likes it, going to aggressive lengths to stop activists documenting what happens in factory farms. Keeping us in the dark makes the ethical issues abstract, not something that busy practical people trying to live their lives should waste time or energy on. There's no individual animal for us to picture in our mind's eye, looking back at us, suffering. Nonetheless, we can be thankful that a few brave campaigners have shown us what goes on. Do not be in any doubt: the meat we eat relies on systematic cruelty that is documented, widespread, and beyond the most sadistic thoughts you can imagine. It's not a question of whether animals are being tortured for our food, it's a question of whether we care enough to stop it.

For me, this is very personal. I love food, I love cooking … yes, all right, I'm very greedy. When we moved to California, Rachel and I decided to raise chickens with our sons Ben and Sonny. It is one of the most pleasing things you can imagine – seeing your children run outside in the morning to let the chickens out of their coop, fascinated as they peck around, excited to collect the eggs. Of course, I see that this is the stuff of parody; that the first thing defenders of our inhuman, industrial food system will say is that objecting to it is all very well – but all very elitist. Big Food is cheap food, and most normal people can't keep chickens; can't afford your fancy-dan free-range, hand-reared, artisanal, grass-fed whatnots. Intensive, 'efficient' production of food is the only way to feed our growing population affordably, it is claimed. This is false, as we shall see, but those who want to see food produced through more human, less barbaric means are often dismissed as being out of touch. You know: 'Let them eat seasonal, organic, locally sourced, fair-trade cake.'

This caricature of 'Bad but Cheap' versus 'Good but Expensive' misses the fundamental point. Why do you think factory food is cheap? It's not because it's inherently cheaper or more 'efficient' to farm animals and process them in a highly mechanised way. We've chosen to make it cheaper as a deliberate act of policy, through direct and indirect corporate subsidies, regulations and laws designed to protect Big Food and crush any challenge to it from those who want to do things differently. 'Most people have little idea just how much they are paying for food in hidden ways,' says Patrick Holden, founding director of the Sustainable Food Trust and one of Britain's most thoughtful food activists. 'The failure to introduce true cost accounting into food and agricultural policy is the biggest single impediment to the wider uptake of more sustainable farming.'[169] Humane food appears to be more expensive because all its costs are included in the price. With factory food, we pay its costs in other ways.

There is a growing cost to our health. Our ability to treat infection is slowly coming under attack as a result of the excessive antibiotic use on factory farms. In the UK, nearly half of all antibiotics are used on farm animals, not humans (in the US it's 80 per cent).[170] This is considered necessary not only to keep animals from dying (because their quarters are so squalid, overcrowded, and diseased) but also to promote quick growth (thanks to antibiotics, chickens that would otherwise take fourteen weeks to mature require only six in a factory).[171] In the last five years, doctors have observed an alarming rise in urinary tract infections (UTIs generally affect one in nine women every year) as well as sepsis, particularly from strains of *E. coli* that are antibiotic resistant. Factory farming isn't responsible for all resistance to antibiotics – we use them for ourselves and even our pets at levels far higher than we should. But the genes in an increasing number of resistant cases have been found to match bacteria found on 'conventionally' (that is, industrially) raised meat – specifically those given antibiotics.[172] In the words of Sir Liam Donaldson, formerly Chief Medical Officer for England: 'Every inappropriate or unnecessary use in animals or agriculture is potentially signing a death warrant for a future patient.'[173] Antibiotics used to promote quick growth in livestock are now doing the same thing to people. According to studies by public-health researchers, 'chronic mass exposure' to antibiotic 'residue' is now believed to contribute directly to *our* growth, increasing our propensity to gain weight above and beyond food's 'nutrition facts'.[174]

While antibiotic resistance threatens everyone (including vegetarians and free-range enthusiasts), those of us who eat factory meat (and even crops from nearby fields) are much likelier to get ill directly from it.[175] First, because the high density of animal confinement increases disease, just as urban slums do among humans. These breeding grounds give us contaminated food: in the United States 69 per cent of shop-bought pork and beef and 92 per cent of poultry is contaminated with *E. coli*.[176] In the UK, in July 2014, the major supermarkets launched emergency investigations into the spread of *Campylobacter* bacteria – which in the UK sickens 280,000 people a year and kills 100 – to as much as two-thirds of all fresh chicken sold in Britain.[177]

It's not just about animal confinement. The problem with our factory system is that food (all of it, not just meat) is combined, mixed, and redistributed so widely that a single sick cow or contaminated batch of vegetables can infect the food supply across the country almost overnight. In a Welsh chicken plant run by major poultry producer 2 Sisters (whose customers include most big supermarkets), an investigation discovered dead chickens routinely being picked off the floor and put back into production lines, a factory floor flooded with chicken guts and water from scalding tanks that had gone more than three days without being cleaned (meaning around 250,000 birds had passed through it) – all in the span of one month. While the company described the allegations as 'untrue, misleading and inaccurate', you can view the images yourself and come to your own conclusions.[178]

This industrialisation of food might look 'efficient', but it creates massive risks that make the whole system inherently fragile: vulnerable to outbreaks that can have a devastating and costly effect. This isn't to say that small-scale farmers aren't susceptible to animal infections, but at least in those cases meat can be more easily isolated and contained. With a national – international – system of collecting, mixing, and spreading food, one 'rotten apple' can cause problems on a vast scale.

'This food, and this way of eating, is killing us'

Factory food goes way beyond meat. Michael Moss, a Pulitzer-Prize-winning journalist at the *New York Times*, spent over four years researching and reporting on the science behind processed food, talking to hundreds of people in (or formerly employed by) the food industry as well as combing through thousands of pages of memos and other internal documents. In his revealing book, *Salt Sugar Fat*, he explains how factory food is engineered to be addictive.

Moss tells the story of Howard Moskowitz, one of the food industry's go-to consultants for fine-tuning its products. A mathematician with a PhD in experimental psychology from Harvard, he got his start in the unlikeliest of places: the US Army, which had called on him to help solve the problem of getting soldiers on the battlefield to eat all of the food rationed to them. (After a while, soldiers would find their ready-to-eat meals boring and not finish them, creating waste and possible energy deficits.) What *would* soldiers eat ad infinitum? White bread. Though it would never get them excited, Moskowitz explains, 'they could eat lots and lots of it without feeling they'd had enough.'[179]

This is called 'sensory-specific satiety'. According to Moss, 'it is the tendency for big, distinct flavors to overwhelm the brain, which responds by depressing your desire to have more.' Eating bland food (like white bread) might fill you up, but you don't feel like stopping. This insight would launch Moskowitz's long career helping food companies make their products more addictive. For over three decades, he's been a paid 'optimisation' consultant for Big Food companies like General Foods, Campbell Soup, Kraft and PepsiCo. 'I've optimized soups,' he says. 'I've optimized pizzas. I've optimized salad dressings and pickles.'

To achieve this, consumers are paid to sit for hours in focus groups, giving their input on every sensory detail you can imagine – taste, touch, the rather creepy-sounding 'mouthfeel', packaging, smell, etc. The data is then processed using a complex statistical method called conjoint analysis. Moss explains: 'It's not simply a matter of comparing Color 23 with Color 24. In the most complicated projects, Color 23 must be combined with Syrup 11 and Packing 6, and on and on, in seemingly infinite combinations.' The goal: to find consumers' 'bliss point'.

How do you attain bliss? In case the title of Moss's book wasn't too much of a giveaway, it's with salt, sugar and fat. Not necessarily more of all of them – there's a 'Goldilocks' point for each – but certainly nowhere close to moderation. The simple truth is that salt is addictive. Sugar is addictive. Fat is addictive. Who cares if eating too much of them makes people unhealthy? Certainly not Big Food. If you're running a factory-food company, the whole point is to get people to eat more and more of your product.

Let's look at sugar in particular. It's everywhere, and in excess. A Müller strawberry yogurt Fruit Corner contains 22.4 grammes of sugar, about the same as a KitKat (23.8 grammes).[180] A typical 330 ml can of soft drink contains 35 grammes of sugar – that's nearly nine teaspoons. Disgusting if you actually imagine scooping each one in, but we don't, because they're easily dissolved (i.e. camouflaged) directly into the food.[181] You'll find added sugar in your sausages, bread, ready meals, soups, burgers, crisps … the list goes on. Subway's Meatball Marinara 6-inch sub has 11 grammes of sugar (about three teaspoons).[182] Sugar is hidden in just about every processed food, mainly because it is addictive.

Making consumers physically addicted to their products is a carefully calibrated science into which the Big Food companies put huge effort. At one point, Frito-Lay, maker of Walkers crisps and other snack foods, was spending $30 million per year at their research centre in Dallas. According to Moss, 500 chemists, psychologists and technicians were put to work, measuring and optimising every variable they could. My favourite tool described by him is the company's $40,000 chewing simulator. They used it to answer questions like how brittle the perfect crisp ought to be: 'People like a chip that snaps with about four pounds of pressure per square inch.' Consider the brand Wotsits. With annual worldwide sales of over $4 billion, it's a big business.[183] Its most important feature, according to food scientist Steve Witherly, is 'vanishing caloric density' – the cheese puff's ability to dissolve instantly on your tongue. 'If something melts down quickly, your brain thinks that there's no calories in it … you can just keep eating it forever.'

As you might expect, this food, and this way of eating, is killing us. The rapid rise of heart disease and diabetes in Western society is directly linked to diet. A report by the UK government's Chief Scientific Adviser Sir David King warned that costs associated with obesity and people being overweight will hit £49.9 billion per year by 2050.[184] That's over £1,200 on average a person will pay annually in extra taxes to subsidise the treatment of diet-related disease.[185] The bottom line is: factory food is toxic, and the only way to understand how it's become so pervasive is to understand the business of factory farming. Not just factory farms for animals, but the farms growing the crops on which this whole industrialised monstrosity is built. It's there that the question of how we've ended up with such a terrible, inhuman system begins to make sense.

'No future in farming'

Matt Rothe always wanted to be a farmer. Raised on a large family farm in Colorado, perhaps the most exciting day in his childhood was the day his father showed him how to use the tractor … and let him drive it. 'It's corn as far as you can see in any direction,' Matt explains. 'And despite the fact that you're only going three miles per hour, you're always making a little progress toward the end of the field, and there's such a sense of satisfaction when you get to that final row, and you turn around, and the whole thing is done.' Rothe had spent all his summers during university at home, working the farm, driving the tractor. It was the family business: soil was in his blood and he loved it. 'I liked planting things in the ground and taking care of them – taking care of the land. I liked seeing it and feeling ownership of it.'

By his final year of university in 1994, Rothe had been doing a lot of thinking about his future. In April, he called his father and told him what he'd decided: he wanted to 'come home and farm'. He thought his father would be thrilled. But instead, his father told him: no, there's just no future in it. What he meant was, no future in farming the way *they* farmed. No future in a family farm. 'It was hard for both of us,' Rothe says. 'I can't imagine being a father and listening to my son and telling him he couldn't come back and run the business – the business that had been in the family for twelve generations.'

But Matt Rothe stuck to his guns. He moved out to California and got a job running one of the best-known suppliers of humanely produced meat in the state.[186] After that, he went to business school. Just as he was finishing his degree, he found out his dad had been diagnosed with pancreatic cancer – a year-long death sentence. Rothe started spending much more time at home, being with his father, helping him manage the farm's affairs, and getting a glimpse into what the business was really like. 'I flew to Colorado nineteen times in nine months,' he says. 'I started taking a look at all the spreadsheets, all of the profit-and-loss statements, the balance sheet.' It turned out the farm was close to bankruptcy. After his father passed away, Rothe and his mother had no choice but to sell. 'There was this feeling of helplessness, of seeing the farm disappear for good in our family. My dad was the twelfth documented generation of family farmers in our family. And there wasn't going to be another one.'

Several months before his father died, the two had been sitting at the kitchen table, and Rothe's dad started to tell his son a story – the same story that, many years before, his own father had told him. It was the story of how the tractor ruined farming.

'It used to be that we had horses, and they did all of our work,' he began. 'The cycle of the day was that you'd get up in the morning, feed the horses, feed yourself, go out in the barn, saddle all the horses, get them all connected, and you'd go out and work in the field until noon. Then you'd come back, get the horses some water, a little food. You would eat. And you'd take the horses back out in the afternoon to work either until they couldn't work any more or you couldn't work any more. And at the end of the day, you'd put the horses back in the stable. Everyone would go to sleep, and you'd get up the next morning and do it again. Then one day they invented the tractor. And this tractor was going to be the saviour for farming. This was going to make farming easier; it was going to make it more profitable. We were all going to get rich: "Go buy a tractor!" Think about it ... you went from a horse, which is one horsepower, to a tractor which is scores of horsepower. It was a giant leap forward in terms of technology on the farm.'

But tractors were expensive. Farmers didn't have a lot of money, so they took out loans to buy them. That wasn't really a problem (after all, the tractor was going to make them exponentially more productive), but then the tractors broke down a lot and needed lots of fuel, so they had to take out loans to *run* them, and then they realised that the tractor was so productive, they were no longer limited by hours in the day but by how many acres they had. Except that without enough acres, they couldn't actually pay off the tractor. So they took out more loans, bought more land, and farmed it like never before.

'Everybody is getting a tractor,' his dad continued. 'All the neighbours now have tractors. Everybody is more productive, everybody is buying more land, everybody is producing more food. And because there's more of it in the market, the prices are declining. The reality is that we're not really any better off financially, because prices have come down as a result of our productivity. And we have all this debt that we have to service. At least with the horse we had the promise of only working a twelve-hour day, because that's all the horse could work. Now we're working all day every day just to service this tractor.'

At that moment, sitting at the kitchen table, listening to his dad in his bathrobe talking about tractors, it all clicked for Rothe. 'My grandfather's story of the tractor is basically an allegory for every technology that's been developed since. That includes artificial pesticides, fertilisers, genetically modified organisms. It includes the specialisation of farming equipment and technology. It's all the same story.'[187] These technologies we've developed – which on the surface have led to highly 'efficient' farming of the same crop in huge fields (much easier for the tractor to plough through) – actually mask the decline of productive capacity in our soils. We produce more calories now than we ever have, but it's an illusion. In reality the underlying asset, the soil, is declining (and not just its fertility: overworked farms leave soil overexposed to wind and water erosion).

As soil health declines, farmers must compensate with more and more nitrogen fertiliser. But not all of it gets taken up by crops. Rather, it ends up in the air (fuelling climate change as nitrous oxide), in our rivers and oceans (killing off entire marine ecosystems), and in our drinking water. And soil is relatively finite, taking 500 years to produce just 2 cm.[188] There are also the pesticides we have to filter from our water; the flooding precipitated by eroded fields; the loss of habitats for critical species (let alone the species themselves) ... the list goes on. In December 2013, the New Economics Foundation attempted to calculate the industrial agricultural system's environmental costs. Their upper estimate came to £7.2 billion a year for the UK alone.[189]

Farming never used to be a depletive act. It was the ultimate symbiotic relationship between man and nature. Though each crop would take something from the soil (how else would it grow?), it would give something back too. Legumes, like clover, would be planted during off-cycles to fix nitrogen in the soil – nitrogen that other crops like vegetables, fruits and grains need to grow well. This is why for generations, farmers would rotate the crops they grew within their fields each season. Meanwhile, grazing livestock would create fertiliser (for free), greatly reducing if not eliminating the need to buy artificial inputs, as well as making waste management a far easier task. Nitrogen fixation – a natural process – converts nitrogen in the air into ammonium in the soil, which can then be picked up by all other plant types and converted to plant protein. Simplistically: no nitrogen, no crops, no food.

The availability of food is obviously a basic requirement for humans, and until the mid-nineteenth century, population growth in Europe was largely constrained by the amount of reactive nitrogen in the food supply. To keep up with demand, reactive nitrogen was mined directly from coal, saltpetre and guano. But then, at the start of the twentieth century, Fritz Haber, a German chemist, worked out how to convert natural gas into nitrogen fertiliser. It was considered nothing short of alchemy. Managing multiple crops on a farm, rotating them so that soil nutrients can be properly restored, isn't conducive to industrial techniques. But the availability of industrial fertiliser made possible the introduction of vast, tractor-able expanses of single crops like corn, wheat, soy, rapeseed and sugar that can be farmed in massive volumes. These are the basic ingredients of the factory food – junk food – that has come to dominate our diet.

As technology, like fertilisers and machinery, made industrial farming possible, the traditional family farms morphed into the giant factory farming corporations that dominate our food supply today – companies like Cargill and Monsanto. As big companies tend to do, these giant agri-businesses turned their market power into political power, successfully lobbying for the things that would make their life easier and the life of the ever-shrinking number of family farms harder. When people say it's elitist to want a more human food system, because factory food at least delivers cheap food for hard-pressed families, tell them about the subsidies. Factory food is 'cheap' because it's subsidised – by you, whether you like it or not. British farmers received £3.2 billion of direct subsidy in 2012,[190] and the vast majority supported food production that was neither sustainable nor humane (96.5 per cent of farms in the UK aren't registered as organic, and about a quarter of all cropland is used to produce cereals for livestock feed.)[191] On top of that there are the indirect subsidies which are even bigger: we pay the financial costs of the health and environmental damage that the big food companies cause – costs which they avoid. This means we pay once for factory food when we buy it; twice when we pay taxes to counter its negative impact on our health and environment, and then a third time through our taxes that subsidise the Big Food companies. Taxpayer subsidies are supposed to pay for things that are good for society but which wouldn't happen without the subsidy – things that wouldn't be delivered by the market. And yet here we are, subsidising commercial activity that harms the public. It's nuts.

We can change this. We can design a food system that's better for our health, better for the environment, better for animals. We can design a food system that is more human.

If Chipotle can do it …

In government, we tried to reduce the harm done by Big Food through voluntary agreements – Responsibility Deals – through which the companies would make their food less toxic. The idea was that this would actually be a quicker way to achieve concrete outcomes like reductions in salt, fat and sugar than going through a process of regulation. But the truth is, such efforts are totally superficial because they don't address the deep structural forces at play. The key to making food more human on a mass scale lies in new business models that can produce better, healthier food systematically. The UK has many excellent small-scale examples of food produced in a more human way. But it's in America, where the worst forms of industrial farming were born (and persist), that entrepreneurs are now creating the building blocks of a new and more human food system.

Just look at Chipotle, the US-based 1,700-branch chain (with locations now in Europe and Canada), serving custom-built tacos and burritos made from freshly prepared, recognisable ingredients. They're proving that fast food can be made at scale using a humane, sustainable supply chain. When one supplier failed animal welfare inspections, Chipotle temporarily stopped serving pork at over a third of its restaurants rather than continue buying and selling the inhumane meat.[192] Chipotle's commitment to food that's produced in a more human way is a key part of its brand, but what's less well-known is that much of Chipotle's ability to buy humane meat at the scale it does rests on the ingenuity of one man determined to prove it was possible.

A little over a decade ago, Steve Ells, Chipotle's founder, read an article called 'The Lost Taste of Pork' in an obscure food magazine called *The Art of Eating*. In it, writer Edward Behr describes the 'best pork' he had ever eaten and details the old-fashioned practices of the farm it came from, run by a man called Paul Willis. After ordering some to try for himself, Ells was hooked. He was determined to make his burritos with meat from farms like Willis's.[193] But how could one small farm supply thousands of restaurants around the world? Paul Willis had the answer.

A down-to-earth, fourth-generation farmer from Iowa, Willis has been raising pigs (all free-range) since the mid-1970s. 'I learned to do this when I grew up, and it was common,' he explains. 'I liked the idea of the animals being out on the pasture. Pigs were part of your crop rotation – we were growing corn, soybeans, oats, and hay – and one of the things you had were pigs.' Over time, Willis was able to grow the farm to over a thousand pigs. Like many other pig farmers around the country, he had built a sustainable, profitable livelihood for himself – one that respected the land, the animals and the community.

Then at some point in the 1980s, Willis started to notice confinement buildings popping up – buildings designed to house (tens of) thousands of livestock packed together as closely as possible. They started out small – individual buildings on farmers' land – but by the 1990s, factory farms had infiltrated the pig industry, and the buyers didn't want to deal with small farms. 'They started to squeeze us out of the marketplace. They would bid us a lesser price or rate our meat poorer quality, since it yielded less.' (Pigs raised outdoors have bigger lungs and hearts, since they use them, running around and doing what pigs naturally do.) But Willis refused to change his ways. 'Going in one of those buildings just convinced me that I just never wanted to raise animals like that.' The sound, the crowded conditions, the concrete, the palpable misery – all have an overwhelming effect on anyone who sets foot in a modern factory farm. 'I think the thing that really knocks me over is the odour – the hydrogen sulfide and ammonia. You can't take enough showers to get rid of it, even if you're in there only a minute. I lived on a farm – grew up with farms: my grandparents, my parents and so forth. And *this* was a brand new smell, something we had never experienced before.'

On his farm, Willis makes sure that his 'pigs can be pigs'. Recognising that they, like humans, require companionship, he never introduces one animal into a social group that's already established. He'll also make 'retreat areas' with straw bales to give timid animals a place to get away from their aggressive peers. (Contrast this with the 80 per cent of pregnant sows in American factory farms, churning out piglets with little respite their entire lives, raised in steel-and-concrete pens which prohibit them from turning around – a practice defended on the grounds that it prevents the cruelly stressed pigs from injuring each other.)[194]

As farms consolidated around him (almost 600,000 small farmers went out of business between 1979 and 2004),[195] or as farmers were forced to 'evolve' with the industry, Willis looked for a way to keep farming the way he knew was right – for him, the animals, the land, and ultimately, people. His answer was also consolidation

– but on farmers' terms, not industry's. 'There were a few people raising pigs in a similar way, so that was the first place I looked – farmers I knew,' Willis recalls. After that, he started reaching out to other local-farmer networks. 'It wasn't finding people to change their ways. It was finding people who were already doing this – trying to get by doing the right thing – and paying them a premium price.' Little by little, welfare standards were established, and, with fellow humane livestock pioneer Bill Niman as a partner, the Niman Ranch Pork Company was established. Today, it comprises 500 farmers and can't increase supply fast enough.[196]

In addition to a price premium, the pork company members receive a guaranteed price floor (to protect against unexpected drops in the market), and are able to use their scale to economise on processing, distribution and marketing. In founding the Niman Ranch Pork Company, Willis and Niman created a business model that would allow farmers to confidently stick to a more human approach, able to compete with the ever-growing pressure of industrialised, mechanised Big Food. Now, thanks to Paul Willis, you can buy humane pork not just at high-end restaurants and grocery stores, but in the mass marketplace – for example the next time you're at Chipotle.

A different, but equally promising, challenge to the industralised food system is being pioneered by Belcampo Meat Company, based in Oakland. Its innovative business model focuses on just one ranch, owning some 20,000 acres in northern California, and the entire supply chain needed to support it. For its 2,300 cattle and 4,000 other animals such as quail, sheep, goats, rabbits and chickens, that means one slaughterhouse and a handful of retail butcher shops (there are five already in California with two more on the way). The farm, the processing, the retail – all in one business. According to founder Anya Fernald, bringing it all together isn't only more profitable; it also assures that standards are upheld. Raising the animals is really only half the battle, after all. You might be the most caring, humane rancher in the world, but you might have to use a third-party slaughterhouse who doesn't share your values. This leaves far too many questions unanswered. Fernald wants to know: 'How was it actually killed? How was the handling leading up to the kill? How long was it sitting on the truck?'[197] She designed Belcampo to make sure there were no missing links in the supply chain.

'One of the key elements of designing the business was asking: what's the human interaction necessary to create truly high-quality food? This doesn't just mean the cutting of the meat and the ageing of the meat,' Fernald explains.' It also means the husbandry of the animals, the attention to detail ... actually watching and curating their health.' The key for Belcampo is bringing everyone together – from the rancher and slaughterhouse cutter to the butcher and customer, such that where your food comes from is no longer some black box – in fact every single piece of meat is completely traceable, since the system is so straightforward and transparent. It's human-scaled.

Fernald acknowledges that Belcampo can't sustainably grow beyond eight or nine stores, but this doesn't mean the model can't. She envisages a multiplicity of 'Belcampos' – each with its own management team, butcher's shops, slaughterhouse and ranch. 'When businesses that are producing food get to a large scale, quality takes a nosedive and communication breaks down.' For a meat model that's focused on health and husbandry to work profitably, she insists, the supporting business structure must be large enough to turn a profit but not so large that it becomes out of touch.

Niman Ranch and Belcampo show us two different ways of raising humane, sustainable meat profitably and at a scale beyond just one-off family farms selling what they produce at the farmers' market each week. But to deliver non-factory food (not just meat but everything else) at a meaningful scale, we must also think about how it's sold.

Booths, a small supermarket chain in northern England, is showing that making a profit and bringing people good, healthy and humane food are not mutually exclusive. Its aim, says chairman Edwin Booth, is 'making really good food choices available to as many people as possible.' Sometimes that means local and organic, but sometimes that means food imported from around the world. It involves a responsibility to customers, but also to suppliers, which takes many forms. There is the labelling, now widespread in all supermarkets, that shows where cuts of meat or produce come from. But unlike the big supermarkets, Booths' butchers actually know the farmers and fishermen, and the company treats them well. Harry Wilson, who raises lamb in Cumbria, is a loyal supplier: 'I don't think consumers understand how tough it can be in farming, about the constant pressure on price,' he says, but Booths does, paying 'market price plus a premium: £4 an animal. It adds up.' And unlike factory-meat buyers who care for quantity over quality, Booths takes the opposite approach. 'We had a conversation last year with a buyer from Booths who said they'd prefer to take good [quality lamb] rather than volume. If we only have 55 that have reached the right weight [as opposed to their typical sixty a week] that's what they'll take … And when we go to our nearby store in Kendal they have a sign up saying which farmer produced the lamb on sale.' This is all part of the company's mission, says Booth. 'We have to be good corporate citizens. We have to care about our suppliers' employees. We have to care about the rural economy.' As the *Observer* food writer Jay Rayner notes: 'I can't for the life of me recall ever hearing anyone from the big supermarkets say anything like this.'[198]

Booths gets it. Farmers have one of the most stressful, underpaid, under-appreciated jobs in the world. We literally need them to survive, yet we squeeze their pay in the name of '50p off'. As a result of good corporate responsibility – and radical transparency – Booths have learned how to do things the right way.

In California, a start-up called Good Eggs is using technology to challenge the industrial food system. It is an online food-retail platform that eliminates most of the extra cost of buying from local, sustainable producers by cutting out the physical store, saving on buildings and wastage. They deliver straight from producers and farms directly to your home. This is not dissimilar from community-supported agriculture or fishery schemes, in which households subscribe to a particular farm to receive a basket of goods each week (you get to decide what you like and how much of it you want). Good Eggs expands access to good food – real food, not fake, factory food – to people who might never otherwise see such items in the supermarket or get to the farmers' market. This expanded reach of even the smallest producers allows them to bring down costs in ways their size would otherwise preclude (not to mention the fact that because of the shortened supply chain, they get to keep more of each sale). What's really revolutionary about Good Eggs is that it fundamentally changes the grocery-shop model to one of production on demand. Instead of baking, say, one hundred loaves of bread, selling out some days and wasting half on the others, the producers on Good Eggs' platform know precisely how much they need to make (you place your order two days in advance). These savings make good food even more accessible.

And now in the UK, a similar business model is being pioneered in a start-up called The Food Assembly. Just like Good Eggs, their online platform allows customers to pre-order their items, so that farmers and producers have a precise count of what they need to deliver ahead of time. But rather than deliver directly to customers' homes, The Food Assembly organises weekly, two-hour 'assemblies' – pop-up markets – where producers and consumers come together to fulfil their orders, not just giving them a chance to meet each other but also cutting down waste and costs.

Jamie and the food revolution

So yes, a more human approach to food is emerging. How can we encourage it? Some have argued that consumer information and education – changing our food culture – holds the key. Ending bad food starts with an appreciation of good food – not just how to eat it but how to shop for it and cook it. No one has done more to advance that cause in the UK over the years than the heroic Jamie Oliver. By turning millions of people onto food, by making it cool to cook, by running fantastic campaigns against bad food with programmes like *Jamie's School Dinners* and *Jamie's Food Revolution*, he is the single best thing that has happened to our food culture. And Jamie himself would be the first to acknowledge that he's building on the work of other great leaders, like Alice Waters in the US, and Carlo Petrini in Italy. Upset by a planned McDonald's restaurant near the Spanish Steps in Rome, in 1986 in Piedmont, Petrini founded an organisation called Slow Food. Since then, Slow Food has become a global movement, coming to represent much more than an opposition to fast food. Its motto, 'Good, clean and fair', captures precisely the opposite of what our food system has become. Every two years, a conference is held in Turin bringing together thousands of farmers, fishers, ranchers, food artisans – and, of course, eaters – from every corner of the earth to share each other's cultures and, most importantly, put a face – a story – behind what's being enjoyed. Slow Food has proposed a 'narrative label' for foods, with details like animal breeds, types of feed, pasture type and location and animal welfare.

Why focus on the narrative? What about all those certification schemes that you see everywhere? Standards, kitemarks, different terms approved by governments and regulators – isn't that the way to change consumer behaviour? The problem is, these bureaucratic schemes are just another black box that consumers don't really understand and can't see into; they're not human – just like GDP for the economy or PISA scores in education. They give a superficial feeling of authority, but with a few exceptions (like the Soil Association's 'organic' mark), they obscure the truth so that a carefully crafted facade can be more easily believed.

In America, there's a TV ad (for an insurance company, as it happens) about a chicken travelling across the country. Wherever it goes – along train tracks, into a diner – it sends selfies back to the farmers who raised it. As the camera pans out from the farmers sitting on their veranda, we see thousands of chickens roaming freely across the countryside to the narrator's message: 'If you're a free-range chicken, you roam free. It's what you do.'[199] This is what you might imagine when you see a 'free range' label on meat you buy in the supermarket. It's what you're supposed to imagine. It's what the words 'free range' literally mean: freedom. Rolling outdoor pastures, animals able to behave naturally, roaming about, eating grass, little bugs, whatever they want.

Well: roaming free may be what you do if you're a chicken in an insurance ad, but it's highly unlikely to be what you do if you're an actual free-range chicken in the real world. It is perfectly permissible, within the relevant EU labelling rules, for 'free-range' chickens to spend most of their lives cramped inside huge indoor barns. What about 'cage free' – sounds good, no? While it's technically true that cage-free chickens aren't housed in cages, farmers can get away with providing them bedded space that is half the size of a piece of A4 paper, and still be completely within the rules.[200] Within both free-range and cage-free labelling schemes, it is perfectly acceptable to treat animals with antibiotics and to carry out cruel and disgusting practices like throwing live chicks into mincing machines.[201]

Of course, there are many wonderful free-range and cage-free farmers who treat their animals much better than required; but they are the exception. And the truly depressing fact is that this is what passes for good in our current system. The free-range and cage-free standards are an order of magnitude better than those applied to meat and dairy products with no animal welfare label at all. But nothing is worse than the use of humane-sounding terms that have no specific standards associated with them at all: terms like 'farm fresh', 'country fresh', 'high animal welfare', 'naturally produced', or 'corn fed'. (This last one is particularly egregious since it is often perpetrated by smart restaurants trying to give themselves an aura of quality. All chickens are 'corn fed'; saying so doesn't tell you anything about whether or not they were raised in horrific conditions.) The use of these terms amounts to deliberate lying by the culinary-industrial complex to cover up factory farming's grotesque cruelty to animals. It is a scandal.

Information is a vital part of making markets work properly, but in the food market today, the information that's supposed to efficiently connect buyers and sellers is not information at all. Despite all the controls and specifications that govern food labelling and advertising, consumers are misled and lied to on a daily basis. Why is it acceptable for my milk carton to feature images of cows meandering on grassy hills when they're actually confined inside and fed unhealthy diets of corn and soy (not the grass their digestive systems were designed to eat)? Why is it acceptable for chickens certified as 'free range' to be held captive indoors for half of their lives? Why don't I have a right to know what kinds of antibiotics were pumped into the bacon I'm about to serve my family at breakfast? What about the TV ad for pasta sauce that suggests it was cooked in some home-style kitchen? How can the Big Food company responsible give that impression when it was actually made in some giant, grey, industrial vat with a whole bunch of chemicals that wouldn't be out of place in a science lab?

As we are misled on animal welfare, so too are we misled about the nutritional value of our food. The latest marketing gimmick from Big Food is to trumpet the vitamins their food contains. But this is a total con. In order to cut costs and increase shelf life, the factory food industry removes actual nutrients during processing. Then, to be able to tout their products' nutritional benefits, processed-food companies add artificial nutrients into the food which their own machines have stripped of natural nutrients. The result is a total deception; food brands advertise the vitamins they've added, signalling to the consumer that no matter how much salt, fat or sugar is present, it has nutritional value and is 'healthy'. Meanwhile, we lose the benefits of nutrients that work better in their natural forms. And worse, we are lulled into a false complacency. While vitamins and nutrients are good for us, they don't help with diet-related diseases like heart disease and obesity. Processed 'health' food is healthy in all the wrong ways. Westerners are really not at risk from vitamin deficiency (compared to the 2 billion in poor countries who are[202]), notes science writer Catherine Price, and yet we eat this 'healthy' processed food that actually make us obese and diabetic.[203] One UK survey found that many cereal bars had more sugar than sugary cereals.[204]

It's not just that loosely regulated claims, certification schemes, packaging and advertising misrepresent what's gone into the food you buy. In many cases, it really is outright lying. One study in Leicester found that over 40 per cent of meat products collected from butchers, retailers, wholesalers, manufacturers, fast-food outlets and caterers contained other species of meat than those which appeared on the labels. In 17 per cent of samples, meat of the undeclared species was the primary ingredient.[205] Fish in the US are so regularly mislabelled that the government actually has a task force devoted to fighting 'seafood fraud'.[206] While 94 per cent of random samples of red snapper taken from retailers across the United States were found not actually to be red snapper, some 74 per cent of sushi bars were found to mislabel their seafood.[207] In the UK, some 7 per cent of cod and haddock is mislabelled; in Ireland, it's a quarter.[208] Meanwhile, 30 per cent of fish in Spain and 32 per cent in Italy is mislabelled.[209] For some specific fish it's far worse: 82 per cent of smoked fish in Ireland and up to 80 per cent of bluefin tuna in Paris is mislabelled.[210]

Carlo Petrini's idea of narrative labelling takes us towards a more human, and more effective answer: just let people see what's going on. There's a simple rule we should introduce that would start to address Big Food's lying and misrepresentation. Any food product must have a reasonable proportion of its packaging (and any promotional materials like TV ads) devoted to showing the precise conditions it was made in. A pack of frozen chicken nuggets would have a photo of the actual farm the chicken came from. A TV ad for hot dogs, a video of the pig pen. That 'home-made' pasta sauce? Let's see a picture of the factory, steel vats and all, not some fake pastiche Italian country kitchen constructed in a studio. To make sure it's all real and above board, there should be a requirement that every part of every facility of every factory farm and every food factory be live-streamed on the Internet so people can see exactly what's going on and track their food if they want to. This would be more effective than any number of regulations and certifications. (I wanted to introduce this requirement in government, but it didn't get anywhere.) Look, I'm not saying all of the packaging and promotion of food products should be truthful; just a reasonable amount – say 20 per cent. That still leaves 80 per cent for lies and deception. Who could object to that?

Well, people who get cross about 'the nanny state', I guess. Hmm. 'It's curious that we're open to social engineering when it's being done by corporations,' says Michael Pollan, a noted American food writer and activist. 'You're socially engineered every time you walk through the cereal aisle in the supermarket. The healthy stuff is down at your feet and the stuff with the most sugar and chocolate is at your eye level – or your child's eye level. That doesn't seem to bother us. But as soon as it's done by elected officials on our behalf, it's anathema.'[211] Kelly Brownell, a professor of psychology and public health at Yale University, argues: 'As a culture, we've become upset by the tobacco companies advertising to children, but we sit idly by while the food companies do the very same thing. And we could make a claim that the toll taken on the public health by a poor diet rivals that taken by tobacco.'[212] Perhaps the best advice is in fact Michael Pollan's: never eat food that has been advertised.

Beating Big Food

But in the end, changing our food culture, consumer pressure … it's not enough. We've had consumer pressure for years and the problem is getting worse, not better. Still today, only 3.5 per cent of

UK farmland is organic. In any case, it's not fair to put the burden for change on consumers when the Big Food producers have all their structural advantages: the subsidies, the lax regulation. To say that people should care more, that they really should shop differently, misses the point. They do care already. But it's such an effort to shop differently. Hardly anyone has the time or inclination to investigate their poultry producer or get up early on Sunday morning for the local farmers' market. People are busy trying to earn a living, raise children, take care of their families. Food may be of great concern to some – as a hobby, as a way of life. But for those whose interests lie elsewhere, for whom grocery shopping happens online between paying the bills and replying to emails, for whom dinner is squeezed between two part-time shifts – why should good food be an out-of-reach privilege? How civilised can a society really call itself if humane, healthy, wholesome food is a luxury for those with the time and money to look for it? We need to make food that is produced in a more human way the norm. That will take much more aggressive action than fiddling around with labels or even TV ads, welcome as that would be.

Step one: we must account for the true cost of our factory food and adjust our tax and subsidy regimes accordingly. Isn't it obvious that we should design food policies to put people first, not the needs of big, bureaucratic, industrialised food companies? Oh, wait – 'people' don't have expensive lobbyists in Westminster and Brussels who can take the right civil servants out to dinner and the opera, offer the right regulators a cushy job as 'Technical Adviser' once they leave public service, or invite politicians to spend agreeable weekends with them in country estates. In the US, 'people' don't make campaign contributions to the right members of the right committees in Congress and state legislatures. No. It's the big food companies that do that. No wonder the system is designed to suit their needs.

What the 'people' can do is put pressure on the politicians to make the changes we need. Just as we have applied the 'polluter pays' principle to companies that damage the environment, we should require food companies to pay for their negative impact on the environment and public health. We already do this for ships responsible for pollution off the coast. Extending a similar 'price correcting' mechanism to food would finally set the true costs of factory food straight. But we can't just focus on the bad. We have to support the good. So we should redirect taxpayer subsidies to farmers and producers who are doing the right thing.

If a government tried to end the factory-food companies' subsidies and make them pay the true costs of their operations, here's what would happen. The bosses of the big food companies would take to the airwaves and say the price of food would go up. Politicians, terrified of doing anything that raises 'the cost of living', would back off. But the 'cost of living' as measured by food prices doesn't include the cost of our dying that the factory-food companies make us pay for through the NHS; local habitats dying that we pay for through taxes; animals dying in disgusting circumstances that spread disease. None of that – and more – is included in the price of factory food, in the cost-of-living figures. That's why nothing gets done. But it's not true that the price of food will go up. The price of bad food will go up, but the price of good food – more human food – will go down. If we stopped subsidising industrial food and instead chose to lower the costs of fresh fruit, fresh vegetables and humanely raised meat, we would save money for the taxpayer and lead happier, healthier, longer lives.

In the absence of such political leadership, here's step two. Beat Big Food at its own game. There is an exciting approach being pioneered in the UK by the prominent City investor Jeremy Coller. He argues that factory farms pose an increasing threat to companies' (and their investors') financial returns, insisting that they create risks for the industry as a whole, but that these are ignored by the markets.[213] He and his foundation have started laying out what these risks actually are. They argue that the factory-farming sector is precariously susceptible to circumstances that, ironically, it has played a large part in bringing about: widespread antibacterial resistance (rendering its antibiotics useless); feed shortages (due to poor soil health or scarcity of fossil-fuel-based fertilisers and pesticides); major food-borne disease outbreak; and increasing awareness and shifts in consumer preference. All could wreck Big Food's business model. So Coller and his foundation insist that the directors of any company in the food industry should assess and report these risks, so their share prices accurately reflect the financial implications of engaging in factory food. This would have the indirect effect of incentivising a more human, more sustainable model. But as an investor himself, Coller takes a more active stance, and promotes the same to his peers. Coller Capital insists on transparency for all its own investments, helping them take animal welfare into account in their investment decision making. This not only allows Coller to avoid companies that refuse to improve their abusive business model but also to argue directly for change in the practices of companies they're already invested in.

A moral imperative

There's one final step we need to take. As I argued at the start of this chapter, animal cruelty is an absolute moral outrage. There really is no incremental improvement, no optimal compromise to be had. We have to be rid of it for good. So I think it's reasonable to take an absolutist policy position, as we do in defence of other moral principles: our abhorrence of torture, child abuse and other forms of cruelty. We don't tolerate a moderate view on rape; nor should we. Over time, our progress as a civilised species has been defined by what is added to this list of 'moral universalisms'. One of the most profound was on the subject of slavery, which used to be ubiquitous. Now of course, it is accepted that slavery is morally wrong.

I think it's time we consider factory farms the same way.

In the introduction to this book, I spoke of the empathy evolution: we have increasingly expanded our moral consciousness to include others less like us. Our ability to empathise is fundamental, its expression recognised in infants as young as one day old.[214] Every time we extend empathy, society moves forward.[215] The philosopher Jeremy Bentham went a step further: slavery was a tyranny, and people shouldn't be treated differently by race. Why, Bentham extended the argument, should animals be mistreated simply because they have a different number of legs or the inability to converse? In his mind, difference created a slippery slope that allowed the cruel and tyrannical domination of one group over another. Who – or what – made up that 'other' group was immaterial: 'The question,' he wrote, 'is not, *Can they reason?* or *Can they talk?* but *Can they suffer?*'[216]

As proud as we are of our history, we also reflect with shame on atrocities committed by our great-grandfathers (and gratitude that we've come as far as we have in our moral evolution). When our great-grandchildren look back on today, they'll shake their heads at our gross abuse of animals. So the right policy response to factory farms is clear. We shouldn't just 'not subsidise' them. We shouldn't just regulate them better, or make them more transparent. We should ban them. To decide how a ban would be applied, we should look to existing definitions – like the practices itemised in the Business Benchmark on Farm Animal Welfare: close confinement, non-therapeutic use of antibiotics and other growth-promoting drugs, routine mutilation (like tail docking and breaking beaks), partially conscious slaughter, and long-distance transport.[217] UK-based Compassion in World Farming argues that animals ought to be free from thirst and hunger, from discomfort, from pain and disease, from fear and distress, and able to behave in a natural way.[218] Their goal is to eliminate factory farming by 2050.[219] And of course, in our open, trading, interconnected global economy, it must happen around the world, not just in one country. But slavery was banned around the world, eventually. Starting with Britain.

Banning factory farms, however we define them, won't just be better for animals; it will make us better humans. In *Eating Animals*, Jonathan Safran Foer offers his own definition. 'Factory Farm: This is a term sure to fall out of use in the next generation or so, either because there will be no more factory farms, or because there will be no more family farms to compare them to.'[220] It's up to us.

CHAPTER 5

BUSINESS

'Out of the blue one day, we were told to build a thirty-foot stage.'

So begins the most powerful political ad of the 2012 US Presidential election. To foreboding music and a montage of black-and-white photographs, Mike Earnest tells his story, and that of his colleagues at a paper plant in Marion, Indiana. Building a stage was an unusual task for mill workers but they did it, quickly and without question. A few hours later they were summoned back to the warehouse where earlier they had set up the stage, and a group of people walked out – the management of the plant. The stage was for them. Assembled in front of the management, the workers were then told that all of them, all three shifts, were fired. Even though the factory was profitable, it wasn't profitable enough; the plant would have to close. And just like that, after years – for some, decades – of employment, they no longer had a job. 'Turns out that when we built that stage, it was like building my own coffin.'[221]

Who was allegedly behind this inhuman treatment of the loyal workers in that plant? The company that bought it and then sold it, Bain Capital, who the ad tells us made $100 million by firing all those workers. And who was behind Bain Capital? The 2012 Republican Presidential nominee, Mitt Romney. Critics of the ad – including Democratic rising star, now Senator Cory Booker of New Jersey – protested that it unfairly distorted Romney's business career and was profoundly anti-business. But to no avail.

Mitt Romney assumed that his exemplary – stellar – track record in business would help propel him to the most powerful job on earth. At a time of economic difficulty, surely the American people would choose an experienced business leader, who has turned around company after company, to turn around America's stagnating economy? It didn't work out that way. In fact, the opposite was the case. It was precisely Mitt Romney's business background that was used by President Obama to destroy him. In the most important and high-profile contest in the spiritual home of capitalism, for week after week, the Obama campaign pummelled Romney with ads attacking him for being a capitalist. 'The Stage' was simply the most effective of many. Later on in the campaign, Obama was accused of attacking small businesses with a speech in which he said: 'If you've got a business, you didn't build that.' More recently, the front-runner for the 2016 Democratic Presidential nomination, Hillary Clinton, said in a speech in 2014: 'Don't let anybody tell you that, you know, it's corporations and businesses that create jobs.'[222]

It's not just the Occupy protesters, it seems. Anti-business sentiment has gone mainstream – even in America, where you could always rely on both major parties (unlike in British political history) to be pro-business. In the UK, the BBC's Business Editor is regularly asked whether he is pro- or anti-business. Imagine the Sports Editor being asked if he or she was pro- or anti-sport. Media companies – most of them businesses themselves, let's remember – serve up a relentless diet of hostile coverage of business, with barely any positive portrayals to compensate. Opinion polls show large majorities of people agreeing that business can't be trusted, is bad for society and so on. Being anti-business these days is the fashionable thing.

In many ways, it's understandable. But it's also dangerous. Our progress as a society and our well-being as individuals depends on business, and it depends on business being successful. In this chapter, we'll explore why it has become so unpopular in recent years. We'll get to the heart of what's gone wrong, and show how we can change things for the better; how business can help build a more human economy. But first, we need to remind ourselves of some basic truths that often get lost in the shouting matches of day-to-day debate.

'A script of hope'

Consider why business – the engine of economic activity – exists in the first place. It's for the simple reason that individuals acting together through a private organisation, pooling resources, skills and labour can produce more than the sum of their parts: not just 'profits' for 'capitalists', but the goods and services we use every day – the innovations that have lifted people out of poverty and the technologies helping to save our natural environment. Without business, government could not provide social safety nets, pensions, free education and health care … Of course, that means businesses have to make profits: if they didn't, they would go out of business, people would lose their jobs and governments wouldn't get their tax revenue. Nor would we get the goods and services and innovation that make our lives better. This positive circle is the mechanism that has helped billions of humans escape poverty and provided them with a quality of life that was unimaginable decades ago. But when you boil it all down, the mechanism is really quite simple. It's just making, selling, and buying goods and services. It's also, as former Chief Rabbi Jonathan Sacks observes, really quite human:

> *In the market economy throughout all of history, differences between cultures and nations have led to one of two possible consequences. When different nations meet, they either make war or they trade. The difference is that from war at the very least one side loses, and in the long run, both sides lose. From trade, both sides gain. When we value difference the way the market values difference, we create a non-zero sum scenario of human interaction. We turn the narrative of tragedy, of war, into a script of hope.*[223]

Of course, the market economy, trade, business: all these things sometimes go awry and, as we will see, bad things happen. But people sometimes go awry and bad things happen; governments sometimes go awry and bad things happen. We don't write off or condemn the whole of humanity or the very concept of government because of it.

The vast majority of companies profit from providing something people want, without doing harm to others. But it's better than that: the things that companies provide can actually help solve some of our most pernicious problems. As we've seen, in education, in health care, in farming, smart, progressive businesses are finding ways to deliver value for their customers, jobs for their workers and profits for their investors while directly improving social or environmental outcomes. Making a profit and not polluting, or making a profit and paying a living wage, are not mutually exclusive. It's self-defeating for anyone who cares about society or the environment to be 'anti-business' or 'anti-capitalist' or 'anti-profit'. It's all about how: how does business behave; how is capitalism carried out; how are profits made? That's what we should focus on, not a generalised condemnation of the whole enterprise.

And that word, enterprise, is very important too. Trace any business back to its origins and you will generally find an entrepreneur. An individual or group of individuals who had an idea, a dream, a mission: to make that better cart; to build that better car; to design that better cargo ship; and now in the twenty-first century to send that better rocket out into space – and back. The very notion of enterprise, the calling of the entrepreneur, is profoundly human. To believe in something; to believe that you can do better than what's out there at the moment; to believe you can persuade other people to buy it from you; to believe it's worth taking a risk with your life, your reputation, your money or other people's money, in order to start a business: that is a uniquely human thing to do. This is what we should remember. Businesses – real businesses – are human. They're about people, about bringing people together in a structured way to benefit each other and society.

David Packard, one of the founders of Hewlett Packard, put it well in a speech to employees in 1960. This quote appears in my earlier book *Good Business*, and I'd like to include it here too:

Why are we here? I think many people assume, wrongly, that a company exists simply to make money. While this is an important result of a company's existence, we have to go deeper and find the real reasons for our being. As we investigate this, we inevitably come to the conclusion that a group of people get together and exist as an institution that we call a company so they are able to accomplish something collectively that they could not accomplish separately – they make a contribution to society, a phrase which sounds trite but is fundamental.[224]

That social contribution of business is achieved through trade. Trade is unique to us as a species and is essential for human progress. We've farmed for around 10,000 years[225] but we've traded for 100,000.[226] Trade was inextricably linked to (and financed) the energy and communication revolutions that were instrumental in connecting disparate cultures from across the globe. Trade isn't just human; it's responsible for society. Science writer Matt Ridley explains that 'through exchange and specialisation, we've created the ability to do things we don't even understand'.[227] No individual knows how to do everything; we are a symbiotic community, in which individuals need to work with others who have different talents. In place of destruction, peaceful economic cooperation ensures progress. Trade rests on a simple premise, however – an implicit promise that if what you do is worthwhile, others will recognise you for it. This basic principle has throughout history empowered people to do great things with their knowledge and skills, to improve some little part of the world, putting food on the table, a roof over heads, and earning a sense of accomplishment, of contribution. Cumulatively, these basics of business add up to human progress and a better society.

Yet there is a deep sense of hostility towards business today – the kind of hostility that led mainstream politicians like Barack Obama and Hillary Clinton to make anti-business pronouncements knowing they would be well received. They're politicians playing to the gallery; that's to be expected. The interesting thing is perhaps not the 'playing' but the 'gallery'. Why is there such strong anti-business sentiment today?

You could say: who cares? Why does it matter if business, trade, capitalism are becoming more unpopular? Well, it's precisely because of those play-to-the-gallery politicians (and by the way, although I've mentioned two US politicians of the Left, you'll find this tendency in all parties in all countries these days). If politicians see the public turn against business, they are far more likely to enact policies and regulations that channel public anger and attack business. And that is self-defeating. If we undermine the climate for business overall (instead of addressing specific grievances that may be justified), that will lead to less innovation, fewer jobs, fewer goods and services that make our lives better, and less money for government to spend on social problems and all the things we say we want. There's another real-world problem caused by anti-business sentiment. If people get the idea that business is basically bad, they won't want to go into it. The whole positive circle of business, trade and capitalism depends on those entrepreneurs feeling confident and supported as they dream and plan and build. We shouldn't be putting them off – we should be encouraging them.

Business gone awry

What all this requires is a much more forensic approach than anything we've seen up till now. While it is self-defeating to be simplistically 'anti-business', it's equally wrong for supporters of business to airily dismiss the public's concerns. The truth is, the Occupy movement makes some very good points. More importantly, although most people wouldn't dream of actually joining an Occupy protest, they share many of the same feelings about business – especially that great demon of our times, 'big business'.

We are angry with companies for paying obscenely high salaries to their bosses and exceedingly low ones to their workers. We are angry that the businesses which caused the economic crisis are doing better than before. We're angry – we're driven mad by – terrible, inhuman, unresponsive, bureaucratic service; the stupid rules and small print; the relentless sales tricks; the systems designed to suit the company rather than the customer; the infuriating phone menus; the impossibility of speaking to a human being; the inability of a human being if we ever do get hold of one to actually understand what we want, to empathise, to take responsibility, to help. We are angry about the homogenisation of our communities by chain stores. We're angry about pollution of the air, land, sea (and mind) caused by irresponsible manufacturing and marketing practices. And we are angry that these problems never seem to improve; in fact, they just seem to get worse. Business is big and getting bigger. Executive pay is high and getting higher. Homogenised high streets are bland and getting blander. Social and environmental problems are grave and getting graver. Customer service is worse and getting … well, you take the point.

On issues that are blatant, corporate culture seems hopelessly tone deaf. Take executive pay. In the UK, median household income has fallen more than 8 per cent since 2008, yet in the last year alone, the median pay of FTSE 100 chiefs is up 50 per cent.[228] According to Incomes Data Services, a research group, FTSE 100 chief executives paid themselves 120 times more than their median full-time employee last year. In 2000, it was 47 times more.[229] In 2014, median full-time pay across the UK was £27,200.[230] For the FTSE 100 executives? £3,344,000.[231]

This isn't just bad for employees; it's bad for business. Between 2001 and 2013, the value of FTSE 100 companies increased 31 per cent; profits, 47 per cent. Director pay? 315 per cent![232] Executives are taking an increasingly larger proportion of the pie, even after driving their firms into the ground. Martin Sullivan was paid $47 million when he departed from AIG (despite a share decline in excess of 50 per cent on his watch and a $182 billion bailout from the US government).[233]

So how does it happen? By design. Professors at the University of Cambridge examined the effect of compensation consultants on compensation. After looking at 1,000 companies from 2006 to 2012, they concluded: 'Overall, our study finds strong empirical evidence for the hiring of compensation consultants as a justification device for higher executive pay.'[234]

The most egregious examples of personal and corporate greed – and other vivid illustrations of business going awry – tend to occur in large companies. As a result, there's a powerful impulse taking hold, based on the idea that big business is bad and small business is good. I understand that impulse. It's emotional, and I sometimes feel it too. But it's simplistic, and doesn't take you very far: some big businesses do bad things, but so do some small businesses. Many big businesses do good things, and we should want them to continue. For example, size can enable innovation to be incubated and deployed in a way that benefits real people in the real world on a scale that's not possible in a small business. General Electric, Samsung and Honda exemplify this in industry; Google, Apple and Amazon in the computer age. Scale can benefit everyone – the company, its employees, its customers; wider society. It goes wrong when companies use their size or market position to get away with practices that hurt consumers, employees, suppliers, the marketplace or society at large. The problem is not business itself; it's not even big business. It's something else, and to discover what that is, we need to look at some specific examples.

Supermarkets

If you want to see a business that hurts consumers, employees, suppliers, the marketplace and society at large, look no further than the supermarkets. They've driven small farmers and other suppliers out of business; they've turned our commercial centres into 'clone towns'. But this is part of the implicit deal we made with them: they got to open in our communities, set up out-of-town stores, drive independent shops out of business. In exchange we got 'convenience' and 'value': twenty-four-hour shopping under permanent bright lights; 'more choices'; 'lower prices'. Come on, look how cheap milk is these days! (Here's why, by the way: milk, a staple item, is used by the major supermarkets as a loss leader to get customers into stores.[235] In 2014, price wars saw Tesco drop its price for four pints from £1.39 to £1 – a price quickly matched by Sainsbury's and the Co-op, and the same that Asda had been at for a year. With the exception of Asda, which has now dropped its prices even further, these stores now charge only 11p more for four pints than two pints.[236] Consumers might benefit in the short term, but in the long term, their good fortune at the checkout is destroying a fundamental industry, putting immense pressure on dairy farmers whose products are sometimes sold for less than the price of water, and often at a loss.)

I know the argument in favour of big supermarkets. They say: consumers are choosing us, and that's why we're big. We're big because we're popular. But are they? Do consumers really have much choice?

Tesco has a land bank that buys up vast amounts of prime real estate. As of late 2014, Tesco owned 4.65 million square metres of land in 310 sites in England, Scotland, and Wales, the majority of which are undeveloped.[237] Tesco might one day hope to build on some of this land, but of course any property controlled by Tesco can't be used by a rival. While the gullible Competition and Markets Authority (CMA) (whose executives and associates might one day – who knows? – find themselves working for or advising Tesco, given the revolving door between regulator and regulated) found that supermarkets weren't holding land to 'impede the entry by rival grocery retailers into local markets' as a deliberate act of strategy, even though they concluded that at 90 sites which 'grocery retailers had prevented from being used for grocery retailing', this practice of 'land banking' acted 'as a barrier to entry in a highly-concentrated local market'.[238] According to a study of the Land Registry by the *Guardian* and aerial photography firm Getmapping, much of Tesco's banked-up property is close to its existing superstores, and Tesco has not allowed rival grocery retailers to develop on its land (despite offers) even though it has no current plans to do so itself.[239] When Tesco and other supermarkets buy land, they place it under what is called a 'restrictive covenant', a legal provision that restricts future landowners in a particular way, in this case by prohibiting the future development of supermarkets on it.[240]

Over the years, the various competition authorities have looked into all this, and each time the message to the big retailers has been basically the same: 'Nothing to worry about here, it's all got up by the press, bit of a storm in a teacup really ... now be a good chap and fix this little thing over here or that thing over there and I'm sure it will all blow over.' None of these verdicts has done anything to change the structure of the market, the fact that a tiny number of big firms controls nearly all (74 per cent) of the supermarket options available to consumers.[241]

So you can't point to consumer choice as evidence that people want this kind of thing. It's not people choosing Tesco; it's people having no choice but Tesco. The implicit justification for land banking and other unfair practices is that they give us cheap prices, so why should we care? Even putting aside the social and environmental costs that they expect others to pay – for example, the taxpayer in the form of wage subsidies to enable their low-paid workers to survive – you could just about go along with this argument if people were making a conscious choice between Tesco and, say, an independent local retailer with a different set of products, prices and ethical values. But there often is no choice. Because of land banking and loss-leading prices, these stores don't face real competition; if they do have a competitor, it might even be owned by the same parent company. In fact, Tesco wanted regulatory permission to increase its local monopolies, arguing that the definition of how far away a competing store could be should be a thirty-minute drive, as opposed to a ten- to fifteen-minute one.[242]

***

But the real joke about our Faustian pact on low prices is that they have not even gone down for consumers. Despite allowing the big four supermarkets such dominant market power and despite some short-term falls, the price of food in Britain has risen faster than inflation and faster than in other countries. Between 2006 and 2015, for example, food prices rose 37.8 per cent in Britain compared to only 23.5 per cent in Germany and 13.3 per cent in France.[243] The Big Four might say they don't fix prices, but if they have so much power and market share that they can attempt hugely expensive strategies like buying up land or selling milk at a loss, or even alleged illegal ones like deliberately delayed payments to suppliers (which the Groceries Code Adjudicator now has 'reasonable suspicion' to investigate Tesco for, http://www. theguardian.com/business/2015/feb/05/tesco-faces-investigation-over-how-it-pays-suppliers), then our rules are surely broken.[244] The concentration of economic and political power in the hands of this small number of big companies shows that regulatory regimes have failed to achieve the kind of real business and real competition we should want to see. Politicians, of course, instead of challenging these destructive, inhuman leviathans, give knighthoods to their bosses and put them on panels to advise them on 'business'. By what stretch of the imagination are these businesses? Why can't we just be honest about it and admit that when it comes to food retailing, Britain is not a proper market economy with real, competitive businesses but a stitched up economy that manipulates prices, punishes farmers and other suppliers, and disfigures our civic and cultural heritage with Communist-style, top-down national uniformity? We're so used to this now, so numbed into accepting this as the way it has to be, that it's my accurate description of it that sounds extreme.

Banks

Probably more responsible than any sector for the current anti-business sentiment, banks are another clear example of what's wrong with business and what needs to be fixed. Banks long ago lost touch with any sense of human scale. When large banks have problems, they become systemic problems that infect everything. One of the people who understands this better than anyone is Nassim Taleb. From the position of an expert insider, he has been the most vocal critic of 'too-big-to-fail' financial institutions – but takes his argument much further and does so particularly effectively through comparisons with nature. Taleb argues that nature never made anything larger than an elephant or whale for a reason – size breeds complexity, which in turns brings risk. As he argues in *The Black Swan*, much of that risk is hidden and is not always where we think it will be. When large institutions – like banks – get too big, the risk of a catastrophic failure multiples:

> *Financial Institutions have been merging into a smaller number of very large banks. Almost all banks are interrelated. So the financial ecology is swelling into gigantic, incestuous, bureaucratic banks – when one fails, they all fall. The increased concentration among banks seems to have the effect of making financial crisis less likely, but when they happen they are more global in scale and hit us very hard. We have moved from a diversified ecology of small banks, with varied lending policies, to a more homogeneous framework of firms that all resemble one another. True, we now have fewer failures, but when they occur ... I shiver at the thought.*[245]

He said this in 2007. If only he knew just how soon he would be proven right.

Think about the big banks, whose lavishly paid executives recently led us to the brink of economic catastrophe. They have an incentive to be enormous and unwieldy so that because they are 'too big to fail', governments have no choice but to rescue them. That was the lesson of the 2008 crisis. Knowing you can't fail is good for business: economists at the International Monetary Fund and the University of Mainz found that when banks are this big they can borrow at a lower rate, as they are implicitly insured by the government. When applied to the liabilities of the ten largest US banks by assets, the implicit interest-rate subsidy from government was about $83 billion a year. For the top five banks – JP Morgan Chase, Bank of America, Citigroup, Wells Fargo and Goldman Sachs – this subsidy was worth $64 billion, roughly equivalent to their typical yearly profits.[246] These so-called businesses wouldn't even be profitable without taxpayer subsidies. Eric Holder, the US Attorney General, has admitted government's impotence: 'I am concerned that the size of some of these institutions becomes so large that it does become difficult for us to prosecute them when we are hit with indications that if you do prosecute, if you do bring a criminal charge, it will have a negative impact on the national economy, perhaps even the world economy.'[247]

The banks' concentration of economic power has been turned into political power. Big banks get in the door of government and have disproportionate say once they do. What do they want? Rules that benefit them. They want to know they'll be fine whatever mistakes they make. Their interpretation of 'doing business' is lobbying government: and it works. In December 2014, Republicans slipped into a $1.1 trillion Budget Bill a measure that allows traditional banks, whose deposits are federally insured, to invest in a wider array of financial derivatives – the same type of risky investments that contributed to the 2008 financial crisis (and that they had been banned from making since the Dodd-Frank financial reform legislation was passed in 2010).[248] As bad as the measure is, how it got in the bill is even worse. Inserted by Kansas Republican Congressman Kevin Yoder (who personally receives more money from the financial industry than any other),[249] it was actually written by Citigroup in 2013 as part of legislation proposed then. A *New York Times* analysis concluded that seventy lines of the eighty-five-line section can be traced directly to the bank.[250] The move was so blatant that one satirical headline in the *New Yorker* read: 'Citigroup to Move Headquarters to US Capitol Building'.[251] The rule is so important to bankers' profits that, according to the *Washington Post*, Jamie Dimon, CEO of JP Morgan Chase, called individual lawmakers personally to urge their support.[252] Dimon is not a businessman any more than his stooges in government are. He's not taking entrepreneurial risks the way real business people do, but precisely the opposite: he's holding government to ransom to protect his company from risk through special favours.

Of course, it's much easier for banks to obtain the political outcomes they want when so many bankers serve in government and so many politicians and regulators work in banks. The revolving door whirs away, at the heart of the incestuous relationship between them. In the UK, Sir Hector Sants joined Barclays seven months after his departure as head of the Financial Services Authority.[253] Sir Jeremy Heywood, the country's top civil servant, spent years as a managing director at Morgan Stanley.[254] James Crosby, former chief executive of Halifax Bank and then HBOS, went on to be deputy of the Financial Services Authority – until he resigned over reports that he had fired a senior HBOS manager for warning of the bank's failure.[255] He rightly handed in his knighthood, but the fact remains that a former bank chief executive was hired to regulate the very institutions whose failure he had allowed to happen. It's no different in the US; before he was Treasury Secretary, Robert Rubin was an executive at Goldman Sachs; afterwards, he became Chairman of Citigroup.[256] Current US Treasury Secretary Jack Lew was Chief Operating Officer at Citigroup.[257] Even Federal Reserve Chairman Alan Greenspan became an adviser to Deutsche Bank in 2007 after leaving office.[258]

It all stinks. The sense of systemic corruption is truly shocking. While they're in the banks, they know they can one day end up supervising them in government. While they're in government, they know they can one day end up in senior positions in the banks. Who doesn't think for one second that these men – yes, they are all men – put the interests of the banks and the untouchable 'financial services industry' before the interests of the people? What is so laughable is that these same grand figures of the Establishment in Britain and America look down their snooty noses at the kleptocracy of Putin's Russia or the rampant bribery in places like India and seem to think they're better than all that. They're worse. At least in Russia the corrupt elites aren't hypocrites too.

Lobbying

Of course, it's not just banking. The way in which big businesses in most severely uncompetitive industries capture the levers of power and use them to serve their commercial ends, rather than fairly competing in the marketplace like real businesses, is one of their hallmarks. No practice exemplifies it better than lobbying, an industry itself these days – especially in places where regulatory power is concentrated, like Brussels and Washington DC. Senator Elizabeth Warren points out that while recent US budget cuts hit programmes for the working poor and middle-income earners, subsidies and tax breaks for businesses that make billions in profit were funded at full level.[259] But it's instructive to look a little lower down the chain too. In Chapter 1, we saw the great promise of decentralised power and how the American states, as 'laboratories of democracy', show the best aspects of decentralised power. They are indeed a great model – unless they've been captured by corporate lobbying.

The American Legislative Exchange Council, or ALEC, is the country's premier forum for legislators, think tanks and corporations to come together to discuss issues. Unsurprisingly for a group run by corporate interests, ALEC pushes for bills that suit corporations. But delegates at ALEC meetings do more than just talk; they actually write legislation in committee. At these meetings, legislators – whose trips to ALEC meetings are often paid for by ALEC through a corporate 'scholarship fund' – are joined by policy analysts and representatives from ALEC's corporate members, who pay between $3,000 and $25,000 to be on a given committee. Together, they write 'model' legislation that aligns with the aims of the corporate sponsors and can be adapted across multiple states – often as a backdoor to legislative outcomes that are difficult to achieve at the federal level or as attempts to undermine federal rules outright. The proposed bill is then voted on by the committee. If a majority of both the legislators and corporate representatives on the committee approve it, it becomes 'model legislation' and is posted on ALEC's website for legislators across the country to use in their own states.[260] Indeed, the broad applicability of model bills is the aim; they feature 'insert state here' placeholders so all that legislators have to do is remember which state they are in.[261] One set of identical ALEC-backed energy bills was introduced in Oregon, New Mexico and New Hampshire; the bills, which benefited companies like ExxonMobil and Koch Industries were, naturally, written at ALEC meetings in which representatives of those companies participated.[262] More than 1,000 ALEC bills are introduced a year, with over 200 passed into law.[263]

ALEC is (unbelievably) considered a charity and according to its 2010 tax filings had lobbying expenditure of – wait for it – $0.00.[264] The ALEC process represents not just one depressing trend – the unfair influence of corporate voices in making laws (since when did *citizens* get to write 'model legislation' that is implemented across the nation?) – but two. This way of doing government is thoroughly centralising: it undercuts the whole idea of localism and policy experimentation by individual states.

Some would argue that businesses writing legislation is not quite as bad as it sounds: at least they understand the issues and so the legislation is less likely to have the errors and unintended consequences that often arise from a bureaucrat's lack of specific knowledge. That is no doubt true: the model legislation written by these companies will, I'm sure, accurately address the relevant issues. But accuracy isn't really the point. The point is accountability: how can people have confidence in their democracy when companies can literally purchase the right to draft legislation while everyone else has to make do with old-fashioned things like voting? When you look at something like ALEC, with the corporate lobbyists cheek by jowl with the legislators, writing the rules that they will play by, you have to ask what this has got to do with real business. With enterprise? With markets?

You may be thinking: well, yes, that's America for you. We don't have that kind of corruption in Britain. Not so fast. Even in countries without massive spending on political campaigns, like the UK, you see the same effects. It's just more subtle. More British. First, remember that while the scale is totally different than in the US, election campaigns and political parties do need to be paid for – to the tune of many millions a year. On the Left, the money comes from trade unions, which is its own form of corruption. On the Right, it typically comes from wealthy individuals; more precisely, Britain's economy being what it is, wealthy individuals in the financial-services sector. This means that politicians end up spending their time in the company of a very narrow fragment of society. Nothing so blatant as the legislation-writing shamelessness of Citigroup in the US – but there's an influence none the less.

Second (and not so much in the spotlight because the focus inevitably falls on politicians) is the lobbying that targets the civil servants who in the UK system actually write the rules and regulations that make such a difference to commercial outcomes for companies. Undisclosed hospitality, gifts, the implicit promise of future seats on boards and consultancy contracts ... all this is part of the very British form of corruption that goes on, most of the time completely hidden from view.

The third way big businesses get what they want from government is more subtle still, but just as powerful. When policy decisions affecting industries are made, big businesses (whether they or their representatives are physically present or not) are often the loudest voices in the room. This is because they have a powerful arm lock on politicians who are terrified of being branded 'anti-business'. They are culturally cowed into writing rules that benefit the dominant existing players, and work to keep smaller, innovative challengers out.

Small businesses are having an increasingly difficult time, and it's no wonder: their competitors have used their power unfairly to bully, cajole, manipulate, and muscle their way into maintaining market share. Take, for instance, the local pub: there were almost 70,000 pubs in 1980, but since then some 21,000 have closed,[265] with over 7,000 shuttered since the financial crisis.[266] Now, some 30 pubs close each week.[267] Ivy House, a South London pub, was the first of 300 to earn the newly established 'asset of community value' status, a policy that Rohan and I developed to try to level the playing field and which allows community groups to buy pubs rather than allow them to be acquired by developers to be torn down. But this kind of tactical response, however worthy, is not the answer.

Politicians who unquestioningly back big business make a terrible error. They confuse big business with all business, and they confuse business with the market. The correct posture, the one that fairly benefits business and society alike, is to be pro-market, pro-competition, pro-enterprise. That does not equate to doing the bidding of our biggest companies.

Business or bureaucracy?

Are you spotting a theme here? Businesses colluding with each other, squeezing their suppliers and squeezing out the competition, trying to achieve their aims through manipulating markets and lobbying government. Whether that's the banks, the supermarkets, the utilities or any number of other industries you could choose, the problem is the same: the concentration of market power. Not business itself, not capitalism itself, not even 'big business' – because not all big businesses behave the way the supermarkets do. Many consumer brands and technology companies, for example, are big. But the barriers to entry in their market are so low, and the ability for consumers to choose alternatives is so high, that simply being big doesn't give you market power, it just means you're doing well – for the moment.

Big market power, on the other hand, is bad for the economy, distorts our political system and is bad for society. If the economic results of oligopoly and lack of competition are a precarious financial system; if the political results are a corrupted political system; then the impact on our society is worse quality of life. With a concentration of market power, we get anonymous big-box stores at the expense of local businesses, customer service and unique community spaces. We get energy companies whose profits between 2009 and 2013 increased from £8 per customer to £48, and are on track to earn over £110 per household.[268] It is all completely inhuman and it explains a lot of the hostility you see towards business these days.

What is the underlying cause? What is it that lies behind businesses becoming so distant from and dismissive of human concerns? We could just blame the people in charge, writing it off to the fact that they're simply the 'greedy capitalists' of caricature. That is simple-minded. It's not the people, any more than in our opening story involving jetBlue we should blame the person. There, we rightly blamed the system, the system that makes people behave in inhuman ways. And it's the same here. It's a structural problem with our economy, and it needs a structural solution. What we are experiencing today is a business landscape dominated by institutions that have become large, sclerotic and driven by their own organisational interests rather than those of the people they touch. Far removed from human scale. The banks, for example, are driven not by any concern for the real people at the receiving end of all the financial trickery: clients are not individuals but figures on spreadsheets. Something wrong was bound to happen when a family's home loan was boiled down to a single letter rating, then tossed together with hundreds of other loans to be sliced, diced, reconstituted, resold, and insured by so-called 'masters of the universe'. Finance has become so big and complicated, so far from the human scale, it's a wonder there haven't been more crises. When billions are moved around in moments, the banks have lost the point that at the core of each financial instrument is a home, a family, a life.

The banks, the supermarkets, the other inhuman institutions that behave in these ways: they have nothing of the entrepreneur, the risk taker about them. They don't want to win by creating better products, they want to win by getting the government to rig the market so they won't be challenged. They are not real businesses at all, they are bureaucracies. These private-sector bureaucracies reduce workers to costs; customers to sources of revenue. I'm not saying that workers don't cost something, or that customers aren't the ultimate source of cash flow. But if you view business as a human endeavour designed to create value for everyone involved, workers are not a cost, they're the people you depend on to create the core value of the business. Customers are not an annoyance to be milked for money and 'handled' as 'efficiently' as possible but people you build a relationship with. Real business is a profound act of mutual benefit that should, accordingly, be founded on mutual respect. But that is totally alien to the modern business-as-bureaucracy where the imperatives of the system and the process, rather than people, always rule.

Real businesses are different. They do not depend on regulatory capture for their commercial success. Real businesses want to do great things – for themselves, obviously, but also for their employees, their customers, their suppliers, their communities, and the wider world. Great entrepreneurs don't rely on loopholes to make profits. Of course they want to win, but they want to win by having the best products and services – not the best lobbyists and lawyers.

Over the past few decades, as globalisation has gathered pace and business has become more bureaucratic and less human, successive campaigns – be they the original anti-globalisers or more recently the 'Occupiers' – have fought for social and environmental justice; stood up for the little people against the big corporations; raised awareness, gained much public support. But as we've seen, nothing has really changed. And now we can precisely identify the reason. The 'anti-business' movement, in all its various forms, with all its valid points, has been aiming at the wrong target.

They've been aiming at the symptoms, not the cause. The cause of the discontent that people feel with business today, the underlying reason for all the specific complaints, is the concentration of economic power in fewer and fewer hands. The transformation of businesses into bureaucracies, practically part of the government; writing their own laws, writing their own rules. And it's not just the activists and the campaigners: we've all got it wrong. We've been tactical, not strategic; superficial, not structural. We've responded to the problems caused by business-as-bureaucracy with yet more bureaucracy, more specific rules and regulations. But as we've seen, the business bureaucracies that cause the social and environmental problems in the first place know exactly how to get around the rules, avoid the regulations, go their own way. The people who are hurt are the small businesses, the real businesses, the entrepreneurs without lawyers and lobbyists to help them.

As the real target comes into view – the concentration of power in the hands of the business bureaucracies – so too does the solution. It's one that we can find deep within ourselves, in a very human instinct.

Fair trade

Just as to trade is human, to compete is human too. If you watch two children, somehow or another they find a way to make whatever game they are playing into a competition. Sure, they have fun. But half the fun is that they are aiming for some sort of purpose, a victory however small. Competition is built into us, even at an early age. And it has helped build the world we live in today.

But it has to be fair. It's not just competition that's hardwired. It's fair competition. Behavioural experiments have shown that we innately care more about fairness than rewards.[269] But you don't need a social scientist to tell you this. Just think about how we feel about cheating in our everyday lives. We love fair competition (Olympic underdogs!), but nothing grates on us more than cheaters (Olympic dopers!). When a number of beloved Major League Baseball players in the United States were discovered to be using steroids, the outcry led all the way to Congressional investigations. This disgust at unfairness is strong and instinctive.

Trade and fair competition – so brilliantly blended by free markets – are naturally and distinctly human, both by themselves and together. So what we need now – the practical, positive, constructive response to 'anti-business' sentiment – is a massive shake-up in our economic structures, to make them more competitive. People in fair competition don't pay each other excessive wages; that only happens in a culture where there's no real competition, and executives can scratch each other's backs while sitting on each other's compensation committees. Competition, on a human scale, would see real diversity on our high streets, not the same old stores. Business at the human scale would place appropriate value on social and environmental costs. It would put people first: customers, workers, suppliers. What we have now is not fair competition; it is not a market economy; it is an economy of bureaucracies, by bureaucracies, for bureaucracies. Except they have the nerve to call themselves businesses. It's when companies have no competitors, or no real competitors, or so few that the dominant players can all get together and stitch things up between them, that the results tend to be bad for society. Lack of competition leads to a lack of accountability, which is what causes bad business behaviour. Of course the vast majority of businesses with little or no competition tend to be big ones. But if we're going to do something constructive about the things we most hate in the modern economic world, we need to move beyond the simple impulse that big businesses are bad, and adopt a more sophisticated approach. Businesses without fair competition are bad. But how should we define 'fair competition'?

We have competition authorities in place today that act according to the mandate set for them by politicians, and their own interpretation of that mandate. But it's a flawed framework. It may stop a business literally becoming a monopoly, but it doesn't prevent the harmful practices of dominant players. The definition of a competitive market should be radically strengthened. The crucial concept is 'barriers to entry' – how easily can new firms enter a market and compete? You should be able to be as big or as small as you want, but you should not be able to prevent other firms from competing against you (either explicitly or implicitly by using incumbent advantages like free current accounts or loss-leading milk prices). This is what the competition authorities should enforce. At the same time, the interpretation of the harm done by anti-competitive practices should be broadened. Today, the competition rules are focused on one thing, 'customer welfare', expressed as 'price, quality, range, and service' (PQRS). In other words, the current competition rules mean that as long as authorities think service is good enough, quality is high enough, price is low enough and range is wide enough – regardless of the harm that's done to achieve those things – then all is well. This obviously neglects harms to society like putting small firms, whether competitors or suppliers, out of business by unfairly using the advantages of scale and incumbency. We need to change that.

There's one more step we should take: a simpler and even more radical way of thinking about this. If the good things about capitalism come from real, entrepreneurial businesses, and the bad things come from those that are basically just private-sector bureaucracies, we need to boost the former and constrain the latter. How do we distinguish?

By returning to the concept of 'too big to fail'.

Imagine that Tesco goes bust. In towns where it has used unfair practices to drive out competition, where will people shop? What will become of its properties? As Nassim Taleb points out, 'should [a megastore, in this case Tesco] go bust (and the statistical elephant in the room is that it eventually will), we would end up with a massive war zone'. Beyond losing access to a grocery, high streets up and down the country would have giant holes that could take years from which to recover. 'It is completely wrong,' Taleb continues, 'to use the calculus of benefits without including the probability of failure,'[270] particularly when those costs are borne by consumers, communities and taxpayers.

Whether a company, in the event that it failed, would need to be bailed out by the government is a good proxy for whether it is a real, entrepreneurial business or a private-sector bureaucracy. In his book *Antifragile*, Nassim Taleb has an ingenious proposal for discouraging such bureaucracies: 'My suggestion to deter "too big to fail" and to prevent employers taking advantage of the public is as follows. A company that is classified as potentially bailable out should it fail should not be able to pay anyone more than a corresponding civil servant … Such limitation would force companies to stay small enough that they would not be considered for a bailout in the event of their failure.'[271]

We should broaden the mandate of the competition authorities to require them to assess whether in their view a particular company, if it failed, would require support from the government. If the answer is yes, it is a bureaucracy, and should be treated as such. These companies would be subject to the same pay and compensation rules as their public-sector counterparts ... including for their senior management. This would have a powerful incentive effect. While almost all such companies would be big, it's obvious that not all big companies would fall into this category – not by a long way. Take Apple, the world's biggest corporation by value. If it went bust tomorrow, there would be no need for government to bail it out. There would be plenty of viable alternatives for consumers, employees, suppliers, shareholders. But if Tesco were to fail, or HSBC, you can bet there's a taxpayer subsidy or bailout on its way. That may well be right and necessary. But then let's not pretend that these corporations are real businesses. They're not: they're basically part of the public sector, so it follows that they should be treated like the rest of it.

Technology's promise

Thankfully, despite the obstacles, there are more and more companies doing things better. And the interesting part is that it is new technology that seems to be leading the way in helping business become more human.

Take Red Dress Boutique. Its founder, Diana Harbour, was bored with her 'secure but soul-sucking' office job, but loved fashion. As an aspiring designer, she decided to build a boutique around curating fashionable but affordable outfits. So she started on eBay, selling outfits from her basement. Realising she needed to expand, she and her husband Josh dug into their savings and opened a shop in Athens, Georgia. After some initial success, they moved online in 2010 – at which point the business skyrocketed: $63,000 in sales in 2010 transformed to $7 million in 2013 and then to over $12 million in 2014, with a net profit of $2 million. Diana had something of value to offer the world, and the Internet enabled her to share it.[272]

Another Internet marketplace, Etsy, unleashes the wares of small designers around the world using a platform that helps them compete with big retailers and global brands. By giving consumers the chance to buy unique items directly from artisans who make them (and to communicate with them as well), Etsy doesn't just support those whose local markets would be too small to survive; it also forges a human connection between maker and consumer. By bringing to market items that might never have been economical to manufacture on any scale or to stock in a store, Etsy also helps makes the world just a bit more different.

A more human economy is one in which people control both their own labour and their own assets. Technology is helping here, linking us in the emerging 'sharing economy'. By enabling people to provide services directly to others without substantial corporate infrastructure or intermediation, the sharing economy builds community in ways that typical corporate-consumer relationships do not. The essence of the sharing economy is that customers receive services not from professionals, but from people like themselves – it's more human by definition.

Airbnb epitomises the sharing economy. It's now a big company that competes with hotels (its latest valuation surpasses Hyatt),[273] but more importantly it is a platform for the actual sharing of assets. Airbnb is transforming the way people travel. It gives everyday people extra income by renting out spare rooms, and they get to meet new and interesting people to boot. Airbnb hosts are completely autonomous; they set their own policies, their own prices, their own schedules. Guests get to connect with real people offering rooms, apartments and houses. Rather than staying in a sterile hotel room, Airbnb connects travellers with a real Londoner, Chicagoan, or Hong Konger. Often Airbnb guests socialise with their hosts and even develop friendships over repeated or reciprocal visits. It's a great example of the argument that in business 'big' is not necessarily bad; that 'big' can be human – as long as it is a real business competing fairly in a real market.

Technology is helping business become more human in other ways, by increasing transparency about how suppliers are treated. More information means better, more conscious choices to improve not just products but the impact of their manufacture, distribution and sale as well. In Chapter 4 we saw how the tech start-ups Good Eggs and the Food Assembly, by cutting out the bricks-and-mortar store, are able to lower the cost of and expand access to fundamentally better food products (not just in quality but social and environmental impact, too). BeGood Clothing, another San Francisco start-up, is doing the same thing.

'We sell online and through our store directly and skip middlemen,' explains co-founder Mark Spera. 'That's how we've been able to offer a disruptively low $15 price point on our T-shirts.'[274] The entire clothing line is made in Los Angeles and San Francisco in good conditions, to workers paid fair wages. And all from materials that are organically harvested and processed sustainably, without the use of harsh chemicals. BeGood has embraced the very human narrative behind each of its garments. At their store and online, each item carries an explanation of the materials and processes involved as well as the people and places along its supply chain. Just as with food, it's essential for a more human economy that we start acknowledging and understanding the non-monetary costs of producing the things we consume.

Because generally, they are pretty high; often horrendous. Consider the children of Savar, Bangladesh. They're dependent on the textile factories that make the clothes we buy in the West. The income their parents earn allows them to go to school. But those factories are also the worst fixture in their lives. In order to export at rock-bottom prices, the companies that own them pay abysmally, are unsafe for the workers – the Rana Plaza disaster in 2013 that killed hundreds occurred just two miles away – and cause a toxic environmental mess that makes everyday living, let alone learning, practically impossible. The reason? Rivers of noxious chemical waste.[275]

Take the ubiquitous pair of denim jeans. Their blue colour might be their most inhuman feature. In countries like China, India and Bangladesh, waste water used to dye and process textiles is routinely dumped untreated, saturating rivers and streams with carcinogens like chromium, lead, cadmium, arsenic and mercury used to create the colours we want. This not only poisons the factory workers and their families who live nearby; it kills off fields and local fish supplies as well. In the Pearl River Delta in China's Guangdong province, the water literally runs blue from the synthetic pigments used to process 200 million pairs of jeans dyed there every year.[276] According to Green Cross Switzerland, 9 trillion gallons of water are used annually in textile production around the world. Most of it is dumped untreated.[277]

In Savar, some of that runs next to the Genda Government Primary School, creating toxic headaches for students and teachers alike: the 'suffocating' odour in the air makes students and teachers feel dizzy, vomit, and lose focus. Occasionally, students faint. Despite protests by parents and opposition by the mayor, the industrial interests win out. According to the school's headmaster, Mohammed Abdul Ali: 'We've never seen the owners take our appeals seriously ... everything is going on as usual. They have a good relationship with the politicians. That is why they don't care.' Every once in a while, a reforming minister or regulator comes to power and attempts to do something but is inevitably stifled. For a short period Munir Chowdhury, an environmental official, held textile factories accountable, conducting raids and imposing fines. He didn't last of course; he was transferred to another department. More often than not, ministers are part of the problem. 'These people who are setting up industries and factories here are much more powerful than me,' says Mohammed Abdul Kader, the mayor of Savar. 'When a government minister calls me and tells me to give permission to someone to set up a factory in Savar, I can't refuse.'[278]

The problem is that the shirts produced in Savar are cheap; the shirts sold at BeGood in San Francisco are, while relatively inexpensive, still not competitive with what's sold to the average Western consumer. But the only reason that sweatshop textiles are cheap is because the businesses that produce them resist rules that might require them to treat people decently. Taxpayers then foot the bill for the harm they cause. So rather than perpetuating the fiction that social and environmental responsibility is an indulgence for the rich, we should be asking why we continue to subsidise companies that offload the true costs of their operations onto others. That's not real business; it's certainly not fair competition or even proper market economics.

Technology can help make these markets more human by improving information. The Internet enables consumers to discriminate on the basis of more than just quality and price: they can increasingly take human and environmental impact into account too. As companies like BeGood raise the bar about how much information is provided about consumer products, social impact becomes a consumer feature just like any other. This has been a winning strategy for firms like Patagonia, the environmentally sensitive (and enormously successful) maker of outdoor clothing. It has used its websites to show where and how its products are made, recently announcing the completion of a seven-year process to make sure all the down feathers used in jackets and sweaters are 100 per cent traceable and cruelty free. One section of their website, 'The Footprint Chronicles', traces the journey of some of their products around a global map, showing images, videos and descriptions of each step along the way.

Or browse the website of Everlane, a much younger clothing maker. On the top of its homepage are links to its main sections: 'Men's', 'Women's', then 'Factories'. When you click on the page, up pops a map pinpointing each part of its supply chain, from leather shops to distribution centres to mills and factories. Each of them has a dedicated page showing basic data like the number of employees, the date it was established, even current time and weather. Further down is a description of which products are made there, how Everlane found this particular factory, details on the materials it sources, and information about the factory's owner. If you scroll down, you can look at high-resolution images taken by Everlane's staff. Back on the individual product pages (which all link to their relevant factory-profile pages), Everlane takes transparency a step further, breaking down where every penny of the purchase price goes – from materials and labour to transport and profit.

The Internet is just the beginning of the effect technology will have on the social and environmental impact of business. Ubiquitous mobile technology will enable a hyper-transparent supply chain we could never have imagined twenty years ago. In previous decades, 'corporate responsibility' meant the occasional, unannounced inspection with the results being filed away or scanned into big PDFs hidden on investor-relations websites. But now, with mobile technology nearly everywhere, we can fundamentally change how we evaluate a company's working conditions, not to mention its overall impact on vulnerable communities.

'The current tool is an audit and certificate,' says David

Bonbright, head of Covox, a human-rights monitoring firm. 'It doesn't tell you how to solve any problems that might arise, just that there *are* problems.' So Covox takes a more human, twenty-first-century approach based on the fact that nearly every worker in the developing world – even the poorest – has a mobile phone. Workers are asked directly about their own conditions; questions like: 'Does your employer treat you fairly?', 'Are working conditions healthy and safe?' and 'Does the company respect your community's rights and behave like a good neighbour?' Every day, a question like this is posed to a different representative sample of workers via text message to their mobiles; this way everyone's voice is heard. The results are immediately reported, collated, and delivered. Now, rather than a twelve- to twenty-four-month lag in discovering that something is wrong on the ground, issues can be discovered and diagnosed continuously. And with basic (anonymised) user data such as gender and age, Covox can gain even further insight about particular issues and how they're affecting workers and their community. It's more than mere compliance, Bonbright explains. 'It's about capturing the voice of marginalised people who are part of the supply chain.'[279]

Tools like Covox aren't in the hands of every consumer yet – but with the trend being set by companies like Patagonia and Everlane, it's likely they soon will be. This is where technology proves itself, when wielded correctly, as an enabler of good business, empowering society to make sure capitalism puts people first.

Technology's peril

However: technology can also be a double-edged sword for transparency, obscuring abuse and harm as much as exposing it. We make a fuss about corporations like Walmart because we can identify their employees; we see them in the aisles and at the tills. But online retailers like Amazon, however innovative and cost-saving for consumers, can hide how they treat their people behind the clean facade the Internet allows them to put up. Amazon's workers are out of sight, and as a result easy to put out of mind. But undercover investigations have revealed employees toiling in warehouses for low wages in slave-like conditions (some walk up to fifteen miles, criss-crossing its massive warehouses, in the span of a ten-and-a-half-hour shift). At Amazon's Swansea facility, employees work fifty-plus-hour weeks at minimum wage. They'll be fired if they take more than three sick days in a three-month period (or get sick twice and show up late by a minute twice, or get sick once and are late four times, and so on). According to one undercover journalist, strict fifteen-minute breaks start wherever the worker happens to be in the warehouse at the time, which could be a long walk away from a place to sit down, and that's after passing through airport-like security to be patted down (to prevent looting).[280] At another warehouse, employees are actually tagged with their own personal satnavs so their movements can be governed 'scientifically' by managers. If employees don't go to the toilet nearest them, they are asked why.[281] Treating people like this is humiliating and undignified.

Amazon has said: 'We're working hard to make sure that we are better tomorrow than we are today.' No doubt they are, but in many big companies it's the absence of human values that allows harm to take place. Bureaucratic systems eliminate basic humanity and the personal connection, kindness and empathy natural to nearly all of us. I don't know him, so I can't be sure, but I sincerely doubt that Jeff Bezos, the remarkable founder and CEO of Amazon would, if he found himself in one of his warehouses with an employee betrayed by the personal satnav as having gone to the 'wrong' toilet, actually ask that employee why. The system, the process, the bureaucracy: these are things that distance people from each other, and that's what we should be attacking, not the idea of business or capitalism or profits – all of which can (and do) deliver wonderful human outcomes in the right circumstances.[282]

Real business: challenging incumbents

While we should never blithely assume that technology is always a force for good, it is clear that technology is enabling the emergence of more human competition to established businesses more quickly and easily than ever before. Amazon emerged to challenge the traditional retail industry; now in an exhilarating turn of the circle, we're seeing more human competitors challenging Amazon. Postmates is a firm that would have been physically impossible to run, let alone conceive, without the latest technology. Postmates resembles Amazon in many ways: it sells a multitude of products in its online store, is based on mobile technology, and delivers products directly to consumers using a network of couriers, not unlike those seen in ride-sharing or meal-delivery services. But there's one big caveat.

'Everything that we're doing is anti-Amazon,' says Bastian Lehmann, the start-up's co-founder. Instead of sourcing and sorting products itself, Postmates sells the products of a network of local bricks-and-mortar retailers. Why bother with the logistics of a warehouse operation when there are stores already fulfilling that function? Instacart, another shopping delivery start-up, takes the same philosophy, delivering from both chain stores and local independent shops. 'We want to use the city as our warehouse instead of building a warehouse outside the city,' says Lehmann of Postmates. 'We want to be part of a city versus saying: "Here's a way that you can save $2 on an item, but nobody in your city earns a dime, but now you have a cheap DVD player – congratulations!"'[283] As innovative as Amazon is, it's already being disrupted. That is real entrepreneurial business, not bureaucracy. The fact that Amazon's challengers are trying to travel the right, more human, road simply offers more evidence of business's power for good. Competition doesn't just force companies to offer better prices or better products; it can force them to think about how best to serve the whole, human community.

Here's another example of the great, dynamic, positive circle that real, competitive business represents. One of the challenges for participants in the sharing economy is the lack of predictability and stability. Working for a large corporation might often seem like soulless drudgery, but at least it's mostly stable: regular hours and a pension. Of course, even the grandest of corporations can go belly up overnight, and there is nothing to prevent you from being laid off without much notice. But workers in the sharing economy experience hourly volatility, often not knowing how much money they'll make in a given day, let alone week or month.

Now, entrepreneurs (once again with technology) are tackling those challenges. Peers, a San Francisco-based organisation with 250,000 members, offers products and services to support so-called 'gig' workers. Take its 'Keep Driving' programme. For $20 a month, it gives drivers for car-sharing services like Lyft or Sidecar access to a temporary car in the event that their own is damaged or stolen. For drivers like San Franciscan Michael Bendorf, whose hybrid Volkswagen was rear-ended in a four-car collision, this service prevented him from losing the $5,000 to $7,000 per month he normally would have earned during the time his car was being repaired. Peers is also filling other gaps that often pop up in the sharing economy, like insurance (many car and property insurers will cancel your policy if you lend, or charge to share, your car or home). Peers now offers a $1 million liability policy – in one-month increments (with no minimum) – for those who make their space available to travellers via Airbnb, HomeAway, FlipKey, or even Craigslist. 'What we're trying to do here is recognise the needs of a new class of worker,' says Shelby Clark, the company's executive director. 'There are hundreds of thousands of people across the country earning money in new ways. While they love the flexibility and that they can start earning right away, at the same time they're encountering new challenges, like making sure they have stable income.'[284]

One of the incumbent advantages that established firms have traditionally had over start-ups and 'gig workers' is that their scale has enabled bulk-buying discounts on things like administration, workspace and insurance. But the Internet is increasingly making this a moot point. While firms like Etsy enable makers to sell their wares online, new payment services like Square allow small shop and restaurant owners to use nothing more than an iPad and a small plastic card reader to process card payments in person. Gone are the days where small entrepreneurs had to choose between 'cash only' or big bulky and expensive IBM cash tills.

With dreary predictability, however, obviously beneficial products and services like these are being confronted by bureaucratic government resistance. Take Tesla, the Palo Alto-based electric-car company founded by serial entrepreneur Elon Musk. With its breakthrough battery technology, Tesla is doing more than almost anyone to make electric cars economical on a large scale. But Tesla's innovations aren't limited to technology – and therein lies the problem. Rather than sell through dealer middlemen, Tesla sells its vehicles directly to the public through its own stores, where customers can explore one or two model vehicles and an example of the battery packs, then use touch-screen terminals to customise their order. What could be wrong with a company that has a product and business model that are both innovative? Well, according to some US states, quite a bit. Since the car industry in America traditionally works through dealerships, those dealers don't take kindly to an approach that disrupts their entire way of operating. Across America, Tesla has had to contend with lawsuits and legislative battles just for the right to sell its cars.[285] In some states, it is only allowed to have 'galleries', where visitors can see cars but where employees are prohibited from discussing prices or how to buy a car. And even those limitations aren't enough in some other states. In October 2014, for example, Michigan, the home of American car manufacturers Ford, GM, and Chrysler – the companies Tesla is disrupting – passed a law that bans even galleries.[286] It's a perfect example of the pattern we see over and over again in today's unfair, uncompetitive, rigged economy: government bureaucrats siding with private-sector bureaucrats and using outdated protectionist regulations to keep challengers out.

As we're seeing throughout this book, technology can work for good and ill. On one hand, it's the great equaliser. As technology increases in power and decreases in price, the costs of employing people's creative capacities continue to fall. Anyone can post a video of themselves making music on YouTube at minimal cost and become tomorrow's superstar. The deeper, more structural point, though, is that technology is enabling a profound transformation to take place in the realm of competition: it's eliminating barriers to entry by making many of the advantages that big or incumbent firms used to have, like economies of scale, irrelevant. Of course technology companies can be bureaucratic just like any other, but usually they are the kind of business we should want to see in every sector. Entrepreneurial tech firms show us exactly what a bureaucracy doesn't look like. In their fights with vested interests (including other, mature tech firms), they demonstrate precisely what happens when you allow innovation to unseat established bureaucracies. (Even better, their products are allowing other firms to escape bureaucracy themselves.)

The Internet, argues leading Silicon Valley entrepreneur and investor Peter Thiel, makes it easy for customers to switch to the best products in a heartbeat. While this ease is what enables the really great businesses to balloon in size overnight, it's what also makes even the most successful, established tech firms so inherently 'disruptable'. Unlike old industries in which control of one bit of infrastructure, like oil wells or pipelines or steel mills or railroads, enabled firms to lock challengers out and charge consumers whatever price they wanted, with the Internet, tiny upstarts can topple giants. Facebook was born in a dorm room and upended the seemingly formidable Myspace. Google became more popular than Microsoft, but Microsoft had put IBM in its place before that. Look at the success of Instagram, WhatsApp and Slack. From nowhere, these companies were built by risk takers who had a vision, and they were rewarded because the market posed minimal barriers to entry for them to let customers try their products. Facebook's acquisition of the first two not only demonstrated the value these entrepreneurs had created but also how susceptible it is to competitive pressure, despite its dominance and market size. And such acquisitions only encourage more innovation.

Competition enables innovation that enriches us all. We need competition not just for our economy to succeed but for our society to flourish. But right now, we are headed in the wrong direction. Look how the politicians, regulators and public authorities, instead of backing this move to a more human economy, are actually fighting it – with a massive regulatory onslaught against new products and services like Tesla, Airbnb and Uber. The political establishment is in the pocket of the economic establishment: all the bureaucrats together. They want to hang onto their power, and it should be our mission to take it away from them. That's the way to address the very real anxieties people have about the role of business in the world today, and to build a more human economy that puts people first.

CHAPTER 6

POVERTY

This is how we deal with poverty today: there is a boy – let's call him Chris – from a poor family in East London. Like so many others across Britain who have to endure the multiple issues surrounding poverty, he has lots of well-meaning people from government trying to help him: social workers, probation officers, mental-health officers. Chris has all sorts of problems: acting out in school; being in trouble with the police; mental-health issues. One day the adults responsible for different aspects of his life decided to hold a conference to discuss his problems. There were going to be eleven professionals present. Chris's mother went to see David Robinson, founder of Community Links, a remarkable organisation that for over twenty-five years has been fighting poverty in some of the country's poorest neighbourhoods. She asked him to come too. 'Why?' he asked. There were, after all, already going to be nearly a dozen people there. She pleaded: 'I need someone on my side.'

How heartbreaking. She saw the social workers, the court officers – all of them – as her son's enemies.[287] As David Robinson says, the well-meaning but ineffectual government assistance was so overwhelming that the mother practically needed a diary secretary to keep up. They were all working on her son's problems piecemeal, with a different caseworker (or more) for each of his problems, pursuing the priorities and processes set by their part of the bureaucracy.

Yes, this is how we deal with poverty today: in a way that is inhuman. Chris and his mother's experience illustrate a broader disease. Today's vast, complex welfare system is clearly not working: how do we spend £120 billion a year fighting poverty[288] and still have poor people? With generation after generation in poverty, we're obviously not dealing with its causes. But the truly remarkable thing, given how much money we spend on it, is that we're not even dealing properly with its symptoms.

The symptoms of poverty

Every year HSBC, the international bank based in London, now under fire for its sterling work helping the super-rich (including its own senior executives) avoid taxes, holds its annual general meeting where shareholders gather to discuss financial results, hear executives speak, and make decisions about the company's governance. These meetings tend to be quite petty; almost entirely predictable. But in 2003 the meeting was quite different. Sir John Bond, the company's chairman, had just finished his address. There was a celebratory mood in the air; much of the assembly had centred around HSBC's planned acquisition of Household International (an American loan company), and William Aldinger, its head, had been persuaded to join HSBC's management. As is customary, Sir John opened the floor to questions.

Up stood perhaps the last person he would have expected to see.

It was a man who was the proud owner of just enough HSBC shares to earn him a spot at the meeting, thanks to a consortium of East End charities that had pooled resources to buy the shares. He was braver than many of his colleagues, who also had things they wanted to say to the Chairman of HSBC but were frightened of speaking out – in case they were fired. The man standing to ask Sir John a question was the man who cleaned his office every night. This is what he said:

'Sir John Bond, distinguished ladies and gentlemen, my name is Abdul Durrant, I work in the same office as the board members, the only difference is I don't operate computers. My function is to operate a mop and bucket. Yes, I am one of the invisible night cleaners. You may be wondering what the hell is a night cleaner doing here: we're supposed to be invisible. Well, I am here on behalf of all the contract staff at HSBC and the families of East London. We receive £5 per hour – a whole £5 per hour! – no pension, and a measly sick-pay scheme. In our struggles our children go to school without adequate lunch. We are unable to provide necessary books for their education. School outings in particular they miss out on. In the end, many of our children prefer a life of crime to being a cleaner ... Sir John, we have met before. Will you consider your previous decision not to review the cleaning contract with OCS, so that I and my colleagues receive a living wage?'[289]

The working poor

Abdul's story touched everyone in the room, particularly Sir John. It wasn't just that the story was moving. Or that people were impressed by Abdul's eloquence despite his being so completely out of place. His story was especially poignant because the board had just discussed the pay package for Mr Aldinger, who was now joining HSBC's management. His salary? £23 million over the next three years. It was a contrast too stark for even the most avowed capitalists in the room. Abdul had made his point.

His situation was not – is not – unusual. He is among the 1.2 million or so British workers (about one in twenty) who earn the legal minimum wage. Another 1.3 million earn within just 50p of it.[290] Worse, many of them really are just as good as invisible. Not only are they hidden from sight because of their night-shift hours but also because of the subcontracted process through which they're employed. 'They're one step or two steps removed from the original employer so it's very difficult to build up a picture of how many are working, in what conditions,' explains Matthew Bolton of campaign group London Citizens. 'Whoever you go to at whatever state of this subcontracting chain, they don't want to tell you.'[291]

These are the working poor. And for them life is terrible, in ways that most of us cannot even begin to imagine. Their struggles are not just about money, but dignity. Financial poverty leads to deprivations and challenges that are inconceivable for the rest of us. According to behavioural economist Sendhil Mullainathan: 'There are three types of poverty. There's money poverty, there's time poverty, and there's bandwidth poverty... . One of the things the poor lack most is bandwidth. The very struggle of making ends meet leaves them with less of this vital resource'[292] – a resource essential to performing simple tasks and getting through life. The poor are worse parents; they forget to take medications; they make bad decisions. But it is not about lack of love or skills. It's simply the inability to cope with so many things at once.[293] The rich can buy time in ways the poor cannot; they hire housekeepers, gardeners, assistants, accountants and nannies. They can go 'away for the weekend'; they take holidays. They can afford to take their time when making financial decisions. They can buy a shorter commute by choosing to live near where they work.

Poor people simply cannot afford these tools. When poor people are constantly worrying about money, they neglect other areas of their lives. Scarcity of money affects scarcity of time, which in turn affects scarcity of mental bandwidth. All of these things feed on themselves, leading to worse and worse decision making. And while most of us might take a break when life feels overwhelming, the poor cannot. 'Poor people can't say, "I'll take a vacation from being poor,"' Mullainathan explains. 'It's the same mental process, but a different feedback loop.'[294] This problem is faced by all poor people, of course, not just the working poor. But the working poor feel it acutely, precisely because they spend most of their waking hours working.

We should remember that the working poor are not some 'underclass', bent on cheating the system. Or even teenagers earning a little extra cash in summertime.[295] In 2011/2012, for the first time ever, over half of the 13 million people in poverty in Britain were from working families; 1.42 million of them had part-time work but wanted full-time work. They're not poor for want of trying.[296] Low pay is often bandied about in political debates as a talking point. But just think about it for a minute. Think about it on an individual, human level.

Imagine if it were you. Imagine if you got up every day, worked to the point where you were so exhausted you couldn't move; worked so hard that you felt permanently, achingly guilty that you weren't spending enough time with your children and were missing moments with them that would literally never come again; imagine if you worked like that but your wages were so low that you still didn't have enough to live on. You'd then have to give up even more of your humanity: your independence, and on top of all the other indignities go to the government and ask for a welfare payment – a handout, even though you were working as hard as you possibly could. Imagine how that would make you feel. This is not just any other issue. This is a scandal.

We ended slavery because it was inhuman and wrong. As we saw in Chapter 4, it is time to end animal cruelty, because it's inhuman and wrong. And now I want to show you how we can end the moral scourge represented by the very notion of the 'working poor'. I'm not arguing this on the basis of 'efficiency' or 'growth' or any other numbers-based objective. I'm arguing this because I think it's morally unacceptable that anyone who works should not be able to live off their earnings.

To understand the modern solution, we have to travel back to nineteenth-century Australia.

The policy intervention most obviously aimed at helping to end poverty pay is the government-established 'minimum wage', based on the principle that no one should work without fair compensation. The minimum wage got its start in 1896 when Australians, having just seen the abolition of slavery, resolved to treat all workers with dignity. They believed that it was morally necessary to recognise workers as human beings, rather than costs of production (which is what many, as slaves, had literally been considered as just a short time before). 'It would demean us all,' argued Alfred Deakin in 1896, a legislator in the state of Victoria and later an Australian prime minister, 'if those who made our food and clothing or tended to our comforts and well-being were treated as inferior beings.'[297] By 1907, Australia's minimum wage had become both a beacon for reformers worldwide and a symbol of pride for many Australian citizens.

In Britain, we owe the roots of the minimum wage to none other than Sir Winston Churchill (a Conservative and economic liberal), who as President of the Board of Trade backed the country's first minimum-wage legislation in 1909. In the bill's second reading in Parliament, Churchill put it as well as anyone: 'It is a serious national evil that any class of His Majesty's subjects should receive less than a living wage in return for their utmost exertions.'[298] He would go on in that same year to create wage councils, which protected and set wages in the 'sweated' industries, a reform that would last over eighty years until the Major government of the

1990s.[299] John Major and the Conservatives (including me, as a junior researcher at the time) made the conventional right-of-centre argument against the minimum wage: that it would distort markets, leading to higher unemployment.[300] With the Trade Union Reform and Employment Rights Bill of 1993, Major abolished the wage councils; the only minimum wage at that point in the UK was in the agricultural sector. When Tony Blair and Labour took power in 1997, part of their manifesto was to restore a wage floor, but instead of doing it industry by industry, they resolved to create a National Minimum Wage. In July 1997, Blair created the Low Pay Commission, an independent body that began setting a minimum wage in 1998.[301]

The actual introduction of the minimum wage comprehensively defeated the arguments of those who had opposed it. It seemed to have no negative impact on employment or the economy more generally, and today the idea has all-party support. Yet still, despite a minimum wage, taking full-time and part-time workers together, 5.28 million people in the UK – 22 per cent of employees – live on wages that are considered below what is reasonable to live on. Over a fifth of British employees don't earn enough from their wages to afford the basic necessities of life, from rent to food to utilities to clothing.[302] Even more depressing is that those with low pay find it hard to advance to even slightly higher positions: almost a quarter of minimum-wage workers have remained at that rate for the past five years.[303]

Earning your own living is widely acknowledged as being essential to human dignity, and psychologists have shown that autonomy and independence are vital for well-being. Yet just under 2 million people are working full-time while being paid by their employers at a level they can't live on.[304] These workers are robbed of their essential human dignity. While it's impossible to know exactly how many work full-time or part-time, some 2.3 million in-work British families qualified for Working Tax Credits in 2013;[305] they worked but instead of being independent, they were forced to rely on welfare handouts from the government. How can the minimum wage be an antidote to poverty when it doesn't provide enough to live on?

None of us should feel comfortable with a society like this. The idea that many people in our economy have to work multiple jobs –

tough, physical, and sometimes demeaning jobs – in order to make ends meet is surely unacceptable. Of course, there's a distinction between part-time and full-time: if you work twenty hours a week you shouldn't expect to make the same as someone who works forty hours. But if you work full-time, you should be paid enough to live on – end of story. There will, of course, always be people on benefits out of necessity (like elderly or disabled people), but society, quite rightly, does not expect them to work for a living. Everyone else should. But for moral reasons, never mind economic ones, there should be no such thing as the working poor.

In Australia – way back in 1907 – the minimum wage became synonymous with a living wage when it was defined as such by the President of the Arbitration Court.[306] It's what Churchill meant, too, when he equated a minimum wage with a living wage. But today the minimum wage is obviously not enough to live on. If it were, we wouldn't need to top it up with welfare payments. Wouldn't it be better – more human – if we dealt with this by paying a living wage in the first place?

The 'living wage' is an amount that's enough to live on if you work full time (defined as 37.5 hours per week),[307] based on the costs of food, housing, energy, transport, basic leisure and so on. While there are various definitions, the most prominent one in Britain is calculated by the Living Wage Foundation, which in 2015 assessed the level as £9.15 per hour in London and £7.85 in the rest of the UK.[308]

The HSBC annual general meeting in 2003, with Abdul Durrant's remarkable speech to Sir John Bond, was a turning point for the living wage. A grass-roots community-organising group called London Citizens, based in the East End, had been running a living-wage campaign since the previous year (they had helped buy Abdul the shares which permitted him to speak). London Citizens' campaign now started to bear fruit: HSBC, and soon many others, would adopt a living wage for all staff on their properties – security guards, cleaners, caterers – everyone. Neil Jameson, who helped start London Citizens and was the driving force behind the campaign, convinced many politicians and employers to see not only the moral imperative of paying their workers a living wage but the good business sense it makes. To date, almost 1,200 employers have been accredited by the Living Wage Foundation, including Barclays, Chelsea Football Club, Goldman Sachs, Lloyds of London, KPMG and Nestle,[309] helping around 60,000 people.

But there are still so many – over 2 million working families in the UK – who make barely enough to survive: 85 per cent of all bar and restaurant employees make below the living wage; 70 per cent of retail employees; 40 per cent of carers.[310] Carers! These 'hard-working people', so beloved of the politicians' slogans, are forced to live in the most inhuman way, and worse, for no real reason; trapped there by political inertia and pointless bureaucracy. Let's examine why.

Do the right thing – it pays

There is an assumption that requiring employers to pay everyone a living wage will cost jobs on a massive scale. As the original opponents of a minimum wage argued, higher wages mean higher costs for employers. The fear is that raising the minimum wage to the level of the living wage might increase incomes for some but could reduce employment overall. The scale of the increase – from a current minimum wage of £6.50 to a London living wage of £9.15 and 'rest-of-UK' living wage of £7.85 – is not trivial. If we're serious about ending poverty for working people, we need to address this legitimate concern.

Let's start by looking at some of the companies that have implemented a living wage. KPMG, the global accounting firm, now insists on it for all its employees and contractors in the UK. According to Mike Kelly, who has spearheaded KPMG's efforts, the board at first had its doubts. 'If you *just* looked at the living wage as a pay differential, it's an additional cost to the business,' he says. So they set out to discover where there were opportunities to enhance productivity by recognising the potential value each worker could deliver. 'You don't just look at it as a wage-rate change,' Kelly explains. 'You should look at it as a way to re-engineer your business to become more people-centred.' In addition to increasing the wage, KPMG reorganised job functions. The building's postmen, for example, were put in charge of stationery during the hours they otherwise would be idle between delivery and collection rounds. Similarly, cleaners used to be on two-hour or four-hour shifts, coming in the middle of the night when no one would see them. But for a lot of the square footage of the building, it really didn't matter if they were there during the day. As Kelly says: 'If you change the shift patterns, so somebody can work eight hours rather than work two hours, catch the bus somewhere, then do another two, now that person can construct a career.'[311] Staff turnover dropped from 47 to 24 per cent; productivity increased as staff stayed on longer (not to mention the fact that they were no longer running around on buses from job to job in the middle of the night), and absenteeism declined.

All right, you might say, that's all very well for a high-end professional services firm like KPMG – they charge huge fees, have big profits; they can afford it. But the living wage would never work in a tough, low-cost, low-margin business, right? A business like fast food or retailing, where every penny counts and companies have to cut their costs to the bone in order to survive? I used to think that too. Until I heard the story of Costco.

Costco is a global discount chain – the second-largest retailer in the world.[312] Its business model is simple: huge warehouses, products stacked high, incredibly cheap. (Although don't assume the quality suffers: it has the exact same organic fruit and vegetables as can be found at upmarket stores at a fraction of a price.) And yet Costco pays its workers way over the living wage. Repeat: way over the living wage. In the US, employees earn, on average, $20.89 per hour, not including overtime. And 88 per cent of employees have employer-sponsored health insurance – a big deal in the United States where there is no free NHS.[313]

For Costco, a living wage is good business. In a letter to Congress in support of a higher minimum wage, CEO Craig Jelinek wrote: 'We know it's a lot more profitable in the long term to minimize employee turnover and maximize employee productivity, commitment and loyalty.' Just consider that 70 per cent of Costco's warehouse managers got their start on the floor, stacking boxes and collecting carts. Turnover is 5 per cent for those who have been there over a year. It's easy to understand where the loyalty comes from: Wall Street investors have asked for decades that Costco lower its benefits and wages. Instead, management has increased them every three years. During the 2009 downturn, when retail shops were laying employees off and cutting pay and benefits, founder (and then-CEO) Jim Sinegal decided to do exactly the opposite: he gave workers a raise of $1.50 an hour. According to Costco Chief Financial Officer Richard Galanti: 'The first thing out of Jim's mouth was, "This economy is bad. We should be figuring out how to give them more, not less."'

How much do these 'generous' policies cost? Admittedly, lower profits in the short term. But in the long term this ethos has paid off. Last year Costco made $2 billion in profits.[314] Its share price has more than doubled since its pre-recession peak. And it's not as if Costco is passing on these costs to customers. It has a general policy to mark items up at no more than 15 per cent of their costs. For Costco, the right thing to do – share more of the value workers create with the workers themselves – has made financial sense, and its investors have come to agree.

Of course every company is different. But Costco demonstrates a fundamental principle: that a living wage is not necessarily bad for business. Even in a sector with as slim margins as grocery and discount retailing, paying the living wage will not doom the company or cause people to be laid off, if the management makes the choice to put people first. And this really is a choice: it's not some immutable law of the market, or the stock market – as the positive investor response to Costco has shown – that stops companies treating employees like humans rather than costs.

Think about the money a company makes as a surplus: it can choose to distribute that in various ways. Simplistically put, a company can choose to invest its profits in new technology or innovative processes; it can give that money to its customers in the form of lower prices (or higher value products for the same prices); it can give the money to its shareholders, or it can give the money to its workers in the form of higher pay and benefits. Obviously, most well-run companies do a combination of these things. But what is the balance? At Costco, it's tilted more towards workers. But elsewhere across the economy, instead of sharing their surplus with workers, companies have been choosing to give it to shareholders. Could that be because senior executives' pay and compensation are now so closely tied to their company's share price? Whatever the motivation, the end result is that over the last ten years, companies on the S&P 500 have spent almost 90 per cent of their profits on shareholder dividends and stock buybacks, according to one analysis.[315]

The most frustrating part is that, as we saw with Costco, treating your workers fairly and paying them a living wage can actually help your business and in the long term help boost your share price. It is a lazy assumption, contradicted by the evidence, that putting shareholders first is the best way to succeed in business. It's especially ironic given the example set by one of America's great heroes of capitalism, Henry Ford. Ford doubled the daily wages of his employees amidst a deep recession in 1914, declaring that: 'If you cut wages, you just cut the number of your own customers. If an employer does not share prosperity with those who make him prosperous, then pretty soon there will be no prosperity to share. That is why we think it good business always to raise wages and never to lower them. We like to have plenty of customers.'[316]

He's not alone. Jack Welch, the former chief of General Electric, recently said that maximising shareholder value 'is the dumbest idea in the world'.[317] Paul Polman, CEO of Unilever, has called it a 'cult'.[318] As Ford knew and as we saw with Costco and KPMG, a living wage on its own can make sense from a business perspective. Better paid employees work harder, are more open to changing job roles to suit their company's needs, and call in sick far less – one UK business that adopted the living wage reported a drop in absenteeism by as much as 25 per cent.[319] Employers enjoy higher morale (among all employees, not just the low-paid ones), an improved reputation, and lower staff turnover.[320]

Another objection you hear to the idea of a universal living wage is that while it may be possible for large or even medium-sized businesses, it would be devastating for small businesses. And that matters a lot when so many of the working poor are in the retail and hospitality sectors, where small firms dominate. It turns out that here too, there's no iron rule – it's a question of choice. If you build higher wages into your business plan, you can make it work; the Living Wage Foundation has certified not just big corporations but small and medium-sized businesses too. Faucet Inn, a small chain of pubs in southern England, is a good example. According to Richard Stringer, the Group's operations director: 'Committing to the living wage is a real opportunity to give more to your staff to ensure that everybody who works for [us] has a balance of work and home life and family life.'[321]

In the US, campaigns against poverty pay are succeeding in a number of places. Seattle, San Francisco, Santa Fe, Washington DC and the State of Maryland have all instituted living wage laws. And these are some of America's most thriving economies. A living wage is not a pipe dream; mandating it (at least for large companies to start with), is possible. A mandate would have the added benefit (which voluntary initiatives like the Living Wage Campaign don't), of not giving some companies an unfair advantage over competitors.

But still, as we saw in Chapter 1, people are irrational. No matter how much evidence you provide, or how many case studies you cite, people will ask: 'How can we afford it?' Business lobby groups will oppose it. Media organisations will condemn it. Politicians won't challenge them. So if we really want to make this happen, we need to make it easier for businesses. Happily, there is a solution: let's call it the 'business-friendly living wage'.

The debate over low pay and the working poor captures only half the argument. It's not just about wages. It's also about taxes – business taxes. Think about what an inadequate minimum wage is. It allows a company to pay workers less than they need to live, because the government will make up the difference through welfare payments. A minimum wage that's too low for people to live on is actually a subsidy to business. In policy circles, the fashionable vehicle for these subsidies is the concept of the 'tax credit' paid to low-wage workers, called the Working Tax Credit (WTC) in the UK and the Earned Income Tax Credit (EITC) in the United States. These give unemployed people incentives to take low-paid jobs instead of welfare. They have partly achieved that aim and done some good in lifting people from poverty,[322] but studies have found that both the Working Families Tax Credit (the predecessor to the WTC) and the EITC benefit some demographic groups at the cost of others.[323] Other research shows that while wage subsidies like this can increase employment, they also depress wages by allowing employers to pay less: one American study found that for every dollar spent on the EITC, only 28 cents were a net benefit to the recipient; 72 cents were captured by the employer in the form of lower wages paid.[324]

In the end, the problem with these schemes is that it's still the government topping up low pay – a subsidy to the employer and an insult to the worker. It's especially shocking that free marketeers and conservatives seem to support these subsidies to businesses, presumably because they are branded 'tax credits'. What a triumph of spin. But it doesn't make it right. And the really mad part is that at the same time as receiving wage subsidies from the government, companies are paying employers' taxes to the government. This is an insane merry-go-round of money: a company pays low wages to its workers; it pays tax to the government; the government then takes the tax and gives it back to the workers because they can't live on their wages.

Let's just list the ways in which this is economic, political, social, moral madness. Economically, it's an unfair subsidy to big business paid for by their workers and by taxpayers. Politically, it contributes to the need for a vast bureaucracy to slush money around the system with nothing but negative consequences. Socially, it perpetuates cycles of welfare and a loss of human independence and dignity. Morally, it invalidates the work of millions of people on whose labour society depends.

Here's a simple way to end it: let's introduce a National *Living* Wage, and cut employers' taxes by the same amount they're paying in higher wages.

In the UK, the Working Tax Credit (WTC) is funded by both employee and employer contributions to National Insurance. While a significant proportion of National Insurance contributions go to pensions and the NHS, they also go to topping up underpaid workers. Between 2012 and 2013, 2,295,000 families received a total of £7.1 billion in WTC benefits, an average of £3,094 per family.[325] According to the Living Wage Foundation and Resolution Foundation, a living wage would increase tax and National Insurance receipts by £2.8 billion. At the same time, many underpaid workers would no longer need as much or even any government welfare to 'top up' their insufficient income. With the accompanying reduction in welfare bureaucracy, it's estimated that the government would save £1.4 billion. Altogether, a living wage would actually have a net positive fiscal impact of £4.2 billion per year.[326] Why don't we take that £4.2 billion and use it to help make the living wage affordable for business? The Resolution Foundation estimates that it would cost business £6.5 billion.[327] If we used that £4.2 billion to reduce companies' National Insurance contributions – perhaps starting with small or medium-sized firms who could least afford a living wage – those refunds would bring the overall cost to business down by almost two-thirds, to £2.3 billion. It's not perfect, but it's a start.

Of course, the introduction of a business-friendly living wage would not do very much about inequality. There will always be a distribution of income, with some at the top and some at the bottom; there will always be a range of 'quartiles' and 'deciles' as the statisticians call them. Some people, with valuable skills and entrepreneurial ingenuity, are rewarded for their talents and contributions to society. Wealth that rewards work and talent is fair and to be expected. In that sense, nothing will end inequality; nor should it. But in the current debate about poverty and inequality, the two concepts are unhelpfully lumped together. If you look at it from a more human, more practical perspective, and recognise that there will always be some people who are poorer than others, why can't we just make sure that even the poorest workers live in dignity?

The causes of poverty

It will take more than a living wage, though, to end poverty. In far too many cases, poverty is generational, handed down like some perverse inheritance within a family. To end poverty, we need to break that cycle. While economic policies can help fight the symptoms of poverty, it is social policy that will help us fight the causes. That has to start with children – like Sasha.

Sasha lives in Bayview, one of San Francisco's poorest communities. Violence is rampant not only in her neighbourhood (she knows three people who have been murdered), but also in her home: her father drinks, and when he's drunk, he hits Sasha and her mother. He's in prison, but the fact that he's not there to abuse them is the only good thing about his absence. Sasha's mother had to work evenings to make ends meet, but because she couldn't find a babysitter for Sasha, she lost her job, and with it, the income to pay the rent. Now they live in subsidised housing, but before that they were homeless for several months. Meanwhile, Sasha – ashamed of herself and her family – is almost always tense with her mother who is depressed (but unable to get effective mental-health treatment because of her lack of insurance). Sasha has a hard time focusing in class, so she misbehaves: she is jumpy and often overreacts to provocation. She was recently suspended for kicking another girl. Her action wasn't justified, but she thought she was being threatened, and after a life in her shoes, it was the only way she really knew how to respond. Sasha is eleven years old.[328]

She is also a patient of Dr Nadine Burke Harris, a local paediatrician. Born to successful Jamaican immigrants, Burke Harris grew up in the wealthy suburb of Palo Alto, about an hour's drive south. Her medical training took her to some of America's best universities: Stanford, Harvard, Berkeley. Yet when she chose where to locate her medical practice, she came to one of the country's most difficult neighbourhoods.[329] Soon after setting up her paediatric clinic in Bayview, Burke Harris grew uneasy. She knew, as we all instinctively do, that being poor is not good for anyone's health. It's difficult to eat right; sleep is often disrupted; taking exercise is harder. But even these basic realities couldn't explain the common health problems she was seeing across her patients – conditions like asthma, learning disabilities, behavioural issues – far in excess of what was normal for children at their age. She began to wonder if these conditions were somehow connected to the children's challenging circumstances. What if her patients' health problems were actually symptoms of something deeper? Something more structural in their lives?

Toxic stress

In 1985, Dr Vincent Felitti was running an obesity clinic in San Diego, California. And he was stumped. Around half the patients who were participating in the programme (designed for those who were at least 100 pounds overweight) were dropping out, and he wanted to know why, especially as they were successfully losing weight. He decided to ask them. He brought a couple of hundred of those who dropped out of the programme into his clinic and asked them a standard set of questions, like: 'How much did you weigh when you started first grade?' 'How much did you weigh when you started high school?' 'How old were you when you married?' For a while, nothing unusual surfaced. Then he made a mistake.

'I misspoke,' he remembers. 'Instead of asking, "How old were you when you were first sexually active?" I asked: "How much did you *weigh* when you were first sexually active?" The patient, a woman, answered: "Forty pounds."' Not quite understanding her, he asked the same question again. Her first sexual experience, it turned out, was with her father when she was four years old. Felitti was dumbfounded. 'I remembered thinking: "This is only the second incest case I've had in 23 years of practice."' So he continued the line of questioning with others. 'About 10 days later, I ran into the same thing. It was very disturbing. Every other person was providing information about childhood sexual abuse. I thought: "This can't be true. People would know if that were true. Someone would have told me in medical school."'

Still not convinced he wasn't somehow biasing his patients, he asked other doctors at the clinic to ask the same thing. Sure enough, of the 286 people interviewed, most of them had been the victims of sexual abuse. For some, eating was a coping mechanism – a 'drug' that made them feel better, soothing depression, anger, fear. For others, being overweight provided a form of protection: in the case of one man, it had prevented other kids from beating him up in the school yard. For one woman, being fat made her an undesirable rape victim (when she was seven, her father told her the only reason he wasn't abusing her sister was that she was fat).

While many doctors were sceptical, Felitti found allies in Dr David Williamson and Dr Robert Anda, epidemiologists at the US Centers for Disease Control. After years researching childhood trauma, determining which questions they would ask, and setting up the questionnaires, they began a trial in 1995. By 1997, they had asked over 17,000 patients passing through a San Diego clinic about ten types of childhood trauma – including sexual, verbal and physical abuse, family dysfunction, and emotional and physical neglect. They would then try to draw correlations between childhood circumstances and health conditions.[330]

The home environment, they discovered, played a crucial role in the health of the people they interviewed – particularly the children. Of the ten specific adverse childhood experiences (ACEs) that they asked about, some two-thirds of the study participants had had at least one.[331] The doctors created a simple scoring system: one point for the presence of each type of ACE in a child's life. For example, if your parents had divorced during your childhood, you had a score of 1. If you were abused and had divorced parents, you had a score of 2. And so on. As traumatic experiences added up – as the ACE score increased – the worse the health outcomes. In the 1998 article in which they published their results, they wrote that compared to someone who had had no ACEs, someone with an ACE score of 4 was 3.9 times more likely to have emphysema or chronic bronchitis, 2.4 times more likely to have hepatitis or jaundice, 1.6 times likelier to have had skeletal fractures. They also found a significant relationship between ACE scores and risk factors for heart disease, liver disease and cancer. Those with an ACE score of 4 or higher were 2.2 times likelier to smoke, 1.6 times likelier to be obese, 4.6 times likelier to have been depressed in the past year, and over 12.2 times likelier to have ever attempted suicide.[332]

Nadine Burke Harris's own experiences in her Bayview clinic – and her hunch that something deeper was going on with her patients than just the symptoms of poverty – led her to Felitti and Anda's research. She realised she was witnessing ACEs taking place ... in real time. Those problems her children were encountering had little to do with health per se: they had everything to do with the family environment of the children. Sasha's domestic problems – the alcoholic father who physically abused her and her mother; the violence and murder all around her – these were not just unfortunate coincidences alongside her health problems. They were their cause. And the connection? A phenomenon called toxic stress.

Not all stress is bad. 'Positive stress' is a mild response to a challenge or exciting event, like an exam or a big sports match or public performance. While it might not feel great in the short term, experiencing positive stress as a child can help build strength and grit. 'Tolerable stress' is severe and negative, but is usually in response to a one-off event, like a death in the family.

If managed with the help of a caring adult, a child can overcome tolerable stress. But 'toxic stress' is different. It is toxic – literally poison. Defined as the 'extreme, frequent or extended activation of [the body's] stress response without the buffering presence of a supportive adult',[333] toxic stress is exactly what you would imagine is created by those Adverse Childhood Experiences – ACEs. In the absence of any compensating warmth, love and affection from at least one parent or primary caregiver, it creates physical, molecular changes in the brain.

When the body senses stress or anxiety, it activates defences that cause chemical and physical reactions. With positive or tolerable stress, this is not a problem because it is temporary. But repeated stress disables the ability to respond correctly. 'If you are growing up in an environment where there are constant threats, the brain adapts in a way that reacts to those threats,' explains Burke Harris. Children exhibit relatively minor symptoms like the inability to sit still. But as adults, they become unable to cope and wind up behaving destructively. 'When we were evolving, the threats were sabre-tooth tigers and lions and bears and this made a ton of sense,' says Burke Harris. 'Whatever it is you'd have to jump on it and beat the crap out of it in order to survive. Nowadays when you do that you end up incarcerated or if you're trying to sit still in a classroom and the kid next to you hits you or pokes you then you end up getting kicked out of class. What we see in children who are experiencing toxic stress is tremendous difficulty in self-regulation.'[334]

Children with toxic stress have higher levels of the long-term stress hormone, cortisol, in their brains. This is a particular problem for younger children because of neuroplasticity (the way our brains physically change and evolve). Neuroplasticity isn't unique to stressed children – everyone's brain architecture and chemistry are affected by experiences. But children younger than five years old are especially vulnerable to environmental stressors. This is because there are two types of neuroplasticity. One is synaptic plasticity (the strength of connections between brain cells); this occurs throughout our lifetimes. The other is cellular plasticity (the number of those connections), which occurs primarily in the first five years of a child's life. Toxic stress – elevated levels of cortisol in the brain – disrupts that development and can cause long-term damage. For children, failure to inhibit the stress hormones in their brain inhibits their own maturation. This permanent, toxic stress leads not just to bad health outcomes for children, but bad life outcomes that are at the heart of the fight against poverty.

The costs of poverty

Welfare costs the UK £120 billion per year.[335] Addiction costs £36 billion.[336] Child poverty costs £29 billion.[337] Educational failure costs £20.2 billion.[338] Crime costs £17.1 billion for the criminal justice system and an additional £24 billion in social and economic costs.[339] These social problems are overwhelmingly concentrated amongst the poor. As the saying goes, some of this 'will always be with us'. But so many of these costs would be reducible, avoidable, if we took more interest in their deep, structural causes rather than just (expensively) addressing the symptoms. This would mean addressing poverty on a more human level, concentrating on the individual person from their very earliest days, and how they end up part of a 'social problem'. All those big numbers, the costs of welfare, crime, addiction, are comprised of individual people with their own stories and circumstances. And one thing we can now say with confidence is that for a vast majority of them, adverse childhood experiences – and the toxic stress that goes with them – are part of their story; part of their circumstances.

We typically attempt to intervene after kids commit crime or drop out of school, but we fail to prevent these problems in the first place. By the time the 'system' even realises that someone like Sasha exists, she is already deeply in crisis and needs lots of costly help to get out. But if we look at where ACEs (adverse childhood experiences) mostly arise, it's at home, in the family context. That's not surprising: the family is the core unit of life. Families care for each other, teach each other, play together, eat together, love together. Most importantly, families raise children. Generally, happy and successful children tend to come from stable, loving families; troubled children tend to come from troubled homes.

There are caveats, of course. Some people who are extremely successful – and sometimes even happy – grew up in homes that were far from being stable and loving. There's a theory that overcoming early adversity was for many of the world's most successful people a direct spur to their accomplishments. But what we don't know, and will never know is: what if the adversity wasn't a spur but a harness, that they achieved amazing things despite the difficulties they experienced at an early age? Imagine how much more might have been possible. And remember, it's not just about avoiding social costs. It's about the benefits too: the benefits to all of us if children develop in the right way from an early age.

Family first

Here's the big idea. The easiest, most effective, most *cost-effective* way to end poverty, reduce inequality, promote better health and well-being, cut crime and anti-social behaviour, spur entrepreneurship and innovation; the best way to achieve the outcomes we all want for our society and economy; the single most valuable thing we can do in government and outside of it to make the world a better place for all, is to invest in the infrastructure that matters most: the human infrastructure of the family.

Most families work well. In their own different ways they do a good job of instilling the character traits that will help children succeed as adults. All we need to do is help the minority of families where that's not happening to get their act together – to become at least as good as the average. That single change would do more to end poverty and improve our society and economy than anything else. And it is possible. We have done much harder things than this. We have mobilised resources on a much bigger scale, more quickly, than would be needed for this. We have put a man on the moon. We have invaded countries.

Now we can end poverty – the human way, if we choose to make sure all families get the help they need so all children get the opportunities they deserve.

We are getting this so wrong at the moment. We leave it far too late to pay attention to the things that matter. A child's path is a little like steering a large ship. Shifting 1 degree at the start is much easier than making a 90-degree course correction later on, hundreds of miles away from harbour. For children, acting early to make sure they're on track means fewer kids will get into trouble as teenagers or young adults. It's a lot harder to help a delinquent youth or a dropout than it is to help a toddler. Social problems begin early and then multiply. Stress, as other recent studies have found,[340] is contagious, adding to cycles of toxic stress in struggling families. And one of the biggest sources of stress is family structure itself, specifically in the form of children raised without their father (or a consistent father figure) in the home. Men who don't stay around to raise their children are one of the primary causes of social breakdown. In the UK, some 76 per cent of young offenders come from households without dads.[341] Families break at different points, but many do so in part because of the stress of having children – and the experience of family breakdown, combined with the circumstances of poverty, leaves an often indelible imprint on the children affected.

Recall David Robinson of Community Links in East London, and the boy with eleven caseworkers. That story doesn't just make the case for streamlining social services for families; it also points to a broader issue. Even when government tries to help people living in poverty, it often does so haphazardly. The problems of poverty don't neatly stack into whatever programme we've created to tackle them. We've seen throughout this book that in many policy areas we try to compensate for their complexity by putting them into neat boxes – 'silos' in policy-speak – thinking that by simplifying or neatly packaging and assigning them to a particular agency, law, or programme everything will be made easier. This is inherently not human; the human world is a messy place and most things are interconnected.

Many chapters in this book overlap with each other, and that's not a coincidence. After all, you can't solve unemployment without thinking about education; you can't think about health without thinking about food. And no social issue can be solved without thinking about our most fundamental social unit, the family. Instead of helping the boy who David Robinson was working with piecemeal – in school, through his probation officer, and in his after-school programme – those efforts should have been put into a broader context: what is his family situation? What is his home physically like? What were his adverse childhood experiences? Is he suffering from toxic stress? To turn around the lives of troubled children and help them escape poverty for good, we don't just need to streamline the help we give them, we need to provide the right infrastructure for them to succeed; we need to help their entire family.

If we fail to take a broad view of a family and its problems, solutions will only be patches that treat symptoms rather than solving the underlying cause. Poverty stems from multiple things going wrong: perhaps the stress of a difficult relationship or a break-up leads to substance abuse and the loss of a job; perhaps someone who has received government assistance and training can't get a job because she can't afford childcare or transport to work. These problems are all related, and those who suffer them are often least equipped to handle them. If you have a stable income or a good social-support network, a break-up or substance abuse can be overcome. But if several of these things happen at once, the missing support network exacerbates the severity of each problem. For children born into families living under these circumstances, they're swimming against the tide from before they're even born.

All this is made much worse, of course, by the scale and distance of government. The parts of government that typically provide services for families are local authorities responsible for many hundreds of thousands of people. It's no surprise that these large bureaucracies end up putting their own systems and procedures first, often in the name of 'efficiency', and the individual circumstances of real people a distant second.

That's why we need organisations like David Robinson's Community Links and why we should give them a much bigger role in fighting poverty. Community Links has two great strengths. First is its multifaceted, 'hub' approach, combining many services in one place. 'Within the hub model there is no wrong door.' According to Robinson, this improves service and reduces the cost for both the individual and the state.[342] That doesn't mean it does everything, but it is an entry point that allows people who need services to access them in a convenient way in a comfortable setting with people they know and trust. This is the other critical strength of Community Links: relationships matter, and they are more easily built and maintained when not spread across a dozen agencies. They're even more powerful when they are organic and come from a person's own volition. No one is mandated to come to Community Links and so it's a source of trusted counsel rather than suspicion. But in the end, however it's organised or delivered, it comes down to the individual, human level: one person working with one family to help its members get their lives back on track. That simple idea was the starting point for one programme I'm especially proud of having helped start in government.

We knew intuitively – and then once we arrived in government had the detailed research to back it up – that a relatively small group of completely broken families suffers and creates the most problems in our society. These families – around 120,000 of them – cost taxpayers some £9 billion annually (£75,000 per family on average).[343] Their interconnected problems – unemployment, debt, substance abuse, violence, educational failure – read like a template for the adverse childhood experiences Nadine Burke Harris is recording in San Francisco. For decades, government at all levels had failed to get a grip of these deep problems, and I was determined that we would be different. I also knew that a traditional bureaucratic approach would never work. We needed something more human, and I knew exactly the person for the job.

If you want to meet the personification of a 'human' civil servant, meet Louise Casey. A former deputy director of the homeless charity Shelter, she came to prominence when Tony Blair appointed her head of the Rough Sleepers Unit in 1999 to solve the decades-old problem of homeless people sleeping out on the streets of London. She succeeded – and went on to take a number of high-profile social welfare-related management positions in government. Her Wikipedia entry describes her as 'known for being outspoken'. You can say that again.

In 2011, we asked Louise to lead a new Troubled Families Unit with a dedicated budget and very clear brief: £448 million in funding over three years to turn around the lives of those 120,000 most chaotic, dysfunctional families by the end of the parliament in 2015.[344] The crucial difference was the approach: a more human one, focusing a family worker on each of these families. The family workers would be given the training and discretion to respond creatively to the very different, human needs of the people they were trying to help. Louise is clear about why a change in approach was needed: 'On the whole, most politicians think there are two ways to get something done in government. One is to pass laws through Parliament. Of course you can get some change through passing laws, but it's a blunt instrument. The other way is through fiscal change. When it comes to poverty or families, either they think they need to change the laws, i.e. introduce a measure to tackle antisocial behaviour, or they think the thing to do is tax credits.[345]

'Large institutions,' she says, 'operate around numbers and targets; they don't operate around people, behaviour, and change.' But that institutional setting is especially problematic for troubled families and their plethora of problems. 'My families have an average of nine very significant problems and multiple agencies around them each operating within their own systems. It's no shock to me that you can often find over fourteen different agencies running around them.' The approach Louise's team takes is to try to work with families to get to the root of their problems. They recognise that these problems are not based in government, so neither are the solutions. Instead, they try to understand exactly how a family – in all its complexity – is really working (or not, in most of these instances). They work on the family's terms, not the government's. For instance, in many cases a family might be receiving state services that are either unhelpful or counterproductive – so the Troubled Families Unit will stop them. In other cases, they work with local councils, police, health, voluntary and community sectors to ensure coordinated, unduplicated services for families. As with David Robinson's Community Links, taking complexity out of these people's lives is one of the best antidotes to their problems.

Perhaps most importantly, instead of being reactive, the unit tries to be proactive, asking how it can prevent a family falling into further crisis. 'I met this girl who lived a life of abuse, handing it on to her three children. [Since she was a drug abuser, the social workers] said "prevention" and prescribed her methadone so she doesn't go out and shoplift any more. That's not prevention!' Louise exclaims. 'That is too late and not enough done. The problem is no one wants to go about it directly. People think that's judging families: some on the Left don't like it because they think it's judging the poor; some on the Right don't like it because they can't accept that these people need help getting back on their feet and it's not just about getting a job.' This is the whole point: we need to get out of an ideological mindset and think about these people as they are, not as our grand political theories paint them. 'I profoundly think that when you're dealing with people like my families, they need an inspirational, sometimes judgemental mentor,' Louise says. 'You need a human being to enter their lives skilfully, lovingly and to create a connection with them where everyone else has otherwise failed to connect.'

Sometimes, the best person can be found within the family itself. Louise's most profound insight on how best to help troubled families is simple. Most parents – even abusive ones – love their children and are their best hope for a successful childhood. 'I can predict the families that have histories of abuse; they have a lack of boundaries. And so what's in the middle of that triangle is poor resilience, poor well-being, no sense of what's right and wrong, no sense of how to create boundaries and relationships with people, how to love well. People beat people even though they love them.' While there is a line to be drawn and kids should be protected from abusive parents, the default reaction shouldn't be for government to swoop in and alienate them. A child's relationship with their parents is the most important relationship in their life and to sever it without working to repair it first is dangerous and short-sighted. That's why we need a different model that works as much as possible within the communities in which children live, a model where we work on their terms, rather than make ideological and presumptuous pronouncements. That is the point of the Troubled Families Unit and its shift to a more human policy approach. It is already showing results: by February 2015, almost 90 per cent of families that received interventions had been turned around.[346]

There are many more families where children are growing up in generational poverty than the truly chaotic and dysfunctional families that are the focus of Louise's work. Without action we can be pretty sure that the children in those families will be the ones who end up on welfare, in the criminal justice system, or at the very least lacking the opportunities that most of us take for granted. As my former colleague in government, Liberal Democrat policy adviser Richard Reeves, puts it: 'The bigger challenge is to help the millions of parents who are not directly threatening their children, but are nonetheless damaging their long-term life chances by raising them poorly. Targeted interventions often seem to make the most sense in terms of making the best use of limited resources. But precisely because they are targeted, they run the risk of creating a stigma.'[347] When I was thinking about our family policies and how to help this wider group without stigmatising them, an answer came to me in the most personal possible way, in the form of one of the great British inventions – an innovation we can trace all the way back to Greater Manchester over 150 years ago.

The human face of social policy

In 1862, the first health visitors were employed by the municipality of Salford; known in those days as 'sanitary visitors', and introduced in response to the high levels of infant mortality and poor living conditions in nineteenth-century working-class areas. The idea was for trained workers to come into people's homes and develop a trusting relationship with families over time, helping with advice on nutrition, health, looking after young children, whatever a family needed. In 1929, health visiting was made a universal statutory service, and it has evolved considerably over time, including its incorporation into the world of professional nursing in 1945, and then fully into the NHS in 1974. But it was my personal, human experience of health visiting, at the time of the birth of my first son, that convinced me that Britain's long tradition of health visitors could be the centrepiece of a revitalisation of family policy.

The key, as with so many of the most successful policy interventions, is the human touch. Health visitors, who first enter your home at a time of great stress and anxiety – the birth of a child – have the potential to become the single best way to help families with problems, way beyond the immediate pressures of caring for a newborn. As with Louise Casey's approach in the Troubled Families Unit, it's all about the human, personalised connection. I know that many families (particularly those living in big cities) have far from positive experiences of health visiting. Despite its rich and proud history, the service has become inconsistent as budget cuts, a rise in caseloads, and a lack of sufficient recruits has eviscerated the ability of many health visitors to provide anything beyond perfunctory assistance. With a ratio that has grown from an average of one health visitor for every twenty families to one for every 362 – and in some cases as many as 1,142[348] – they can scarcely develop a rapport with families, let alone become trusted advisers. After an initial check or two, their overwhelming workloads often rule out any meaningful interventions except for the worst cases. But this is clearly something that can be changed. Home visiting can be much more than an early-warning system; it can be a central component of a more human family policy.

Home visitors could offer a lot more than just checking that a baby is well fed and looked after: they should be trained for the fully fledged family work that the best of them already perform. They can identify relationship problems, parenting problems, substance-abuse problems, mental-health issues – and then direct families to locally available help and support. It's natural for health visitors to be the primary connection between the state and families. They are already in the home and, unlike other agents of government, are trusted people who have forged bonds with parents and children that can be built upon. They are the human face of social policy.

We know this approach really works. From its origins in the British Industrial Revolution, home-visiting services have been emulated in many other countries. One of the most evaluated social-policy interventions anywhere in the world is the Nurse-Family Partnerships service first developed by David Olds, professor of paediatrics, psychiatry and preventive medicine at the University of Colorado in Denver. It is very similar in intent to the concept of health visiting, although in the United States it has been focused on low-income families since it was conceived in the early 1970s. Now pretty much a national programme, it exists in forty-three out of fifty states, and there is a dedicated national non-profit to help replicate and improve it. A study by the RAND Corporation showed that children in the programme end up being arrested less, while their mothers have fewer children and spend less time on welfare. For high-risk mothers, each dollar invested in Nurse-Family Partnerships produced $5.70 in value.[349]

In the UK, we've seen through the experiences of David Robinson and others that families living in poverty are already overburdened with too many social workers and state agents. A health visitor can be a coordinator of care; when operating properly, a guide to the best that the state, voluntary and private sectors have to offer and the definition of a more human public sector. That's why, in government, we chose to overhaul the health-visitor service by investing in recruitment, training and organisation. If we reinvigorate the programme with a new sense of purpose, along with the resources and staff to bring down the visitor-family ratio, we can revolutionise the practical help that families get, creating a ladder out of poverty.

I wrote in Chapter 1 about the terrible waste caused by government's short-term approach. Our children are not line items on budgets; their childhoods are not measurable in quarterly increments. The early interventions I've described in this chapter are the most effective (and for those who count money, cheapest) way to solve big social problems. But they don't mesh well with the political calendar. Poverty is a complex, difficult issue that takes time, effort, and resources to solve. But the old bureaucratic approach has made little headway – except to expand the bureaucracy. A more human way is better: in the short term, a living wage to make sure that no one who works full-time is poor. For the long term, fighting the causes of poverty through one-to-one help for the families where poverty is a cycle that needs to be broken. Building the right support for families is like the construction of great physical infrastructure: you won't see results immediately, but in the end it will be hugely effective and worthwhile. That's how we will end poverty for good.

CHAPTER 7

INEQUALITY

In many ways, Sebastian Thrun personifies Silicon Valley. A German computer scientist, his career spans success in academia, as a professor at Stanford; industry, as an engineer at Google and founder of its Google X lab; and now in start-ups, as the founder of Udacity, which (as you'll see) is a business aiming to revolutionise how we learn. He is responsible for much of the technology – from self-driving cars to wearable computing – that might represent the future. Sebastian is among the world's foremost authorities on artificial intelligence and automation. But he's worried about the future. On the one hand, technology will make us so productive that the cost of goods, Sebastian speculates, could become almost nothing. We have the potential, he thinks, to reach new heights of human creativity as a result. However, there will be a significant cost:

'The thing I can't wrap my head around with artificial intelligence is its effect of doing away with the value you bring to the table in terms of labour. The ability to contribute is diminishing. There are fewer and fewer jobs where people can go home satisfied in the evening and say I did something amazing today.' That, he thinks is 'eating into the middle class, eating into employment', and will have serious social, economic, and political ramifications. 'The world where people can contribute productively is limited to a small number.' Sebastian's uncertainty reflects the central economic question of our time: what can we do about stalled social mobility and our increasingly unequal society?

The symptoms of inequality

I believe in the positive power of business and the market economy. But something has gone wrong. An economic recovery is happening, but most people are not seeing the benefit. Capitalism doesn't seem to be working at the human level, even though the overall figures tell a positive story. Economic growth no longer lifts household incomes in the way it used to. Since the financial crisis, GDP has recovered (surpassing its pre-crisis size) but median income remains flat. The wealthiest 10 per cent, however, are capturing a greater share of the pie.[350]

The economic forecasters at EY Item Club predict that median pay in real terms will go down from £18,852 in 2008 to £17,827 by 2017.[351] Despite falling unemployment and rising employment statistics, more and more people lack fulfilling, steady work: they are working part-time (and having to rely on a second job or benefits to make ends meet)[352] or are underemployed in jobs that don't use the skills they acquired in the education system.[353] Meanwhile, the prospects for long-term, secure job growth are dim: long-term unemployment has increased as unemployed workers find it harder and harder to return to work.[354] The British economy might have jobs, but these jobs won't fill the long-term void left by an economy hobbled by increasingly low worker productivity[355] and stagnating wages.[356]

One factor is the way businesses account for investment. Recall from Chapter 1 the myopic way we account for infrastructure in government. A similar problem infects business, according to the world's leading management guru Clay Christensen. He describes three types of innovation: empowering innovations, sustaining innovations, and efficiency innovations. Empowering innovations create new sectors of the economy, bringing products and services to the masses in new ways, leading to many new jobs. Think Ford's Model T or Intel's chips. A sustaining innovation is neutral; it improves the empowering innovation but creates few new jobs because it basically replaces it. 'Whenever Toyota sells a Prius,' Christensen says, 'they don't sell a Camry.' He believes it's the third type, efficiency innovations, that are at the heart of our problems. Efficiency innovations allow firms to make the same product for the same customer, but more cheaply. Walmart, according to Christensen, lowers costs by about 15 per cent, but also lowers retail employment in the areas it enters by around the same amount. This is good for consumers but harms the overall economy.

In the 1980s, the spreadsheet was introduced into the daily life of businesses. For the first time, management consultants could pinpoint the different ways to make a profit: invest in innovations that make a profit over time or those that do so quickly. Empowering innovations take years to develop; efficiency innovations might return capital in a year or two. Not surprisingly, executives, with their pay linked to short-term share-price gains, chose the latter. More profits – but fewer jobs. Banks are 'awash with capital' but small businesses can't get funded to expand their enterprises, and our economic recoveries generate fewer jobs each time. According to Christensen, it's the accounting software that has misdirected invest-ment in this way. Higher rewards for shareholders, lower rewards for workers.[357] So if you want someone to blame for inequality, blame Dan Bricklin, the inventor of the spreadsheet. A bit, anyway.

Fifty years ago, many low-skilled and undereducated workers shifted from a stable, decent-paying job in the fields to a stable, slightly-better-paying job in a factory, right out of school. The labour market was 'more flexible', according to American economist Tyler Cowen, 'because the technologies of those times often relied on accompanying manual labor'.[358] Few new jobs today are like that. Princeton economists Alan Krueger, Judd Cramer and David Cho have documented a permanent class of long-term-unemployed workers for whom the main economic policy levers – like tax cuts, or interest-rate changes – simply don't work because they lack the skills to do the jobs that are available.[359] And even higher education isn't guaranteeing success. According to one report, as many as a third of university graduates are underemployed – doing jobs that don't require their degrees.[360]

This – and by extension, inequality – is going to get worse. Jobs already lost in manufacturing will soon be lost in the clerical, administrative and professional classes: doctors and lawyers too. (Despite the training and specialisation that goes into them, many of these careers – both individual jobs and entire professions – will be made obsolete by offshoring, replacement by robots or an algorithm, or both.) A report by Oxford economists Carl Frey and Michael Osborne estimates that some 47 per cent of America's jobs will be lost to automation over the next decade or two.[361] Of those that remain, many will be 'bullshit jobs', according to LSE anthropologist David Graeber:

the kind of jobs that even those who work them feel do not really need to exist. A lot of them are made-up middle management, you know, I'm the 'East Coast strategic vision coordinator' for some big firm, which basically means you spend all your time at meetings or forming teams that then send reports to one another … And then think about the ancillary workers that support people doing the bullshit jobs: here's an office where people basically translate German formatted paperwork into British formatted paperwork or some such, and there has to be a whole infrastructure of receptionists, janitors, security guards, computer maintenance people, which are kind of second-order bullshit jobs, they're actually doing something, but they're doing it to support people who are doing nothing.[362]

These problems of economic inequality are exacerbated by structural inequality. In recent decades, we saw the emergence of something close to a meritocracy in which the best could rise to the top and anyone who worked hard could have a stable, middle-class life. But that is increasingly hard. Globalisation and technology delivered the initial blow, but those who have succeeded in this new world are now piling on their advantages and cementing them for their children through marriage, parenting and education choices. Those who have 'made it' are inadvertently shutting down opportunity for the rest of society. We need solutions to this structural, family-based inequality too.

The big trends

So we know the problems. We see these giant, overwhelming forces that seem to be way beyond the control of any country or government, and we wonder if anything can be done; whether we just have to accept our fate and do what we can to help people cope with the worst effects. We get angry about it. We protest. And over the last few years, as I've seen some of the terrible failings and destructive consequences of global capitalism, I too have been tempted by the arguments of the anti-capitalist, anti-globalisation movement. On many occasions, I have felt emotionally with them. So are they right?

Let's see. Paradoxically, as inequality has become a problem in the West, global inequality is at its lowest rates ever; the number of people in poverty worldwide has been halved in twenty-five years.[363] So to 'stop' or even 'slow down' globalisation (whatever that means) because we fear its impact on ourselves would be selfish and short-sighted. Remember how deep a human instinct it is to trade: we would hurt ourselves not just economically but in our evolution as humans, reversing centuries-long progress as economic cooperation brings humanity closer. Inhibiting globalisation would mean closing ourselves off and moving backwards: less connected, less empathetic, less human. Emotionally I sometimes feel like yelling: 'Enough! Let's stop these out-of-control global corporations and faceless money-shuffling plutocrats gambling with everyone's savings in a luxury casino called the financial markets and go back to a blissful prelapsarian state where we all just grow our own produce and trade with each other in a charming local economy!' But it's really not the answer. It's not rational. Even if it were possible, it would do more harm than good: people would be hurt, mostly poorer people in other countries who are desperate to participate in the global economy that we so lightly disparage.

What about technology then? Does the answer to inequality lie in stopping technology – or at least checking its remorseless advance? This is also an easy conclusion to reach – especially for me, someone who refuses to have a mobile phone (much to the irritation of those close to me) and who is prone to emotionally charged rants about how technology is 'ruining our lives'. Trying to tame technology may also seem the obvious conclusion from the very idea of this book: after all, if we want things to be 'more human'; if we're 'designing a world where people come first', surely we should put human beings and the decent, well-paid jobs they need ahead of the latest 'inhuman' technology? Right?

Wrong. Again, it's important not to let emotions lead us down a self-defeating path. We need to take a step back from whatever contemporary concerns we may have about technology and look at the big picture. We need to remember our history. The moment when I really understood the impact of technology on humanity was when I read the first volume of Robert Caro's biography of Lyndon Johnson, *The Path to Power*; specifically, Chapter 27. There you will find a description of life in the Hill Country of Texas in the 1920s (where the future President grew up), before electricity. It is a vivid portrayal of what life was like for women before technology intervened. Then, the 'drudgery of housework' didn't just include washing clothes, mopping floors, or cooking. It was inconceivably worse:

> *Without electricity, even boiling water was work ... If the source was a stream, water had to be carried from it to the house, and since, in a country subject to constant flooding, houses were built well away from the streams, it had to be carried a long way. If the source was a well it had to be lifted to the surface—a bucket at a time. It had to be lifted quite a long way: in the hills it was a hundred feet or more. And so much water was needed! ... the average family farm used 200 gallons, or four-fifths of a ton, of water each day—73,000 gallons, or almost 300 tons, in a year ... On the average, the well was located 253 feet from the house—[so] to pump by hand and carry to the house 73,000 gallons of water a year would require someone to put in during that year 63 eight-hours days, and walk 1,750 miles.*[364]

Worse, without electric heaters, they also had to haul wood to fuel their stoves. Then there was the lack of refrigeration. Caro quotes one woman: 'We didn't have refrigerators, you know, and without refrigerators, you just about have to start every meal from scratch.'[365] There was laundry day: laundry was done outside by hand in a tub. Imagine physically scrubbing clothes, 'agitating' them like an electric washer, carrying them in heavy wet tubs (three tubs of water per load – and remember how hard it is to get water), then wringing them out, then 'punching' the clothes. This was hard, physical, onerous, labour. 'Living was drudgery then,' Caro quotes one person who endured it. 'Living—just *living*—was a problem. No lights. No plumbing. Nothing. Just living on the edge of starvation. That was farm life for us. God, city people think there was something fine about it. If they only knew ...'[366]

Any time you think technology is a bad thing for humanity, just read those passages and be thankful that you are alive now. Technological progress can free us to spend time on things that are more pleasurable and creative than domestic and professional drudgery. Think about the incredible impact even basic technology, like the washing machine, had on the lives (and life chances) of women. The early- and mid-twentieth century's wave of household innovation meant more time to be human. There is no reason to believe that the technology of today and tomorrow will be different.

Human productivity

So despite sometimes being emotionally drawn to the notion that the answer to rising inequality is to stop, slow down, or reverse the powerful forces (globalisation and technology) that have contributed to it, it's not what I think. On balance, these forces are positive for humanity. So what *is* the answer?

Over the last few years, the debate has focused on education, skills and training – increasing the individual productivity of workers, and the overall productive capacity of the economy as a whole. But our current training infrastructure doesn't do nearly enough to combat inequality and promote social mobility. It's not just that we have a dearth of skilled workers. We have too many under-skilled (but more often than might be expected, overeducated) people fighting for positions at the bottom, because they're not qualified for the jobs at the top. This massive skills gap means we have the paradox of not enough competition for the most highly paid jobs (driving high wages for the few even higher) and tremendous oversupply of low and unskilled workers at the bottom (driving low wages for the many even lower). Our inability to match skills training to economic needs is one of the biggest factors driving income inequality. As *The Economist* put it: 'Boosting the skills and earning power of the children of 19th-century farmers and labourers took little more than offering schools where they could learn to read, write and do algebra. Pushing a large proportion of college graduates to complete graduate work successfully will be hard and more expensive.'[367]

None of this is news. For as long as I can remember, politicians on all sides have been reciting some version of the mantra that education and training are the keys to success in the future, and that we need to equip people with the skills to do well in the twenty-first-century economy. Well, yes. We've been hearing (in my case, saying) that kind of thing for years. Education and training policies have come and gone: new curricula, new ways of organising training, apprenticeships, private-sector partnerships, skills strategies, training and enterprise councils, you name it. The trouble is, none of it seems to have made any difference.

Then I had what is described these days as an 'aha moment'. At lunch in a former schoolhouse in East London in September 2013, Rohan and I were talking about this issue. I was expressing the kind of frustration I've just outlined here: that despite all my instincts, I was feeling increasingly hostile to things that I knew I supported intellectually – the market economy, global capitalism, technology – because on a human level, they just didn't seem to be working. What do we do? His response was that 'training' – a word and policy area that is very much the poor relation in Westminster politics; a subject that rarely gets debated in the editorial pages of our newspapers or leads the agenda on news and current affairs programmes – so much less glamorous a term than 'inequality', really is a big part of the answer. We just need to think about training completely differently, in a more human way, to understand the reality of people's lives. In short, we need an infrastructure that makes it possible for every single adult to benefit from repeated bursts of training throughout their life – by designing it in a way that fits in with their life. More important than that, we need to understand that the barriers are often in the mind, in people's attitude to training. So we need a total change of culture; a shift in which self-improvement isn't just for TV reality shows but a constant process, for people from all walks of life.

As I write this, I am in the midst of readjusting my own career, shifting from policy implementation in Downing Street to teaching at Stanford University and creating a technology business in Silicon Valley. My experience shows how the idea that still dominates education today – that we get trained for our careers in our late teens and early twenties and then are done – is preposterously antiquated. I could never have predicted where I'd be today when I was at university. We are ill-served by a system and a culture that assumes we've filled our brains once we're finished with secondary or higher education.

Changing this should not be a burden: to learn is one of the most human qualities there is. Game designers worked this out a long time ago – video games are addictive precisely because they constantly challenge players to improve, and reward them when they do. Once you've mastered a new level (usually having failed a couple of times first), it's that sense of accomplishment, being recognised for a newly improved ability, that keeps players going – not to mention a temporary high when the chemical dopamine is released in the brain.[368]Achieving competency is an innate psychological need, directly related to well-being.[369] This is learning in action. And it's one of the most distinguishing characteristics between humans and other animals.

But in Britain we start with a cultural disadvantage: the idea that training is more for the tradesman than everyman; it's the plumber who trains, not the chief executive. Where American executives attend business school and executive education to learn and reinvent themselves, for British executives, seeking more education is too often an admission of inadequacy. This attitude starts at the top. The cultural norm in the highest echelons of British society is to glorify the gifted amateur and innate ability; if you work too hard, it's a sign that you aren't talented or clever enough – it's 'bad form' to show you've tried. Honestly. If we ever want people to improve themselves so they can make the most of their potential, we have to move beyond this complacency, this idea that people are 'set' once they finish school or university and start their careers.

The anti-training culture has pernicious effects on all aspects of British society, from politics and the competence of government and administration to the performance of the national football team. (We throw children into playing competitive matches at an early age but woefully underemphasise training them in the basic skills they need to excel.) Every human has within them a desire to learn and improve and it's a terrible competitive disadvantage if the national culture is to mock or denigrate this instinct. If we could get over this hang-up, we would have a better chance of solving so many problems we seem to be stuck with, and look confidently towards the rest of this century instead of grumpily fearing the worst. We have to normalise readjustment and reinvention throughout life. This is the key to social mobility.

Long term, this culture will change if our behaviour changes. And that's more likely to happen if we design our training policies with people's real needs in mind. In further education, for example, the debate is always about fees and funding. But for those who drop out or don't even start, the real barriers are more complex: things like difficulty getting to class, family obligations, health problems, pregnancy, even the burdens of a current, unfulfilling job.[370] Now it turns out that many of these barriers can be overcome by the very thing that automates jobs away: technology.

'Nanodegrees'

Back to Sebastian Thrun. He was an early pioneer of what we now know as MOOCs – massive, open, online courses. In 2012, he decided to put his Stanford Artificial Intelligence course online and was astonished to see that within days 160,000 people around the world were participating. It gave him the idea for his next venture. Udacity is an antidote for the middle-aged out-of-work (or bored in-work) person who realises that in order to be competitive again, they need to learn a new skill, like coding. 'A lot of people in life are stranded because of the lack of lifelong learning,' Sebastian says. In his view, though, learning is only one piece of the puzzle. Accreditation is just as important. Imagine, he says, a teacher who also has computer science skills and wants to leave education to work at a tech company. 'You might be a really great software engineer, but you will never get a job at a company like Facebook because your CV will say "high school, high school, high school". So the model today buckets people in life, with the choices they make early on restricting choices they make later, leading to poverty and social immobility.' That's why training is in fact such a vital weapon in the fight against inequality. We just have to rethink how it is designed and delivered.

Sebastian's solution: Udacity's 'nanodegrees'. Nanodegrees are for those who have neither the time nor the inclination to pursue a conventional degree programme. They are short, online courses for people who want to learn a specific skill, either to be more competitive for a job or to improve on the one they are already doing. Many are created in partnership with employers (like AT&T, a telecoms company) – so nanocourse users know that the skills they learn will improve their employability. Nanocourses are structured with the utmost flexibility: you go at your own pace, on your own devices, and can repeat sections as often as you want. 'Learning for a dedicated period of time in a dedicated physical location is something we can only really afford in our youth when we have no obligations: no family, no kids, no mortgage,' Sebastian says. Nanocourses benefit from technology that allows learners to overcome distance – the first hurdle – but more than that overcome the pace of the traditional classroom, which forces students to go through a course at the same time as everyone else. 'Ideally,' Thrun says, 'you have a teacher–student ratio of one to one, but in any setting right now that's uneconomic.' So Udacity takes advantage of technology to make available the best professors (by circulating their lectures on an almost unlimited scale) paired with the intimate, personalised learning environment that an individual needs. Since there are so many users on each course, Udacity can invest the resources to create the best class possible, while costs per person are still negligible.

As mobile technology advances, its flexibility enables incremental learning any time and anywhere. Thrun likens it to 'toothbrush technology', borrowing a term from Google co-founder Larry Page: something you do for a short time at least twice a day. 'It's individualised in so many ways that people still have the freedom to live their lives in a normal way ... you can learn on the weekends, on the bus, on the toilet even!'[371] Here is an instance of technology making lifelong learning more human. You can see how it could help create a new social norm that training is what everyone does all the time, their whole lives. Like going to the gym, picking up new skills and knowledge should be one of those things you just do as part of normal life: a practical step towards a more mobile society and less unequal economy.

Just as the skills we use will change with ever-greater frequency, so too will our careers. Rather than bemoan this fact, we should design policies that help. The Danes get this. Their policymakers aim not for job security but employment security. Labour law makes it intentionally easy to hire and fire employees; it's a two-way street. Though this results in a large number of dismissals during downturns, it allows firms to adapt to changing circumstances and workers to end up where they can add the most value. A quarter of Danish private-sector workers change jobs each year, but to smooth these transitions the unemployed are guaranteed a relatively generous benefit (up to 90 per cent of a normal salary for the lowest paid workers)[372] as well as education, skills training, or subsidised work placement (if not placement in a new job).[373] To prevent firms from under-investing in skills development (one downside of high employee turnover) 'continuing vocational training' – a hallmark of the Danish system – is generously funded by the state. Individuals can work towards part-time degrees or certificates at universities or training centres.[374] No wonder Denmark has one of the lowest rates of inequality in the world.[375]

It's not just about getting people into work: to address the problems of stagnant wages and inequality we need to boost the skills of already-employed people so they in turn can keep boosting their potential. In Britain, the retail chain John Lewis is starting to think like this. It's a good employer on many fronts, always trying to help its employees ('partners') be more productive. Here's an example: like most large retail stores, John Lewis has armies of delivery drivers bringing online orders and bulky items to customers' doors. As appliances have become more complicated, shoppers have started to pay for items not just to be delivered but installed as well. John Lewis thought: who better to install something than the person already on site, carrying it from the van to the front door? Many delivery drivers have therefore been trained to install the products they carry. Such specialised training 'increases the contribution they are able to make', which, according to chairman Charlie Mayfield, means John Lewis is 'able to pay them more'.[376] It's a simple, practical example of the principle of lifelong training being put into practice. Beyond better pay and productivity, John Lewis's model helps tackle inequality in a practical, human way by giving its employees an ownership stake in the company. That's why they're called 'partners'.

This relates to another factor (beyond business's accounting practices and people's skills and training) that is driving economic inequality: returns to capital are greater than returns to labour,[377] so those who own a piece of the economy benefit much more from it than those who just receive wages. If trends in this wealth gap continue, it might not even matter what job you have; if the only thing you have is a job, you will be falling behind. We should do much more to encourage companies to back employee ownership the way John Lewis does.

By allowing people flexible jobs and the ability to make money from assets they aren't using, many have trumpeted the 'sharing economy' as an answer to the problem of capital being in fewer and fewer hands. It may well be part of it, as we saw with Airbnb in Chapter 5, but there are companies frequently described as being part of the sharing economy where people are 'sharing' not an unused asset, but simply their labour: companies like DoorDash, which brings food from restaurants, and TaskRabbit, which lets people outsource errands and small tasks. Whilst this may be convenient for users of the services, let's not fool ourselves into thinking that this is going to help in the fight against inequality; it may in fact make it worse. As Leo Mirani deftly explains in an article on *Quartz*, this part of the 'sharing economy' is the latest incarnation of an old-fashioned service relationship in places with a large-enough concentration of rich people who are willing to pay for mobile convenience:

Of the many attractions offered by my hometown, a west coast peninsula famed for its deep natural harbor, perhaps the most striking is that you never have to leave the house. With nothing more technologically advanced than a phone, you can arrange to have delivered to your doorstep, often in less than an hour, takeaway food, your weekly groceries, alcohol, cigarettes, drugs (over-the-counter, prescription, proscribed), books, newspapers, a dozen eggs, half a dozen eggs, a single egg. I once had a single bottle of Coke sent to my home at the same price I would have paid had I gone to a shop myself.

The same goes for services. When I lived there, a man came around every morning to collect my clothes and bring them back crisply ironed the next day; he would have washed them, too, but I had a washing machine.

These luxuries are not new. I took advantage of them long before Uber became a verb, before the world saw the first iPhone in 2007, even before the first submarine fibre-optic cable landed on our shores in 1997. In my hometown of Mumbai, we have had many of these conveniences for at least as long as we have had landlines – and some even earlier than that.

It did not take technology to spur the on-demand economy. It took masses of poor people.[378]

San Francisco, where many of these services originated and are now based, Mirani points out, has more severe income inequality than Mumbai does. So let's not kid ourselves: much of the sharing economy is simply a modern version of the service economy. While parts of it can indeed give people a stake in the economy, it will only ever be part of the solution.

The causes of inequality

Training, lifelong learning – even parts of the sharing economy – might alleviate some of the problems associated with rising inequality. But we need to go deeper. We saw in the previous chapter that for many, poverty has an immediate and straightforward solution in the living wage. But for those for whom poverty is not just about a lack of money but dysfunction at home, we saw that we have to look to more structural roots; longer-term solutions like interventions in the family. Inequality likewise has symptoms and causes. An economy-wide skills mismatch is a symptom whose solution is more and better training, but its causes are much deeper; indeed, we've already discussed two of them: technology and globalisation. But as we've also discussed, to attack either of these would do us more harm than good. Interestingly, there is a third cause of inequality, potentially more pervasive than the other two combined. It is structural, often family-based. And this one warrants vigorous attack.

Today's debate around inequality often focuses on 'the 1 per cent', the bankers and CEOs making millions or billions of pounds for often no justifiable reason. While they certainly contribute to inequality overall, they represent just a small part of the problem. The wider affluent classes: the lawyers, doctors, engineers, and middle-tier executives – often products of public schools and Oxbridge – are also contributing to inequality, but their contribution is less financial than cultural and behavioural. They are entrenching privilege for their children.

With all their environmental advantages – from safe neighbourhoods to good nutrition to access to tutors, music lessons, extracurricular activities and travel – the children of the rich are lapping their poorer peers, even when the latter are naturally brighter. As the economist Leon Feinstein famously showed, while students from high socio-economic backgrounds with innate ability maintain their trajectory, similar students from low socio-economic backgrounds don't just regress over time, they are eventually overtaken by initially low-achieving children from high socio-economic backgrounds.[379] Affluent children are not succeeding just because of nepotism (although there's plenty of that around), but their success is undeniably a function of the family and social infrastructure into which they are born, an infrastructure that enables them to be exceptionally well prepared for the challenges of the modern economy. The world remains merit-based, but it's a meritocracy in only a partial sense of the word. Yes, the winners are qualified for their positions, but too many losers fall short not for lack of effort or intellect but because their starting point is so far back that they were never really even competing.

Some of this 'affluent glass ceiling' is explicit. Consider professional licences. While obviously a doctor or lawyer should be licensed, it is increasingly common for a licence to be required to practise moderate-skill jobs like being a childcare worker or teeth whitener. In the 1950s, only one in twenty workers needed a licence in America; now three in ten do.[380] Why might this be? Well, as author and commentator Reihan Salam argues, professionals don't want the competition; dentists want to maintain the exclusive right to clean teeth, so they have erected an artificial barrier to those who wish to do it. As a result, those who might enter slightly higher-skilled fields for better opportunities find themselves facing expensive credential schemes and onerous requirements.[381] This has made mobility more difficult while entrenching the privileges of those already occupying these higher-status professions. Inequality is further ingrained when the affluent marry each other. Their 'assortative mating', as it has been called, doesn't just result in high-earning, two-income families, but in brighter offspring, who by inheriting brainy genes from brainy parents inevitably do well in the educational rat race themselves (their test scores, for instance, near perfectly correlate with income).[382]

As a result of all these phenomena, inequality perpetuates itself. Those who are on the winning side of technology and globalisation don't just enjoy those benefits now; they pass them along to their children, creating what *The Economist* calls 'an hereditary meritocracy'.[383] For those displaced in today's economy, the outlook is grim: where your economic station is inherited, the consequences of being adversely affected by technology and globalisation aren't just for your own life, but for your children's and grandchildren's, too. As with poverty, inequality has the regrettable feature of worsening itself. So in the same way, we need to come back to the real source of the inequality: what goes on at home, in the family. Children not born into affluence need better schools and eventually better training, but even more, they need better support from the start. If we're going to fight inequality, chucking bricks at the most successful will be largely futile; we have to narrow the gap by raising up those being left behind.

Family, again

What do the inequities look like in practice? They're small things, really, but they start early and can quickly add up to a profound impact before children even get to primary school. For instance, research shows that hearing lots of words (both in quantity and variety) is important for a child's development. More affluent and educated families speak to their children significantly more often and with a larger vocabulary than their poorer and less educated counterparts. By the age of three, rich kids have heard some 30 million more words than their poorer peers, creating a 'word gap' that leaves poor children academically and developmentally behind.[384] 'Maybe the reason that rich, smart parents had rich, smart children wasn't genetics,' says George Kaiser, an American billionaire working to address these gaps, 'but that those rich, smart parents also held their kids, read to them, spent a lot of time with them.'[385] The resulting inequality is staggering and proves the need for stronger programmes in early childhood.[386]

Early interactions, developmental psychologists tell us, can make a huge difference to a child's well-being. Something as simple as skin-to-skin contact between a baby and its mother is incredibly valuable. According to developmental psychologist Ann Bigelow: 'Particularly in the newborn period, it helps calm babies: they cry less and it helps them sleep better. There are some studies that show their brain development is facilitated – probably because they are calmer and sleep better.' And it helps the mothers (and fathers) too: she says they are less depressed, more sensitive to their babies' cues, and gain better responsiveness from the babies. Another important interaction: simply by responding to infants, usually by repeating motions back to them, parents show their children that they are causal agents and have an interactive role to play in the world. According to Bigelow: 'Seeing [their behaviour] reflected back helps [babies] understand themselves … The more experience babies have with someone who is going to be emotionally engaged with them, the better off they're going to be.'[387]

It's easy to airily assume that all this is known by and comes naturally to every parent. Not at all. Educating, encouraging, and helping parents to interact with their children in constructive ways is step one on the road to a more equal society. We know now that the quality and style of parenting received by a child is a better predictor of success than anything else – including the economic circumstances of the family.

There is not, nor should there be, one 'ideal' family or parenting approach. But there are some circumstances that are more ideal than others. Of course, it's about making sure that children grow up in a loving home, but a word that comes up over and over again in any discussion of child development and family policy is 'stable'. Stability is what gives children the structure within which to grow and develop and thrive; it is one of the best things we can give children, both for their own happiness and flourishing and for that of our society and economy too. That's why marriage is so important, and so connected to the argument about inequality.

Marriage is increasingly the preserve of the university educated and well off.[388] Working-class and non-university-educated women who still want children are now more willing to have them without a father in the home. While many judge women for bringing children into the world in less than ideal situations, think a bit about their situation – especially when compared to their university-educated peers – before forming an opinion: 'College-educated young adults can see a good future, where they're likely to find a good partner, pool two incomes, and they're willing to wait to have kids till they can do that,' according to Andrew Cherlin, a sociologist who's studied long-term family and social trends. Less-educated women, on the other hand, 'don't see the possibility of finding partners with good incomes. And many are unwilling to give up the opportunity to have a child by waiting.'[389] For some of those without a university (or even high-school) education and sparse hopes for career advancement, it doesn't matter: parenthood is the one marker of adulthood they can attain.

Studies have consistently shown that children whose parents are married, or who live together and marry later do better in behavioural, cognitive, and health outcomes than those who just live together.[390] Both groups do better, though, than children whose parents divorce or who never marry at all. Children born into families with delinquent dads fare the worst.[391] And yet stability increasingly eludes us as today's adults often put their needs before those of their children. Family breakdown in the UK has risen dramatically: according to the Office of National Statistics, the divorce rate has nearly doubled since 1971 from 5.9 divorces per thousand married population to 10.8 per thousand. (If you go back further, things really have changed: in 1858, there were only 24 divorces across all of Britain).[392] And as we're divorcing more, we're marrying less: compared to fifty years ago, the marriage rate has dropped from 67 marriages per 1,000 unmarried men to 22.1, and 52.4 marriages per 1,000 unmarried women to 19.9.[393] Parents (mostly mothers), are increasingly comfortable bringing up children not only outside marriage, but on their own.

For the well off and educated, however, their children start life not only with the advantages of wealth and education but also with stability. It's no wonder they leap ahead. For the worst off, the problem of instability is especially acute, which is why anyone who cares about inequality needs to care about finding ways to help parents maintain their relationship in the first place, so broken homes can be avoided. This all gets back to Louise Casey's point from the previous chapter, which is that a child's parents are the best agents for good in that child's life, no matter how imperfect. And as simple a fact as that is, our culture today has tacitly approved separated families. Because the issues involved are so highly personal and intimate, we have hesitated to take a position or make a judgement. If two adults decide they can no longer live together: well, that's their business and no one else's, right?

Wrong – not if they have young children. When the costs and benefits affect everyone – as they do – we can't just privatise this issue. It's a matter of social responsibility, not just personal choice.

We gloss over the real and difficult responsibilities of bringing up a family. You could argue that in the past, cultural leadership on the social responsibility of family life was provided by the Church. But with the decline of faith in countries like the UK[394] (a decline marked not just in lower levels of religious observation but in lower levels of religious leadership – witness the increasingly pathetic and irrelevant men who have been head of the Church of England) a dangerous vacuum has been allowed to develop in how we view these responsibilities. It seems as if the socially acceptable position is to prioritise the personal choice of the parents. But that's the wrong priority. If you care about future opportunity and a more equal society, the interests of children should be the priority.

If it's better for people – and society – when children grow up in stable, loving homes, then a more human way of tackling inequality means accepting that marriage is a vital issue of public policy. But this has often been misunderstood (or deliberately distorted) as a simplistic assertion that married couples make better parents than their unmarried counterparts. Of course that's not true. The argument is about family stability. Marriage is what social scientists call a commitment device. It creates inertia in the relationship, and stable relationships lead to better life chances for children.

The value of a commitment device is never tested more than during the unprecedented stress that arrives with children; child rearing, studies tell us, directly contributes to making already unstable relationships even less stable.[395] 'Children do seem to increase happiness [while] you're expecting them, but as soon as you have them, trouble sets in,' Harvard psychologist Dan Gilbert explains. 'People are extremely happy before they have children and then their happiness goes down, and it takes another big hit when kids reach adolescence. When does it come back to its original baseline? Oh, about the time the children grow up and go away.'[396] While having children strains all couples' relationships with each other, the commitment device of wedding vows helps keeps them together,[397] and this is overwhelmingly in the interests of children unless something terrible is going on. While

37 per cent of cohabiting couples split up by their child's fifth birthday, less than 6 per cent of married couples do. And though marrying after the birth of a child helps, those couples still have a significant gap with couples that were already married before.[398]

What we feel – and increasingly, scientifically know – about child development in the context of family structure is one of the reasons we should support marriage equality. Encouraging marriage is not about promoting some traditional or moral view about what's right or wrong for adults; it's about what's best for children – and the evidence suggests that children are better off being raised by a married gay couple who provide a stable, loving home than by an unstable, unmarried straight couple.[399] Even if you're not persuaded by the evidence in support of the collective benefits of marriage, there's now a strong body of work highlighting the individual benefits. It turns out that marriage is just better for you than the alternative. According to Gilbert, married couples are on average happier, healthier, wealthier, live longer, and even have better sex.[400] (How does he know?)

While many have argued that the link between marriage, happiness and family stability is tenuous – correlation rather than causation – new evidence debunks them, showing that marriage leads to happiness and improved well-being. A 2014 paper using data from the UK's Annual Population Survey showed that even taking premarital happiness levels into account, 'the married are still more satisfied' and that marriage helps people through midlife dips in unhappiness.[401] According to co-author Shawn Grover 'Marriage may be most important when there is that stress in life and when things are going wrong.'[402] Spouses are friends, and that friendship helps get each other through difficult times. 'The biggest benefits [of marriage] come in high-stress environments,' says John Helliwell, the study's other co-author. 'People who are married can handle midlife stress better than those who aren't because they have a shared load and shared friendship.'[403] Married couples are happier; happier couples are more stable; homes which are more stable give children a better chance to rise. That's why the growing marriage gap between the rich and the rest is so alarming.

It goes without saying that there are circumstances in which single parenthood is the better option. A parent in an abusive relationship should get out of it, in the interests of both themselves and their child. But we need to work to avoid those drastic outcomes. Being in a relationship is hard; being a parent is harder and more stressful. While children can bring out the best in us, they can also bring out the worst, especially when there are underlying tensions between a couple that bubble to the surface.

Today there is unnecessary stigma attached to relationship support, but if society considered the taking of professional relationship advice as a sign not of a bad relationship but a good one, we would go a long way – in a very human way – towards strengthening family stability across our whole society and helping improve the life chances of every child. Even the couples with the best relationships could use a bit of outside perspective to help them get through the most tumultuous times.

Another important change that would reduce inequality is a greater expectation of shared parenting. Our social norms around family life have failed miserably to catch up with the transformation in the role of women in society and the economy over the last few decades. This is the cause of much of the stress that undermines many marriages today. As former high-flying US government official Anne-Marie Slaughter points out, while mothers feel obliged to put their families ahead of their work, men are often praised for their sacrifice of home life (and valuable time with their children) in service to their careers. 'Why should we want leaders who fall short on personal responsibilities?' Slaughter asks. 'Ultimately, it is society that must change, coming to value choices to put family ahead of work just as much as those to put work ahead of family.'[401] This is exactly right; professional culture must value family life for both mothers and fathers. Let's make it easier for mothers to be professional women and for professional men to be fathers.

Generous paternity leave would be a good start. The first few weeks and months after a child is born is when a renegotiation of domestic duties take place; if the mother is at home and the father at work, the mother often ends up by default taking over more domestic duties. By sharing those duties with fathers, mothers get a fairer deal in the long run.[404] Paternity leave also helps mothers avoid the stigma of new motherhood in the workplace. Mothers often face brutal challenges upon having children, with workplace policies and cultures that make it difficult if not impossible to resume their careers. Those with access to paid maternity leave are likelier to return to their prior employer, and 97.6 per cent of them make the same salary or more upon returning. On the other hand, 30.6 per cent of women who have to change where they work experience a pay drop.[405]

But paternity leave at the start isn't enough; we need to help parents spend time with their families throughout their growing up. If both parents (especially fathers) continue to make efforts to share parenting and household duties, it will make for a happier and more stable marriage (which is in turn good for their children, both now and in the future).[406] This means better family leave and giving workers more control over their hours so they can choose what to prioritise. For example, while we have plenty of evidence from neuroscience and elsewhere that the early years of a child's life are crucial, we mustn't neglect other important stages. Parents with teenagers know that it's actually in those later years (when emotional and physical development can cause all sorts of problems as well as joys and opportunities), that children need their parents around, just to talk to them, spend time with them. Inequality can be rooted in something as mundane as how often a family eats together.[407]

Employers tend to see paid family leave as harmful to business. But in a study of California's family leave law, the authors found that 'the vast majority of employers reported that it has had a minimal impact'; indeed, some employers even reported cost savings.[408] While maternity leave doesn't hurt business, the lack of paternity leave does harm women. Many are cast aside for promotion ahead of time, because their bosses know they might soon be taking anywhere from a few months to a few years off.[409] If fathers took similar leave, such discrimination would obviously decline; after all, if everyone who became a parent took leave, there would be less reason to discriminate against the mothers who biologically have to. Obviously mothers (and fathers) might choose to remain at home in the long run – that's a perfectly valid choice – but in an age where women are breaking down barriers in the workplace, shouldn't the norms around parenting change too? While maternity and paternity leave don't seem like issues of inequality, they really are: they can help close the gaps between upper-income and lower-income families and between men and women in the workplace.

Helping parents

Precisely because being a parent is so hard, there is not one parent in the country who would not benefit from better information and support on parenting. In fact, let's not beat around the bush, there's not one family, not one parent, who wouldn't benefit from parenting education.[410] But even more than the stigma attached to training that we saw earlier in this chapter, or the stigma attached to seeking relationship support, the stigma associated to parenting and anything that sounds like 'parenting classes' is massive. That is a terrible shame, a silly prejudice that has a direct impact on inequality. Octavius Black, founder of an excellent new parenting programme in the UK, Parent Gym, observes that 'challenging someone's parenting skills is one of the strongest challenges to their identity';[411] it smacks of government intervention and the nanny state. But so many lives would be improved if it was as normal to learn about being a better parent as it is to learn how to drive. It's already seen as completely normal to buy parenting guides, to read the books and magazines – there are even parenting apps. But there's something about parenting classes that is socially unacceptable – a fear of looking foolish in front of others, an admission of incompetence, or even a punishment.

I saw this first hand when I was developing our family-policy agenda in government. As you'd expect, I spoke to experts in the theory of parenting education, and worked with some fine civil servants with fantastic knowledge and commitment. But nothing was as striking for me as attending some classes in person. Even though I was there for the purposes of policy research, I took part myself (I could hardly just sit at the back taking notes if I were really trying to understand the experience). And I learned, even in a few two-hour sessions, incredibly useful tips and techniques that have made a real, practical difference. The most amazing thing, though, was talking to the other parents afterwards. Without exception, they used the same phrase to describe the experience: 'This has changed my life.' Perhaps most interesting was the testimony of parents who had been sent to the classes by a court or local authority or some other arm of the state because their children were considered out of control. These parents were even more enthusiastic than those who had signed up voluntarily, but they all told me some version of the same story: 'I had to be dragged kicking and screaming to come to this but after the first one I could see it would change my life.' (That phrase again); 'I wish someone had told me about this years ago, it would have changed everything.' Another parent recounted through tears how her relationship with her seven-year-old son had completely transformed just over the course of the eight weeks she'd been going to the sessions. One reason seems to be a very human one: the fact that you're there with a small group of other parents. You can be honest about your anxieties and learn from each other. Everyone has trouble with parenting; there's great relief in realising you're no worse at it than most people.

Parenting courses are not incredibly onerous, but they are a commitment. Typically, the ones that work best are eight to ten weeks long, with a one-and-a-half or two-hour session once a week, run by a professional coach for a group of around ten parents at a time – either couples or lone parents. Some take place in the evenings; some use school facilities and run classes for parents in the mornings after they have dropped their children off. There are many, many providers of parenting classes, and as you'd expect, some are great, some are all right, and some are terrible. What we need to see is a massive opening up and 'mainstreaming' of this market – a little like the exercise and fitness market, perhaps. There was a time when there were practically no gyms anywhere except in schools, universities and army barracks: now they're everywhere. There was a time when having a personal trainer, yoga teacher or some other kind of fitness guru meant that you were a Hollywood celebrity or multimillionaire; when the idea of going to an exercise class was right up there in the weirdness stakes along with eating organic food and drinking herbal tea. Now all this is becoming mainstream, and my question is: if it's socially acceptable to learn how to look after ourselves, don't you think we might take the same approach when it comes to looking after our children?

In government, we took a small step in that direction with a pilot programme in 2012. The idea was to help stimulate a market for parenting courses by giving people vouchers that they could spend with approved providers in their area. To reduce the stigma and make the whole thing seem normal and not part of some welfare scheme, we worked with Boots, which helped give out the vouchers in their stores. The pilot was broadly successful, increasing both demand and supply for parenting courses, but perhaps more importantly, it did actually decrease their stigma.[412] Nonetheless, public awareness is still low and we have much more work to do to create a culture more receptive to parenting support. Here's the bottom line: we need to make parenting education aspirational. Instead of being seen as something that's done to you by the government because you're a bad parent, it needs to be something everyone chooses to do, because it's part of being a good parent. This single change could be the one that makes the most difference to long-term, structural inequality.

Combining these family interventions with the new approach to training that we saw at the beginning of this chapter would grow opportunity. But failure to get this right reinforces inequality, one of the most urgent questions of our times. Technology is making obsolete many tasks once done by people. And those who have the resources and education keep entrenching their advantages while those who don't, fall behind. The former is an inescapable fact. The latter is not.

Rather than lament change, we should embrace it as a chance to make work more human and opportunity more abundant. We once washed clothes using washboards; now we have washing machines. We once stoked furnaces by hand with coal; now we fuel furnaces through gas lines. Have we suffered for it? No, we've become only more prosperous. Let's forget those inhuman jobs and instead focus on the skills that are most human and create our economies around them. People are innovative, they are creative, they are caring, they are nuanced. Let's create an economy that embraces these qualities. We should be happy to rid ourselves of the automated, mind-crushingly boring, administrative, cubicle jobs and the back-breaking, dehydrating, physically dangerous factory and agricultural ones; wouldn't those workers be the first to agree that they'd be better off if they did something that engaged them as people, not workhorses? They would be better off in terms of wealth, health and general well-being, but so would the rest of us. Imagine how advanced our world would be if everyone had the chance to innovate, create, be entrepreneurial, share their passions. We'd be far richer in every conceivable way.

This will only happen, though, if, on a fundamental level, we shift the way our system works. No one would argue against more tailored training, more lifelong learning, or more attention to the skills that will build resilience in a new, dynamic economy. But such a shift within the existing system will just make things incrementally better. We must completely rethink what training means to society as a whole. Training has to become the normal thing to do. Yes, a CEO's experience will be different (in content and context) than a factory worker's, but both should continually seek improvement, and we should help them attain it. Just making training available (even if completely subsidised) is not the whole answer. It has to be relevant and engaging. It has to be enjoyable, convenient. People are on their phones all day – because the content there is engaging. Those who join sports leagues or music groups practise for hours on end both because they want to do well themselves but also because they don't want to let their teammates down. Learning can be just as addictive, just as socially rewarding; but we've settled for tedious books, tutorials, and lessons, because 'that's just what learning is'. Sebastian Thrun tells the story of one student who became so engaged with a course that she stayed up all night to complete it. Now, I don't advocate insomniac learners, but shouldn't this be where we set the bar?

The debate around inequality is often focused on outcomes: who's rich and who's not. That's the wrong way to look at it. Instead, we should be examining mobility: who is falling behind because they aren't getting a fair shot? Yes, this includes the workers who are dropping out of the labour force because they lack skills; but it also includes their children (and those of the larger middle classes) who are losing out on the chance to get ahead because of their home and family life. Giving everyone the chance to compete fairly and on the same terms is the very essence of a democratic market economy: that's a meritocracy.

No one wants to see a society with a few people at the top doing incredibly well and everyone else struggling – but that really seems to be where we're heading. We can go in a different direction if we cast the inequality debate in more human terms: making it normal for every individual to train and gain skills all the way through life; giving better support to parents so we bridge the gaps between the least-well-off and best-off children. That is the basis of a more human economy, where opportunity is more equal.

CHAPTER 8

CHILDHOOD

Children are vulnerable, so we protect them. Children need nurturing and guidance, so we put their needs first. These are basic, human instincts – but today we're getting childhood all wrong: simultaneously over-protecting and under-protecting.

It's human to fall in the playground and hurt yourself; it's human to be lost or bored. If we over-protect our children, we inhibit their development, mentally, physically, and emotionally – and risk them developing unhealthy fears and behaviours. But it's also human to be a child during childhood, and while we're over-protecting children's play with ridiculous, risk-averse health-and-safety measures, we are at the same time under-protecting them, allowing children to experience the adult world prematurely because we're too lazy to properly invigilate or too weak to say no. We think we're being kind, but we're doing real and lasting harm.

There is a particular problem with technology. Devices have brought children entertainment and education, but they've also erased the boundaries between the child and adult worlds. We need better policing of the border between children and technology, because unconstrained, unlimited access to the Internet prematurely exposes children to unhealthy sexual norms, inhibits their cognitive abilities and disturbs normal social interactions. Perhaps worst of all, technology is resurrecting old ideas of misogyny, setting back one of our society's greatest recent achievements.

Let's not blame 'kids today' for these trends: it's our fault for putting up senseless boundaries while failing to set up sensible ones. But it's not too late; we can turn things around. We need to – because children are humans, too.

Over-protection

Berkeley, California is famous for its world-class university, periodic outbursts of student radicalism, and – if you care about food and where it comes from (see Chapter 4) – for Alice Waters's pioneering restaurant Chez Panisse. But there's something else Berkeley ought to be famous for: the most extraordinary and wonderful children's playground you've ever seen. The Berkeley Adventure Playground is built by the people who use it, constructed of salvaged wood, old rubber tyres, scraps of sails – all decorated with graffiti-like smears of paint. Enter with your young children and you are handed a container of nails and a hammer. Walk around and you'll see children as young as six and seven sawing pieces of wood. No safety equipment. No bossy rules. Just families having fun, being creative, and above all being human. All this in the land of the waiver, the lawsuit and the helicopter parent. It's a little bit terrifying, and it's hard to believe you're actually in America.

The people who run the Berkeley Adventure Playground understand the true essence of children's play. As did British landscape architect and children's advocate Lady Marjory Allen of Hurtwood, who popularised adventure playgrounds in Britain after the Second World War.[413] But in recent years, we've managed to dehumanise it. Whether as parents or policymakers, we have become so irrationally fearful of every risk that we've outlawed and restricted and regulated children's lives to the point at which things seem to be designed more for our peace of mind than our children's recreation and benefit.

This mindset has so conquered our collective psyche that those who want to give their children more leeway are ostracised, even penalised. Brooklyn mother Lenore Skenazy's nine-year-old son wanted to experience some independence, so she and her husband armed him with a MetroCard, some quarters for a phone, $20 in cash and a map – and left him at a department store that sat directly above a station for their local subway line. Forty-five minutes later, exhilarated, he returned home. When she wrote up this positive experience, she was quickly dubbed 'America's Worst Mom'.[414]

Skenazy, a middle-class mother, was relatively lucky in that the only punishment she got was name-calling. Consider the shocking experience of Debra Harrell, a single mother in Tennessee. Harrell is one of the millions of low-paid, over-stressed workers we met in Chapter 6 where we saw the importance of a proper living wage; she works hard to support herself and her daughter but can't afford childcare. Rather than having her nine-year-old daughter sit in the McDonald's where she works all day, Harrell gave her a mobile phone and let her play in the local park down the street. Parkgoers, suspicious of a child playing by herself, reported her to the authorities. Harrell was arrested, charged with unlawful neglect of a child, and subsequently fired. Since Harrell is a single parent, her daughter was then taken from her home and placed in the care of local social services.

What a shameful story. What a terrifying insight into the twisted minds and arrogant overreach of modern bureaucracies. Following a public outcry, at least Harrell now has her daughter and job back. But imagine the ordeal she has had to go through. Imagine how much worse off Debra Harrell's daughter is, living forever with the experience of having an imprisoned mother and spending time in public-sector care. All this because a mother trusted her daughter and let her play outside.

This over-protective attitude is harming children. Whether it's aggressive bureaucracy removing any remotely challenging play equipment from playgrounds, or panicking over the idea that a child might encounter a single germ or piece of dirt, we are cutting away at the basic humanity of childhood experience. By trying to create a risk-free existence for our children, we are gradually shutting them off from the world. Neighbourhoods friendlier to cars than kids; public space appropriated for shopping rather than playing; energy and investment going into superficially more captivating indoor alternatives – particularly involving technology. We ply our kids with electronics to keep them busy (and give us a breather); we prevent them from playing outside because we fear what might happen to them. But we forget that an important part of many of our own childhoods involved engaging in the world, not being 'protected' from it.

Of course to a certain extent, caution is natural and proper: our instincts and emotions guide us to protect our children, after all. But it's gone way too far. The dreary and soulless trend towards the avoidance of any risk reflects good instincts and good intentions that have been perverted by a culture of hysteria, lawsuits, and puffed-up bureaucracies.

'Playground safety', for example, is mostly a solution in search of a problem, argues the play expert Tim Gill in his book, *No Fear*. Despite the occasional sensational headline, serious playground injuries are rare, deaths even more so. The facts show that a child has about a one-in-sixteen chance of being injured in a playground and only a one-in-two hundred chance of receiving an injury requiring medical attention.[415] Nonetheless, when something does go wrong, it is amplified hysterically in the media: tragic accidents are emotional and emotion makes for better stories. But while the overdramatisation of danger to children may generate more clicks, sell more newspapers, keep a few more viewers from turning off the local news, it also breeds fear of previously uncontemplated risks. The result is an illogical debate that leads to unnecessary rules, irrational insurance policies and a whole new miserable, exhausting world of paranoid language, bureaucracy and culture to enforce it all. Parents, terrified for their children, and insurers, terrified of lawsuits, have pushed for new guidelines and regulations on anything that touches children's lives. But since, as Gill writes, 'there was little or no attempt to look systematically at accident data or to place playground accidents in a wider context', these trends merely 'reinforced the idea that playgrounds should be free of risk', leading to policies that put the prevention of any injury whatsoever over the goal of having the best playgrounds for children.[416]

This is terribly wrong. We shouldn't ignore passionate parents, but we shouldn't make policy decisions to mollify them either – because rather than solving problems, parents' unjustified fears have created new ones. Go to any public playground today and you'll see that the equipment is increasingly dull and uninspiring, making playtime less fun and less adventurous. This is not just a shame; it stunts crucial aspects of child development, as we will see. Even worse, some safety rules have actually made children less safe! For example, it turns out that the cushioned safety surfacing often required to be in place to break children's falls is really only meant to prevent serious head injuries – an extremely rare occurrence – and in fact leads to more broken bones.[417]

What's more, safety surfacing is so expensive it means that other more cost-effective ways of keeping children safe are ignored. A cost-benefit analysis found that spending up to £250 million over five years on playground safety surfacing (the amount needed to install and maintain it for Britain's playgrounds) would have saved one child's life during that time. Of course, every child's life is incalulably precious. But imagine how much more agony could be spared if resources were invested in more cost-effective ways of protecting children from genuine danger – such as road traffic, which typically kills well over 150 children and seriously injures around 10,000 over a comparable five-year period.[418] If you want to be statistically brutal (but accurate) about it: making our children infinitesimally safer at playgrounds condemns them to die elsewhere at a much higher rate.

It's important we understand the root causes of all this. It's too easy just to blame parents' emotions, or the media. In fact, insurance companies, fearful of the ubiquitous lawsuit, have instituted guideline changes every time a new safety issue arises. These actions might protect them from litigation, but they mean that every organisation that builds or operates a playground or similar facility has one more rule to comply with. Why? Because if they're sued by a disgruntled parent, someone might point to these 'guidelines' and ask them why they didn't comply. In the age of tighter budgets, staving off a potential lawsuit and making playgrounds as cost-effective as possible is a much higher priority than making them fun and rewarding.

Hard at play – or hardly playing

But play is being undermined and distorted in more places than playgrounds. Our society increasingly sees play as a neat and tidy occupation that should occur in prescribed ways. When children try to break out of these artificial shackles, they – especially boys – are deemed to be 'troublemaking' or 'antisocial' for perfectly innocent offences like making noise, hitting things (and occasionally each other), and climbing trees. Of course there are risks for our children; there always have been and there always will be. But we should focus on the real hazards, not imagined ones. Society has worked itself into a frenzy that the world is ever more dangerous. But it's not true. Consider child abduction: compared to forty years ago, we perceive a growing threat, although it's no more likely to happen than in the 1970s. The odds of a child being kidnapped and murdered by a stranger are one in 1.5 million.[419] We fear that our children might be assaulted by strangers, but they are far likelier to fall victim to an abusive relative or family friend.[420] Instead of working harder to protect children from domestic abuse, we teach them to avoid strangers – the vast majority of whom would be a source of help should they ever need it.

The consequence of these trends is that our children increasingly live and play in a stifling, boring, risk-free world with places that are wild and free – like the Berkeley Adventure Playground – few and far between. Instead of letting them explore parks and meadows, too often we keep children locked up as virtual prisoners of their parents and caregivers. In 1971, 80 per cent of British seven- or eight-year-olds walked to school on their own; by 1990, it had dropped to 9 per cent.[421] 'Today's children,' writes British author Jay Griffiths, 'are enclosed in school and home, enclosed in cars to shuttle between them, enclosed by fear, by surveillance and poverty and enclosed in rigid schedules of time. These enclosures compound each other and make children bitterly unhappy.' We instinctively distrust children, forgetting that they can handle themselves much earlier and far more effectively than we give them credit for. When parents do trust their children, society condemns them. In 2010, writes Griffiths, 'two children, aged eight and five, cycled to school alone and their headmaster threatened to report their parents to social services.'[422]

In our attempts to shield children from risk, we've not just made their play dull, or wasted public money on largely pointless safety measures; we've also inadvertently hampered children's development. The life lessons that come with play are some of the most essential. Amongst other things, high quality, unencumbered, imaginative, and adventurous play teaches children resourcefulness, entrepreneurship, hand-eye coordination, creativity, cooperation and social skills. A sense of adventure is not only an integral part of being a child, it is essential for their biological, human development. When doctors want to inoculate a patient against a disease, they make a vaccine containing a bit of the disease so that the body can identify it and learn to overcome it. This is the only way vaccines work. Fear works in much the same way. If children are to mature by tackling their fears, they have to be exposed to them. They need to take risks when they play. A Norwegian study by early-childhood education professor Ellen Sandseter found that safe play is actually detrimental to the process of child development. She found that children were exhilarated when exposed to stimuli they had previously feared. As they gradually matured and mastered new skills and explored new environments, their natural (and perfectly healthy) inhibitions – which protected them from any serious danger – correspondingly declined. In other words, the thrill helped them overcome their phobia. If they didn't experience risky play, they didn't overcome their natural phobias, which then became pathologised and unhealthy later on. Exposure to feared stimuli generates an exhilarated emotional response.[423] Sandseter concluded that lack of risky play might lead to an increase in psychopathy and neuroticism as children grow up.

Play is essential, but not just to any one child's development; it's essential for the development of humanity itself. This is obvious to those who observe it up close. What is play but tinkering, trying new things, new combinations, new rules, new roles, new ideas? Play is the essence of experimentation, of risk taking, of innovation. Play leads to progress.

'Free Range Kids'

The good news is that we don't have to do anything too radical to make play more human. The Berkeley Adventure Playground isn't the only example of enlightened thinking; advocates of play (and the fantastic playgrounds they support) exist all around the world, and the movement is growing. But it is nonetheless still under attack, and we need to support those who are fighting back. Like London Play. As councils and communities eliminate adventure playgrounds or build dull new ones, organisations like London Play campaign against such moves while developing their own playgrounds that engage children and facilitate play in fun and educational ways. They have also sought to shed light on both real and imagined dangers. For example, knowing that cars are a legitimate concern, London Play has experimented with closing down streets for periods and setting up temporary play spaces (like a life-sized Monopoly board with each house on the street a different property).

Paul Hocker, London Play's development director, has been struck by how naturally play comes to children, even when they are exposed to new things. When London Play did its first street closure in 2009, kids were so excited, they couldn't wait to start. When they did, it was 'like something out of a Disney film', with children 'flying out' of their homes, 'dragging all sorts of objects and plunking them on the road'. Even though they'd never played on the street before, 'within about ten minutes, there was this very rich, stimulating play space that they had just created from bits and odds and ends they had. They didn't need to be told what to do. And that's the secret of the work,' Hocker says, 'to provide children with the space and the licence to play and play freely. As much as society changes around children, how children play remains the same.'[424]

So one solution is simply to create more permanent play spaces – both formal as with London Play, and informal. It just needs to be made more of a priority in the planning and development process. It is a choice that could be made. Of course, there needn't be just one model for reforming play. In the UK, adventure playgrounds often discourage parental involvement; the idea being that children better develop their independence away from the anxious eyes of over-protective mothers and fathers. For children without easy access to the outdoors, organised 'forest schools' have emerged whereby children regularly visit woodland sites, in all weather, not only to play in a way that provides healthy exposure to nature but also to learn skills in survival, ecology, craft, self-regulation and teamwork. Finding more ways for children to play outside is crucial; as London Play's Hocker says: 'The more kids outside, the safer it is.'

But even if we make playtime more human and convince the powers that be (from parents to policymakers) that real play is fine and needs to be supported with more and better play spaces, perhaps the biggest threat to play is the new rat race that discourages it altogether in favour of hyper-organised and didactic leisure activities. Although for many over-scheduled children (of over-achieving and over-anxious parents) in places like London and New York, 'leisure' is hardly the word. You have to feel sorry for these kids. Their parents have bought into the anxiety that football and even piano lessons aren't enough, so we have to add Mandarin lessons, the violin, ballet, extra maths – extra everything with expensive tutors. And all of these activities must be structured and supervised with benchmarks and rankings. But as crazy as this sounds, parents are under immense pressure; we have been led to believe that if our children aren't doing everything, they won't do well in nursery or primary school or the endless standardised tests, and so will fail to get into a good university. And then their lives are basically over.

The world that awaits our children as they enter adulthood will indeed be a challenging, perhaps scary place. But the more that 'experts' go on about how competitive and unforgiving the world will be – how poor, plodding British children have absolutely no chance against the crazed, pint-sized learning machines of Asia; how any child without an armful of qualifications will be lucky to have anyone give them the time of day let alone a job – the more that real and reasonable expectations of parents transmogrify into a demented obsession with filling every child's every waking hour with career-enhancing content. As a result, we're crushing playtime, recreation, balance for children just when they need it most.

Here's an idea: don't worry so much. Let your children climb that tree or use that tool. Don't supervise them 24/7 and certainly don't plan their playtime for them. Give them time to form their own interests and use their imagination instead of placing them in every extracurricular activity under the sun. Lenore Skenazy (the New York mother who let her son take the subway on his own) has started the Free Range Kids movement to advocate for just this kind of parenting. In her book and on her website, Skenazy draws attention to the social norms we've embraced as parents without really thinking through their ramifications. She points out that the idea of even having to define a 'free-range kid' is ridiculous: thirty, forty, fifty years ago, being a kid and being a free-range kid were one and the same thing. But now, parents are made to feel guilty about everything from not breast-feeding to not buying the right knee pad for playing outside. Meanwhile, we need to listen less to the hype about dangers to children and focus on the things that really threaten them. For example, the idea of 'stranger danger' is an outdated and unhelpful one. We need to teach our children how to talk *to* strangers so they know who to turn to in case of real danger.

This is not to say that there aren't some children who need better support and supervision. Education writer Paul Tough points out that while risk is indeed elusive for the richest children, it is a daily occurrence for the poorest and most vulnerable kids. Their problem is that they have no support to overcome their challenges and develop character. While rich children can benefit from risk, poor children are overwhelmed by it, suffering adverse consequences like toxic stress. As one critic put it in a review of Tough's book, there are two childhood extremes: 'For rich kids, a safety net drawn so tight it's a harness; for poor kids, almost nothing to break their fall.' Helping children develop character by persevering through the challenges of childhood and adolescence is how we can help them succeed.[425]

We need to let children explore the world on their own terms. And we need to recognise that play is natural – naturally human. Rather than fight it, let's harness it productively. All of those involved with the upbringing of children – parents, policymakers, educators, coaches, neighbours – need to step back and think: are we really protecting children or are we allaying our own fears instead? Chances are, if you're a parent reading this, you had a carefree childhood. You survived. Your children will too.

Under-protection

A carefree childhood doesn't mean total freedom. There is an important sense in which we are not protecting children enough. It is bizarre that at a time when adult life is being extended in dramatic ways upwards – people are living longer, working longer, staying active longer – we also seem determined to extend adult life downwards, forcing (or at best, allowing) children to become consumers earlier, to become sexual earlier and to take on board at an earlier and earlier age the very adult burdens of stress and anxiety. Why? What's the hurry? Our culture mocks notions of childhood innocence. We don't treat children like children any more. We are, in fact, inhuman towards them because we treat them like something they're not: adults. This threatens not just the healthy development of an entire generation; it also stands to reverse one of society's most important advances of the last fifty years, that of women's emancipation.

Leaning out

At long last, women are now taking up roles of power and influence, asserting equality at work, and claiming their place in areas previously the sole domain of men. We've seen the success of strong women who forged a path for others – pioneers like Virginia Woolf and Gloria Steinem; Germaine Greer and Betty Friedan – and those who have taken it up, like Margaret Thatcher, Hillary Clinton, Christine Lagarde, Janet Yellen and Mary Barra. For the first time ever, in 2015 all the top jobs in an American city, Washington DC – mayor, police chief, schools commissioner – were held by women. In Nordic countries, gender equality has been the social norm and practical reality for decades. Obviously there's further to go. Pay inequality, offensive stereotypes, sexism and gender gaps persist. In the 2010–15 UK Parliament, only 148 members of the House of Commons were women – 23 per cent.[426] Just seven women currently lead FTSE 100 companies.[427] Despite all the barriers she's broken, even Hillary Clinton had to put up with Barack Obama commenting on her clothes in a televised debate during her 2008 Presidential bid. Women, even successful ones, 'still can't have it all', as former Princeton University professor and State Department official Anne-Marie Slaughter put it.

Thankfully, we have great champions today. As Secretary of State and subsequently, Hillary Clinton has been a tireless advocate for women's emancipation, economic empowerment and leadership. Despite being shot in the face, Pakistani teenager Malala Yousafzai continues her campaign for the rights of girls simply to go to school. One of the latest advocates for women can be found in Silicon Valley: with her book *Lean In*, Facebook executive Sheryl Sandberg called on women to overcome the forces holding them back professionally. But there's some irony in the fact that the latest leader to carry the flag of gender equality is the chief operating officer of a technology giant. That's because the biggest threat to gender equality in the world today comes from technology; from something that is, literally before our eyes, reversing feminism's hard-fought gains. And that is the smartphone.

The fundamental battle on gender equality is in the mind. Gender equality is rooted in people's attitudes, whether it's women's attitudes about their role in life, society and the economy; men's attitudes about theirs; or both about each other. In my generation, that battle is being won. We are moving firmly away from obnoxious and imprisoning attitudes about women. We reject anachronistic stereotypes of women as housewives, mothers and nothing more; as sex objects, subordinate to men, defined by appearance rather than brains or talent. Those attitudes are just not socially acceptable any more. Recent generations have won these changes and moved society towards true gender equality.

But when we look at what's going on with young children and teenagers and ask whether progress is being made (let alone maintained), the answer is no. Young people are increasingly being exposed to depictions of and attitudes towards women that we thought we'd consigned to the history books: as sex objects defined by looks.[428] Children's clothing is ever more sexualised: one study found that almost 30 per cent of pre-teen clothing had 'sexual' characteristics that highlighted breasts, buttocks, or slimness.[429] While cultural pressures like impossibly high standards in beauty, fashion, and grooming are communicated across all age groups, they have a significant effect on impressionable girls.[430] This has real world consequences. Self-objectification is common in young girls and women and has been found to impair cognitive function (because young women are so distracted by worrying about their body image)[431] and cause emotional distress.[432] Shame, anxiety and self-disgust occur in pre-teen girls.[433] And it is causing unnatural and frankly scary behaviour. Driven by images and videos of models, pop-culture icons, and porn performers showing the perfect wax, as well as the consequent expectations of boys, girls as young as twelve are starting to shave their pubic hair.[434]

The assault on gender equality is not happening in the political arena, where progress at the legislative and regulatory level (even the representative one) is steady, if slow. It's not happening in the workplace, where despite the need for more change, as we saw in the previous chapter on families, women's equality is becoming gradually accepted. No, the assault on gender equality is most evident in the younger generation and its culture. And we can be even more precise than that. Is the problem at school? No – the complaints you hear about schools and gender tend to go in the opposite direction: concerns about 'political correctness gone mad'. Is it at home that women's role in society is being sent back to the dark ages of sexism and objectification? Hardly. In fact, the potentially disastrous unwinding of progress towards equal treatment of men and women is happening in the place where young children spend more and more of their time: the online world. Specifically, their gateway to that world: the smartphone and other mobile Internet-enabled devices (MIEDs). Nearly four decades after Susie Orbach published *Fat is a Feminist Issue*, we can today agree on the twenty-first-century update: Phones are a Feminist Issue. For children, this is where we need more protection, not less.

Sexualised childhood

The average British child receives his or her first mobile phone at the age of twelve; nearly one in ten receives one before the age of five.[435] A third of children aged five to fifteen have a smartphone, and two-thirds of twelve- to fifteen-year-olds do;[436] nearly half of three- to four-year-olds own some kind of device, while a majority of those aged eight to fifteen have three or more.[437] Let me repeat: more than half of these children have at least three media devices. While these figures change slightly with income, they broadly cut across all socio-economic demographics. So after that barrage of numbers, let's just agree the simple points: it is normal for young children to be inundated with technology; they're using it to go online without supervision, and these trends are accelerating.[438] A big majority of parents (84 per cent) say they monitor their children on the Internet, ranging from asking them what they've been doing to actively checking their browser history or sitting beside them as they use it.[439] But when the device in question is a *mobile* Internet-abled device (MIED), then of course, parents cannot always watch what their child is doing. Nor can they know what content their children are viewing on another child's MIED – or when their child is not at home. Consider: while parents *say* they maintain some sort of vigilance, 40 per cent of eight- to eleven-year-olds report no direct supervision when they're online – at home or elsewhere.[440]

The ubiquity of smartphones has enabled the ubiquity of pornography and other sexual or sexualised content (for example in music videos) not suitable for children. Over half of twelve- to fifteen-year-olds use the Internet to view sexually explicit material,[441] and a significant number of children are exposed to explicit context at ten or eleven years old.[442] This premature sexualisation is a terrible scourge because it gives children incorrect notions of healthy sex and relationship dynamics. It inculcates in young, impressionable minds – starkly and brutally – the idea we have fought to banish from our culture: that women's primary role is as the object of sexual gratification for men.

For many children, pornography is what they think real-life sex is, or should be. As most online porn is created for men and is often aggressive if not violent, MIEDs are creating in this generation absolutely shocking, dark patterns of expectation and behaviour when it comes to sex. Young girls think they have to look and behave like porn performers, shaving their bodies and taking part in sexual activity that is often painful and disturbing to them, like anal sex or sex with more than one boy at a time. Boys, meanwhile, are freed from any moral or cultural restraint to treat girls with respect or affection. The shared understanding of what sex means today is the grim, inhuman, exploitative version that the porn industry has manufactured.

These concerns are real. Young people increasingly report that they learn about sex from pornography; some 45 per cent of young men believe it is educational, and three-quarters of young women believe it puts pressure on girls to act and look 'a certain way'.[443] Consequently, young men expect girls to conform to the fantasised version of sex they see in porn, and are themselves, unsurprisingly, more likely to be sexist.[444] Men who watch porn are more likely to see women as sexual 'playthings'.[445] Worse, that education is one of violence: in the years 2009 to 2012, 4,562 minors committed 5,028 sex offences in Britain.[446] The children, some of whom were as young as five, 'mimicked' behaviour seen in porn, often viewed online.[447] As many as one in three had victimised family members. 'When you interview young women about their experiences of sex, you see an increased level of violence: rough, violent sex.' That, according to Professor Gail Dines, a leading anti-porn campaigner, 'is directly because of porn, as young boys are getting their sexual cues from men in porn who are acting as if they're sexual psychopaths'.[448] Men can be victims, too: Irish and Canadian researchers have found that exposure to porn directly affects male perceptions of body image and self-esteem.[449] 'Pornography,' adds Dines, 'is sexually traumatising an entire generation of boys.'[450]

Yes, I know, porn has never exactly been good on this account. And yes, children have always happened across the proverbial copy of *Playboy* or *Hustler* or whatever in their father's drawer. But the scale and nature of it today is completely different from anything our society has ever seen before. At younger and younger ages, children are spending more and more time on smartphones,[451] the biggest source of pornography in the UK.[452] They're watching it more easily, earlier and more often. And the nature of what they're watching is radically different. Before Internet porn, there was regulation, of sorts. The kind of material that was available at the local sex shop or on the top shelf of the newsagents or on Page Three of the *Sun* might have degraded women, but it wasn't in the same league of depravity that any child can access today with a couple of clicks on their MIED.

We know that things are bad when it's the porn editors who say so. Martin Daubney is the former editor of *Loaded*, a men's magazine that features plenty of sexual imagery of women. Accused of peddling pornography, he 'agonised' that his 'magazine may have switched a generation onto more explicit online porn'. When he set out to investigate the effects of this culture on young people, it was worse than he imagined. 'I used to be sceptical that porn was as damaging a force as the headlines and David Cameron – who recently said it was "corroding childhood" – suggest … but what I saw … changed my opinion of pornography forever,' he wrote in an op-ed in the *Daily Mail*.[453] He describes attending a panel of young teenagers assembled by sex-education consultant Jonny Hunt, who asked them to write A-to-Z lists of all the sexual terms they were familiar with. It turned out that the adults had insufficient vocabulary.

'"Nugget, what's that?" asked Jonny,' Daubney recalls. '"A nugget is a girl who has no arms or legs and has sex in a porno movie," chortled one young, pimply boy, to an outburst of embarrassed laughter from some.' More shocking were the mundane answers. 'For example, the first word every single boy and girl in the group put on their list was "anal".' After one teenage boy described a pornographic scene featuring bestiality (which is illegal), Daubney asked him where he saw it. 'Facebook,' the boy told him. 'It just pops up whether you want it or not, sometimes via advertisements. You don't have any control on your home page.'

So this is what's happening today. Children are fed a steady diet of submissive and abused women as norms. Their idea of proper sexual behaviour is that boys can get away with whatever they want and girls think they should allow it. Porn, Daubney concludes, 'is the most pernicious threat facing children today'. And while this is an issue that reflects broader societal trends, and while in the well-known phrase, smartphones are the 'sewer not the sewage', these devices have done as much as anything in recent years to objectify women and turn back the clock on feminism, as girls' images of themselves and their identity and potential are reversed.

But the most tragic part of the triangle of sex, MIEDs, and young people isn't even exposure to pornography – it's that they expose themselves. Law-enforcement officers around the world have long battled child pornography, but they are increasingly wondering how to battle child pornography committed by the victims. Technically, minors who possess nude images of even themselves run afoul of child-pornography laws, but as one columnist put it, charging them as paedophiles 'makes as much sense as charging a kid who brings a squirt gun to school with possession of an unlicensed firearm'.[454] And so police officers, school administrators and parents are left in a grey area, desperate to communicate the severity of 'sexting', as the perky euphemism goes, without ruining their children's futures.

An otherwise unassuming rural region in central Virginia, Louisa County became the centre of a firestorm in early 2014 when a sexting scandal erupted after a local high-school girl saw her naked image on an online bulletin board and her mother reported it. Journalist Hanna Rosin of the *Atlantic* spent several weeks there to try and understand the ordeal that followed. Police started with the girls whose pictures were on the site and the boys who followed them on Instagram. Every interview yielded more names of high-school students who had sent or received 'sexts'; the confiscated smartphones started to pile up. It became quickly apparent that to the teenagers being interviewed by the police, no crime had been committed; no harm had been done. While some girls (like the one whose mother initiated the investigation) were indeed humiliated, many of the girls Rosin interviewed felt more mortified that they had to discuss the images with police officers.[455] Donald Lowe, the police officer leading the investigation, said that his characterisation of the girls evolved from 'victims' to 'I guess I'll call them victims' to 'they just fell into this category where they victimised themselves'.[456]

The problem with smartphones is that they amplify and escalate normal 'teenagers-being-teenagers' behaviour into something much worse. As Rosin writes, technology has the power to turn an otherwise private experience into a public hell. Where once a girl might have flashed a boy she liked in an empty room and that was the end of it, now that 'flashing' has a permanent record. Kids who illicitly forward these pictures without permission are unquestionably committing sex crimes and the majority who do so might know it's wrong, but they certainly don't think of themselves as criminals. Are these 'youthful indiscretions' no worse than anything that previous generations did? They may or may not be, but one thing is clear: because of the technology and its ubiquity, the consequences are far worse.

Vulnerable children, under pressure from a sexualised culture and social life, bear the brunt of sexting's exploitation. Boys now expect sexual pictures from girls, flattering and cajoling them until they cave in, but then immediately think of the girls as 'thots'– best translated ('that ho over there') as 'slut' or 'whore' – when they send a picture. The boys Lowe interviewed told him that sharing nude pictures was 'nothing unusual. It happens all the time.' When Rosin asked students how many of their peers they thought sexted, the answer was 'everyone'.[457] But such actions are evidence of a culture that doesn't just normalise sexual behaviour for youth, it pushes children who are far too young into it. The ubiquity of phones and the Internet is bad enough when it exposes young people to porn and unhealthy and backward attitudes toward sex, violence, and the opposite sex. But by eliminating all but the smallest barriers to communicating explicit material of oneself or another far and wide, MIEDs haven't just spurred this behaviour, they've often, as in sexting, created it.

'I'd like to learn how to have a conversation'

A common response to all this is: 'Well, yes, I know, it's terrible, but really, what can we do about it? The Internet and phones and technology – they bring all these good things but they bring some bad things too and we just have to accept it and do the best we can to deal with the worst parts of it. You can't turn the clock back.'

You can't turn the clock back. You've got to take the rough with the smooth. You can't put the genie back in the bottle. These are some of the clichés that are bandied about in any discussion of the impact of the Internet on society. Generally, I would say they're probably true. Generally, it's true that the Internet is like all new technology that becomes widely adopted: it has become widely adopted because people find it useful and good, and accept its downsides as part of the price you pay for the far larger upsides. Generally, I agree that you can't and shouldn't try to turn the clock back. Generally.

But the issue I'm talking about in this chapter is not general. It's specific. The issue is: children having unsupervised access to the Internet. Not children using technology, or children using tablets, or smartphones, or going on the Internet, or even children owning mobile phones. The issue is unsupervised access to the Internet. That's a pretty narrow, specific issue. And there *is* something we can do about it. More to the point, I believe there's something we must do about it because MIEDs are putting at risk one of the best and most important social changes in human history: the empowerment of women. It's great that Sheryl Sandberg's Lean In Foundation created a partnership with Getty Images to create a new library of stock images showing women in traditionally male professional roles.[458] Now let's see some action on smartphones too. As mobile phones became camera-phones and then smartphones connected to the Internet, it was like handing young people the keys to the drinks cabinet; it was only a matter of time before something went horribly wrong. Technology ran way ahead of our ability to handle it; for many young people, navigating the intersections of the Internet, mobile devices, and social media has been a baptism of fire. Just as with alcohol, we need to keep it away from our children unless we're there to supervise – not least because phones are not just a feminist issue. They are a developmental issue too.

Smartphones and tablets hurt our children in other ways as well as distorting their view of sex and gender.

We know what a good childhood looks like – and it turns out that modern brain science backs up what we knew by instinct all the time. The things that are generally associated with happy children who go on to be successful adults are human things – including time spent with people who love them, physical activity,[459] walking and spending time in nature,[460] and playing. Traditional toys, argues Brian Verdine, a postdoctoral fellow at the University of Delaware in Newark, are much better than "electronic toys and apps" at helping children learn spatial skills. 'Skills, including early geometry and knowing the names of shapes, help kids learn the math skills they pick up in kindergarten,' he says. 'And if they already have those (before they begin school), they are ahead of the curve.'[461] None of these things are provided by smartphones, tablets and other MIEDs, and yet an increasing – and alarming – proportion of children's time is being diverted from the positive things we know are good for them. The diversion comes from the devices given to them by their parents and marketed to them by big businesses with no sense of restraint about how and where to make money.[462]

'Parents see that children will watch these screens and look like they understand, but they are not looking and perceiving in a way that is helping them learn,' says Marsha Gerdes, a psychologist at the Children's Hospital of Pennsylvania. 'Kids are not learning as much as when they are actually looking at their parent's face and listening to them sing a song when they are watching a pattern on a screen.'[463] Research has shown that children who play with blocks do better in maths later on,[464] and yet children are spending between two and four hours a day on screens.[465] It should alarm us that devices are now more popular than traditional toys.[466] As we saw earlier, the problem of over-exposure to screens and tech is pretty evenly spread across the income groups. But the difference is, middle- and upper-class families at least have the money and the time to build positive physical (not screen-based) experiences into their children's lives. Not so for poor families, where the device can be a blessed relief from the stresses of parenting in difficult circumstances. You can understand why – but it doesn't make it right.

When we allow children to shut out the world to focus on devices, studies are starting to tell us, we harm not just social relationships but basic human abilities. Chief among them is the skill of conversation. In a 2012 TED Talk, Sherry Turkle, an MIT professor who has studied the interaction between people and technology, recounted a recent conversation she had had in the course of her research: 'An 18-year-old boy who uses texting for almost everything says to me wistfully: "Someday, someday, but certainly not now, I'd like to learn how to have a conversation."'[467] Turkle found that people increasingly eschew conversations because they can't control what is said. In text messaging, email, and social media, they can. What's more, people can customise their communications, tuning in and out without having to endure one second of content they don't care about. But there are costs. As Turkle puts it: 'You can end up hiding from each other, even as we're all constantly connected to each other.' Among those who go online, 71 per cent of twelve- to fifteen-year-olds, 20 per cent of eight- to eleven-year-olds and even 5 per cent of five- to seven-year-olds say they have a social-media profile on a site or app.[468]

And they – our children – are suffering the consequences; ironically, more connectivity actually dehumanises. In her book, *Alone Together*, Turkle writes about an encounter she had with a teenager: '"There is a difference between someone laughing and someone writing that they're laughing." He says, "My friends are so used to giving their phones all the attention … they forget that people are still there to give attention to."'[469] This phenomenon is leading to slightly tragic new rules of etiquette, like the number of people in a group who can acceptably be looking down at their screen at any one time.[470] Neglected friendships are one thing, but what about parents neglecting their children? When parents spend so much time on their devices, it is, Turkle says, problematic for their children. 'These kids are extremely lonely. We are giving everybody the impression that we aren't really there for them. It's toxic.'[471] While it's bad enough to be experimenting on ourselves with screens and devices, we also run great risks that the connectivity enabled by technology will have outsized impact on impressionable children. As we learned with the work of Nadine Burke Harris in Chapter 6, children are especially affected by neuroplasticity. Keeping that in mind, imagine how much it affects you – then imagine your children, who now have to grow up in this toxic environment, unable to access any space that's technology-free or without a device. We're experimenting with their very ability to think.

We are not powerless

MIEDs are incredible inventions and fantastic tools for all sorts of things. They facilitate learning through education programmes and apps, allow parents to keep in touch with their children, can save time and hassle and enhance our daily lives. They can free us from drudgery to spend time on things of more value. Without question, children need to be comfortable with and adept at using computers. But since there are undeniable adverse side effects, we should try to address them, rather than sticking our heads in the sand, assuming there's not really anything we can do about all this, that we have to 'take the rough with the smooth', 'can't turn the clock back', 'can't put the genie back in the bottle', etc., etc.

That response is weak, feeble, pathetic. Of course it's possible to protect our children while enabling them to successfully navigate our technologically advanced, connected society. This is not a generalised, existential problem with technology, or the Internet. It is a highly specific, narrow, solvable problem: how do we prevent children (and our society) suffering the negative consequences of unsupervised child access to the Internet?

There are lots of well-meaning efforts. You now see a steady stream of books and articles on 'digital detoxing' and similar self-denying ordinances; advice to parents on how to limit their children's screen time. Turkle recommends we establish 'sacred spaces' at home and at work away from our devices so we can reflect on our thoughts and connect with others. We as parents should certainly avoid apps that encourage the shortening of our attention spans and mean less time with our children. A new app called Spare5 lets people do brief, mechanical tasks on their smartphones for money when they have a few minutes, like labelling different kinds of shoes for an online retailer. It's creative enough as a business idea, but really, what have we become, that every minute of every day must be spent occupied on a device? More promising are 'digital detox' apps like RescueTime and

Anti-Social. But while these can help solve some of the problems of adult over-reliance on tech, I don't think the 'self-denying ordinance' approach comes close to being the solution we need for children.

One serious way forward lies in the design of tech products themselves. Many of the biggest tech companies have put huge amounts of effort into building versions of their core products that prevent children from seeing adult content on the Internet. Examples include Apple's Family Sharing, Google's Safe Search and YouTube's Safety Mode (full disclosure: my wife Rachel is a leading advocate for child protection efforts within Google). There are also apps like NetNanny that claim to offer the same kinds of protections. Another version of this argument is that parents should not give children smartphones with data plans, thus limiting their use to phoning and texting.

These are all positive steps to address the problems we've seen in this chapter. But they don't go far enough. First, phones and tablets are increasingly sophisticated and while parents may have options for more control, children are often two steps ahead. There are too many stories of children easily getting around various child-protection controls for anyone to have confidence in this approach. But there's an even more serious objection, and it's rooted in a very human concept we've seen a few times already in this book: social pressure. This problem of children seeing adult content and being able to use the Internet to harm themselves and others; this phenomenon of phones as a feminist issue, phones as a developmental issue, phones as an antisocial issue; it's not a product issue, a technical issue: it's a behavioural issue.

It's not just about whatever controls or restrictions you as a parent put on your child's use. It's about everyone else's children and their access to the Internet on whatever devices their parents have allowed them. However much some parents might not wish their children to have these devices outside the home or classroom, unsupervised; or whatever controls they successfully (or unsuccessfully) place on their own children's usage, they simply have no way of supervising their access to other children's devices. What do you do if you don't want your children to have an MIED? Should they be stigmatised for not having them when they face peer pressure if they don't?[472] I'm obviously alert to the risk that my own children might lose out because they aren't carrying the latest smartphone, tablet or 'wearable'. As a parent, I will be forced to decide between what I believe to be good for my children's emotional and neurological development and what is best for them socially. That's a terrible choice, for me and for all parents. And that's why we need a fundamental rethink: this problem is not an individual problem, it's a collective one, like pollution, and that's how we need to deal with it. Unconstrained, unsupervised Internet use by children is mental pollution and there is a simple solution for that kind of thing – one we know well and are used to applying.

Here's a way we could make life easier for parents, better for children, and retain the benefits of technology while making life more human. We need to create a social norm that children should never have access to the Internet without supervision. Since the principal method through which children access the Internet unsupervised is through smartphones or other MIEDs, that's where we have to take the fight. Just as we've banned smoking or drinking for under-sixteens because we think those things are bad for them, we should ban smartphones and other mobile Internet-enabled devices for children too – to protect under-sixteens from unsupervised content. They could still have so-called 'feature phones' to call their parents in an emergency or send text messages, but they would not be able to view pornography (and other illicit video and photo content) or take and post pictures of themselves whenever they wanted. Establishing this as a norm would licence parents' enforcement of what would be an (inevitably) unpopular rule: 'It's not my fault, it's the law.'

Of course, children should have the benefits of the Internet when they're learning, exploring, and connecting with the world. As we saw in Chapter 2, technology can help students and teachers alike. But all of this can be achieved under supervision, in the home with parents and at school. If we allow uncontrolled use, devices will dominate our children's lives, to the detriment of making friends, gaining tactile knowledge, and playing outside – in short everything that makes childhood so wonderful, vital, human. That's why we need more protection. That's why we need a ban.

I realise this might sound extreme or fanciful but you can't tell me it's impossible. It's not. My family is living proof of it. Our sons do not have phones or tablets, only use a computer at school, and at home have perhaps a half-hour or so of screen time three or four days a week, watching videos, not TV. I myself do not have a smartphone and no, I don't say this from some cabin in the woods but a few miles from Stanford and as the CEO of a tech start-up and husband of a Google executive. I feel perfectly connected and perfectly happy not to be chained to screens.

Some will say: 'How can you justify something as draconian as banning kids from having smartphones or tablets?' I think it's reasonable to put the burden of justification on them: 'Could you please explain why you want children to have unsupervised, unlimited access to the Internet?' For those who think such a ban is unenforceable in a practical sense, and who point to underage drinking and smoking despite similar bans, I'd say of course: no ban ever achieves complete, 100-per-cent compliance. But they can be made to be effective in the vast majority of cases and perhaps most importantly, a ban helps set a social norm; it draws a line; it upholds society's standards and collective sense of right and wrong.

As society adapts to the digital age, we need to push back a bit and make the digital age adapt to us. On the one hand, technology – especially in the form of mobile devices – has built a whole new world of progress. On the other hand, devices have unintended and serious negative side effects that we need to recognise and address if we are to maintain a healthy relationship with technology and retain our humanity. Ending children's unsupervised access to the Internet is a step in the right – and more human – direction.

Being a parent has always been hard, and seems ever harder. But as in so many other areas of life, we now have the evidence to know what our children need and what they don't. They need the freedom to play, to interact in the world, to discover themselves; they don't need the freedom to roam the Internet. We can't make childhood perfect, but we can set sensible rules and boundaries that best suit our children's very real limitations, needs and aspirations. We should allow children to have a childhood that's more human.

CHAPTER 9

SPACES

Walk down East London's famous Brick Lane, pulsing with life and energy at the intersection of the worlds of art and fashion and music and tech start-ups and waves of immigrants who have made this incredible place their home over the centuries, turn into Hanbury Street and soon you'll come to a building as intriguing and important as any that have been created in the world these past few years.

The first things you'll see are trees – carefully selected to make sure one of them is flowering, whatever the season. Then you'll notice a strange, bubble-shaped glass wall emerging from the side of the building. Go in and you'll be struck by the colours – amazing, bright colours. Poke around a bit. There's a café, desks, Mid-century furniture, offices. But everywhere there are plants – not just stuck in pots as you'll find in the beige-topia office buildings the world over but plants that are actually growing up and along the walls and columns. Hydroponically, if you please. What is this place?

I'm so proud to say that it's the first Second Home, a business that Rohan started as an expression of his belief that our physical surroundings have a huge part to play in the quality of our lives: our personal lives, and, as in the case of Second Home, our working lives. With his business partner Sam Aldenton and two thrillingly inventive Spanish architects, José Selgas and Lucía Cano, Rohan is showing in a practical way what we can achieve by aiming higher when it comes to designing our surroundings. (The *Architectural Review* asked rhetorically whether Second Home is 'the best office in the world'.)[473] According to Selgas and Cano: 'Everything for us is related to how the brain works, whether that is a homespace or a workspace. The brain is more related to nature. If you are in an artificial rectangular space, your brain is restricted.'[474] As a result, Second Home is full of nature; there are plants everywhere inside and out, and to reflect the natural world, there are no right angles in the whole building. As Rohan says: 'We didn't evolve with straight lines.'[475]

But Rohan's vision is not simply about melding nature and people. It's also about making people more comfortable in their environment. 'Space is not just a commodity,' he says. It's about 'community and serendipity'; it has to be 'curated'. People want to interact with one another, so Second Home works to ensure a diverse community where people and ideas can cross-pollinate. But Rohan and Sam also understand that people want time and space for themselves. They've designed Second Home for both, enabling members to regulate their own social interaction. For example, side entrances and exits allow you to avoid seeing others if you just want to slip in and out.

Second Home is a living, contemporary manifestation of a phrase that has come to capture the essence of why spaces matter. In 1943, Winston Churchill was asked to comment on the design of the new House of Commons building in Westminster. He explained his view that the physical characteristics of the building would have a major influence on how the politicians who used it would behave, and ultimately on the policies that resulted. He quipped: 'We shape our buildings, and afterward our buildings shape us.'[476] This essential truth has been forgotten by far too many architects and city planners – despite how obvious it seems. In Chapter 1 we looked at the idea of human-centred design in the context of government and public policy. In this chapter we're going to apply the same principle – 'human-centredness' – to the design of the physical space around us.

Paradoxically, the more sophisticated we've become, the more our physical interactions with the world have become thoughtless and unnatural. Look at the buildings and public spaces we use every day. Why are so many of them so terrible? Why is so much of the man-made world seemingly designed without any regard for us – the people who actually have to live in it? We have settled for industrially designed and manufactured homes and offices, suburbs that are 'good enough' – but our inhuman attitudes towards the built environment make many aspects of our lives much worse. Schools and hospitals resemble factories instead of places of nurture while playgrounds are too nurturing, leading to the harmful over-coddling of our children. We need places that work on a human scale and a human level.

I know that might sound old-fashioned; quaint, even. But what is it that increasingly divides us from a physical world that is smaller, flatter, and more accessible than ever? Often, it's a misguided modernity. The quest for the new – which Nassim Taleb calls 'neomania' – can be dangerous. Progress can be wondrous but only in pursuit of the right ends. It is human to constantly push forward, and that has often led to fantastic results. But progress purely for its own sake is not helpful. When the built world becomes too planned, too logical; it no longer reflects the people – humans – who live in it. Our brilliant architects and urban theorists might be perfectly rational, but cities and buildings aren't rational, their inhabitants even less so. And so in the course of 'modernising' or 'improving' we have often ended up with outcomes that are theoretically sound but inhuman to their core.

Unless you're in the unadulterated outdoors (for more on that, see Chapter 10), the space that surrounds you was designed by someone; ostensibly for you and others like you who at some point might find themselves there. But this is not say that it was designed with your actual needs in mind. And this can have severe consequences.

In 1931, German psychologist Kurt Lewin proposed what would come to be known as Lewin's equation: $B = f(P, E)$ – that is, behaviour is a function of a person and his or her environment. This was groundbreaking at the time: most psychologists assumed a person's habits and behaviours were a result simply of the type of person they were. Lewin thought otherwise. 'Only by the concrete whole which comprises the object and the situation are the vectors which determine the dynamics of the event defined,' he remarked when the theory was first proposed.[477] The idea that your situation could shape your behaviour as much as internal characteristics gained additional heft a few decades later. Psychologists in the late 1960s coined the term 'situationism' to describe the overwhelming influence that external factors have on a person's behaviour (as opposed to mood, personality, and preferences). In the ensuing decades, experiment after experiment in the lab as well as in the real world has proved this to be the case, lending even more weight to those wartime words of Winston Churchill. Our surroundings play such an important role in determining how happy, healthy and productive we are; it's time we made them more human.

Homes, not housing

The most obvious place to start is where we should most feel 'at home': our actual homes. Home is where we rest and recharge, raise our families, bond with friends. Home is an intimate place; it should be the haven from which you make your daily adventures into the world. Of course for many around the world, even the rudimentary basics of a home like dryness, warmth and running water are still unattainable luxuries. And homelessness remains a shocking problem in the developed world, too. But for the vast majority who live in basic, structurally sound dwellings, home – in its deepest sense – is still an elusive concept.

Britain suffers from two problems where homes are concerned. First, there aren't enough of them. There are some 2 million households on waiting lists in the UK[478] despite enough readily available land for at least 1.5 million.[479] A quarter of adults under thirty-five still live in their childhood bedrooms, even though 72 per cent of them are working.[480] Only 140,150 homes have been built on average annually in the past four years[481] – far fewer than the 240,000 needed each year.[482] In 2013, fewer homes were built in England than in any year since 1949,[483] except for 2010.[484] Moreover, the idea that there's 'not enough land' is a myth: urban landscape accounts for only 10.6 per cent of English land, 3.4 per cent of Northern Ireland, 1.9 per cent of Scotland, and 4.2 per cent of Wales.[485]

The second problem is with what's being built. They are barely homes at all. They are factory houses. Consider this: 31 per cent of homeowners today would not choose a home built in the last ten years;[486] British homes are on average the smallest in Western Europe.[487] The average new home is only 818 square feet. (In Australia, it's 2,217 square feet; Denmark:1,475. Even crowded Japan's average is more than 70 per cent larger than in the UK.)[488] Even worse, because the number of bedrooms is used as a key metric when selling houses, developers increasingly take advantage of the fact by carving additional, useless rooms into already small spaces. They have no problem charging more for the extra walls.[489] But what use is a child's 'bedroom' without a table for building toys or doing homework, without shelves for books, without room to play?

Both these problems – not enough homes, not good enough homes – are structural. They are caused by the nature of the market, dominated by fewer and fewer big housebuilders, whose dominance continues to grow. Medium-sized companies have closed down at the rate of 60 per cent since the recession and small builders have declined by half.[490] The five largest builders were responsible for 20 per cent of house completions in 2008–9. In 2012–13, their share rose to 33 per cent.[491] This is not a proper market; these are not proper businesses. They are bureaucracies, just like the ones we met in Chapter 5, manipulating and lobbying their way to dominance while giving people a worse and worse service. The factory houses they build sell because there's little choice and there's a housing shortage. As a result, the houses are also getting more expensive. Property prices increased 4,268 per cent between 1971 and 2012. The authors of a report by KPMG and Shelter point out that if chicken prices increased at a similar rate, a typical supermarket broiler would now cost £51.33.[492] And the industrial housebuilders' market power means they have no need to care about what people actually want from their homes.

A report from Ipsos MORI and RIBA found that many homeowners find the 'feel' and 'character' of a home to be more important than many practical considerations.[493] Developers and politicians might dismiss this as sentimental, but how a home feels to you strongly affects how you feel in it. This is vital for physiological as well as psychological well-being. Human-centred design principles teach us that homes ought to be flexible, both for different everyday uses and for the long term. And it's obviously a fallacy to think that every person and family, in all their uniqueness, would want the same thing: people are different. Yet the houses built by the big developers are all the same. How is it that we can customise things as trivial as our burgers or cars yet have almost no say over our homes unless people have the money to pay for extensive (expensive) remodelling? We need a complete shake-up of the so-called housing 'market' so people can choose what they want rather than meekly accept whatever the big bureaucratic housebuilders offer. It's absurd that people keep referring in Britain to a 'housing market'. The market for new homes is no more a market than the GUM store in Communist Moscow was a 'supermarket'.

Imagine a completely different future, a more human one. Imagine that it's standard practice for every family to be involved in the design of their home. Technology – combined with good policy – could make it happen. London-based architect, Bruce Bell, is part of that future.

As a product-design student at the Royal College of Art in the early 2000s, Bell had nearly unlimited access to the latest in manufacturing technology. Hundreds of different machines, from punch presses (that cut holes in things), to routers (that hollow out areas of a surface), to wire benders (that bend wires), were his to experiment with. In the last decade or so these already powerful machines have been extraordinarily enhanced by technology; by digital control. Product designers can now achieve precision that could only have been dreamt of before. Now, you can get any idea you want test manufactured on a one-off basis at high quality and low cost, in very little time.

But Bell didn't go into industrial design; he went to an architecture firm, building homes, not products – and still in very old-fashioned ways. Having just learned cutting-edge manufacturing techniques at the RCA, it killed him that he would draw something to the millimetre on the computer and 'the contractor would still be using a hammer and saw, measuring things with a tape measure'. He wanted to find a way to replicate the magic he had experienced with digital fabrication, where the product would materialise in real life just as precisely as it was illustrated on the screen. Bell set out to transform the way we build houses.

After experimenting with different machines and techniques, he settled on one simple tool: a CNC router (CNC stands for 'computer numerical control'), which basically cuts shapes out of timber boards by 'drawing' the design with a mechanical cutting bit that moves up and down from above. Now it would be possible to 'print' the whole house: the walls, doors, window frames, floors, and ceilings could all be cut out of specially engineered wood and 'joined' together with practically no gaps in between, like Lego blocks. After some prototyping, a process was created and a London-based company, Facit Homes, was born. They soon discovered a second advantage to the CNC machine: it was easily transportable. This was revolutionary: bringing the machine to site meant the architect, builder and homeowner could be standing next to the house in progress, notice something they didn't like, change a component's design, and have it manufactured and placed almost immediately. 'We can stay flexible and not be restricted by the tools that we create. We can respond to any design scenario, any client situation,' Bell says.

What Bruce Bell and Facit have done is far more consequential than any of the individual homes they've designed and built. They're showing that the future of housing really can have people at its centre. Rather than vainly exhorting the massive bureaucratic homebuilders to change their practices to adopt human-centred design, Facit's technology makes it possible for every home to be an act of personal expression, based on the needs, desires and circumstances of individual people and families.[494]

A more human future for housing is one where we become a nation of 'self-builders' – a country that allows individuals and families to pull together the land, financing, design and construction of their own homes. 'Self-building' doesn't mean that you literally have to build your own house. It could mean hiring a firm like Facit to give you total personalisation of your home. Self-building meets the needs of those who will actually live in the house and liberates them from the homogenising dictates of local planners and 'volume' builders. But today only 10 per cent of new homes in the UK are self-built. In Austria it's 80 per cent; in Germany, Belgium, Italy, Sweden, Norway and France it's around 60 per cent.[495] Why are we so uniquely standardised and centralised? We have a fond self-image in Britain as a creative, entrepreneurial nation of rebels and upstarts compared to the bland, boring, sheep-like dullards of Europe. When it comes to housing, it's completely the other way round. We are the ones who pathetically submit to the grey tyranny of the identikit house, while the rest of Europe enjoys the freedom of domestic self-expression. Again, why? It's not a simple question, but the overwhelming reason – and the reason the big housebuilders have been able to achieve their baleful dominance – is the limited availability of land. In other countries, local councils have to make space available for development by people and not just big housebuilding companies.

Consider the Homeruskwartier district in Almere, a city of 200,000 people half an hour east of Amsterdam.[496] The local authority drew up street plans in 2006[497] and then made plots – ranging from under 86 square metres to 1,200 – available to local people to buy their own plot and design whatever they wanted.[498] Over 1,000 homes have already been built with thousands more on the way.[499] The project has drawn comparisons to the neighbourhoods that run along Amsterdam's famous canals: 'They did the same as we are trying to do,' explains Jacqueline Tellinga, a driving force behind Homeruskwartier. 'The plots were parcelled out, the buyers were given a few guidelines over things such as height, but after that it was left to the individual.'[500] The result? The most incredibly quirky, interesting, human neighbourhood you can imagine. Each house not only fulfils the needs of those who live within; it is an outward expression of their personalities. One house, painted bright red, is set up as a beach house, with sand and lounge chairs in the back yard. One row of homes imitates Amsterdam's canals, with the bottom floor even forming the wall of a canal along the back. In another house, the owner decided to use strips of Teflon as the side facade. People got homes that suited their needs precisely. For one family, that was a garage large enough for their boat. For another, it was an attached granny flat. Each resident received an A4 sheet of paper that specified their plot, its dimensions, and a few restrictions – nothing about design, though. 'We wanted to give the people complete freedom in aesthetics as part of our ideology of trusting people,' Tellinga explains. 'Who are we to decide what kind of aesthetic they have to use?'[501]

Another Dutch city, Nijmegen, has been similarly inspired. With a little more restriction, it's offering residents a choice of twenty-nine 'flat-pack' designs. In addition to giving local architects work (over twenty local firms collaborated with the city to contribute to the catalogue), the fact that each can be easily assembled helps keep costs down without sacrificing design quality.[502] Local architects understand the community and its complexity. They understand local needs; they get its vernacular. Moreover, employing local architects keeps whatever profits are made in the community, rather than having them siphoned off to some housebuilder's corporate headquarters.

In the UK, such a wonderful way of building a neighbourhood is made impossible for no other reason than weak political will. It's certainly not cost (self-built homes in the UK cost about 60 to 75 per cent of their final value),[503] nor is it lack of demand. According to an Ipsos MORI survey, there are more than 6 million people in the UK looking to get involved in a custom-build project in the next year.[504] There's plenty of land, but you can't just buy a plot and build a house. Instead, the land is portioned off in large chunks and sold to one of the handful of volume homebuilders who hold them in land banks. Barratt, Berkeley, Persimmon and Taylor Wimpey – the four largest developers – collectively held 300,000 plots as of December 2013.[505] Many plots that receive permission for building on remain vacant. In 2013, the Local Government Association estimated that across the UK, there were some 380,000 plots altogether that had achieved planning permission but on which the houses had yet to be completed; 152,000 of them hadn't been even started.[506]

You might think this makes the marketplace ripe for rival upstarts, but housebuilding is as much locked up by policy and government as by the big private firms involved. Planning rules make it very hard to enter the market, since you need to begin siting land and seeking approval years in advance. When authorities make land available to build on, they tend to do so in large tracts – tens of thousands of plots at a time – making them functionally available only to huge firms for huge developments. But even once the land title changes hands, slow approval holds things up. It's so complicated and takes so long that only a large, bureaucratic developer can interact with the planning bureaucracy itself.

People on both sides argue about who's to blame. The industry says it's moving as fast as it can – that it's government that slows them up. People in government say that the homebuilders carefully calibrate the pace of their building to maximise profits, rather than the number of people moving into homes. But the truth is that the whole system is wrong and needs to be replaced with one that puts people first. Bureaucratic planning authorities and 'factory homebuilders' combine to create a disaster. This is not the way to build homes. Your home is a local, personal thing. You know what you want. There are legions of people – architects, contractors, carpenters, plumbers, electricians – with the skills and talents to translate your needs and wishes into a design and construction. Why do we need big bureaucracies to bungle something we've been doing ourselves perfectly well for millennia? And now with technology we can do it ourselves even more easily, less expensively, and better. Just as with banks and supermarkets, we've allowed a too-big-to-fail system to dominate an industry that is more important than most: it's providing fundamental infrastructure.

Meanwhile, localised not-in-my-back-yard sentiments prevent affordable housing from being built in many towns and villages – the very affordable housing those areas need to stop their economic decline. Of course, if you already have a home, the system's working great. But it's people who don't yet live somewhere who need the homes built. That's why real neighbourhood control of housing needs to be accompanied by financial incentives for those neighbourhoods to accept new housing.

Once you allow your mind to wander outside the bizarre, centralised paradigm that is the housebuilding system of today, the solution is really quite simple. Land that's sited or zoned for houses – regardless of who owns it (non-builders own 45 per cent of the permitted home sites in London)[507] – has to be opened up. We must commit not just to building more homes but to making them affordable and human-centred. The best way to do this is to break open the bureaucratised planning and building process. If individuals and families or small and medium-sized firms have the financing, they should be as free to build on housing plots as the large developers. Innovations – whether it's new policies, development models, or design and construction technology itself – that move us in this direction have to be encouraged. We desperately need to make the housing system more human.

Space and the quality of everyday life

Home might be where the heart is, but when it comes to the communities in which we live and work, many urban planners and architects seem to have followed only their heads. Obsessed with their own notions of rationality, they spent the twentieth century experimenting with our neighbourhoods, often with awful results. There is no more iconic example of inhuman architecture than the work of Swiss architect Le Corbusier who inspired many of France's urban housing projects in the mid-twentieth century – high-rises that have mostly served to isolate poor individuals from the rest of the community. The very term he used to describe his buildings is exactly what's wrong with them: 'machines for living in'. It's hard to imagine a less human approach. One of its best critiques was offered by Jane Jacobs, who had studied social housing as a reporter for *Architectural Forum* in the 1950s. As Canadian journalist Robert Fulford reports:

> *On paper [the housing developments] looked fine, but when Jacobs visited them she discovered that the open spaces were empty of people. Planners had segregated residences, retail stores, business offices, and schools, an arrangement that was tidy but also inhuman and uninteresting. An environment created out of goodwill and careful thought had turned out to be boring, dangerous, and ultimately unliveable. The new developments had literally been planned to death: they left no room for happy accidents, and no room for life.*[508]

If ever there were an advocate of human-centred design, it was Jacobs. In her classic – and now thankfully influential – book, *The Death and Life of American Cities*, she lays out both her critique of and antidote to the 'visionary' planning that typified public projects in the mid-twentieth century (and government programmes more generally today). Jacobs's legitimacy derived not from theory (which she ignored) or any advanced degree (which she lacked) but from street-level observations of people themselves and how buildings and streets influenced their interaction. She was only concerned about how cities worked 'in real life' (as she put it), because that was the only way to understand how to plan, rebuild, or develop a neighbourhood for economic and social success.[509] For 'planners' to be captivated by their own visions of order and beauty was to forget about how people actually lived. If you pick up her book, which reads as much as a work of literature as an urban planning guide, you might be surprised at the simplicity of many of her suggestions and the length she devotes to each. There's an entire chapter discussing the need for short street blocks (with many possible routes to any given destination, an area 'opens up'), another on old buildings, and four chapters on pavements. To many, these are trivial features that merely enhance a city's functions; to Jacobs, they were central to its fundamental vitality.

These issues are brilliantly brought to life in that most iconic of cities, Paris. It is a place that tells a powerful tale of contrasts, providing a juxtaposition between a human, Jane Jacobs world and an inhuman, Le Corbusier one.

It was the late nineteenth-century modernisation of French Emperor Napoleon III which set the stage for this dichotomy. When he seized power as emperor in 1852, Napoleon III had an almost 'messianic' plan for Paris, telling the municipal council in 1858 that his vision was of Paris 'responding to its highest calling'.[510] In 1853, he appointed Baron Georges-Eugène Haussmann, a Parisian native from an Alsatian family who had been prefect in various cities around France, to be the new 'Prefect of the Seine'. Paris was an old city even in the 1800s and had many ills. The medieval streets were difficult to navigate and often impassable, paved with stones that 'offered an uncertain footing for pedestrians and horses alike' and made of dirt that the 'slightest rain … turned into black mud'.[511] Paris was, according to French writer Maxime du Camp, 'on the point of becoming uninhabitable. Its population [was] suffocating in the tiny, narrow, putrid, and tangled streets in which it had been dumped. As a result of this state of affairs, everything suffered: hygiene, security, speed of communication and public morality.'[512] Much of this stemmed from lack of good plumbing and sanitation; sewers overflowed and emptied into the Seine, which was in turn a source of drinking water.

Napoleon and Haussmann were determined to modernise Paris. They knew that a city, as a physical space, encompassed a complex ecosystem; accordingly, writes historian Colin Jones, they 'saw themselves as physician-urbanists, whose task was to ensure Paris's nourishment, to regulate and to speed up circulation in its arteries (namely, its streets), to give it more powerful lungs so as to let it breathe (notably, through green spaces), and to ensure that its waste products were hygienically and effectively disposed of'.[513] Haussmann channelled his patron's dictatorial powers by aggressively attacking the city in order to change it. In one sense his reforms were the epitome of inhumanity: instead of rebuilding piecemeal, he demolished whole neighbourhoods to recreate Paris in a neater grid, building wide avenues on straight axes to ease movement in the city. The new apartments that lined them were uniform and modern, in the now famous Haussmannian style. But they were in the service of human outcomes: Haussmann created wide avenues so pedestrians could have spacious promenades; he built new buildings to modernise living spaces and allow light to come to the streets, and he employed engineer Jean-Charles Alphand to construct several huge new parks to give all Parisians access to green space, 'green lungs' for the overcrowded and polluted city.[514] He fulfilled some of Parisians' most basic human needs, creating a modern plumbing system that brought fresh water from outside the city while disposing of waste in a sanitary manner – but he also promoted their aspirational ones by building the Opéra Garnier as a monument to culture. There's no doubt today that Paris is a beautiful, modern city.

That is, at its centre. When you contrast the centre of Paris with its *banlieues*, or suburbs, full of housing projects (called *Habitation à Loyer Modéré*, or 'rent-controlled housing') inspired by Le Corbusier, you find a different, sadder story. These built-up utopias are cruel traps: residents have sunlight and fresh air but are left in thrall to whichever gang controls the banks of lifts. More fundamentally, Le Corbusier forgot that as people move through life, they want different kinds of residences: urban apartments for young people, then space for raising a family, and then a pleasant retreat for retirement. 'If you don't vary the housing units in a given neighborhood – if you fill entire quarters of the city with standard-issue monoliths – you condemn upwardly mobile people to constant movement,' observes American journalist Christopher Caldwell, who has studied the *banlieues* in great depth. 'The only people who develop any sense of place are those trapped in the poverty they started in.'[515] At first glance, Haussmann's Napoleon-era reforms and the construction of the Le Corbusier-inspired high-rises seem similar: both stemmed from top-down visions of hubristic planners; both, too, had 'more human' goals at their centres.

But despite the inhuman process, Haussmann's vision in Paris worked. The *banlieues* did not. Central Paris is beautiful, with plentiful transport connecting mixed-use buildings everywhere. On almost every street, the ground floor is a shop or business with offices and housing above. The *banlieues*, on the other hand, have become synonymous with disaster, most recently burdened by massive riots in 2005. The rioters – mostly first- and second-generation North Africans – had plenty of grievances: unemployment, racism, France's failure to integrate them into society. But their grievances were exacerbated by the inhuman architecture of the *banlieues*. By concentrating the city's poorest, most desperate, and most violent residents, French planners inadvertently created a powder keg, which duly burst when three youths from a *banlieue* – thinking they were being chased by the police – hid in a power station and were electrocuted; two died, a third was gravely injured, and an entire community of young people rose in rebellion against the society they felt was responsible. Neighbourhood design did not cause the weeks of ensuing riot, but the daily indignities of inhuman architecture and planning certainly contributed to them.

The reason that central Paris 'works' is because with different types of people using the same streets at all times of day, Haussmann inadvertently created a 'Jacobsian' city; there are always, in her famous phrase, 'eyes on the street' to watch over it. The *banlieues*, with their isolated, single-use buildings dominated by gangs, are the precise, inhuman opposite.

One of the marks of a great, human neighbourhood is that you can't really tell where it begins or ends; one area just flows into the next. Sooner or later, you know you're somewhere special, but the precise moment never really announces itself.

For decades, it was pretty easy to know when you had entered St. Lawrence, Toronto. Situated close to the bustling downtown, Toronto Harbour, and the Canadian national railways yard, the neighbourhood had once been a busy port area but by the 1960s had grown blighted and vacant. But affordable housing was high on the agenda of 1970s Mayor David Crombie, and despite its grittiness, St. Lawrence offered prime real estate in the heart of the city. The city-hall bureaucrats were nervous about any sort of large new development, especially if it were to be led by the government. Prior years and decades had already been scarred by grand efforts at urban renewal in the style of Le Corbusier and like-minded city planners around the world. Toronto's leaders had fresh memories of their own: Regent Park, a 1950s 'tower-in-the-park' housing project near downtown had fallen into disrepair and crime after ten years, and the 1960s high-rise development of St. James Town just to the north is ridden with crime to this day.

But 1970s Toronto would be different. Jane Jacobs moved there from New York in 1968 and had already begun influencing its activists and politicians alike. Mayor Crombie and Michael Dennis, the city's housing commissioner, were eager pupils of her ideas and prepared to throw out the existing textbooks on urban planning in favour of a completely new approach. Their first move with St. Lawrence was to bring in an outside architect, Alan Littlewood, at Jacobs's recommendation (perhaps his appeal was precisely that he had no formal planning degree). From the start he saw the project as a process of 'invisible mending'.[516] That is, rather than raze entire city blocks and rebuild a 'utopian' community, Littlewood kept as much of the neighbourhood's original features (and historic brick character) as possible, tucking new housing in where he could among its existing roads and buildings, as well as its treasured mid-nineteenth-century structures like the wedge-shaped Gooderham flatiron building, the Cathedral Church of St. James, St. Lawrence Hall, and St. Lawrence Market (which now houses what *National Geographic* magazine has called the world's best food market).[517]

St. Lawrence would come to typify the recommendations Jacobs had made in her seminal book a decade before. It would be more human. To prevent the *banlieue* problem à la Paris, the neighbourhood was built to appeal to a broad spectrum of individuals and families, using a variety of dwelling types (apartments, condominiums, houses) to meet the needs of residents of all ages and incomes (so both market and social housing were intermixed). And unlike most new developments at the time, which kept traffic strictly separated from pedestrians with long and wide 'superblock' roads next to large parks and plazas, St. Lawrence preserved its nineteenth-century street grid of short, frequent blocks. This allows for the type of serendipitous 'street ballet' adored by Jacobs. She writes:

Under the seeming disorder of the old city, wherever the old city is working successfully, is a marvelous order for maintaining the safety of the streets and the freedom of the city. It is a complex order. Its essence is intricacy of sidewalk use, bringing with it a constant succession of eyes. This order is all composed of movement and change, and although it is life, not art, we may fancifully call it the art form of the city and liken it to the dance, ... an intricate ballet in which the individual dancers and ensembles all have distinctive parts which miraculously reinforce each other and compose an orderly whole. The ballet of the good city sidewalk never repeats itself from place to place, and in any one place is always replete with new improvisations.[518]

St. Lawrence has been successful because the long-term realities of people were put before the (often short-sighted) needs of planners, developers and bureaucrats. Unlike many ego-driven projects, the place is special precisely because it doesn't immediately appear to be anything special. It's the people who live there, flourishing, who take centre stage.[519] Not a machine, but a community for living.[520]

Space and function

Today, although our public spaces on the outside give the appearance of having evolved beyond Le Corbusier cubes, the facades of most buildings merely obscure the ugly truth within: that we are living and working in machines as much as (if not more than) ever before. Too much of our built environment – public and private – is designed to maximise overall 'efficiency' and minimise cost rather than serve our most human needs.

This inhuman approach to space contributes to any number of problems – from environmental harm and social unrest, as in Paris's *banlieues*, to poor workplace productivity. Marlon Nieuwenhuis, a psychologist at Cardiff University, found that adding plants to otherwise spartan offices increased productivity 15 per cent[521] (Second Home has 1,000 of them). A study by Northwestern University and the University of Illinois at Urbana-Champaign found that office workers with window exposure to natural light slept longer and better, were more physically active, and enjoyed better overall quality of life than their counterparts without.[522] Of those spaces that aren't explicitly 'broken', many just serve their minimal function – think of windowless classrooms, soulless offices, treeless streets – processing people through the day rather than providing the setting in which they can lead happier and more fulfilled lives. In a twist of irony, the spaces we live and work in are often designed to better serve other machines (cars, lorries, computers) than humans.

According to Carlo Ratti, a designer and architect who works on the nexus of technology and the physical world at MIT, technology could help change this.[523] The original computers were so large that to use them people had to work in large, dark, air-conditioned rooms – often squirrelled away in basements. 'The machine determined the physical condition of the space around it,' he says. 'It was 90 per cent machine, 10 per cent human.' Now, technology has literally untethered us. The advent of small, powerful and mobile devices coupled with ubiquitous wireless Internet access allows us to work anywhere – even outside. And this 'ubiquitous computing' marks a profound shift in how we design spaces. There is a paradox, Carlo says, in that when technology is all around us 'we can focus much more on the architecture, on the human side of things, and design offices, homes and buildings around people instead of around machines'. Indeed, the whole reason we can discuss open-plan offices or flexible homes is because technology (and the appliances that enable it) is no longer the limiting factor in building spaces. We can focus on our environments in other ways, like helping us to be healthier, more productive, more creative; in short, more human. And we are getting better and better at it.

Around the world, school administrators, factory owners, and office managers observe at first hand the difference that can be made by space designed with people in mind. What's most exciting is when companies choose to make space more human as a competitive advantage – the thinking behind Rohan's Second Home. Steve Jobs famously insisted that the toilets at Pixar Studios (creators of hits like *Toy Story* and *Finding Nemo*) be located in the centre of the building so people from different departments would run into each other throughout the day, sparking spontaneous human interaction and creative collaboration.

If any company understands the importance of putting people

at the centre of the design process, it's Herman Miller, which makes some of the most ergonomic furniture in the world. For many years, though, the human-first principles they applied to their furniture-making didn't extend to their workers. After a transformative factory redesign – infusing both the manufacturing and office areas with natural light; connecting different parts of the building by an indoor, bamboo-plant-lined 'boulevard'; and adding and expanding operable windows throughout the plant – they saw employee happiness and sense of belonging skyrocket and productivity significantly improve.[524] The executives of SnowPeak, a Japanese camping-gear company, thought they would create better products if they could observe their customers using them. So the company adapted the concept of a factory store: they created a 'factory camping ground'. When they built their headquarters, they sacrificed large amounts of land around the building so that loyal (and perhaps curious) customers could come and camp in view of the windows.[525] As a result, product designers and makers can see exactly how their equipment is used and better understand what works and what doesn't. SnowPeak's commitment to transparency works both ways. There are no solid walls or doors; all is glass. No space is off limits, so staff and customers can fully see what's going on and can give feedback. And while everyone can see in, all you need to do is turn toward an outside 'wall' to see the beautiful mountains beyond – a constant reminder of the company's mission to connect customers with nature.

While some aspects of space design are unequivocally 'better' (as we saw with homes), different spaces suit different needs, especially in the workplace. When companies configure office space, they have to consider what their aims are and how space can help achieve them. Companies that want internal groups to work together effectively and creatively will likely want an open plan; those that want to mix up employees from different departments might add flexible seating. But where individuals need to be productive on their own, companies might want to keep the traditional model – or at least a more enlightened variant of it.[526] That means considering employees' needs, not just the corporate view. Open-space offices might boost creativity, but they can also create anxiety, with employees paranoid that their bosses are watching what they're up to. Balancing open and private space is critical; employees need room for themselves, whether to think, work, or simply have a phone call without fear of eavesdroppers. In one recent survey, 88 per cent of the most satisfied workers were those who could work where they wanted.[527] The key, as Rohan is showing in Second Home, is to give workers a choice so they can adjust to their own preferences.

The power of space to enhance creativity, productivity, or employee health needn't be limited to the workplace, though. Thoughtful architects have shown that extending more human design to our schools can improve pupils' performance as well. In Finland, whose excellent schools we discussed in Chapter 2, it should come as no surprise that educators are equally thoughtful about school design. School architects in Helsinki consider questions such as whether the structure allows pupils and staff to break their routines and try new things; whether the environment fosters creativity, enabling observation and investigation of everyday phenomena; whether the building protects against violence and bullying; even whether the school welcomes visiting parents.[528]

Space as solution

Spaces, as we have seen, can have an immense impact on daily life and can help us be more human in our homes, workplaces, and play spaces. But they can also help solve social and environmental problems. In 1982, James Q. Wilson and George L. Kelling put forward their famous 'broken windows' theory – that visible, physical signs of disorder signal crime as an acceptable norm, perpetuating further crime.[529] Small fixes to the physical environment, such as cleaning up graffiti and litter as well as repairing broken street furniture like park benches, can have more of an impact on crime than direct police intervention, or increased social services.[530]

In Lowell, Massachusetts, authorities identified thirty-four crime 'hot spots' and proceeded to clean half of them up. They found that in the half where litter was collected and debris removed, there was a 20 per cent drop in police calls.[531] At the University of Groningen in the Netherlands, psychologists substantiated the same effect. They left an envelope with a €5 note clearly inside half sticking out of a postbox. When the street was orderly, 13 per cent of passers-by took it (the rest pushed it back in); when the area was surrounded by litter, 25 per cent took it; and when the postbox itself was covered in graffiti, the number increased to 27 per cent. Disorder on the street doubled the propensity of passers-by to become thieves.[532]

Street-level nudges can be remarkably effective for other problems as well. Sweden's Vision Zero programme, which aims to eliminate road deaths, has given Sweden one of the best road-safety records in the world.[533] Since it started in 1997, annual road deaths have come down by four-fifths compared to 1970 despite a doubling of traffic.[534] The Vision Zero programme has a simple but radically human-centred message: 'In every situation a person might fail, the road system should not.'[535] The Swedes have thus tried to design a road system nationwide that aims to maintain and increase mobility but never at the expense of people's lives. They understand that people make mistakes, but believe that death should not be the consequence of making one on the road. This is not, the Swedes argue, any different from how we approach other systems: 'If you take a nuclear power station, aviation, a rail system, all of them are based on the idea that they are operated by people who can make a mistake,' says Claes Tingvall, the director of traffic safety at the Swedish National Road Administration. With that in mind, roads are designed in Sweden so that while mistakes might cause an accident, there are no fatalities or serious injuries. 'You have to take the human in our behaviour into account when you design the road transport system. It is understanding that we will never be perfect,' says Tingvall. For example, knowing that drivers will try to overtake other cars on two-lane roads, Sweden has installed '2+1' roads, in which each direction of traffic takes turns using a middle third lane to overtake. In its first decade, that one improvement saved 145 lives.[536]

My favourite example of more human design for public space is from the Netherlands. Consider how Amsterdam became one of the most bike- and pedestrian-friendly cities in the world, with cars used for only 22 per cent of all trips (the rest are by bike, public transport, or foot).[537] In the early 1970s, Amsterdam was like most urban environments around the world: traffic-clogged and dangerous. At rush hour, streets resembled car parks; the air was choked with exhaust fumes. Car accidents killed more than 3,000 people annually across Holland in the early 1970s, including over 500 children.[538] In 1972, one group of children living in central Amsterdam had had enough. The neighbourhood, called De Pijp ('the pipe'), was about 100 years old, five times denser than the rest of the city, and not built for the cars that the 40,000 inhabitants brought with them and filled the streets with.[539] Pupils at one of the local schools started a petition to make the streets less convenient for cars and safer for children like them, launching a campaign that quickly outgrew the tiny classroom from which it started. They even took matters into their own hands, temporarily closing a street to physically demonstrate the need for a safe place to play.

This was part of the birth of a larger movement – Stop de Kindermoord ('stop child murder') that would transform streets in Amsterdam and greater Holland. It wasn't easy – when residents decided to turn a small part of a street into a car-free zone, there were violent protests (there's a famous video of an irate driver picking up and throwing a roadblock children had erected). Despite the violent backlash against the anti-car campaign, the children, supported by their teacher, stuck to their guns. All they wanted was a safe place to play. And through their action they started a worldwide urban-design movement which today has mainstreamed pedestrian zones, bike lanes, street furniture, tree planting and so on. The children recognised that the space they lived in was not designed for their human needs – to play, to walk to school, and to socialise with their friends and families – and they did something about it. One group of children, in one school in Amsterdam. What a lovely, inspiring tale of more human social change.

In many cases, making space more human is really just about recognising how people actually behave in certain contexts (as opposed to how we assume they do) and designing our environments with this in mind. A Stanford University project that Jason (the Jason who, along with his brother Scott, helped me write this book) was involved in, designing a 'concept home' that would be net-zero-energy, shows how a human-centred approach can help solve environmental problems too. Jason first mapped all the places people interact with their homes in ways that consume energy (light switches, thermostats and so on). His team's key insight was that few people actually want to waste resources; we just do so because there are small, seemingly insignificant barriers that for reasons of forgetfulness, lack of attention, or even just laziness get in our way. If the team could remove as many of these barriers as possible, people's intention to either save money, do good for the environment, or simply avoid waste would be less impeded.

Of the handful of innovative products his team developed and built in the house, my favourite was a 'room switch' that would make the people at Nest (producers of beautiful and practical home services like thermostats) blush. 'We wanted to rethink the whole idea of the light switch,' Jason says. There are all sorts of different electronic items plugged into the wall that draw energy, even when they're off – device chargers, televisions, kitchen appliances. Jason and his team wanted to design a 'light' switch that worked for the whole room – one that could turn everything off, not just the lights. 'Simplicity was important – part of the reason people don't unplug things is because it's a pain.' The solution, as is so often the case, lay right in front of them. Most of the team had Apple laptops, which have what are called 'trackpads'. They're touch-based, but instead of a screen, you touch an opaque surface. As Jason puts it: 'You can achieve an incredible amount of functionality based on your gestures and how many fingers you use to draw them.' With the 'room switch', you could turn off every electrical appliance with one touch, or select individual ones with different gestures.

There's a broader point to be made here. Today, energy is at once one of the most personal and impersonal ingredients of our lives. It fuels our cars, heats our rooms, lights our homes, cooks our food, and allows us to communicate with the outside world. Our modern economy – not just the phones and tablets in our pockets but also the vast data centres, mobile-phone towers and Internet routers – depend on energy. But we aren't really in control of it. Since fossil fuels dominate where our power comes from, energy has had to be 'big' (and therefore removed and obscured from daily human life) simply to get it out of the ground and into a consumable form. The tremendously high costs of producing energy on the scale we need it have meant that only a handful of large players could conceivably do it. Unsurprisingly, given energy's central role in the modern world, these big energy companies have become dominant forces in the economy and in government too, with our leaders forced into shaming geopolitical positions, in hock to oppressive, sometimes hostile regimes who, by controlling our oil and gas supplies, get to decide how we respond to their abuses (or, in the case of Russia and Ukraine, invasions).

Until now, if you as an individual wanted to do anything about the energy you used, the most you could do was turn the thermostat down, install curly light bulbs, or buy a hybrid car. All the same, if you were consuming any amount of energy – no matter how much 'less' – you were still dependent on big, dirty power. But new technology and smart design of spaces means we can change all that. We can move to a more human system: we can put people in charge of their own energy. Smart meters (there are now over 500,000 installed across the UK)[540] give homeowners an increasingly transparent view into their use of energy. And as devices like thermostats – or Jason's 'room switch' – become more advanced and connected, we're getting a precise view of our energy-use patterns as well as the means to do something about it.

It's not just how we consume energy that is changing, but how we produce it too. Thanks to huge advances in both performance and cost, the proliferation of distributed (as opposed to centralised) technologies means we can incorporate energy production into the immediate spaces around us, ending Big Energy's stranglehold on our lives. Solar panels can already turn roof space into a power station. But now imagine if every surface facing the sun could do the same – only much, much more efficiently. Imagine a world in which solar panels, thanks to advances in nanotechnology, have microscopic ridges that improve their energy-absorption capacity from 20 or 25 per cent conversion of light to useful energy, to 80 per cent efficiency.[541] This is in the foreseeable future, according to the Braun Research Group at the University of Illinois. In fact, it's not difficult to imagine a future of cells embedded into windows, flexible films and even paint. Recent advances in 'quantum dot' technology, in which energy-absorbing solar cells are manufactured as nanocrystals, would free us from the material limitations of current photovoltaics, which are brittle, heavy and flat. Quantum dots, if commercialised, could be sprayed or painted on curved and uneven surfaces, even onto thin sheets of plastic and rolled up – for easy shipping anywhere.[542] Distributed energy, personalised data and tailored controls are bringing the formerly distant and long arc of energy production and consumption down to the human scale.

Spaces and human impact

'First life, then spaces, then buildings – the other way around never works.' At seventy-eight years old, Danish architect Jan Gehl still has strong opinions about the way our cities are designed. He's spent the past fifty years developing the principles of what makes a city 'liveable' and leading an unwavering campaign for 'architecture that considers human scale and interaction.'[543]

I was fortunate to be introduced to Gehl's work by Richard Rogers, who (along with that other great British architect, Thomas Heatherwick) has taught me so much about architecture and urban design, and who is a fantastic champion for the future of cities. 'Cities – like books – can be read, and Jan Gehl understands their language,' he writes in the foreword to Gehl's book, *Cities for People*. 'The street, the footpath, the square, and the park are the grammar of the city; they provide the structure that enables cities to come to life, and to encourage and accommodate diverse activities, from the quiet and contemplative to the noisy and busy. A humane city – with carefully designed streets, squares, and parks – creates pleasure for visitors and passers-by, as well as for those who live, work, and play there every day.' Denser and more sustainable cities, Rogers adds, are the future, but only if we build them with space to walk, cycle, and breathe in, with 'beautiful public spaces that are human in scale, sustainable, healthy, and lively'.[544] Like the thinking of Jane Jacobs, Rogers's and Gehl's philosophies of cities resonate with me deeply.

It turns out that Gehl might not have learned the language of cities at all had love not intervened. It was 1960, and like all formally trained architects at the time, he was perfectly prepared to build exactly those types of 'modern cities' that Jane Jacobs would soon complain about – cities that, as he puts it, were full of 'high rises and a lot of lawns and good open space – good windy spaces'.[545] Had he not met Ingrid Mundt, a psychologist who would become his wife, his life might have turned out drastically different. As someone who studied 'people rather than bricks' as Gehl puts it, Mundt inspired a host of conversations among their combined peers. Why weren't architects interested in people? Why weren't they paying attention to how architecture could 'influence people's lives'? Why couldn't they work out how to make cities that would make people happier?

Gehl's philosophy was forever changed: 'Brasilia, the capital of Brazil, is a great example. From the air it's very interesting. It's interesting for a bird or eagle. From the helicopter view, it has got wonderful districts with sharp and precise government buildings and residential buildings. However, nobody spent three minutes to think about what Brasilia would look like at the eye level ... Nobody was responsible for looking after the people.'[546]

In 1965, they created the PSPL: a 'public space/public life' survey in Siena, Italy. The initial goal was simple: keep track of the number of people in a public space and what they were using it for.[547] Such 'street-level' observations would inform recommendations for improvements to various neighbourhoods. Fast-forward half a century, and Gehl has now surveyed cities around the world. His focus is almost entirely on considering the city, however large, at the human scale. To him, that's the only way to understand the effect architecture ultimately has on people.

From São Paulo and Amman to Brighton and New York, Gehl and his team spend weeks surveying people at all times of day, watching how they interact with the urban space in question: where they walk, where they spend time, what they do. Just as in Siena, he and his firm can take this base knowledge and use it to advise clients on questions of urban design and masterplanning. In all these years, his goal remains the same: to create 'cities for people'. Through this work, Gehl has created a list of twelve criteria for any public space, based on what he and his colleagues believe are the things people need from their urban environments. They span three categories: *protection* (from traffic, crime and pollution); *comfort* (to be able to walk, stand or sit, converse and play without impediment), and *enjoyment* (of the weather – hot, cold, rain or snow – and of aesthetic qualities). Their approach is meticulous, combining highly studious ethnography with traditional surveys to capture every on-the-ground detail. In one project aimed at improving London's walkability, surveyors counted thousands of pedestrians, measured precise distances between kerbs and pavement obstacles (like rubbish bins and street poles), and keenly observed every sort of behaviour they could catalogue – from mothers enlisting passers-by to help carry a pushchair down steps, to how many people cross against a red signal. They even compare measurements between weekdays and weekends, summer and winter. Though they don't provide a score per se, their reports are exhaustive, combining qualitative and quantitative elements including photographs, graphs and annotated maps to give planners a sense of where they are strong and where they are deficient in each category.[548]

To do this for every space, from schools to offices, houses to neighbourhoods, would be extreme. But Gehl is onto something. We don't need specific measurements or a points system to be able to assess whether a space fulfils human needs. Acknowledging them during its design is half the battle. So here's a simple way for us to make our spaces more human. Today, every building that's constructed has, at the very least, basic safety standards that it has to pass, as well as extra hurdles like environmental impact reports. On top of that, almost every type of space is subject to seemingly endless rules and regulations, standards and requirements.

What I propose is far simpler: a report – nothing too long or onerous; let's call it a Human Impact Report. No specific regulations or requirements. Just a short, straightforward statement of how any development – home, office, city block or neighbourhood redevelopment – fulfils each of Gehl's twelve criteria. In the spirit of 'nudging' outlined in Chapter 1, the point here is not to create another layer of burdensome bureaucracy. Rather, it's that if architects, planners, designers, builders and engineers are just prompted to start thinking along these lines, that simple act will end up making a difference – because it will make people think. It will make people think about people. And when this becomes part of the planning vernacular; when buyers, tenants, residents, citizens, and everyone else who occupies a space is exposed to these questions (and how builders answer them), 'human-ness' will become a real competitive advantage. Imagine that – a system in which developers and builders and architects and urban planners compete with each other to make the world around us more human.

That's a world I'd want to call home.

CHAPTER 10

NATURE

There's a classic speech that American park rangers are trained to deliver whenever they catch a child trying to make off with a 'natural' souvenir. 'You are supposed to calmly kneel down and say, "I saw you picking the flower. That is so pretty! Now think about what would happen if every child picked a flower,"' explains Matthew Browning, a former park ranger at Mount Mitchell State Park in North Carolina. 'And then they are supposed to have this moment of guilt.' One day in 2009, Browning saw a fellow ranger give the speech to a boy, about eight years old, in the park's restaurant. Instead of picking flowers, the boy had picked up a small handful of 'rocks'. In fact, it was gravel that the rangers had bought at the local supply store to spread over the road. Browning had an epiphany at that moment. 'It made me sick. The boy was crestfallen. He was so excited about coming to the park that he wanted to take a little memento back with him. More than feeling empowered or excited to protect the natural world, now he is going to associate going to state parks with getting into trouble.'[549]

But it's not just picking flowers and rocks that get you into trouble. Mount Mitchell – and most parks for that matter – prohibit all sorts of things: going off the official footpath, climbing trees, shouting, playing with sticks, digging holes … you name it. Disillusioned, Browning left the park and enrolled in graduate school to study the recreational use of natural areas. Hearing about so-called 'nature play areas' in Europe where children were allowed to play with abandon, he set off to Sweden to observe some at first hand. He ended up finding one near just about every primary school he visited (Sweden has a lot of forests). 'They all had plenty of forest and plenty of kids playing in the woods.' Browning didn't interact much with the children, preferring to observe rather than interrupt. But there was one boy, about twelve years old, who he recalled meeting one day: 'He was talking about how he would break branches and build forts and throw rocks. He had a knife with him. He said: "I carve sticks into spears and stuff like that."' So Browning asked him if he would ever stick the knife into a tree. The boy was shocked: '"No! It would hurt the tree; it would hurt the tree just like it would hurt me."'

This twelve-year-old's instinct highlights the human instinct of wanting to connect with nature. In 1984, the world's leading evolutionary biologist E.O. Wilson introduced the biophilia hypothesis, which he describes as the human 'urge to affiliate with other forms of life'.[550] He uses it to explain the fact that for much of human history, we've surrounded ourselves with plants and animals (either domesticated in our homes, gardens and communities, or close by in adjacent parks). You even see it in zoos, where animals exhibit unnatural behaviour when their pens don't mimic the natural environments from which they come.[551] It's an inborn desire we all share.

Indeed, study after study has substantiated the important beneficial effects of nature on human health and well-being. Views of nature and natural settings reduce stress and improve attention; walking in it even more so.[552] Though running reduces anxiety and depression wherever it is done, Swedish researchers have found the effects are amplified when it is done in nature.[553] The fortuitous design of a suburban Pennsylvania hospital allowed for the biophilia hypothesis to be tested directly in a sort of natural experiment: some rooms faced a stand of deciduous trees, while the others faced a brick wall. The patients with the views of trees had shorter hospital stays (by almost a day on average) and required fewer pain medications.[554]

Unnatural behaviour

Despite nature's great importance to us, we've systematically disconnected from it and destroyed it. For most of our history, we've gone out of our way to conquer the natural world. We've tilled the land, hunted – then domesticated – animals, cut down forests, dammed rivers, mined mountains, built cities. Now, we're manipulating genetics with biotechnology and even toying with the idea of engineering the climate (to fix the damage we ourselves have inflicted). We have tried to bend nature to human will. We have tried to make nature … more human.

For generations, this relationship worked because the scale and power of nature so exceeded that of human civilisation. Our efforts to conquer nature enabled our survival and progress as a species without, it seemed, doing nature much harm. But over the most recent phase of human history we have become much more mechanised and industrialised. As humanity began to outpace its natural context, the costs of our way of doing things became apparent. We saw pollution, spoilt landscapes and filthy cities. In 1952, London was hit by the Great Smog, a combination of cold weather and windless conditions that trapped air pollution (mostly from burning coal) for four days in and around the city, creating smog so thick that it is estimated to have prematurely killed at least 4,000 people.[555] A similar event killed nineteen people in Donora, a small mill town in south-western Pennsylvania, just four years before that. There, weather conditions led to toxic smoke from the town's steel and zinc mills blanketing the town for five days in a row.[556]

We reacted; the pendulum swung a bit towards conservation, and we cleaned things up. A bit. Earlier progressives like Theodore Roosevelt had championed the cause of nature, greatly expanding its protection through the National Park system.[557] But the inexorable march of industry went on throughout the twentieth century. A decade that saw a high-water mark of environmental awareness and activism in the 1960s and '70s – Earth Day, the Environmental Protection Agency, Clean Air and Water Acts – then receded into an era of cheap plastics, mass manufacturing, and ever-growing urban sprawl and fossil fuel consumption. As quickly as we learned our lessons, it seems, we swiftly forget them. So today, we live with a tomorrow that has never been more at risk.

Humanity's hubris – our hubris – was thinking that we could endlessly extract from nature with little or no adverse consequences. Our fundamental mistake, according to the influential twentieth-century economist E. F. Schumacher, was to treat nature like an infinite bank account from which we could forever make withdrawals. But such an adversarial relationship is a fallacy: if man won his battle with nature, 'he would find himself on the losing side'.[558] Despite our best efforts, there's just no way to bend all of nature's vast, incomprehensible complexity to our human rules and institutions. We have to realise that nature isn't just humanity's support structure; humanity is a *part* of nature. Our careless manipulation of it is not only unnatural; it is irrevocably harmful both to nature and, ultimately, to ourselves.

We've now destroyed 17 per cent of the Amazon rainforest – that's nearly one-fifth – more than 3.1 times the land area of the entire UK.[559] We lose over 20 million acres of tropical forest per year.[560] There is now estimated to be at least 268,940 tonnes of plastic floating in our oceans, according to a 2014 report from the Five Gyres Institute in Los Angeles (an organisation set up for the express purpose of studying the issue).[561] Rather than biodegrade (the way organic material would), plastic just breaks down into smaller and smaller pieces, devastating the wildlife that ingests it. Coral reefs occupy less than a quarter of 1 per cent of the marine environment but house a quarter of known fish species. In the 1970s, live coral covered half of the Caribbean's reefs; today it covers 8 per cent of them.[562] According to the International Union for Conservation of Nature's latest 'Red List of Threatened Species', 41 per cent of amphibians and 26 per cent of mammals are currently under threat of extinction. Precision is difficult, since many species are still undiscovered, but estimates suggest we are losing between 500 and 36,000 species each year.[563] All said, we've endangered or driven to extinction countless species, we've destroyed irreplaceable habitats, and we've polluted our air and waters to dangerous levels.

One of the most impactful meetings I ever had was when Rohan took me to meet E. O. Wilson at Harvard University. He is recognised as being one of the first theorists to discuss and advocate for 'biodiversity', that is, variation among genes within species, species within ecosystems, and ecosystems among each other. As he puts it, we risk losing '"genetic encyclopedias" millions of years in the making',[564] embodying countless medical, biotechnical and agricultural opportunities (49 per cent of cancer-fighting drugs, for instance, are derived from natural products).[565] According to Wilson, we stand to reduce at least half of the earth's remaining plant and animal species to extinction or critical endangerment by the end of the century; such cataclysms (of which the earth has had five so far, the last one having brought an end to the dinosaurs) take 5 to 10 million years to repair. 'We are, in short, flying blind into the environmental future,' Wilson says.[566]

To forestall the sixth mass-extinction event which he speaks of, we have to get more serious about conservation. According to a December 2014 assessment by the science journal *Nature*, a loss of 690 species per week (the upper end of estimates) would bring such an event about by the year 2200.[567] Wilson's bold vision (what he calculates is necessary to avoid ruinous biodiversity loss)[568] is to set aside half of the earth for conservation or restoration (Half Earth). Crucially, it's not just making sure that land already out of civilisation's way remains protected (though this is important). It's making sure that all of the world's ecosystems have at least some protected areas where nature can 'do its thing'. In some cases this will require restoration; in others, it might mean paying landowners to ensure parts of their land remain undeveloped (but still accessible for light use). It also means threading these protected areas together so that as habitats shift with a changing climate, wildlife is able to migrate – perhaps hundreds or even thousands of miles through accessible 'corridors', like the White Hawk Project adjoining the Corcovado National Park in Costa Rica.[569] In order to preserve the Park's incredible biodiversity (some 2.5 per cent of the world's total), the White Hawk Project purchases and maintains land abutting the Park in order to create wildlife corridors using conservation easements, which restrict development and land use for ecological benefit.

When our family, along with Rohan and his wife Kate, holidayed near the Park in April 2015, we learned about the White Hawk Project first hand from Lana Wedmore, our ecolodge's owner and the project's founder. What is so amazing – but equally frustrating – about Lana's work is that compared to the massive sums spent by government, often ineffectively, fighting climate change, she's asking for a pittance. And yet here is a solution that not only contributes to global climate efforts but conserves land for ever and tangibly saves species from extinction, today. Even more tangibly, visiting the Corcovado National Park exposed all of us to the rainforest and showed us first hand the true value of nature and its protection. This kind of direct exposure to nature has got to be the best way to instill in everyone – especially children – a conservation ethos that lasts a lifetime.

It seems hardly necessary by now to justify why this would be worthwhile. The unknown human value that will one day derive from the biodiversity preserved (and stimulated) by a globally connected wilderness alone makes ambitions like Half Earth and projects like White Hawk easy to justify. But it's also the benefit of having truly natural nature (such a phrase would seem ridiculous if it weren't necessary) local to everyone. We would be infusing our modern, sophisticated landscape with pristine nature, side by side, everywhere.

Throughout this book, I've discussed how we need to make our world more human. But when it comes to nature, we've already made the world too human. We've distorted our idea of what nature is and should be, because we've misunderstood our part in it. So now we need to fundamentally rethink humanity's relationship with the natural world which we inhabit, moving the pendulum back towards the system of our ancestors, in which we benefit from nature while simultaneously giving back to and coexisting with it.

Natural capital

Nature isn't just beautiful, it's practical. Nature can help us prevent floods, dampen tidal waves, filter water, and clean the air. Nature is increasingly being recognised by engineers – not just environmentalists – as a way to provide essential services we otherwise would trust to machines and concrete and steel. It actually has a term devoted to it: green infrastructure. Nature provides many 'services' to us when left in its natural state. For example, it saves our lives and communities in times of natural disaster. Flooding and storm surges can be softened, if not stopped, by wetlands and marshes that absorb the brunt of the impact. When authorities built sea walls to protect against annual floods in the Humber Estuary in Yorkshire and Lincolnshire, they inadvertently killed off the wetlands that had formed natural barriers. So when flood waters hit, the walls held back some water but without the wetlands to block the storm surge, flooding was actually worse. To solve the problem, sea walls have now been deliberately breached so that the wetlands return to their natural state – a move that will create £11.5 million of net benefit over the next fifty years in terms of saved farmland and property compared to the damage the standing sea wall would have led to.[570] In Boston, Massachusetts, the Army Corps of Engineers found that annual flooding of the Charles River would cost $17 million a year if not for wetlands protecting the city.[571] Wetlands can be particularly crucial during extreme events: a long-standing rule of thumb holds that for every 2.7 miles of wetlands, a hurricane storm surge can be reduced by as much as a foot.[572] When Hurricane Katrina hit New Orleans in 2005, it found a city built out too far to the ocean's edge – with 1,900 square miles of natural wetlands having been destroyed and developed between true land and the Gulf of Mexico.[573] Without these natural shock absorbers, the flooding wasn't just destructive; it was devastating. Thankfully, some wetlands were still intact: scientists estimate that if there had been none left, the flood waters would have been 1 to 2 metres higher.[574]

While some environmentalists might scoff at putting a price on nature, not to do so is to completely devalue it and let others take advantage – and destroy – its enormous wealth. Depleting natural resources might not cost money, but it isn't 'free'. Take, for example, the conversion of mangrove swamps in southern Thailand into shrimp farms. One report found that such conversions yield around $1,220 a hectare. But these profits fail to consider the costs of losing the mangroves. After five years, the farm is depleted, requiring intensive and expensive rehabilitation. And while used as shrimp farms, the mangrove swamps fail to provide wood for local communities, nurseries for local fish farming and a barrier against storms. In total, the implicit costs equal $12,392 a hectare, an entire order of magnitude greater than the profits from shrimp farming.[575] Yet because the costs are borne by the 'public' while the profits are earned privately, the decision was a foregone conclusion: profits were made; natural capital was lost. The argument – and a compelling plan – for rigorously accounting for nature is brilliantly set out in Dieter Helm's latest book, *Natural Capital*. A proper plan for protecting our environment should start by just implementing that.

Nature doesn't only mitigate the impacts of future disasters; it provides us with essential services every day – often cheaper and more reliably than man-made infrastructure can. In the American state of Maine, about 15 per cent of the population, mostly in the greater Portland area, gets its water from Sebago Lake. The lake covers 30,000 acres, and the area that supplies it is more than 50 miles long.[576] Because of the area's pristine condition, the Portland Water District has long operated under a federal waiver allowing it to draw its water without many of the typical filtration requirements that are otherwise necessary in other geographies. Recently, though, the lake's water quality has deteriorated, as run-off from upstream land development and population growth has increased. The typical approach would be to invest in 'grey' infrastructure (so-called because of the colour of the excessive cement usually involved) – in this case, 'membrane filtration' technology. An analysis by the World Resources Institute found that this would cost between $102 million and $146 million. Investing instead in conservation and restoration of the surrounding forest ecosystem – green infrastructure – at a cost of between $34 million and $74 million would deliver $70 million in savings.[577] It turns out that natural forest land is just more efficient at keeping our water clean (one study estimates that for every 10 per cent increase in forest cover in a source area, there is a corresponding decrease of about 20 per cent in water treatment costs.)[578] And yet our human habits, Australian ecological economist Robert Costanza estimates, destroy $23 trillion each year of the $142.7 trillion in these 'services' (not just clean air and water and storm protection but also waste decomposition, crop pollination, renewable energy sources, and raw materials, to name a few) that our natural ecosystems provide us.[579] But despite these powerful arguments, the environmental movement is losing.

People understand what they can see, hear, touch and smell. At that level, I think most people really do care about the environment – even if they hate green politics and can't stand talk of climate change. I've yet to meet someone who is in favour of dirty air and water, dead forests, or poisoned landscapes. Or someone who doesn't enjoy, if they get the chance, spending time in the mountains, at a lake, or at the beach. Behaviour that could be described as 'environmentalist' is really just showing our love of nature. Pretty much everyone is in favour of that. But by branding and politicising environmentalism, we've made good stewardship a question of saving the entire planet: an unrelatable idea.

So while our local actions do indeed have global impacts, these impacts have to be talked about at the human scale, otherwise their real meaning becomes obscure. Climate change doesn't mean 'global sea level rise' (though this may happen), it means that farmers lose their crops and livelihoods, entire species of animals and plants are lost forever, and centuries-old villages are wiped out by the sea.

The other problem with the big global-environmental argument is that it diffuses responsibility. Elinor Ostrom won the Nobel Prize in economics for demonstrating the tragedy of the commons, in which behaviour that benefits the individual at the group's expense leads to everyone doing it (until the whole group is out of luck). When problems are made to seem big, the individual actions we take to both create and solve them have the same illusion of insignificance. Noble as fighting for 'parts per million' is, it just doesn't mean anything if you're not a scientist. We have to make sure that nature is accessible to everyone so that everyone can have their own experiences, their own memories to draw from, their own reason to care that we don't destroy it all.

As much as the communications revolution (not to mention high-definition television) has enabled us to more vividly experience exotic ecosystems and animals across the world, there is no substitute for the real thing. The key to making us environmentalists, conservationists, good stewards (or really, just conscientious human beings), is exposure to what we otherwise wouldn't care about. So the answer to the threat to nature is not a new law, or a new government programme, or an ad campaign or any of the other traditional levers of bureaucratic action. It's something more human than all of that. It's the simple act of being in nature, walking in nature, playing in nature, getting out into nature, seeing the world's wonder. When you begin to comprehend your place on the planet in the midst of everyone and everything else, it all suddenly comes into perspective. But of course, this theme has been true throughout the book – empathy through human connection and experience.

This is what politicians and conservationists have got wrong. While often well-meaning, their efforts have morphed the environmental movement into Big Green, the bureaucracy and politics of which have needlessly made the environment a contested and partisan one. The environment is not a battlefield of Left versus Right; it's actually about loving the world we live in, our home. People – all people – want blue skies and clean air and safe water, but you'll never convince people to be greener if you make it all about carbon dioxide. Yes, we have to highlight how nature can actually, tangibly help us in our own daily lives. But 'green' is nature, animals, parks, the countryside. It's about where people want to go on holiday or spend free time with their families. It's about the joy of fresh air and beautiful scenery.

We should start with children. It's not just about a respect for and understanding of the natural world, its importance to us, and the necessity of sustainability and conservation. It also helps child development. Children need to engage in the world if they are to be properly educated. As we saw in Chapter 8, a significant part of their development comes from exploration and adventure, and there is no better place to do that than in the natural world.

But this is a big hurdle. I've seen it at first hand. When I grew up, spending time in nature was not the social norm. Now, here in Northern California where it is very much part of the culture, I've chosen, for the first time in my life, to do strange things (for a confirmed urbanite) like go camping. Camping! How horrific. Actually not. It is no exaggeration to say that our children and their friends are never happier than when out in the woods or wherever we go in nature. It is cheaper – and better – than any number of toys or trips to theme parks or visitor attractions.

The worst part of all this is that for wealthy people, nature is perfectly normal. People with money buy the home in the country, the house by the beach, the lodge in the mountains, the villa on the lake. The rich have made nature fashionable, with eco-tourism and luxury brands and philanthropy. They wouldn't think of keeping their kids inside all the time. But the second you suggest that everyone else should get better access to nature, it's suddenly just that – a luxury, a waste of money that we can't afford (because, gosh, what would happen to those PISA scores?). Why? Why is nature a necessity for rich people but a luxury for poor people? Why is nature less important than maths or art or history?

'Shopping is not a hobby'

Connecting people with nature will become increasingly urgent as humanity continues to urbanise. Since 1950, the urban population has gone from 30 per cent of the global population to 54 per cent today, and is expected to reach 66 per cent by 2050.[580] Cities represent a prosperous and in some respects more sustainable future. But for all its modern, hipster vibe, urbanisation comes with a significant drawback: the more we live in cities, the further we are from nature and the closer we get to forgetting its importance altogether. We risk what some are calling 'nature deficit disorder'.[581]

But how do you persuade people to change? We obviously need a new strategy, and in this there is a role for the human touch. At the moment, when we try to distil nature into human terms, what results is a dangerous abstraction. We need to bring people's interaction with nature back to a human, visceral level. Nature must be experienced.

Many parents want their children to experience nature but don't know how to go about it. There are too many barriers, many of which, as we've seen throughout this book, are simply inherent in our inhuman world today: families live too far away from natural spaces, parents have unrealistic fears of the outdoors, teachers lack enthusiasm for leaving the classroom, technology too easily entertains and distracts children.[582] The key is to start the process early, with a proper communication of the interconnection between nature and society. Jason and Scott fondly remember their grandparents sending them the magazines *Your Big Backyard* and *Ranger Rick*, published by the National Wildlife Federation in America, which, by helping them understand the importance of nature as children, shaped a lifelong environmentalist ethos in them. Those magazines worked because they explained nature in children's terms.

The same principle guides author Christiane Dorion, who has developed a creative way to communicate complex environmental and scientific concepts through her pop-up children's books.

'Children are naturally interested in the natural world,' she explains, so she tries to identify 'the questions they are interested in learning about'. And it turns out that children are indeed fascinated by the water cycle and weather patterns – just not when described in those words. Instead, Dorion poses questions that children have actually asked her – Where does rain come from? What's inside the earth? How do plants live? – and then answers them in surprisingly rich detail while keeping it all age-accessible. They might not understand biodiversty loss or climate change, but they come to intuit how small things in their lives connect directly to the wider world. Dorion jokes that parents tell her they keep reading her books after putting their children to bed, since they never learned these things when they were younger.[583]

If applied correctly, technology, like Dorion's books, can play a helpful role too. Researchers at Stanford, MIT and Harvard are working on various projects to create virtual-reality simulators that put users directly into otherwise inaccessible natural circumstances. For instance, a simulation created at Stanford transforms users into a pink coral, so they can see what happens to reefs over time. During the simulation, sea urchins, sea bream, sea snails and fish interact around 'you'. Over the course of thirteen minutes, the simulation progresses through a century, and the environment changes around the reef as it is degraded by acidification (an urgent problem currently facing all the world's oceans).[584] Species which are present at the start disappear and even the pink coral skeleton that the users embody disintegrates. Early studies suggest that conveying the gravity of human effects on the environment in such a personal way has a significant impact on attitudes, which the researchers confirmed in follow-ups with participants afterwards.[585] 'One can viscerally experience disparate futures and get firsthand experience about the consequences of human behavior,' says Jeremy Bailenson, the director of Stanford's Virtual Human Interaction Lab, which ran the simulation.[586] And with the advent of virtual-reality headsets like Oculus VR, zoos, parks and schools can increasingly use these technologies as a complement to their real-world programmes.

The studies done around virtual reality and nature prove that we need to empathise with nature to care about it. But it's also pretty ridiculous that we have to reduce nature to a virtual-reality headset. All the book learning in the world won't change the simple fact that children need to touch nature for themselves. It must be palpable. It must be emotional. Nature must be experienced at first hand. That's why programmes like Vida Verde are so crucial to this effort.

Vida Verde is an educational camp and organic farm in California's Santa Cruz mountains dedicated to getting children from all backgrounds into nature. 'There are thousands of children who live thirty miles from the ocean, and they've never actually seen it,' explains Laura Sears, who founded the organisation with her husband, Shawn, in 2001. 'We've seen kids who come to Vida Verde who've never spent time walking on uneven surfaces.' Shawn and Laura bring groups of no more than thirty children at a time from different inner-city schools in the San Francisco area for three days and two nights to their 23-acre property. The children learn experientially, classifying plants and animals on walks; learning about mammals whilst milking the resident goats, and birds whilst collecting hens' eggs; and understanding the sea whilst running barefoot in the sand (many for the first time in their lives) or exploring rock pools – all in the same lesson, of course. 'It's a beautiful thing to let these children start to discover and explore and let their guard down,' Laura says, 'and just be in this gorgeous environment that they maybe never thought they'd ever get to be in.' (As an aside, making children excited about nature also excites them about wholesome and natural food. The meals of the programme come from the animals and plants grown at the farm; and the children participate in their harvest and preparation.)

'Kids do really well being outside, using all their senses and bodies to learn, not just reading something or hearing it,' Shawn explains. Being there and doing it makes it real for them. For the first time, they can really connect to the place where they live, and their teachers can use this in the classroom from there on to connect lessons to real life. Teachers report that children engage in their studies as they haven't in the past. Perhaps more importantly than this, nature can be harnessed as a tool for teaching very human lessons about relationships, trying new things, determination, and working together. In one activity – the goat hike – small groups of students use teamwork to herd resident goats across a river, through the thistles, and up a mile-long hill on a steep, sometimes tricky path. 'It's a physical challenge. They simply have to work together to make it,' says Shawn. 'You see students who don't necessarily talk or hang out with each other otherwise doing it because it's needed. People just breaking down and treating each other like human beings – and walking away from the experience with fresh eyes for those around them and new friends.' Such programmes are so important. Jason and Scott – northern Californians themselves – remember that when they were sixth-graders (they're twins), everyone in their peer group went to a camp like Vida Verde, where many of them camped for the first time. They spent a week hiking, exploring marshland, running basic experiments in the forest (not to mention growing emotionally by being away from their parents for the first time). Nearly every state school in the region participates in these types of programmes, providing a valuable link for schoolchildren to receive an education in nature.

You can predict the objections. 'Well, that's all very well if you live in Northern California in one of the richest and most naturally beautiful places on earth but what about the real world where you don't have incredible nature on your doorstep? Or incredible wealth to preserve it? Or incredibly rich families who can pay to send their kids to experience it?'

Well – here's the thing. None of this is preordained or determined by geography, finances, or anything else. It's about priorities.

At the moment, across the world, consumerism is the social norm and nature is not. We choose to build Westfield shopping centres. Why? Why do we need more of those? Why do we think it's acceptable for children to spend a weekend afternoon going shopping? As my sister-in-law has pithily remarked: 'Shopping is not a hobby.' But for many people in rich countries today, that's exactly what it is. We can change that. The norm has certainly flipped before: when workers spent most of their time in the fields, bronzed by the sun, the elite stayed inside. But with the advent of the factory and then the office cubicle, that norm switched. Once workers' skins grew pale under artificial lights, the rich jumped at any chance they could to develop a tan, setting themselves apart – the 'leisure' class.[587] But the outdoors shouldn't be a function of fashion. It should be something everyone enjoys from the richest to poorest, that everyone rightly feels entitled to experience as a human, without stigma. We must choose to make this a priority; we must choose to collectively pay for it; we must choose to require it. Nature should be a fundamental part of our human experience. More than anything else, nature should unify us.

One of the many reasons I would love to be mayor of a city is to show what can happen when we take a radically different – a revolutionarily different – approach to land use.

When it comes to the physical presence of nature in our lives, we could easily incorporate woodlands and wetlands and natural habitats right in the middle of our towns and cities. Not just parks, but real, wild nature. There are some great examples – in Los Angeles, I visited the Ballona Wetlands, which is near Playa del Rey. Here where you'd least expect it – in bustling LA, surrounded by a highway to the east, private homes to the south, a strip mall to the north, and a tourist beach to the west – are 600 acres of open space that state officials are trying to restore to its former glory.[588] The wetlands here once stretched for miles in either direction up and down the coast, but were carved out into developments around fifty years ago. Even in Ballona, there is hardly any wetland left. For centuries, Berliners have enjoyed the Grunewald forest, covering more than 7,000 acres in the western part of the German capital.[589] In Knoxville, Tennessee, locals recently championed the preservation of 1,000 acres of forest along the Tennessee River waterfront. Just 3 miles from downtown, residents and visitors there can use its more than 40 miles of trails to walk, mountain bike, run, or just explore.[590] And of course, there's London's Hampstead Heath, 790 acres of rambling hills and woodland, dearly loved by dogs and visitors alike.

But these are exceptions. How about designing a world where they're not?

If we do make space for nature in the midst of our modern world, how do we make sure that children grow up in it – not through a once-a-year field trip, but all the time? Well, we know exactly how to do it – we just need to make the choice. There are countless national and local organisations – notably the Scouts and Cubs and Girl

Guides – dedicated to giving children fun experiences in nature. We could easily make nature an expectation for every child, just as we expect them to learn maths (or now, coding). It's actually more important than either of those or any other academic subject because the kinds of experiences you gain when you spend time in nature, with others, help build your character in ways (as we saw in previous chapters) that are far more useful in the twenty-first century than anything academic.[591] But instead we insist on locking children up in windowless, soulless boxes from eight in the morning for the rest of the day. Madness. But amidst the strange priorities that have infected today's world, the argument I'm making – that we should expect all children to spend time in nature as a basic, substantial part of their education – is more likely to be seen as crazy.

Nature must be made more accessible in another way too. Remember North Carolina park ranger Matthew Browning and the twelve-year-old boy he saw being chastised for playing in nature? The way things stand now, nature is seen a museum, where we can look but not touch. How do we expect to get excited about nature if we can't engage with it? The typical sheltered life of the twenty-first-century family might make us feel safe, but we are not better off as a result. We cannot survive without nature; we are inextricably linked. Nature is not harmless but it is far from harmful. We must engage with it, understand it, and raise our children in it. And if we do, we will not only improve everyone's happiness and well-being today, but we will also do something much more significant. We will bring up a generation of people who really understand and respect nature and humanity's place within it.

Because when it comes to the natural world around us, it's time we were a little bit less human.

CONCLUSION

This book has ranged across many aspects of life. From food to government, the economy to health care, I've argued that we need to redesign, reorganise, and reconsider our world in terms more suited to the way we truly, naturally, humanly are. From the beginning I haven't promised to cover everything. But I hope that the idea behind *More Human* will help give you a framework for thinking about your own life and how you relate to everything from your civic participation, to your interaction with the light switch, to your lunch. I've talked about how to make our institutions more human, our products and services more human, even our buildings more human, but what about the essence of our humanity, our relationships with one another? How do we make those more human as well?

To be human is to love, to accept, and to empathise with each other, but it is just as human to hate, ostracise, and blame. Witness the ethnic, sectarian, and nationalist tensions across the globe today. From the Middle East, where Israelis and Palestinians are killing each other, to Iraq and Syria, where Muslims are killing each other (and those who get in their way), to Ukraine, where Russians and Ukrainians are killing each other too. And you needn't look only to war zones to see the divisions that engulf the world. For as much progress as we've made, we've returned to the world of the scapegoat, the world of the 'other'. Jews are blamed for problems in Hungary, Muslims in France, Turks in Germany, Mexicans in America, and Poles in Britain. Supporters of human understanding might look at the world today and easily sink into a deep despair, wondering if we have learned anything from the horrors of our past.

The problem with this thesis is that the terrible version of ourselves that we see in all of those war-torn or even just economically depressed places is not the true us. It is the anxious us, the ignorant us, the fearful us. In so many of these places, tensions are unleashed not out of a sense of true racism, xenophobia, or anti-Semitism, but out of political expediency. People like Nigel Farage in Britain, Marine Le Pen in France, or Viktor Orbán in Hungary tap into a national discontent because they know that it's so much easier to blame someone else for your problems. But the funny thing is that while rhetorically or theoretically we might blame the immigrant or the minority, in practice, on a day-to-day basis, in our real human lives, we do not.

Despite the national opprobrium sometimes directed at Polish migrants to Britain, locals find they are pleasant neighbours, and employers find them to be hard workers. One study found that between 1995 and 2011, European migrants had a net positive contribution of £4 billion to Britain (as opposed to a negative contribution of £591 billion for native Britons).[592] 'The Polish Paradox', as *The Economist* called it,[593] is true elsewhere. In America, successive waves of immigrants have faced racist and xenophobic treatment only to be accepted once they start integrating into society and Americans realise they are perfectly decent people. Proximity and contact are thus the ultimate antidotes against insularity and prejudice, a point proven by the steady evolution of public opinion on gay rights. It turns out that once people realise one of their neighbours, friends, colleagues, or relatives is gay, their homophobia turns into tolerance and then acceptance and then comradeship. It's easy to hate strangers on TV and in far-away parades. It's much harder to hate a group to which your son or daughter belongs. Republicans in the United States have traditionally been dead set against gay marriage and other gay rights, but several prominent party members have come out in favour of both, almost solely because of their personal experiences. Former Vice President Dick Cheney, a stalwart conservative, prominently broke with his boss President George W. Bush on the issue of gay marriage out of concern for his lesbian daughter, Mary. More recently, Republican Senator Rob Portman, a former member of President Bush's cabinet, changed his position on gay marriage when his son came out. He said that learning his son was gay caused him to examine his stance 'from a new perspective, and that's of a dad who loves his son a lot and wants him to have the same opportunities that his brother and sister would have – to have a relationship like Jane [Portman's wife] and I have had for over 26 years'.[594]

When confronted on their prejudices by their own children, people tend to evolve and overcome them; after all, if you can't empathise with your child, who can you empathise with? Gay people are relatively blessed with the fact that anyone might be gay; even ardent homophobes might end up with a lesbian cousin or a gay nephew. But for those of different ethnic, racial, national, and religious backgrounds, such genetic serendipity is impossible. And while we have come further than ever before in human history, we need to push ourselves to always engage with those who are different.

Obviously, overcoming difference is most keenly felt at home where de facto segregation and misunderstandings sometimes result in subtle (and not so subtle) discrimination and conflict. And it shouldn't be diminished; lack of mutual understanding can lead to grave injustices, civil unrest, and even tragedy – witness in America the gross disparity between violent deaths afflicting black and white populations. But when those differences fester, as is happening around the world, we see something worse: terrorism, war, and genocide.

We live in an age when we can travel to and communicate with every corner of the world. If we stop talking to one another, helping one another, being human to one another, we undermine our common humanity. Britain is lucky to have the ability to be an actor on the world stage, and we have come to the aid of many under existential threat, from the people of Sierra Leone to the peoples of Kosovo and Bosnia to the people of Libya. Certainly, engaging in armed conflict is a decision that should be made with a heavy heart and the answer surely should not always be 'yes'. But by remembering that we have a heart, we can make a substantial difference in the lives of millions. We can distribute humanitarian aid; we can rebuild communities; we can advise nascent governments. We have to remember that we are all flesh and blood. We all suffer. We are all human.

That's why we need to bolster ways of relating to one another to avoid conflict and reduce strife. Not just economic ties (whose importance we saw in Chapter 5), but also things like the informal, or so-called 'track two' and 'track three' diplomacy between academics, artists, students, civil-society groups, and tourists in countries around the world – including problematic places like North Korea, Iran and Russia. We should continue to build upon the ties that diplomats nurture. Exchanges, visits and summits – personal, human contact – should underpin important international relationships. When world leaders spend time at summits, they don't just negotiate; they also develop rapports that enhance future relations and nip brewing crises in the bud.

Being more human with one another is crucial to bridging cultural divides and living in a more peaceful world. If we are to be a successful global society, this is imperative. But it's sometimes much more basic than that. We need to ask ourselves what it is meaningfully to interact with each other on a daily basis. Civility is not just for the advice columns; it is incumbent upon us all to practise it. And in a world in which technology has rapidly changed social interactions, litigating technology's role would be a good start. As we have seen, mobile phones and the Internet have fundamentally altered how we communicate with each other, for good and bad. Technology helps us learn in our own time, with courses customised to our needs. Mobile phones give parents the comfort of letting their children push the boundaries of independence. And Skype connects distant friends and relatives across oceans, time zones and continents. Through the advent of big data, we now have more capacity to understand and control our own existences than ever before. But technology has its problems. It can be manipulated by nefarious actors. It has led to the scourge of pre-teen and teenage sexting. It has changed our neurology. Perhaps most importantly, it has changed how we live our lives. Too many people, it seems, now live not for the moment but for the Likes and Retweets; they would too often rather hang out online than in person. Staying connected to others is wonderful, but not if its cost is disconnecting from reality and from tangible, actual, people.

In technology as in so many other areas, you could say: no, the status quo is human. You could ask, as we did at the beginning of this book: why is a world designed by humans not already, by definition, 'more human'? Well, in much the same way that all the social-science theories that explain human behaviour as rational fail to take into account our own irrationalities, our institutions fail to live up to their own standards too. Sometimes when we created our institutions, we simply didn't know what was or wasn't human. Behavioural science is a rather novel field and until recently, many of us really did believe that people were perfectly rational. But because we weren't (and still aren't), even our 'rational' institutions turn out imperfectly. We fell victim to the hubris (another human trait) that we could outsmart nature, that we could outsmart even ourselves. Cities were built based on how planners believed we should live, not how we actually would. Education systems were designed based on how we once thought children learned and what they needed for success, not on what actually matters now and for the future. That's why it's so important to embrace the science – the human insights – in fields like behavioural economics, neuroscience, psychology, and biology that allows us better to know ourselves, better to pinpoint interventions, and better to help people flourish.

That's not to say that we shouldn't theorise or experiment until we get it right – tinkering is human too, after all – but we should understand the limits of designing any system, product, service, or environment without connecting with the people who will be involved in it on a daily basis as consumers, providers, recipients, residents, patients, or students. We are on the cusp of transcending 'just theory' in many fields simply because we increasingly have easy access to all the data. We should embrace the science that allows us to determine exactly what causes certain behaviours and outcomes and how we can better help people thrive, while acknowledging its limitations. And we should recognise that what is human for some of us is not human for others. Sometimes values clash, and it's up to us to realise when they do and arbitrate the outcomes so that they are as human as possible for as many as possible. Sometimes that means making a judgement between two values; in cases like those, there's not necessarily a right or wrong answer.

We also must remember that everything is interconnected: children don't just need good families, wholesome play, and limits on mobile Internet-enabled devices – they need liveable homes and safe streets, access to nature, and food and schools not made in or designed as factories. For our economy to flourish, we need to treat workers as humans, require fair competition, and enable people to fulfil their potential, but we also need to plan for the long term, combat poverty at its roots, better educate our future workforce, and lessen the stranglehold of vested interests over our regulatory regimes.

As we saw, some themes are woven throughout. Whilst we must be wary of technology, we must also allow for its near limitless possibilities. And we must remember that the importance of families pervades every issue, from education to poverty to jobs to inequality, which is why government should redouble its efforts at early and comprehensive family interventions. Government itself is formally covered in Chapter 1, but government, regulation, and public policy play a role in every issue in this book. The best way to make change, after all, is through our political system, as I will argue in the Postscript.

In fact, as I said from the outset, in many ways we need a revolution in our society to counteract its many ills. Some are obvious – dissatisfaction with government, unfair wages, the power of rich elites – but others are less so, like the surreptitious harm of smartphones, the attack on proper play, and the absence of human-centred design in policymaking. We need sweeping institutional changes, like bans on factory farms; and sweeping attitudinal changes, like how we relate to nature. Above all we need a more human world to be accessible not just to the elites, which is why we need to reinvigorate our democracy: in government, and in our schools, businesses, and communities, too.

More – or less – human?

In this book, I've argued that more human values, scale, design, products and policies are all good things; that we should aspire to make everything in our lives as human as possible. I've just argued for a revolution in doing so. But while we know what a more human world would mostly look like, there's an interesting exception emerging, a field in which, as it gets more human, the result is more inhuman.

This is the field of robotics and artificial intelligence. Artificial intelligence (AI), simply defined, is the field of trying to create intelligence synthetically. We already have many basic versions of it, from IBM's Watson to Apple's Siri to Google's self-driving cars. Perhaps the ultimate expression of AI is the 'singularity' hypothesis, which as articulated by futurist Ray Kurzweil, predicts 'the union of human and machine, in which the knowledge and skills embedded in our brains will be combined with the vastly greater capacity, speed, and knowledge-sharing ability of our own creations'.[595]

If this sounds like science fiction, you're right. But excitingly (or alarmingly, depending on your view) reality is in many ways already catching up with science fiction. Think about Steven Spielberg's 2002 film *Minority Report*. While our world doesn't yet resemble his, we have developed many of the technologies his characters use, like automated cars, facial-recognition software, personalised advertising, predictive crime fighting (they used mutated psychics called 'precogs'; we use big data and analytics), gesture-based computer interfaces, and even jet packs.[596] As exciting as that may be, it also means that the future is arriving sooner than we think. And we have to determine what we want it to look like.

Technological optimists like Kurzweil and Google's Larry Page believe that automation and robotics will free us up for more human endeavours. There is certainly a good argument for this; after all, as we saw in Chapter 7, even basic technologies have saved people from the most difficult and arduous tasks. Surely keeping people occupied in that way is inhuman? And surely liberating them to do more meaningful tasks or to spend more time in leisure is the more human alternative? Maybe AI is simply tomorrow's version of a mundane task that can be automated. We don't fear our washing machines; why fear whatever's coming next? As Rollo Carpenter, the founder of AI software firm Cleverbot, says: 'We cannot quite know what will happen if a machine exceeds our own intelligence, so we can't know if we'll be infinitely helped by it, or ignored by it and sidelined, or conceivably destroyed by it ... I believe we will remain in charge of the technology for a decently long time and the potential of it to solve many of the world's problems will be realised.'[597] For some roboticists, replacing people has never been the goal. 'There are seven billion people in the world, and almost all of them are very good at being people,' says Helen Greiner, co-founder of iRobot (which made the Roomba vacuum-cleaning robot) and CEO of CyPhyWorks. 'We're not trying to duplicate people. We're trying to help them; make them more efficient, better at their jobs; empower them to do more with robotic technology.'[598]

To naturalist and science writer Diane Ackerman, 'surpassing human limits is so human a quest, maybe the most ancient one of all',[599] and AI is simply the next limit. Indeed, pushing the boundaries of AI might be one of the most human things we can do. In her latest book, *The Human Age*, she writes:

> *I find it touchingly poetic to think that as our technology grows more advanced, we may grow more human. When labor, science, manufacturing, sales, transportation, and powerful new technologies are mainly handled by savvy machines, humans really won't be able to compete in those sectors of the economy. Instead we may dominate an economy of interpersonal or imaginative services, in which our human skills shine.*[600]

On the other side of the argument, technological pessimists like Elon Musk and Stephen Hawking believe that for every great technological advance, we take a step towards human obsolescence. 'With artificial intelligence, we are summoning the demon,' Musk says. 'You know all those stories where there's the guy with the pentagram and the holy water and … he's sure he can control the demon. It doesn't work out.'[601] For example, scientists are building robots that can literally feed (power) themselves: engineers at Bristol Robotics Laboratory are building the EcoBot III, which can convert flies into fuel, while the US Defense Department-funded EATR (Energetically Autonomous Tactical Robot) uses cameras and sensors to find organic matter like leaves, which it can then pick up and burn as fuel.[602] Perhaps while robots perform mundane tasks, this is perfectly fine, but what happens when we can't stop a robot from overpowering us, because we've taught it to feed itself? These pessimists fear at best that AI will supplant jobs (fuelling inequality by leaving the working class with nowhere to go) and challenge the boundary between life and artificiality. But at their worst, they fear the very supplanting of humanity as a species. 'The development of full artificial intelligence,' Hawking warns, 'could spell the end of the human race.'[603]

We therefore have to ask ourselves real questions about AI's potential impact. In the short term, artificial intelligence could cause inequality on a massive scale, more even than we have seen with automation, globalisation and family disparities in Chapter 7; it could permanently lock out huge segments of society from the economy. Today, robots enhance things we can't do, like compute, position us using satellites, perform dangerous tasks, connect to a grid. They are largely unthreatening. But what if computers start to do what we've thought of as essentially human tasks: thinking critically, creating, caring, applying values and reason? What if computers become more like us?

And what if they become more like us but lack central human qualities? 'Ultimately,' writes Sherry Turkle, whose life's work has involved human interactions with machines, 'the question is not whether children will love their robotic pets more than their animal pets, but rather, what loving will come to mean. [Think of] the young woman who was ready to turn in her boyfriend for a "sophisticated Japanese robot"; is there a chance that human relationships will just seem too *hard*?'[604]

Perhaps even more profound a question is: what does it mean if robots don't die? In his 2005 commencement speech at Stanford, Apple founder Steve Jobs spoke of death's great power: 'Death is very likely the single best invention of Life. It's Life's change agent.'[605] Despite Ray Kurzweil's insistence that humans will achieve immortality through biotechnology and advanced medicine, death is, for now, one of humanity's defining traits. While human qualities like love and death might be the great divider between humans and artificial intelligence, a dearth of such characteristics – particularly if robots have many other unfathomable powers and abilities – might be dangerous. What if, like dystopian visions of the future in film and literature, artificial intelligence overtakes us because it exploits those differences or sees them as weaknesses? If it comes down to it, can humans with hearts beat machines with just brains?

If that's the case and AI is inevitable in the long term, we have to ask ourselves how much we could even control it. Stephen Hawking doesn't think we could: AI, he warns, 'would take off on its own and re-design itself at an ever increasing rate … Humans, who are limited by slow biological evolution, couldn't compete, and would be superseded.'[606] We might literally bring about the means to our own destruction, locking humanity out of our own society. These are obviously vast, deep questions, and I don't pretend to know the answers to them. (But I don't feel too bad about it because the brightest minds in the field don't either.) That's why the debate about artificial intelligence is important: it's about not just the future of humanity, but its definition. And yet that debate is cloistered in Silicon Valley and biotech and medicine and nanotech; it is not taking place in public forums, in the press, in Parliament, in the public eye. We hardly know it is happening; how can we have an opinion about it? As futuristic technologies become more and more available, people will want them. While not all will result in an artificial intelligence per se, new technologies that merge man and machine carry with them vast implications that need to be considered.

Take the work of Hugh Herr, an MIT scientist and engineer who lost both legs below the knee in a rock-climbing accident. He used that accident as inspiration for what has become his life's work. 'I reasoned that a human being can never be broken. Technology is broken. Technology is inadequate. This simple but powerful idea was a call to arms to advance technology for the elimination of my own disability and ultimately the disability of others.' At his lab at MIT and in his private company, Herr has developed incredibly advanced prosthetics that are customised in every sense of the word.

> *I began by developing specialized limbs that allowed me to return to the vertical world of rock and ice climbing. I quickly realized that the artificial part of my body is malleable, able to take on any form, any function, a blank slate through which to create perhaps structures that could extend beyond biological capability. I made my height adjustable. I could be as short as five feet or as tall as I'd like. Narrow, wedged feet allowed me to climb steep rock fissures where the human foot cannot penetrate, and spiked feet enabled me to climb vertical ice walls without ever experiencing muscle leg fatigue. Through technological innovation, I returned to my sport stronger and better. Technology had eliminated my disability and allowed me a new climbing prowess.*[607]

Herr recognises the potential to improve our quality of life across the board. He and others have started to experiment with exoskeletons, applying the same technology that has made him a better climber to perfectly healthy people. And while his work is confined to prosthetic limbs, he sees on the horizon relief for all sorts of disabilities and other physical impairments. 'It's not well appreciated,' he says, 'but over half of the world's population suffers from some form of cognitive, emotional, sensory or motor condition, and because of poor technology, too often, conditions result in disability and a poorer quality of life. Basic levels of physiological function should be a part of our human rights. Every person should have the right to live life without disability if they so choose – the right to live life without severe depression; the right to see a loved one in the case of seeing impaired; or the right to walk or to dance, in the case of limb paralysis or limb amputation.' And he is optimistic that this will soon come to pass. 'We the people need not accept our limitations, but can transcend disability through technological innovation,' he says. 'Indeed, through fundamental advances in bionics in this century, we will set the technological foundation for an enhanced human experience, and we will end disability.' When Rohan and I met him in Cambridge, Massachusetts, it left a profound impression. And the seed of an idea for a policy response.

Ending disability would be great, but how will we grapple with adding extra ability? What will it mean to compete in sport? How much of a human is it ethical to replace? Should we be allowed to amputate limbs to obtain new, artificial ones?

These are all important questions about the rapidly approaching future in AI, robotics, and biotechnology; questions that bring up an important axiom: just because we can, should we? Stanford University has announced a century-long study of the effects of AI on society.[608] 'Artificial intelligence is one of the most profound undertakings in science, and one that will affect every aspect of human life,' says Stanford President John Hennessy. 'Given Stanford's pioneering role in AI and our interdisciplinary mindset, we feel obliged and qualified to host a conversation about how artificial intelligence will affect our children and our children's children.'[609] Hennessy is right: this is a necessary conversation – but it's one which we need to bring out in the open. Stanford is still Silicon Valley. In Britain we need more discussion: sooner, more informed, more integrated into daily life and debate. I don't know the answer, but I definitely want to do that most human thing: argue about it.

Luckily, we in Britain have a precedent for situations such as these. After the world's first baby conceived by *in vitro* fertilisation (IVF) was born in 1978, the British government assembled a committee in 1982 to examine the ethical considerations of this new advance. The committee, chaired by philosopher Mary Warnock, delivered a report that managed a consensus on the ethical framework for IVF without judging or making moral pronouncements.[610] After the report, the government established the Human Fertilisation and Embryology Authority (HFEA) in 1990, a public body that now independently regulates IVF treatment, human embryo research, and human cloning.[611]

As we grapple with the challenging existential questions that artificial intelligence and robotics present, we need to establish a body like the HFEA to study it intelligently, carefully, delicately – and above all publicly. That's the conclusion Rohan and I came to after meeting Hugh Herr at MIT. The HFEA has worked precisely because it has not overstepped its bounds and has avoided moralising, preaching, or presuming to set political priorities. Similarly, any such body for AI could be an impartial arbiter to moderate the discussion among our best minds – engineers, scientists, doctors, ethicists, policymakers, and philosophers – making sure that whatever we do, we walk into the future with the best possible knowledge of its implications.

Even if it is on bionic legs.

THE FIRST STEP

In this book I've talked about many changes. Some are things we can each start doing individually, like spending more time in nature with our children. Some are changes that businesses can make, like choosing to pay a living wage. But to be honest, the vast majority of the changes proposed in this book are things that will have to come from government. That's not surprising: much of my thinking on the issues I talk about in *More Human* has taken place either in, or preparing for, government. This is also how it should be. In a democracy, our political system is the only institution that truly represents us: our wishes, our rights, our aspirations. All governments make rules, limit excesses, lock up wrongdoers, protect what should be protected and forge ahead where progress is needed. Democracies are different though, in that their legitimacy stems not from force, God, or birthright, but from the authority of our votes. That is democracy's promise – and why democracy must be the solution.

But because of people's almost total lack of confidence these days that government can change anything much, I understand that the arguments in this book could seem out of reach. How are we supposed to change all these things? Where do we even start? What is the first step?

The first step is fixing our democracy.

Democracy is in crisis: it seems to serve the people no longer, but vested interests. Throughout this book I've railed against those interests. Of all the bad that they do, perhaps their worst impact is the hold they have over our governments. It seems today that political legitimacy stems not from votes, but money: the more of it you have, the more that government pays attention to your concerns.

We have, in some ways, regressed. Corruption used to be the norm in most countries, democratic or otherwise. Power was inherited and bought; political appointments traded for favours in a system under which the elites literally owned the state. But while it is no longer so explicit, in the capitals of Western democracies the ascent of big money and its lobbyists means that while there is no explicit quid pro quo, it is hard to mistake what donors intend when they give money to political parties and campaigns. Or what business people want when they take politicians and civil servants to dinner, the opera, the Brits, Wimbledon. We may no longer have aristocratic courts and inherited offices, but our democracies are increasingly captured by a ruling class that seeks to perpetuate its privileges. Our democratic systems, once thought inviolable, have, in the apt word used by political scientist Francis Fukuyama, 'decayed'. America, where the rich and powerful buy the outcomes they want from the political system, is not in any proper sense of the word a democracy, it is a donocracy. The EU is no better: spend time in Brussels and you will find in the European Parliament and Commission a vast, stinking cesspit of corporate corruption gussied up in the garb of idealistic internationalism.[612]

The fewer people in control, the fewer people who need to be influenced and swayed. At least in America, economic, cultural, and political power is dispersed. In the UK, centralisation is a gift to the vested interests. When the corporate bosses, the MPs, the journalists – and the authors of books like this – all go to the same dinner parties and social events, all live near each other, all send their children to the same schools (from which they themselves mainly came), an insular ruling class precipitates. They flit and float between Westminster, Whitehall and the City; regardless of who's in office, the same people are in power. It is a democracy in name only, operating on behalf of a tiny elite no matter the electoral outcome. I know because I was part of it. While there is no conspiracy (and I know from personal experience that almost all politicians and officials have good intentions), the assumptions, the structures, the rules that govern our lives are not subject to anything as unpredictable as the will of the people. No wonder voters feel that others' voices are being heard more than their own. It's because it's true.

From the rise of the Tea Party and Occupy movements to the protest parties in Europe to UKIP and the nearly successful vote for Scottish independence, it's clear that our political systems – in the UK, America, and Europe – are not translating people's wishes into action. We need to change that: we need to make democracy work as it was intended to, as a vehicle for real people power, not the plutocrat power we have today.

We need to start by getting fresh voices in the conversation. People's political views are more nuanced than the simplified two-party model that Britain's ossified electoral system forces onto them. Many of the ideas and proposals in this book would be at home in parties across the political spectrum; others wouldn't be welcome anywhere. In a true democracy, this is fine. Hardly anyone is a 'dyed-in-the-wool' anything, anyway. We don't need politicians to tell us what platform aligns with our identities – with the information we now have access to, we can make up our own minds. Yet in public life, you have nowhere to go if you take the Conservative view on taxes, Green views on the environment, and Labour views on social justice. Our views are as complex as we are, but our politics are not. Our views are not 'politician'; they're human. We need our politics to reflect this.

That's why I started my company, Crowdpac. We want to give politics back to people – starting in America. We want to give everyone, not just the rich and powerful, the chance to have their voices heard. Changing the political system – especially the role of money and elite influence – is essential. As Lawrence Lessig, a Harvard law professor and a leader in American campaign finance reform puts it: 'It's not that mine is the most important issue – it's not. Yours is the most important issue. But mine is the *first* issue – the issue we have to solve before we get to fix the issues you care about.'[613] It comes back to that first step: fixing our democracy.

Fixing our democracy is the first step in moving towards a more human world. We need to take power out of the hands of the big money donors and the big unions and big business and put it back where it belongs – in the hands of the people. Make it easier for more independent, and independent-minded, candidates to run for office. Give people confidence that it's worth getting involved. Make the representatives we have, actually representative. As long as the same people control the conversation in London or Brussels or Washington, things will stay the same. So we need more grass-

310 • MORE HUMAN

roots, interactive, accountable politics. We need to make politics more human.

That's where you come in. If you agree with the ideas in this book, and want to see them actually come to something, I can tell you exactly what you need to do. You won't necessarily like the answer, but I'm going to tell you anyway. I'm going to tell you the truth.

You need to run for office. Run for Parliament.

If that's too scary, run for your local council. But one way or another, get your hands on the levers of power. If enough of us do it, we can really change things. One independent-minded person who wants to see more human politics enacted, on their own, is not going to change anything. But a handful on a council? Now you're talking. A couple of hundred in Parliament? That's a revolution.

We can do this. We really can. We can take back our democracy and make the world more human. But it will only happen if you – yes, you – take that first step and run for office. I know it's daunting, I know it's off-putting. I know you'll be worried about the kind of people you'll have to deal with, becoming a public figure, having actual responsibility for things. But that's what democracy is. And the trouble is, we've allowed it to be captured by the insiders and the vested interests and the people with money and influence. They're counting on you to be put off by it all, to be put off by the hassle, the complexity, the difficulty. That's their bet: that you don't actually care that much. That you don't really want change.

Prove them wrong.
Take back our democracy.
Make the world more human.

The first step? Right now, go to www.morehumancampaign.org.

ACKNOWLEDGEMENTS

Number one: my amazing wife Rachel Whetstone, whom I love and respect in equal measure and without whom my recent adventures – moving to California, teaching at Stanford, founding a tech start-up – would literally not have been possible. I also appreciate her putting up with days of family disruption during the production of this book (especially Christmas in Beaver Creek, 2014; Jody and Vivienne, thanks to you too). And of course, Ben and Sonny, who have forever changed how I see the world.

One more thing on Rachel. As everyone who knows us is aware, we have strong opinions and tend to express them. But we try and hold back – in public at least – when it comes to each other's work. When I was in government, Rachel had clear views on what we were doing but never aired them. It's the same with me and Google (where Rachel works today), and I hope you will understand that for the most human of reasons – family harmony! – I'd prefer to express my views in private. Sorry to disappoint, but there are few references to Google in these pages.

That I have a platform to write this book is something I owe to one person above all others: David Cameron. I will always be grateful to him for giving me the incredible honour of working in government. He and Sam are remarkable people and true friends. As I write this, it is not clear whether David will serve as Prime Minister beyond 2015 but whether he does or not, history will record that he did so with great distinction and an uncommon sense of duty.

There are too many good friends and former colleagues in government to thank here personally but I want to single out George Osborne, Michael Gove and Oliver Letwin for their special contribution to my political and policy education; Michael Heseltine, David Young and Ken Baker – heroic political figures, all three – for the immense privilege of working with them and the inspiration they have given me; and Andrew Lansley who helped me take that first, vital step into this strange but fascinating world. I will never be able to thank Maurice Saatchi, Jeremy Sinclair, Bill Muirhead and the wider Saatchi 'family' enough for all they've done for me personally and in everything I've been able to achieve professionally.

Also essential in developing the ideas in this book: my friend and former business partner Giles Gibbons. Our time working together at the company we founded, Good Business, was a hugely fertile one for my understanding of the social problems addressed in *More Human*, and how they might be solved.

Many people helped turn *More Human* into reality. Gail Rebuck at Penguin Random House first encouraged me to write this book and helped me hone its theme. The team at WH Allen – Ed Faulkner, Elen Jones, Lucy Oates and copyeditor Mary Chamberlain – have been amazing partners; I can't quite believe how smoothly (most of) it has happened, and in record time. Georgina Capel and Rachel Conway at Capel & Land; Rae Shirvington, Shona Abhyankar and Caroline Butler at Ebury Publishing, and Fiona McMorrough and her team at FMcM have been a pleasure to work with and invaluable on the business and promotional side.

Writing on so many topics has meant reaching out to experts, thinkers, and doers in all of them. Jason, Scott and I feel privileged for having been able to talk to people doing such awe-inspiring work. Many are cited, but some provided feedback and insights without expectation of credit and I'd like to thank them here.

My first teaching assistant at Stanford, Chelsea Lei, was extremely helpful in constructing an early case study. Sarah Stein Greenberg has proven an indispensable colleague at the Stanford d.school and, along with Mel Kline Lee, Jenny Stefanotti and Brent Harris, helped us consider the possibilities of human-centred design in government. Francis Fukuyama at Stanford provided valuable feedback on our government chapter and the history of bureaucracy. Bill Eggers of Deloitte and William Simon of Columbia University likewise affirmed our thinking on government reform. Charlotte Alldritt discussed with us the fascinating findings of the RSA's City Growth Commission. Sir

Simon Jenkins usefully critiqued our arguments on localism and schooling.

Lucy Heller of Ark and Sir Anthony Seldon of Wellington College were insightful and provocative on education. Jamie Heywood's inspiring journey and thoughtfulness were instrumental to our healthcare thesis. Sten Tamkivi and Daniel Vaarik educated us on Estonia's advances in e-health; Jason Oberfest of Mango Health did the same for the intersection of health and mobile devices; Camilla Cavendish helped us understand key aspects of the structure of the NHS. I'm extremely grateful to Liz Kendall MP for pointing us toward the need to discuss end-of-life care. Patrick Holden of the Sustainable Food Trust and Lord Melchett of the Soil Association helped clarify our thinking on agriculture and food policy. Conversations with Matt Rothe directed us to some of the latest and most interesting innovations in sustainable food. Isabel Oakeshott gave valuable feedback on the food chapter manuscript. Philip Lymbery of Compassion in World Farming provided detailed and timely answers to our numerous questions on factory farm conditions.

John Fingleton, former head of the Office of Fair Trading, John Gibson, my former No. 10 colleague now at Nesta, and Christine Varney, former US Assistant Attorney General for Antitrust, proved stimulating sparring partners when discussing competition and helped us create a more rigorous chapter on business. Louise Casey, one of Britain's most inspiring advocates for families and children, helped us set the tone for our poverty chapter; David Robinson of Community Links was similarly inspirational, as was Taryn Gaona, a former teacher and now my children's wonderful nanny. Michael McAfee of PolicyLink gave us a close look at the complexities surrounding the education of a child in poverty. Neil Jameson and Sarah Vero of the Living Wage Foundation, Michael Kelly at KPMG, Conor D'Arcy of the Resolution Foundation and Steve Mobbs of Oxford Asset Management helped us understand the debate around wages. Sir Charlie Mayfield, chairman of the John Lewis Partnership, provided tremendous insight into the challenges of improving low-paid workers' skills and compensation. Sebastian Thrun, founder and CEO of Udacity, proved extraordinarily thoughtful on the issue of workers and technology, and artificial intelligence.

James O'Shaughnessey, another former colleague at No. 10, helped us greatly with our arguments on housing policy in the chapter on spaces. Former Toronto Mayor David Crombie, Alan Ricks of MASS Design, Nash Hurley of VITAL Environments and Carlo Ratti of MIT proved similarly inspirational on architecture and design. Former Pentagon official Paul Stockton, Scott Jacobs of Generate Capital, Teryn Norris of the U.S. Department of Energy, John Thorpe of Thameswey Energy and Will Dawson and Giles Bristow of Forum for the Future helped us think through our complicated relationship with energy. Sarah Butler-Sloss of the Ashden Trust and David Beach at Stanford provided keen insight and incredibly useful examples and contacts for case studies. Our conversation with children's author Christiane Dorion on teaching nature remains one of the most delightful of the entire writing experience.

A number of people had valuable insights on our themes writ large, including Matthew Taylor and Adam Lent of the RSA, Jim Adams at Stanford, Nick Pearce of IPPR, Geoff Mulgan of Nesta, David Halpern of the Behavioural Insights Team, retired diplomat Sir David Manning and Nassim Taleb of New York University.

A handful of people went above and beyond in their assistance. Richard Young of the Sustainable Food Trust spent a huge amount of time offering technical assistance to help us understand agricultural policies and the effects of antibiotic use on farms. Mark Schurman at Herman Miller is as close to a living library on the subject of office design as there can be and was exceptionally generous with his time and knowledge. Zac Goldsmith, who has done incredible work on energy and the environment, helped steer us in the right direction many times and provided valuable connections.

Jason and Scott want to thank the ever-perspicacious Todd Johnson of Jones Day, Banny Banerjee of Stanford ChangeLabs, and Paul and Iris Brest of Stanford Law School and the Creative Commons Foundation, respectively. Thanks to Peter, Lisa, and Julianne Cirenza, who welcomed us into their London home during our travels, and Peter, for his astute observations and feedback on the financial sector. Finally, thanks to Paul and Sheri Bade – Mom and Dad – whose support, understanding, guidance and love is the very human foundation of this, one of our proudest accomplishments.

I want to thank those who laboured through early drafts to give me great feedback: Jenni Russell (who also spent an inordinate amount of effort connecting us with people to talk to); Dieter Helm (my tutor at Oxford) who helped me think through the broad themes of the book as well as the technical aspects of infrastructure and competition; and Kate MacTiernan.

Jason and Scott have been a double joy to work with. (Everyone should have twins helping them with their book!) They complemented each other and me in the best ways as they helped me research and write *More Human*, diving into the project head first (and putting up with me for a year and a half of it). This book couldn't have been produced without them and I'm so grateful for their hard work.

And then finally, I must thank the person who has been central to this book throughout its life: from the years we spent together developing and working on many of the ideas in *More Human*; to the confidence he gave me that this was a project worth pursuing; to the book's structure, and comments on drafts at every stage … my closest friend, and former colleague in government, Rohan Silva, to whom this book is dedicated.

NOTES

Introduction

1   jetBlue has acknowledged and apologised for this incident. The actual dialogue is not verbatim transcript as the incident actually occurred but was based instead on Devereaux's recollection as expressed in various media appearances since the incident. For more, watch her interview here: Jennifer Devereaux, interview by Tamron Hall, *NewsNation with Tamron Hall*, MSNBC, 19 June 2014.

2   Jeremy Rifkin, *The Empathetic Civilization: The Race to Global Consciousness in a World in Crisis* (New York: Jeremy P. Tarcher / Penguin, 2009).

3   For more on the nuanced and complicated history of bureaucracy, see: Francis Fukuyama, *Political Order and Political Decay* (New York: Farrar, Straus and Giroux, 2014), 15–18, 68–71.

4   Alfred D. Chandler, Jr., *The Visible Hand: The Managerial Revolution in American Business* (Cambridge, MA: Harvard University Press, 1977).

5   Michael A. Mitt, David King, Menna Krishnan, Marianna Makri, Mario Schjren, Katsuhiko Shimizu and Hong Zhu, 'Creating Value Through Mergers and Acquisitions: Challenges and Opportunities, in *The Handbook of Mergers and Acquisitions*, eds. David Faulkner, Satu Teerikangas and Richard J. Joseph, (Oxford: England Oxford University Press, 2012)

6   Evgeny Morozov, *To Save Everything, Click Here: The Folly of Technological Solutionism* (New York: Public Affairs, 2013), xii.

7   One 2015 study called the decline in real wages, which it estimates have fallen about 8 to 10 per cent since 2008, to be 'unprecedented'. Though real wages have been ticking up in recent months, this has been due to inflation rather than real wage growth. For more, see: Stephen Manchin, *Real Wages and Living Standards*, (London: LSE, 2015), http://cep.lse.ac.uk/pubs/download/EA024.pdf.

8   Nicholas R. V. Jones, Annalijn I. Conklin, Marc Suhrcke, and Pablo Monsivais, 'The Growing Price Gap between More and Less Healthy Foods: Analysis of a Novel Longitudinal UK Dataset', *PloS one* 9, no. 10 (2014): e109343.

Chapter 1. Government

9   Alex Singleton, 'Obituary: Sir John Cowperthwaite', *Guardian*, 8 February 2006.

10   Francis, *Evangelli Gaudium: Apolistic Exhortation on the Proclamation of the Gospel in Today's World* (Vatican City: Libreria Editrice Vaticana, 2013).

11   Zachary Karabell, *The Leading Indicators: A Short History of the Numbers That Rule Our World* (New York: Simon & Schuster, 2014), 68.

12   Diane Coyle, *GDP: A Brief but Affectionate History* (Princeton, NJ: Princeton University Press, 2014), 114.

13   Joseph Stiglitz, Amartya Sen (both Nobel Prize winners), and Jean-Paul Fitoussi.

14   Diane Coyle, 'GDP Is A Mirror on the Markets. It Must Not Rule Our Lives', *Guardian*, 20 November 2014, http://www.theguardian.com/commentisfree/2014/nov/20/gdp-markets-short-term-victorians-value.

15   Robert F. Kennedy, 'Speech at the University of Kansas' (speech, University of Kansas, Lawrence, KS, 18 March, 1968).

16   Dieter Helm, interview by authors, 21 November 2014.

17   Anthony King and Ivor Crewe, *The Blunders of Our Governments* (London: Oneworld Publications, 2013), 243.

18   Jane Jacobs, *The Death and Life of Great American Cities* (New York: Vintage Books, 1961), 13.

19   'Preterm Birth (Fact Sheet 363)', *World Health Organization*, November 2014, http://www.who.int/mediacentre/factsheets/fs363/en/.

20   'Who Are We?', *Embrace*, 2015, http://embraceglobal.org/who-we-are/our-story/.

21   Sadly, Tversky died before their joint work was recognised, so technically Kahneman is the laureate, though he accepted it on behalf of them both. For their seminal paper, see: Daniel Kahneman and Amos Tversky, 'Choices, Values, and Frames', *American Psychologist* 39, no. 4 (1984): 341.

22   Ronald G. Fryer Jr., Steven D. Levitt, John List and Sally Sadoff, 'Enhancing the Efficacy of Teacher Incentives Through Loss Aversion: A Field Experiment', No. w18237, *National Bureau of Economic Research*, 2012.

23   David Brooks, 'The Character Factory', *New York Times*, 1 August 2014.

24   Robert B. Cialdini, Linda J. Demaine, Brad J. Sagarin, Daniel W. Barrett, Kelton Rhoads, and Patricia L. Winter, 'Managing Social Norms for Persuasive Impact', *Social Influence* 1, no. 1 (2006): 3–15.

25   Jerry Sternin, 'The Viet Nam Story', http://www.positivedeviance.org/about_pd/Monique%20VIET%20NAM%20CHAPTER%20Oct%2017.pdf.

26   Mauricio Lim Miller, 'When Helping Doesn't Help', *Huffington Post*, 7 May 2012.

27   Anne Stuhldreher and Rourke O'Brien, *The Family Independence Initiative: A New Approach to Help Families Exit Poverty*, (Washington, DC: New America Foundation, 2011).

28   David Bornstein, 'Out of Poverty, Family-Style', *New York Times*, 14 July 2011.

29   Stulhdreher and O'Brien.

30   Lim Miller, quoted in Bornstein.

31   David Brooks, 'Stairway to Wisdom', *New York Times*, 15 May 2014.

32   Editorial Board, 'Mr. Bratton Reverses to Go Forward', *New York Times*, 13 September 2014.

33   'Measure for Measure', *The Economist*, 30 November 2013.

34   Michael Sanders and Elspeth Kirkman, 'I've Booked You a Place. Good Luck: A Field Experiment Applying Behavioural Science to Improve Attendance at High-Impact Recruitment Events', No. 13/334 (Bristol, England: Department of Economics, University of Bristol), 2014.

35   Richard H. Thaler and Cass R. Sunstein, *Nudge: Improving Decisions About Health, Wealth, and Happiness: Revised and Expanded Edition* (New York: Penguin Books, 2009), 110.

36   Richard H. Thaler and Shlomo Benartzi, *The Behavioral Economics of Retirement Savings Behavior*, (Washington, DC: AARP Public Policy Institute, 2007).

37   Owain Service, Michael Hallsworth, David Halpern, et al., *EAST: Four Simple Ways to Apply Behavioural Insights*, (London: The Behavioural Insights Team, 11 April 2014), 11.

38   Rohan Silva, interview by authors, London, 17 September 2014.

39   Ibid.

40   Duncan Green, 'Robert Chambers: Why Don't All Developments Do Immersions?', *People, Spaces, Deliberation (The World Bank)*, 6 September 2012, http://blogs.worldbank.org/publicsphere/node/6091.

41   Ken Tatham, interview by authors, 16 December 2014.

42   'Local Elections', *France in the United States, Embassy of France in the United States*, 20 December 2013, http://www.ambafrance-us.org/spip.php?article518.

43   Polly Curtis, 'French Civil Servant's Confession Strikes a Chord in Drive to Shrink State', *Guardian*, 23 March 2011, http://www.theguardian.com/world/2011/mar/23/french-civil-servant-bored-workforce.

44   Irène Couzigou, 'France: Territorial Decentralisation in France: Towards

Autonomy and Democracy', in Carlo Panara and Michael R. Varney, eds., *Local Government in Europe: The 'Fourth Level' in the EU Multi-Layered System of Governance* (New York, Routledge, 2013), 75.

45   In England, the average electorate of a council authority in 2014 was around 161,000. For more details, see this table published by The Local Goverment Boundary Commission for England: https://www.lgbce.org.uk/__data/assets/excel_doc/0006/22839/NEW-Copy-of-Counties-Pivot-Table-2014.xlsx.

46   'BBC Poll: One in Five "Disillusioned" with Westminster', *BBC News*, 31 October 2014.

47   Nicco Mele, *The End of Big: How the Internet Makes David the New Goliath* (New York: St. Martin's Press, 2013), 29.

48   For more, see: Peter Schuck, *Why Government Fails So Often: And How It Can Do Better* (Princeton, NJ: Princeton University Press, 2014), 193.

49   House of Commons Committee of Public Accounts, *Department of Health: The National Programme for IT in the NHS*; Twentieth Report of Session 2006–07, HC 510 (London: The Stationery Office, 2007) EV 18.

50   Ibid., EV 19, Nicholas Timmins, 'The NHS Electronic Records Are Two Years Late', *Financial Times*, 29 May 2006.

51   Anthony King and Ivor Crewe, *The Blunders of Our Governments* (London: Oneworld, 2013), 195–200.

52   House of Commons Committee of Public Accounts, Department of Health, *Review of the Final Benefits Statement for Programmes Previously Managed Under the National Programme for IT in the NHS*. (London: National Audit Office, 2013); Department of Health, National Audit Office, *The National Programme for IT in the NHS. An Update on the Delivery of Detailed Care Records Systems* (London: The Stationery Office, 2011).

53   King and Crewe, 195–200.

54   Alan Milburn quoted in Fraser Nelson, 'Milburn: How I Can Help Gordon Brown', *Spectator*, 19 May 2007.

55   There are 16 authorities that currently have directly-elected mayors. Some are a legacy of the *Local Government Act 2000*. When the Coalition came to government, it wanted to devolve more power to cities, so the *Localism Act 2011* was passed to give the largest 12 cities in England after London (Birmingham, Leeds, Sheffield, Bradford, Manchester, Liverpool, Bristol, Wakefield, Coventry, Leicester, Nottingham and Newcastle-upon-Tyne) the chance to adopt elected mayors or not. The councils of Leicester and Liverpool adopted the mayoral system in December 2010 and February 2012. The rest of the ten cities held referendum in May 2012; only one, Bristol, decided in favour of a directly-elected mayor. Since then, in an agreement between Chancellor George Osborne and its ten local councils, Manchester will hold elections for a metropolitan mayor in 2017. For more, see: House of Commons, *Directly-Elected Mayors*, by Mark Sandford, SN/PC/5000 (London: House of Commons Library, 2014); 'English Mayoral Elections and Referendums', *BBC News*, 4 May 2012; and 'George Osborne: Greater Manchester to Have Elected Mayor', *BBC News*, 3 November 2014..

56   When activists tried to prevent Muslims from building a community centre in Manhattan near the site of the 9/11 attacks, Bloomberg took the politically risky but morally correct stand for religious freedom.

57   'Local Elections', *France in the United States*.

58   Charlotte Wildman, 'The "Chicago of Great Britain": Growth and Urban Regeneration in Liverpool', in *The History Boys: Lessons from Local Government's Past*, Simon Parker and Joe Manning, eds. (London: New Local Government Network, 2013), 29–37.

59   Martin Fackler, 'District in Tokyo Plans to Extend Rights of Gay Couples', *New York Times*, 13 February 2015.

60   Robin I. M. Dunbar, 'Neocortex Size as a Constraint on Group Size in Primates', *Journal of Human Evolution* 22, No.6 (1992): 469–493.

61   Jan De Ruiter, Gavin Weston and Stephen M Lyon, 'Dunbar's Number: Group Size and Brain Physiology in Humans Reexamined', *American Anthropologist* 113, no. 4 (2011): 557–568.

62 Drake Bennett, 'The Dunbar Number, From the Guru of Social Networks', *Bloomberg Businessweek*, 10 January 2013.
63 See note 45 of this chapter.
64 This process describes the Democratic caucuses; the Republicans use a simplified format that does not involve as much debate and moving around.
65 David P. Redlawsk, Caroline J. Tolbert, and Todd Donovan, *Why Iowa?: How Caucuses and Sequential Elections Improve the Presidential Nominating Process* (Chicago: University of Chicago Press, 2011), 124.
66 Ibid., 8.

Chapter 2. Schools
67 Se-Woong Koo, 'An Assault Upon Our Children', *New York Times*, 3 August 2014.
68 Data from Statistics Korea as reported in Yewon Kang, 'Poll Shows Half of Korean Teenagers Have Suicidal Thoughts', *Wall Street Journal*, 20 March 2014.
69 Ibid.
70 Jason Pittman, interview by authors, Mountain View, CA, 5 November 2014.
71 'Cost of Outcomes Associated with Low Levels of Adult Numeracy in the UK', *National Numeracy and Pro Bono Economics*, 2014.
72 Jouachim Wuttke, 'Uncertainty and Bias in PISA', in *Pisa According to Pisa: Does Pisa Keep What It Promises?*, eds. Stefan Thomas Hopmann, Gertrude Brinek, and Martin Retzl (Vienna, Austria: Lit Verlag, 2007), 241–263.
73 William Stewart, 'Is Pisa Fundamentally Flawed?', *TES Connect*, 27 September 2014. https://www.tes.co.uk/article.aspx?storycode=6344672.
74 Aleksander P. J. Ellis, Bradford S. Bell, Robert E. Ployhart, John R. Hollenbeck, and D. R. Ilgen, 'An Evaluation of Generic Teamwork Skill Training with Action Teams: Effects on Cognitive and Skill-Based Outcomes', *Personnel Psychology* 58, no. 3 (2005): 641–672.
75 Angela L. Duckworth, and Martin E. P. Seligman, 'Self-Discipline Outdoes IQ in Predicting Academic Performance of Adolescents', *Psychological Science* 16, no. 12 (2005): 939–944.
76 'IBM 2010 Global CEO Study: Creativity Selected as Most Crucial Factor for Future Success', *IBM*, 18 May 2010, https://www-03.ibm.com/press/us/en/pressrelease/31670.wss.
77 Joshua Wolf Shenk, *Powers of Two: How Relationships Drive Creativity* (Boston, MA: Eamon Dolan, 2009).
78 James J. Heckman, 'Skill Formation and the Economics of Investing in Disadvantaged Children', *Science* 312, no. 5782 (2006): 1900–1902.
79 Jenni Russell, 'Let's Put Character Above Exam Results', *The Sunday Times*, 5 June 2011.
80 Willem Kuyken, Katherine Weare, Obioha C. Ukoumunne, Rachael Vicary, Nicola Motton, Richard Burnett, Chris Cullen, Sarah Hennelly, and Felicia Huppert, 'Effectiveness of the Mindfulness in Schools Programme: Non-Randomised Controlled Feasibility Study', *British Journal of Psychiatry* 203, no. 2 (2013): 126–131.
81 William T. Harris, 'Elementary Education', *North American Review* (1895): 538–546, 15.
82 Marjukka Liiten, 'Top Favorite: Teaching Profession' (in Finnish), Helsingin Sanomat, 11 February 2004, cited in Pasi Sahlberg, *Finnish Lessons: What Can the World Learn from Educational Change in Finland?* (New York: Teachers College Press, 2010), 72.
83 Sahlberg, *Finnish Lessons*, 125.
84 Ibid., 127.
85 Ellen Gamerman, 'What Makes Finnish Kids So Smart?', *Wall Street Journal*, 28 February 2008. See also Sahlberg, 65.
86 OECD, *Education At a Glance: OECD Indicators* (OECD Publishing, 2014).
87 Tim Walker, 'How Finland Keeps Kids Focused Through Free Play', *Atlantic*, 30 June 2014.
88 PISA Interactive Data Selection – Variable ST42003 ('Math Anxiety – Get Very Tense'), *OECD*, 2012.

89   Editorial Board, 'Small Schools Work in New York', *New York Times*, 18 October 2014.

90   Rebecca Unterman, 'Headed to College: The Effects of New York City's Small High Schools of Choice on Postsecondary Enrollment', *MDRC*, 2014.

91   See for instance: News Corporation Amplify, amplify.com; Pearson Learning, https://www.pearson.com/learning.html; Disney Education Programs, http://dep.disney.go.com; McGraw-Hill Education, http://www.mheducation.com; Houghton Mifflin Harcourt, http://www.hmhco.com.

92   Peter Hill and Michael Barber, *Preparing for a Renaissance in Assessment* (London: Pearson PLC, 2014).

93   The Juárez Correa story is heavily adapted from Josh Davis's profile of him in *Wired*. Josh is one of the greatest unearthers of amazing human stories. For the original article, see Joshua Davis, 'How a Radical New Teaching Method Could Unleash a Generation of Geniuses', *Wired*, 15 October 2013.

94   Anthony Seldon, *An End to Factory Schools: An Education Manifesto 2010–2020* (Surrey, England: Centre for Policy Studies, 2010), 9–10.

95   Jeff and Rachael Thomas, interview by authors, 9 October 2014.

96   Sylva Liebenwein, Heiner Barz and Dirk Randoll, 'Zusammenfassung zentraler Befunde: Waldorfschule aus Schülersicht' (in German), in *Bildungserfahrungen an Waldorfschulen* (VS Verlag für Sozialwissenschaften, 2012), 5–12.

97   'Sean Coughlan, 'Is Five Too Soon to Start School?', *BBC News*, 8 February 2008.

98   OECD, 'PISA 2012 Database Tables' (OECD, 2012), http://www.oecd.org/pisa/keyfindings/PISA-2012-results-snapshot-Volume-I-ENG.pdf; UNICEF, 'Child Poverty in Perspective: An Overview of Child Well-Being in Rich Countries', *Innocenti Report Card* 7 (Florence, Italy: UNICEF Innocenti Research Centre, 2007).

99   Dana Nicholls and Peggy Syvertson, 'Sensory Integration', *New Horizons for Learning, Johns Hopkins School of Education*, 2012.

100   Susan R. Johnson, 'A Developmental Approach Looking at the Relationship of Children's Foundational Neurological Pathways to their Higher Capacities for Learning', 7 May 2007.

101   David Elkind, interview by Neal Conan, 'Can You Make Your Baby Smarter, Sooner?', *Talk of the Nation*, (NPR, 28 October 2009).

102   Susan R. Johnson, 'A Developmental Approach'..

103   Sebastian P. Suggate, Elizabeth A. Schaughency and Elaine Reese, 'Children Learning to Read Later Catch Up to Children Reading Earlier', *Early Childhood Research Quarterly* 28, no. 1 (2013): 33–48.

104   Masha Bell quoted in Luba Vangelova, 'How the English Language Is Holding Kids Back', *The Atlantic*, 9 February 2015.

105   Philip H. K. Seymour, Mikko Aro, and Jane M. Erskine, 'Foundation Literacy Acquisition in European Orthographies', *British Journal of Psychology* 94, no. 2 (2003): 143–174.

106   Wendy Ellyatt, Al Aynsley-Green, Richard Layrd, et al., 'The Government Should Stop Intervening in Early Education' (signed letter to the editor), *Telegraph*, 11 September 2013.

107   Jeff Sandefer, email to authors, 3 September, 2014.

108   Perhaps one of the reasons there are so many standardised tests is the profits they make: Pearson makes $85 million per year just in the state of Texas on test administration. College Board, the private company responsible for the SAT, makes over three-quarters of a billion dollars in revenue annually. For more, see: Matthew M. Chingos, *Strength in Numbers: State Spending on K-12 Assessment Systems*, (Washington, DC: Brown Center for Education at the Brookings Institution, 2012) and 'Agenda Materials: College Board Forum 2014', *The College Board*, 27–29 October 2013.

Chapter 3. Health

109   This original figure came from data analysis reported by the Health Care Commission. Subsequent investigations in the public inquiry determined

that a specific number couldn't be established with certainty but that the level was much higher than it should have been. The head of the public inquiry explained that while he was asked to conduct individual investigations for everyone that died, he deemed this 'impracticable'. There were, however, investigations of three of the cases referenced in this paragraph. See: Robert Francis, *The Mid Staffordshire NHS Foundation Trust Inquiry: Independent Inquiry Into Care Provided by Mid Staffordshire Foundation Trust, January 2005 – March 2009*, vol. 1 (London: The Stationery Office, 2010), section C.

110 These anecdotes from the Mid-Staffs scandal are from the following sources: Claire Ellicott, 'NHS Hospital Scandal Which Left 1,200 Dead Could Happen Again, Warn Campaigners', *Daily Mail*, 9 November 2010; Sarah Boseley, 'Mid Staffordshire NHS Trust Fined for "Avoidable and Tragic Death"', *Guardian*, 28 April 2014; 'Stafford Hospital: The Victims of the Hospital Scandal', *BBC News*, 6 February 2013; 'Stafford Hospital: Q&A', *BBC News*, 25 March 2013; and Tracy McVeigh, 'Scandal of NHS "Death Factories"', *Observer*, 11 August 2002.

111 Quotes from *The King's Fund Report* and Joyce Robins (of the charity, Patient Concern, quoted in 'Hospitals "Are Medical Factories"', *BBC News*, 3 December 2008.

112 Brendan M. Reilly, 'Physical Examination in the Care of Medical Inpatients: An Observational Study', *Lancet* 362, no. 9390 (2003): 1,103.

113 Abraham Verghese, 'A Doctor's Touch' (presentation, TEDGlobal 2011: The Stuff of Life, Edinburgh, Scotland, September 2011).

114 'Hospitals "Are Medical Factories".'

115 Ibid.

116 Jeremy Hunt quoted in Randeep Ramesh, 'Give Each NHS Hospital Patient A Single Consultant, Says Jeremy Hunt', *Guardian*, 23 January 2014.

117 Joanna Goodrich and Jocelyn Cornwell, *Seeing the Person in the Patient* (London: The King's Fund, 2008), 9.

118 In addition to the sentiments of the patients, advocates, and politicians quoted above, similar conclusions were reached by *The King's Fund Report*, *The Darzi Report*, and *The Cavendish Review*. For more, see: Goodrich and Cornwell, *The King's Fund Report*, Ara Darzi, *High Quality Care For All: NHS Next Stage Review Final Report* (The Darzi Report), 7432 (London: The Stationery Office, 2008), and Camilla Cavendish, *The Cavendish Review: An Independent Review into Healthcare Assistants and Support Workers in the NHS and Social Care Settings* (London: Department of Health, 2013).

119 Verghese, 'A Doctor's Touch'.

120 'Introducing the Vscan Family,' *GE Healthcare*, 2015, https://vscan.gehealthcare.com/introducing-vscan-family.

121 Priit Kruus, Peeter Ross, Riina Hallik, Reelika Ermel, and Ain Aaviksoo, 'Wider Implementaiton of Telemedicen in Estonia,' (Tallinn, Estonia: Praxis / Center for Policy Studies, 2014).

122 Responding to author's question at speech: Toomas Ilves, 'Evolving Into a Genuinely Digital Society' (presentation, Green Library, Stanford University, Stanford, CA, 23 May 2014).

123 Ali Parsa, interview by authors, 28 October 2014.

124 James Heywood, interview by authors, 9 October 2014.

125 Stefan Larsson, 'What Doctors Can Learn from Each Other' (presentation, TED@BCG Singapore, Singapore, October 2013).

126 Nassim Nicholas Taleb, *Antifragile: Things That Gain From Disorder* (New York: Random House Trade Paperbacks, 2014), 338.

127 Alice G. Walton, 'Steve Jobs' Cancer Treatment Regrets', Forbes, 24 October 2011.

128 Julie Steenhuysen, 'Overuse of Heartburn Drugs is Risky: Study', *Reuters*, 10 May 2010; Health and Social Care Information Centre, National Statistics, *Prescriptions Dispensed in the Community: England 2002–12*, (2013).

129 Ian Forgacs and Aathavan Loganayagam, 'Overprescribing proton pump inhibitors'. *BMH* 336; no. 7634 (2008): 2–3.

130 Virgina A. Moyer, 'Vitamin, Mineral, and Multivitamin Supplements for the Primary Prevention of Cardiovascular Disease and Cancer: US Preventive Services Task Force Recommendation Statement', *Annals of Internal Medicine* 160, no. 8 (2014): 558–564.

131 Marion Nestle, quoted in Michael Pollan, *In Defense of Food: An Eater's Manifesto* (New York: Penguin Press, 2008), 62.

132 Taleb, Antifragile, 342.

133 Jeanne Whalen, 'How Glaxo Marketed a Malady to Sell a Drug', *Wall Street Journal*, 25 October 2006.

134 Steven Woloshin and Lisa M. Schwartz, 'Giving Legs to Restless Legs: A Case Study of How the Media Helps Make People Sick', *PLoS Medicine* 3, no. 4 (2006): e170.

135 Health and Social Care Information Centre, National Statistics, *Prescription Cost Analysis England 2013*, (3 April 2014), 109; Health and Social Care Information Centre, National Statistics, *Prescriptions Dispensed in the Community: England 2003–13*, (2014), 28..

136 IMS Institute for Healthcare Informatics, 'The Use of Medicines in the United States: Review of 2011' (2011), 29.

137 Michael Anderson, quoted in Alan Schwarz, 'Attention Disorder or Not, Pills to Help in School', *New York Times*, 9 October 2012.

138 Nancy Rappaport, quoted in Ibid.

139 Ibid.

140 John N. Mafi, Ellen P. McCarthy, Roger B. Davis, and Bruce E. Landon, 'Worsening Trends in the Management and Treatment of Back Pain', *JAMA Internal Medicine* 173, no. 17 (2013): 1573–1581.

141 Victoria Sweet, 'The Efficiency of Inefficiency' (presentation, TEDxMiddlebury, Middlebury, Vermont, 9 March 2013).

142 Victoria Sweet, *God's Hotel: A Doctor, a Pilgrimage, and a Journey to the Heart of Medicine* (New York: Penguin, 2013), 49–50.

143 Sweet, 'The Efficiency of Inefficiency'.

144 Francis W. Peabody, 'The Care of the Patient', *Journal of the American Medical Association* 88 (1927): 876-82.

145 Sweet, 'The Efficiency of Inefficiency'.

146 Dennis McCullough, *My Mother, Your Mother: Embracing "Slow Medicine," the Compassionate Approach to Caring for Your Aging Loved Ones*, (New York: Harper, 2008), 55.

147 'Woman Dies After Farewell to Horse at Wigan Hospital', *BBC News*, 7 November 2014.

148 While the figures vary across different surveys, a majority prefer to die at home. The National Audit Office puts the figure between 56 per cent and 74 per cent (see: National Audit Office, *End of Life Care* (London: The Stationery Office, 2008) 5); while a report by the non-profit Cicely Saunders International puts the figure in England at 63 per cent (see: Barbara Gomes, Natalia Calanzani, and Irene J. Higginson, *Local Preferences and Place of Death in Regions within England 2010* (London: Cicely Saunders International, 2011), 11).

149 Barbara Gomes et al., *Local Preferences*.

150 NAO.

151 McCullough, 48.

152 Charles Leadbeater and Jake Garber, *Dying for Change* (London, Demos, 2010).

153 Irene J. Higginson, Ilora G. Finlay, Danielle M. Goodwin, Kerry Hood, Adrian G. K. Edwards, Alison Cook, Hannah-Rose Douglas and Charles E. Normand, 'Is There Evidence that Palliative Care Teams Alter End-of-Life Experiences of Patients and Their Caregivers?', *Journal of Pain and Symptom Management* 25, no. 2 (2003): 150–168.

154 Leadbeater and Garber.

155 Keshia M. Pollack, Dan Morhaim and Michael A. Williams, 'The Public's Perspectives on Advance Directives in Maryland: Implications for State Legislative and Regulatory Policy', Health Policy 96, no. 1 (2010):57–63.

156 'Advance Care Planning: National Guidelines', *Concise Guidance to Good Practice* 12 (Royal College of Physicians, 2009).

157   Chana Joffe-Walt, 'The Town Where Everyone Talks About Death', *NPR*, 5 March 2014.

158   Department of Health and Human Services, Office of the Inspector General, *Medicare Atypical Antipsychotic Drug Claims for Elderly Nursing Home Residents* (Office of the Inspector General, May 2011).

159   Ina Jaffe and Robert Benincasa, 'Old and Over Medicated: The Real Drug Problem in Nursing Homes', NPR, 8 December 2014.

160   While the US government sponsors Medicare for all senior citizens, many also have private medical insurance.

161   Department of Health and Human Services.

162   Ina Jaffe and Robert Benincasa, 'Nursing Homes Rarely Penalized for Oversedating Patients', *NPR*, 9 December 2014.

163   The Pathstone story is heavily adapted from Ina Jaffe's reporting for NPR: Ina Jaffe and Robert Benincasa, 'This Nursing Home Calms Troubling Behavior Without Risky Drugs', *NPR*, 9 December 2014

164   Cavendish, *Cavendish Review*.

165   Camilla Cavendish, interview by authors, 8 September 2014.

166   The structural organisation of the NHS is commonly misunderstood. While the NHS is a monopoly provider, it is made up of some hundreds of trusts, commission groups and community providers, in addition to thousands of GP practices. Most of these organisations, like local hospital trusts, are independently run – foundation trusts even more so. This means that they often contract out themselves, have differing standards of training, care, and even uniforms. However, their funding is still determined by the Treasury in London, so while they are local and nominally independent, Whitehall's power of the purse means they have to pay close attention to government policy or else risk losing funding. According to Camilla Cavendish, this means that while they are independent, the various trusts have little incentive to innovate or compete against each other because any new service or programme requires justification to the Treasury to be funded. (Interview with Camilla Cavendish, 25 September 2014.)

167   Ibid.

168   Cavendish, *Cavendish Review*, 82.

Chapter 4. Food

169   Patrick Holden, email to authors, 23 December 2014.

170   For British figures, see: 'Antimicrobial Resistance – Why the Irresponsible Use of Antibiotics in Agriculture Must Stop', *Alliance to Save Our Antibiotics*, (June 2014), 5. For American figures, see the *PolitiFact* analysis in: Becky Bowers, 'Rep. Louise Slaughter Says 80% of Antibiotics Are Fed to Livestock', *Tampa Bay Times*'s *PolitiFact.com*, 15 October 2013.

171   Antibiotics don't work for every disease on factory farms. Porcine epidemic diarrhea; a virus, emerged and spread so quickly that some workers resorted to puréeing the intestines of dead piglets and feeding it back to the mothers in order to 'vaccinate' them. I imagine access to pasture, more humane conditions, and a natural diet would have been equally effective at keeping them healthy, but this almost certainly would have been less profitable. See: Nick Kristof, 'Is That Sausage Worth This?', *New York Times*, 20 February 2014. See also: 'Fight Cruelty: Chicken FAQ', *ASPCA*, 2015, http://www.aspca.org/fight-cruelty/farm-animal-cruelty/chicken-faq; and 'Welfare Issues for Meat Chickens', *Compassion in World Farming*, 2014, http://www.ciwf.org.uk/farm-animals/chickens/meat-chickens/welfare-issues/.

172   For more, see: Maryn McKenna, 'How Your Chicken Dinner Is Creating a Drug-Resistant Superbug', *The Atlantic*, 11 July 2012; and Cólín Nunan and Richard Young, '*E.coli* Superbugs on Farms and Food', *The Use and Misuse of Antibiotics in UK Agriculture* 6 (Bristol, England: Soil Association, 2012).

173   Liam Donaldson, *150 Years of the Annual Report of the Chief Medical Officer: On the State of Public Health 2008* (London: Department of Health, 2009): 32–9.

174   L. Trasande, J. Blustein, M. Liu, E. Corwin, L. M. Cox, and M. J. Blaser, 'Infant Antibiotic Exposures and Early-Life Body Mass', *International Journal*

of Obesity 37, no. 1 (2013): 16–23; Illseung Cho, Shingo Yamanishi, Laura Cox, Barbara A. Methé, Jiri Zavadil, Kelvin Li, Zhan Gao et al., 'Antibiotics in Early Life Alter the Murine Colonic Microbiome and Adiposity', *Nature* 488, no. 7413 (2012): 621–626.

175 While *E.coli*, mad cow, salmonella, and other such outbreaks are indeed likelier to happen in concentrated animal feedlots than on less dense pastures, food disease is always an inevitability – however humane or sustainable the operation is.

176 James R. Johnson, Michael A. Kuskowski, Kirk Smith, Timothy T. O'Bryan, and Sita Tatini, 'Antimicrobial-Resistant and Extraintestinal Pathogenic Escherichia coli in Retail Foods', *Journal of Infectious Diseases* 191, no. 7 (2005): 1040–1049.

177 For emergency investigations, see: Poultry Processors and Retailers Respond to the Campylobacter Claims', *Guardian*, 23 July 2014. For campylobacter figures in Britain, see: 'Campylobacter', Food Standards Agency, https://www. food.gov.uk/science/microbiology/campylobacterevidenceprogramme.

178 Felicity Lawrence, Andrew Wasley, and Radu Ciorniciuc, 'Revealed: The Dirty Secret of the UK's Poultry Industry', *Guardian*, 23 July 2014.

179 Howard Moskowitz, quoted in Michael Moss, 'The Extraordinary Science of Addictive Junk Food', *New York Times Magazine*, 24 February 2013.

180 'Müller Fruit Corner Strawberry,' *Müller Dairy*, 2012, http://www.mullerdairy. co.uk/nutrition-information/fruit-corner; 'KitKat Collection: 4 Finger Milk Nutritional Information,' *Société des Produits Nestlé S.A*, 2015, http://www. kitkat.co.uk/content/kitkatcollection/FourFinger.

181 Larry Hand and Madeline Drexler, 'Public Health Takes Aim at Sugar and Salt', *Harvard School of Public Health Review*, Fall 2009.

182 '6-inch Low Fat Subs: Nutritional Information', *Subway*, http://www.subway. co.uk/assets/pdf/subway-nutritional-values-uk.pdf.

183 Manny Fernandez, 'Cheese Whatevers, City Has Them by the Handful', *New York Times*, 4 August 2010.

184 Bryony Butland, Susan Jebb, Peter Kopelman, K. McPherson, S. Thomas, J. Mardell and V. Parry, Foresight: *Tackling Obesities: Future Choices, Project Report* (Government Office for Science, 2007).

185 This assumes a projected UK population of 77 million, per ONS estimations. In 2015, fewer than half the population paid personal income tax, so we conservatively estimate the tax base in 2050 at 40 million individuals. See Office for National Statistics, 'UK National Population Projections – Principals and Variants, 2012-2087', http://www.ons.gov.uk/ons/interactive/uk-national-population-projections---dvc3/index.html. and 'Number of Individual Income Taxpayers by Marginal Rate, Gender and Age, 1990–91 to 2014–15', https://www.gov.uk/government/uploads/system/uploads/attachment_data/file/404149/Table_2.1.pdf.

186 Niman Ranch, profiled in more detail on page 131.

187 Story written from Erik Olesund, 'How the Tractor Ruined Farming', *Green Grid Radio*, 28 June 2014, and from interview by authors, Stanford, CA, 24 October 2014.

188 'Soil: Protect European Soil From Environmental Damage', *European Environmental Bureau*, 2015, http://www.eeb.org/index.cfm/activities/biodiversity-nature/soil/.

189 Stephen Devlin, Thomas Dosch, Aniol Esteban and Griffin Carpenter, *Urgent Recall: Our Food System Under Review* (New Economics Foundation, November 2014).

190 Parliament of the United Kingdom, *Agricultural Incomes and Subsidies* (2012 Data).

191 'Soil Association 2014 Organic Market Report Reveals Growth in Organic Sales for the First Time in Four Years', *Soil Association*, 13 March 2014, http://www.soilassociation.org/news/newsstory/articleid/6650/soil-association-2014-organic-market-report-reveals-growth-in-organic-sales-for-the-first-time-in-fo.

  50 per cent of the UK's total croppable area is dedicated to cereal production and 49 per cent of cereals are used to feed livestock. (Source: author's calculations from Department for Environment, Food and Rural Affairs,

Department of Agriculture and Rural Development (Northern Ireland), The Scottish Government, Rural and Environment Research and Analysis Directorate, Welsh Assembly Goverment, The Department for Rural Affairs and Heritage, *Agriculture in the United Kingdom*, 2012 (National Statistics, 2013)).

192 Ilan Brat and Sarah Nassauer, 'Chipotle Suspends Pork Sales at a Third of Its Restaurants', *Wall Street Journal*, 13 January 2015.

193 Allison Aubry, 'Antibiotic-Free Meat Business Is Booming, Thanks to Chipotle', *NPR*, 31 May 2012.

194 As defended by the pork industry. See: Rick Berman, 'Commentary: Playing Chicken with Pork', *PORK Network*, 28 February 2013, http://www.porknetwork.com/pork-news/Commentary-Playing-chicken-with-pork-193903501.html?view=all.

195 Nathanael Johnson, 'Swine of the Times', *Harper's Magazine*, May 2006.

196 Paul Willis, interview by authors, 12 November 2014.

197 Anya Frenald, interview by authors, 20 October 2014.

198 Jay Rayner, 'Booths: The Honest Supermarket', *Observer*, 13 November 2011.

199 Geico Insurance, 'Free Range Chicken: It's What You Do', 8 March 2015, https://www.youtube.com/watch?v=3v1wFKKWMCA.

200 Bedded space is technically defined as 'littered' space. While EU regulations require slightly more total space per bird, they make no requirements for its material. For more, see: Council Regulation (EC) 1999/74 of 19 July 1999 laying down minimum standards for the protection of laying hens [1999] OJ L203/53.

201 European Commission Decision No. 543/2008/EC (Poultrymeat Standards), 2008, O.J. L 157/46 Philip Lymbery, email to authors, 29 March 2015.

202 Klaus von Grebmer, Amy Saltzman, Ekin Birol, Doris Weismann et al., 'Global Hunger Index: The Challenge of Hidden Hunger, Synopsis', *International Food Policy Research Institute*, 2014.

203 Catherine Price, 'Vitamins Hide the Low Quality of Our Food', *New York Times*, 15 February 2015.

204 According to Dr Alex Richardson, a research fellow at Oxford University. See: Andrew Purvis, 'Running on Empty Carbs', *Guardian*, 22 March 2009.

205 Leicester City Council, 'Council Meat Tests Highlight Labelling concerns', 3 November 2014, http://news.leicester.gov.uk/newsArchiveDetail.aspx?Id=f2792.

206 Department of State, Department of Commerce, Action Plan for Implementing the Task Force Recommendations (Presidential Task Force on Combatting IUU Fishing and Seafood Fraud, 2015).

207 Kimberly Warner, Walker Timme, Beth Lowell and Michael Hirshfield, 'Oceana Study Reveals Seafood Fraud Nationwide', Oceana (2013).

208 Stephen Evans, 'Mislabelled Fish Slip Into Europe's Menus', *BBC News*, 2 April 2013.

209 Various studies reported in: 'Seafood Fraud', *Oceana*, http://oceana.org/sites/default/files/euo/OCEANA_fish_label_english.pdf.

210 For Ireland, see: Dana D. Miller and Stefano Mariani, 'Smoke, Mirrors, and Mislabeled Cod: Poor Transparency in the European Seafood Industry', *Frontiers in Ecology and the Environment* 8, no. 10 (2010): 517–521. For Paris figures, see: 'Seafood Fraud', *Oceana*.

211 Michael Pollan, quoted in Ezra Klein, 'Big Food: Michael Pollan Thinks Wall Street Has Way Too Much Influence Over What We Eat', *Vox*, 23 April 2014.

212 Kelly Brownell, quoted in Moss.

213 For more, visit: 'Animal Welfare', *Jeremy Coller Foundation*, http://www.jeremycollerfoundation.org/programmes/animal-welfare.

214 J. Kiley Hamlin, 'Moral Judgment and Action in Preverbal Infants and Toddlers Evidence for an Innate Moral Core', *Current Directions in Psychological Science* 22, no. 3 (2013): 186–193; Abraham Sagi and Martin L. Hoffman, 'Empathic Distress in the Newborn', *Developmental Psychology* 12, no. 2 (1976): 175.

215 Rifkin, 359.

216 Jeremy Bentham, An Introduction to the Principles of Morals and Legislation (Chapter XVII, Paragraph 122), 1789.

217 Nicky Amos and Rory Sullivan, 'The Business Benchmark on Farm Animal Welfare: 2014 Report', *Business Benchmark on Farm Animal Welfare* (2014), 35.

218 'Farm Assurance Schemes & Animal Welfare: How the Standards Compare: 2012', *OneKind* and *Compassion in World Farming*, 2012, http://www.ciwf.org.uk/media/5231246/standards_analysis_exec_summary.pdf.

219 'Philip Lymbery: Chief Executive', *Compassion in World Farming*, 2014, http://www.ciwf.org.uk/about-us/our-staff/philip-lymbery/.

220 Jonathan Safran Foer, *Eating Animals* (New York: Back Bay Books, 2009), 59.

Chapter 5. Businesss

221 Priorities USA Action, 'Stage', *YouTube* video, 1:02, 23 June 2012, https://www.youtube.com/watch?v=oLo0Jwj03JU.

222 Angei Drobnic Holan and Nai Issa, 'In Context: Hillary Clinton and Don't Let Anybody Tell You That Corporations Create Jobs', *Tampa Bay Times*'s Politifact, 30 October 2014, http://www.politifact.com/truth-o-meter/article/2014/oct/30/context-hillary-clinton-and-dont-let-anybody-tell-/.

223 Jonathan Sacks, 'The Dignity of Difference: Avoiding the Clash of Civilizations', *Foreign Policy Research Institute*, July 2002.

224 David Packard, quoted in James C. Collins and Jerry I. Porras, 'Building Your Company's Vision', *Harvard Business Review*, September 1996.

225 Estimates vary and range from as little as 6,500 to as much as 14,000 years ago. For various sources, see: Felipe Fernández-Armesto, *The World: A History, 2nd ed.* (London: Prentice Hall, 2010), 31–56; Peter Watson, *Ideas: A History of Thought and Invention, From Fire to Freud* (New York: Harper Perennial, 2005), 53; *Collins Atlas of World History*, ed. Geoffrey Barraclough (Ann Arbor, MI: Arbor Press, 2003), 38.

226 Matt Ridley, 'When Ideas Have Sex' (Lecture, TED Global 2010, Oxford, England, July 2010).

227 Ibid.

228 Median household income figures calculated from ONS data on median household income and the Bank of England's inflation calculator. For more information on median pay, see: Simon Lowe, 'Plotting A New Course to Improved Governance', *Corporate Governance Review 2014*, (Grant Thornton UK LLP, 2014), 32.

229 'FTSE 100 Directors' Total Earnings Jump By 21% in a Year', *Thomson Reuters* and *IDS*, London, 13 October 2014.

230 Office for National Statistics, *Annual Survey of Hours and Earnings, 2014 Provisional Results*, 2014, http://www.ons.gov.uk/ons/rel/ashe/annual-survey-of-hours-and-earnings/2014-provisional-results/stb-ashe-statistical-bulletin-2014.html.

231 'FTSE 100 Directors' Total Earnings Jump'.

232 Data compiled by Robert Colvile from Income Data Services, FTSE, and Bloomberg. See Robert Colvile, 'Yes, CEOs Are Ludicrously Overpaid. And Yes, It's Getting Worse', *Telegraph*, 13 October 2014.

233 Reuters, 'A.I.G. Pays Its Ex-Chief $47 Million', *New York Times*, 2 July 2008; author calculations from Yahoo Finance; Timothy G. Massad, 'Overall $182 Billion Committed to Stabilize AIG During the Financial Crisis Is Now Fully Recovered', *Treasury Notes (U.S. Department of the Treasury)*, http://www.treasury.gov/connect/blog/Pages/aig-182-billion.aspx.

234 Jenny Chu, Jonathan Faasse and P. Raghavendra Rau, 'Do Compensation Consultants Enable Higher CEO Pay?', *New Evidence from Recent Disclosure Rule Changes*, 23 September 2014.

235 Patrick Holden, 'The Price of Milk', *Sustainable Food Trust*, 16 January 2015, http://sustainablefoodtrust.org/articles/price-milk/.

236 Julia Glotz, 'Sainsbury's and Co-op Follow Tesco with Milk Price Cuts', *The Grocer*, 5 March 2014.

237 A *Guardian* investigation and analysis conducted in 2014. Simon Goodley and Leila Haddou, 'Revealed: Tesco Hoarding Land That Could Build 15,000 Homes', *Guardian*, 26 June 2014.

238 Competition Commission, *Market investigation into the Supply of Groceries in the UK*, (London: UK Competition Commission, 2008), 11.

239 Goodley and Haddou, 'Revealed'.

240 Tanya Pilgrim, 'The End of the Supermarket Sweep?', *Pennington Manches*, 8 October 2012, http://www.penningtons.co.uk/news-publications/archive-news/2012/the-end-of-the-supermarket-sweep/.

241 'Grocery Market Share', *Kanter World Panel*, http://www.kantarworldpanel.com/en/grocery-market-share/great-britain.

242 Antony Seely, 'Supermarkets: Competition Inquiries Into the Groceries Market', *House of Commons Library Standard Note: SN03653* (2012); Competition Commission, *The Supply of Groceries*, 72.

243 'Consumer Prices', *OECD*, 30 March 2015, https://stats.oecd.org/index.aspx?queryid=221.

244 Groceries Code Adjudicator, *Notice of Investigation*, 5 February 2015, https://www.gov.uk/government/uploads/system/uploads/attachment_data/file/401349/Notice_of_Investigation_final.pdf.

245 Nassim Nicholas Taleb, *Black Swan: The Impact of the Highly Improbable Fragility*, (New York: Random House, 2010), 182.

246 Kenichi Ueda and Beatrice Weder di Mauro, 'Quantifying Structural Subsidy Values for Systemically Important Financial Institutions', *Journal of Banking & Finance* 37, no. 10 (2013): 3830-3842 and The Editors, 'Why Should Taxpayers Give Big Banks $83 Billion a Year?', *Bloomberg View*, 20 February 2013.

247 Rex Nutting, 'Transcript of Holder's Admission on Too-Big-To-Jail Banks', *Market Watch*, 7 March 2013.

248 Peter Schroeder and Kevin Cirilli, 'Warren, Left Fume Over Deal', *The Hill*, 10 December 2014.

249 Matt Fuller, 'Republican Champion of Dodd-Frank Changes Goes After Elizabeth Warren', *Roll Call*, 28 January 2015; 'Rep. Keven Yoder: Top 20 Industries Contributing to Campaign Committee', *OpenSecrets.org*, 2 February 2015, https://www.opensecrets.org/politicians/industries.php?cycle=2014&cid=N00031502&type=I&newmem=N.

250 Eric Lipton and Ben Protess, 'Banks' Lobbyists Help in Drafting Financial Bills', *New York Times*, 24 May 2013.

251 Andy Borowtiz, 'Citigroup to Move Headquarters to US Capitol Building', *New Yorker*, 13 December 2013.

252 Steven Mufson and Tom Hamburger, 'Jamie Dion Himself Called to Urge Support for the Derivatives Rule in the Spending Bill', *Washington Post*, 11 December 2014.

253 'Barclays Appoints Hector Sants', *Barclays*, 12 December 2012, http://www.barclays.com/news/2012/12/barclays-appoints-hector-sants.html.

254 'Sir Jeremy Heywood, Cabinet Secretary and Head of the Civil Service: Biography', *British Goverment*, https://www.gov.uk/government/people/jeremy-heywood.

255 'Sir James Crosby Resigns from FSA', *BBC News*, 11 February 2009.

256 'Robert Rubin', *Council on Foreign Relations*, http://www.cfr.org/staff/b292.

257 'About: Secretary of the Treasury Jacob J. Lew', *US Department of the Treasury*, 5 June 2014, http://www.treasury.gov/about/Pages/Secretary.aspx.

258 'Alan Greenspan to Consult for Deutsche Bank Corporate and Investment Bank', *Deutsche Bank*, 13 August 2007, https://www.db.com/presse/en/content/press_releases_2007_3606.htm.

259 Elizabeth Warren, interview by Michael Krasny, *Forum*, 88.5 KQED FM, 7 May 2014.

260 Alison Fitzgerald, 'Koch, Exxon Mobil Among Corporations Helping Write State Laws', *Bloomberg*, 21 July 2011.

261 John Oliver, 'Last Week Tonight with John Oliver', television (2014, HBO), https://www.youtube.com/watch?v=aIMgfBZrrZ8.

262 Fitzgerald.

263 John Light, 'Frequently Asked Questions About ALEC', *Moyers & Company*, 28 September 2012, http://billmoyers.com/content/frequently-asked-questions-about-alec/.

264 Janie Lorber, 'Former IRS Official Demands Investigation of ALEC', *Roll Call*, 1 July 2012 and Peter Overby, 'Conservative Group's Charity Status Draws Questions', *NPR*, 19 April 2012.

265 Christopher Snowdon, 'Who's Killing the British Pub?' *Institute for Economic Affairs Blog*, 10 December 2014.

266 Danny Hakim, 'Saving an Endangered British Species: The Pub', *New York Times*, 17 February 2014.

267 Mark Gilbert, 'British Pubs Cry in Their Beer', *BloombergView*, 12 December 2014.

268 Ofgem, *The Revenues, Costs and Profits of the Energy Companies in 2013*, Ofgem, 2013, https://www.ofgem.gov.uk/ofgem-publications/90701/css2013summarydocument.pdf, 7; Ofgem, *Supply Market Indicator for January 2015*, Ofgem, 29 January 2015, https://www.ofgem.gov.uk/publications-and-updates/supply-market-indicator-january-2015.

269 That we dislike cheating is no surprise, of course, but it's telling that we will, as humans, give up some of our reward in a transaction if it means penalising someone who has cheated. In repeated versions of the 'Ultimatum Game', psychologists allow a participant to divide an amount of money between themselves and a second participant however they choose, with the caveat that if the second person rejects the offer, neither gets anything. While the economically rational decision would be to accept any offer above 0, it's almost always the case that if the second participant feels short-changed, they are more likely to retaliate by rejecting the money – hurting themselves – in order to punish the first participant.

270 Taleb, 282.

271 Ibid., 391.

272 'Red Dress Boutique', *SharkTank Blog*, http://sharktankblog.com/business/red-dress-boutique/.

273 Tim Bradshaw, 'Airbnb Valued at $13 B Ahead of Staff Stock Sale', *Financial Times*, 23 October 2014.

274 Mark Spera, quoted in Angela Salazar, 'BeGood Clothing's New Line – Organic Cotton and Silk Basics', *SF Gate*, 12 September 2014.

275 Jim Yardley, 'Bangladesh Pollution, Told in Colors and Smells', *New York Times*, 15 July 2013.

276 Emily Chang, 'China's Famed Pearl River Under Denim Threat', *CNN*, 27 April 2010.

277 'Dye Industry: Fact Sheet', Green Cross Switzerland, 2012, http://www.greencross.ch/nc/en/print/news-info-en/case-studies/environmental-reports/ten-most-dangerous-sources-of-environmental-toxins-2012/2012/dye-industry.html.

278 Mohammed Abdul Ali and Abdul Kader, quoted in Yardley.

279 David Bonbright, interview by authors, Palo Alto, CA, 24 October 2014.

280 Journalist Carole Cadwalladr spent a week working in Amazon's Swansea factory. She recounts her experience here: Carole Cadwalladr, 'My Week as an Amazon Insider', *Observer*, 1 December 2013.

281 Simon Head, 'Amazon's Sick Brutality and Secret History of Ruthlessly Intimidating Workers (Excerpt of *Mindless: Why Smarter Machines Are Making Dumber Humans*)', *Salon*, 23 February 2014.

282 In addition to undercover investigations cited above, you can view video from another by the BBC's *Panorama*; *Panorama*, television (2013, BBC), http://www.bbc.co.uk/programmes/b03k5kzp. In its response, Amazon also said that it 'adhere[s] to all regulations and employment law'. While its response is no longer posted on its website, it is quoted here: Matthew Jarvis, 'Amazon Response to BBC Panorama Worker Criticism,' *PCR*, 26 November 2013.

283 Bastian Lehmann, quoted in Farhad Manjoo, 'Amazon Not As Unstoppable as It Might Appear', *New York Times*, 18 December 2014.

284 Carolyn Said, 'Peers Helps Uber, Lyft Drivers Get Back On Road After Accidents', *San Francisco Chronicle*, 4 December 2014.

285 Mark Rogowsky, 'After the New Jersey Ban, Here's Where Tesla Can (And Cannot) Sell Its Cars)', *Forbes*, 15 March 2014.

286 'Michigan Becomes 5th US State to Thwart Direct Tesla Car Sales', *Reuters*, 22 October 2014.

Chapter 6. Poverty

287 David Robinson, interview by authors, London, 24 September 2014.

288 The amount spent on welfare in Britain annually. For more, see Andrew Hood and Paul Johnson, 'What Is Welfare Spending?', *Institute for Fiscal Studies*, 4 November 2014, http://www.ifs.org.uk/publications/7424.

289 Abdul Durrant, quoted in Nick Cohen, 'A Tale of Two Cities', *Observer*, 19 October 2013.

290 'Press Release', *Resolution Foundation*, 1 October 2014, http://www.resolutionfoundation.org/media/press-releases/a-record-1-2-million-workers-to-benefit-from-first-real-terms-minimum-wage-rise-for-six-years-today/.

291 Matthew Bolton, quoted in Dominic Casciani, 'Secret Life of the Office Cleaner', *BBC News*, 19 September 2005.

292 Sendhil Mullainathan, quoted in Maria Konnikova, 'No Money, No Time', *New York Times*, 15 June 2014.

293 Sendhil Mullainathan and Eldar Shafir, *Scarcity: Why Having Too Little Means So Much* (New York: Time Books, 2013), 160.

294 Mullainathan, quoted in Konnikova,.

295 Kayte Lawton and Matthew Pennycook, *Beyond the Bottom Line: The Challenges and Opportunities of a Living Wage* (London: IPPR and Resolution Foundation, 2013).

296 Tom MacInnes, Hannah Aldridge, Sabrina Bushe, Peter Kenway and Adam Tinson, *Monitoring Poverty and Social Exclusion, 2013*, (York, England: Joseph Rowntree Foundation, 2013).

297 Alfred Deakin, quoted in Marilyn Lake, 'Minimum Wage Is More Than a Safety Net, It's a Symbol of Australian Values', *The Age* (Melbourne, Australia), 10 April 2014.

298 Winston Churchill, Hansard HC Deb 28 April 1909, vol. 4, cols. 342–411.

299 Alan Manning, 'The UK's National Minimum Wage', *CentrePiece*, Autumn 2009.

300 Labour economists David Card and Alan Krueger found a minimum wage in one jurisdiction they studied increased hiring by 13 per cent. See: David Card and Alan B. Krueger, 'Minimum Wages and Employment: A Case Study of the Fast Food Industry in New Jersey and Pennsylvania', *National Bureau of Economic Research*, no. w4509, 1993.

301 Manning.

302 Jack Kennedy, Tim Moore and Annabel Fiddes, *Living Wage Research for KPMG: Structural Analysis of Hourly Wages and Current Trends in Household Finances, 2014 Report* (Henley on Thames, England: Markit, 2014), 5..

303 Adam Corlett and Matthew Whittaker, *Low Pay Britain 2014*, (Resolution Foundation, 2014), 29.

304 The other low wage earners work part-time. Lawton and Pennycook, *Beyond the Bottom Line*.

305 HM Revenue & Customs, *Child and Working Tax Credits Statistics: Finalised Annual Awards in 2012–13* (London, National Statistics, 2014).

306 Lake.

307 'Working Paper: Uprating the UK Living Wage in 2014', *Centre for Research in Social Policy, Loughborough University*, 2014.

308 'What Is the Living Wage?', *BBC News*, 2 November 2014.

309 These are a selection of the almost 1,200 Living Wage employers as of March 2015. For a comprehensive list, see http://www.livingwage.org.uk/employers.

310 Cameron Tait, *Work That Pays: The Final Report of the Living Wage Commission* (London Living Wage Commission, 2014), 33.

311 Mike Kelly, interview by authors, London, 25 September 2014.

312 *Global Powers of Retailing 2015: Embracing Innovation* (Deloitte, 2015).

313 Unless otherwise noted, all facts and quotes related to Costco come from: Brad Stone, 'Costco CEO Craig Jelinek Leads the Cheapest, Happiest Company in the World', *Bloomberg Business*, 6 June 2013.

314 'Costco Wholesale Corp', *MarketWatch*, 29 March 2015, http://www.marketwatch.com/investing/stock/cost/financials.

315 William Lazonick, Profits Without Prosperity', *Harvard Business Review*, September 2014.

316 Henry Ford and Samuel Crowther, *Great Today and Greater Future* (1926; reprint, Kessinger Publishing, LLC, 2003), 198–99.

317 Jack Welch, quoted in Francesco Guerrera, 'Welch Condemns Share Price Focus', *Financial Times*, 12 March 2009.

318 Paul Polman, quoted in Eric Reguly, 'Time to Put An End to the Cult of Shareholder Value', *Globe and Mail* (Toronto, Canada), 26 September 2013.

319 Tait, 18.

320 Lawton and Pennycook, 18.

321 Richard Stringer, quoted in Citizens UK, 'Living Wage Week 2013', *YouTube* video, 3:48, 3 November 2013, https://www.youtube.com/watch?v=7Xz0ylCLBgE.

322 The EITC has in part. See: Suzy Khimm, 'How Paying No Federal Income Tax Helps the Poor Get Off Welfare and Into Work', *Washington Post*, 18 September 2012.

323 Richard Blundell, Alan Duncan, Julian McCrae, and Costas Meghir, 'The Labour Market Impact of the Working Families' Tax Credit', *Fiscal Studies* 21, no. 1 (2000): 75–104; David Neumark and William Wascher, 'Minimum Wages, the Earned Income Tax Credit, and Employment: Evidence from the Post-Welfare Reform Era', *IZA Discussion Papers*, No. 26100, 2007.

324 Jesse Rothstein, 'The Unintended Consequences of Encouraging Work: Tax Incidence and the EITC', *Center for Economic Policy Studies*, Princeton, NJ: Princeton University, 2008.

325 HM Revenue & Customs, *Child and Working Tax Credits Statistics*, 13 (author's calculations).

326 Tait, 25.

327 Lawton and Pennycook, 38.

328 'An Unhealthy Dose of Stress: The Impact of Adverse Childhood Experiences and Toxic Stress on Childhood Health and Development', *Center for Youth Wellness*.

329 Paul Tough, 'The Poverty Clinic', *New Yorker*, 21 March 2008, 25–32.

330 This story is drawn from the following article: Jane Ellen Stevens, 'The Adverse Childhood Experiences Study – The Largest, Most Important Public Health Study You Never Heard of Began in an Obesity Clinic', *ACES Too High News*, 3 October 2012, http://acestoohigh.com/2012/10/03/the-adverse-childhood-experiences-study-the-largest-most-important-public-health-study-you-never-heard-of-began-in-an-obesity-clinic/.

331 Nadine Burke Harris, 'The Chronic Stress of Poverty: Toxic Stress to Children', *The Shriver Report*, 12 January 2014; Vincent J. Felitti, Robert F. Anda, Dale Nordenberg, David F. Williamson, Alison M. Spitz, Valerie Edwards, Mary P. Koss et al., 'The Relationship of Adult Health Status to Childhood Abuse and Household Dysfunction', *American Journal of Preventive Medicine* 14 (1998): 245–258.

332 Those who suffer from toxic stress are 2.2 times as likely to suffer from ischemic heart disease, 2.4 times as likely to have a stroke, 1.9 times as likely to suffer from cancer, 1.6 times as likely to suffer from diabetes, 12.2 times as likely to attempt suicide, 10.3 times as likely to use injection drugs, and 7.4 times as likely to be an alcoholic. For more, see: 'An Unhealthy Dose of Stress'. For the original study, see: Feletti et al.

333 As defined by the American Academy of Pediatrics; for more, see: Sara B. Johnson, Anne W. Riley, Douglas A. Granger and Jenna Riis, 'The Science of Early Life Toxic Stress for Pediatric Practice and Advocacy', *Pediatrics* 131, no. 2 (2013): 319–327.

334 Nadine Burke Harris, interview by authors, San Francisco, CA, 6 October 2014.

335 Andrew Hood and Paul Johnson, 'What Is Welfare Spending?', Insitute for Fiscal Studies, 4 November 2014, http://www.ifts.org.uk/publications/7424.

336 'No Quick Fix: Exposing the Depth of Britain's Drug and Alcohol Problem', part of *Breakdown Britain II*, (Centre for Social Justice, 2013).

337 Note that this figure includes spending on welfare services to address the consequences of child poverty, loss of income and tax receipts of workers who earn less for having been impoverished as children, and benefits spent on them as adults. It likely overlaps with welfare, child poverty, and educational

failure costs. For more, see: Donald Hirsch, 'An Estimate of the Cost of Child Poverty in 2013', *Child Poverty Action Group*, 5 June 2013.

338 As noted earlier, a report published by National Numeracy and Pro Bono Economics written by analysts from the National Audit Office estimated the costs innumeracy to be £20.2 billion, with a low estimate of £6.7 billion and a high estimate of £32.6 billion. For perspective, the £20.2 billion figure represents about 1.3 per cent of the British economy. See 'Cost of Outcomes Associated with Low Levels of Adult Numeracy in the UK', National Numeracy and Pro Bono Economics, 2014.

339 National Audit Office, *The Criminal Justice System: Landscape Review (Report by the Comptroller and Auditor General)* (National Audit Office, 7 March 2014), http://www.nao.org.uk/wp-content/uploads/2015/03/The-Criminal-Justice-system-landscape-review-summary1.pdf.

340 Veronica Engert, Franziska Plessow, Robert Miller, Clemens Kirschbaum and Tania Singer, 'Cortisol Increase in Empathic Stress Is Modulated by Emotional Closeness and Observation Modality', *Psychoneuroendocrinology* 45 (2014): 192–201.

341 *Fractured Families: Why Stability Matters* (London: Centre for Social Justice, 2013), 60.

342 David Robinson, *Out of the Ordinary: Learning from the Community Links Approach to Social Regeneration* (London: Community Links, 2010), 19.

343 Department for Communities and Local Government, *Tackling Troubled Families* (British Government: 15 December 2011), https://www.gov.uk/government/news/tackling-troubled-families.

344 'Troubled Families', *Local Government Association*, 29 January 2015, http://www.local.gov.uk/community-budgets/-/journal_content/56/10180/3691966/ARTICLE.

345 Louise Casey, interview by authors, 7 November 2014.

346 *Troubled Families: Progress Information at December 2014 and Families Turned Around at February 2015*, Department for Communities and Local Government, 10 March 2015, https://www.gov.uk/government/publications/troubled-families-programme-progress-information-at-december-2014-and-families-turned-around-at-february-2015.

347 Richard Reeves, 'Bringing Up Baby', *New Statesman*, 29 January 2009.

348 'Helping New Families: Support in the Early Years Through Universal Health Visiting', (Conservative Research Department), https://www.conservatives.com/~/media/Files/Downloadable%20Files/Helping%20new%20families.ashx.

349 See Nick Kristof, 'The Way to Beat Poverty', *New York Times*, 12 September 2014, which discusses the study or the study itself: Lynn A. Karoly, M. Rebecca Kilburn and Jill S. Cannon, *Early Childhood Interventions: Proven Results, Future Promise* (Santa Monica, CA: RAND Corporation, 2005).

Chapter 7. Inequality

350 'Global Wealth Databook 2014', *Credit Suisse Research Institute*, October 2014, https://publications.credit-suisse.com/tasks/render/file/?fileID=5521F296-D460-2B88-081889DB12817E02, 126.

351 'Consumers Face "Lost Decade" as Spending Squeeze Bites', *BBC News*, 29 September 2014.

352 From November–January 2013 to November–January 2015, the number of people needing second jobs *rose* while number of overall jobs increased. Meanwhile, we've also seen increases in the number of part-time workers. See: Office for National Statistics, *Labour Market Statistics, March 2015: Unemployment by Age and Duration*, 2015, http://www.ons.gov.uk/ons/pulications/re-reference-tables.html?edition=tcm%3A77-353568#tab-Unemployment---economic-inactivity-tables.

353 Office for National Statistics, *Underemployment and Overemployment in the UK, 2014*, 2014, http://www.ons.gov.uk/ons/dcp171776_387087.pdf.

354 World Bank, *Long-Term Unemployment (% of Total Unemployment)*, 2015, http://data.worldbank.org/indicator/SL.UEM.LTRM.ZS?order=wbapi_data_value_2012%20wbapi_data_value%20wbapi_da_tavalue-last&sort=asc.

355 Alina Barnett, Sandra Batten, Adrian Chiu, Jeremy Franklin and Maria Sebastia-Barriel, 'The UK Productivity Puzzle', *Bank of England Quarterly Bulletin* Q2 (2014): 114–128.

356 Office for National Statistics, *Annual Survey of Hours and Earnings, 2014 Provisional Results* (2014), http://www.ons.gov.uk/ons/rel/ashe/annual-survey-of-hours-and-earnings/2014-provisional-results/stb-ashe-statistical-bulletin-2014.html.

357 Clayton Christensen, 'The Capitalist's Dilemma' (Lecture, RSA, London, 23 September 2013).

358 Tyler Cowen, 'Automation Alone Isn't Killing Jobs', *New York Times*, 6 April 2014.

359 Alan B. Krueger, Judd Cramer, and David Cho, 'Are the Long-Term Unemployed on the Margins of the Labor Market?' *Brookings Papers on Economic Activity* (2014): 229–280.

360 Jaison R. Abel, Richard Deitz, and Yaqin Su, 'Are Recent College Graduates Finding Good Jobs?', *Current Issues in Economics and Finance*, 20, no. 1 (2014).

361 Carl Benedikt Frey and Michael A. Osborne, 'The Future of Employment: How Susceptible Are Jobs to Computerisation?' (2013).

362 David Graeber, quoted in Thomas Frank, 'David Graeber: "Spotlight on the Financial Sector Did Make Apparent Just how Bizarrely Skewed Our Economy Is In Terms of Who Gets Rewards"', *Salon*, 1 June 2014.

363 Laurence Chandy and Geoffrey Gertz, *Poverty in numbers: The Changing State of Global Poverty from 2005 to 2015*, (Brookings Institution, 2011).

364 Robert Caro, *The Path to Power, vol. 1 of The Years of Lyndon Johnson* (1981; reprint, London: Pimlico, 2003), 504.

365 Ibid., 506.

366 Ibid., 513.

367 'The Future of Jobs', *The Economist*, 18 January 2014, 28.

368 Matthias J. Koepp, Roger N. Gunn, Andrew D. Lawrence, Vincent J. Cunningham, Alain Dagher, Tasmin Jones, David J. Brooks, C. J. Bench and P. M. Grasby. 'Evidence for Striatal Dopamine Release During a Video Game', *Nature* 393, no. 6682 (1998): 266–268.

369 Richard M. Ryan and Edward L. Deci, 'Self-Determination Theory and the Facilitation of intrinsic motivation, Social Development, and Well-Being', *American Psychologist* 55, no. 1 (2000): 68.

370 *Removing the Barriers to Learning: Exploring Adult Perceptions and Attitudes to Participation in Further Education, Part One: Research Report*, Deloitte and Department for Employment and Learning, February 2012, http://www.delni.gov.uk/removing-the-barriers-to-learning-part-one-research-report-final-for-publication-feb-2012.pdf; Department for Business Innovation & Skills, *Motivation and Barriers to Learning for Young People Not in Education, Employment or Training*, BIS Research Paper Number 87, February 2013, https://www.gov.uk/government/uploads/system/uploads/attachment_data/file/182518/DFE-RR009.pdf; Department for Education, Thomas Spielhofer, Sarah Golden, Kelly Evans, Helen Marshall, Ellie Mundy, Marco Pomati and Ben Styles, *Barriers to Participation in Education and Training* (National Foundation for Education Research, March 2010).

371 Sebastian Thrun, interview by authors, Mountain View, CA, 11 November 2014.

372 For up to two years as long as the worker's unemployment insurance contribution has been paid.

373 'Flexicurity', *Denmark: The Official Website of Denmark*, http://denmark.dk/en/society/welfare/flexicurity/.

374 Thomas Bredgaard and Arthur Daemmrich, 'The Welfare State as an Investment Strategy: Denmark's Flexicurity Policies', July 2012, http://ilera2012.wharton.upenn.edu/RefereedPapers/BredgaardThomas%20ArthurDaemmrich.pdf.

375 'OECD Income Distribution Database: Gini, Poverty, Income, Methods, and Concepts', OECD, 19 June 2014, http://www.oecd.org/social/income-distribution-database.htm.

376 Charlie Mayfield, interview by authors, 22 October 2014.

377 Edouardo Porter, 'A Relentless Widening of Disparity in Wealth', *New York Times*, 12 March 2014.

378 Leo Mirani, 'The Secret to the Uber Economy: Wealth Inequality', *Quartz*, 16 December 2014.

379 Leon Feinstein, 'Very Early', *CentrePiece*.

380 Morris Kleiner, *Reforming Occupational Licensing Practices*, (Washington, DC: Brookings Institute: Hamilton Project, 2015), 5.

381 Reihan Salam, 'The Upper Middle Class is Ruining America', Slate, 30 January 2015, http://www.slate.com/articles/news_and_politics/politics/2015/01/the_upper_middle_class_is_ruining_all_that_is_great_about_america.html.

382 'America's Elite: An Hereditary Meritocracy', *The Economist*, 24 January 2015, 17.

383 'America's New Aristocracy', *The Economist*, 24 January 2015, 9.

384 Betty Hart and Todd R. Risley, 'The Early Catastrophe: The 30 Million Word Gap By Age 3', *American Educator* 27, no. 1 (2003): 4–9.

385 Ann Bieglow, quoted in Nicholas Kristof, 'Oklahoma! Where the Kids Learn Early', *New York Times*, 10 November 2013.

386 Feinstein, 'Very Early'.

387 Katherine Harmon, 'How Important Is Physical Contact with Your Infant?' *Scientific American*, 6 May 2010.

388 Andrew J. Cherlin, Elizabeth Talbert and Suzumi Yasutake, 'Changing Fertility Regimes and the Transition to Adulthood: Evidence from a Recent Cohort', In *Annual Meeting of the Population Association of America, Boston, MA, May* 3 (2014).

389 Cherlin, quoted in Olga Khazan, 'The Luxury of Waiting for Marriage to Have Kids', *Atlantic*, 17 June 2014.

390 Susan L. Brown, 'Family Structure and Child Well-Being: The Significance of Parental Cohabitation', *Journal of Marriage and Family* 66 (2004), 351–367.

391 Terry-Ann Craigie, Jeanne Brooks-Gunn, and Jane Waldfogel, *Family Structure, Family Stability and Early Child Wellbeing*, No. 1275 (2010).

392 Figures come from Table 3a. See Office of National Statistics, *Divorces in England and Wales, 2012*, http://www.ons.gov.uk/ons/rel/vsob1/divorces-in-england-and-wales/2012/stb-divorces-2012.html.

393 Office of National Statistics, *Marriages in England and Wales (Provisional), 2012* (Office for National Statistics, 2014).

394 Census figures show that between 2001 and 2011, self-professing Christians dropped from 71.7 to 59.3 per cent of the population in England and Wales. While overall numbers of those in a faith were buoyed by the sharp rise in Muslims (1.2 million more since 2001, including one in ten Britons under twenty-five); a quarter of the British population professes no faith at all, up from 15 per cent in 2001. For more, see: 'Religion' in National Statistics, *2011 Census: Key Statistics for England and Wales, March 2011* (Office for National Statistics, 2012), http://www.ons.gov.uk/ons/rel/census/2011-census/key-statistics-for-local-authorities-in-england-and-wales/stb-2011-census-key-statistics-for-england-and-wales.html#tab---Religion; 'Census Shows Rise in Foreign-Born', *BBC News*, 11 December 2012.

395 Jean M. Twenge, Keith W. Campbell, and Craig A. Foster, 'Parenthood and Marital Satisfaction: A Meta-Analytic Review', *Journal of Marriage and the Family*, 65 (2003), 574–583.

396 Dan Gilbert, quoted in Kate Devlin 'Marriage Without Children the Key to Bliss', *Telegraph*, 9 May 2008.

397 Niko Matouschek and Imran Rasul, 'The Economics of the Marriage Contract Theories and Evidence', *Journal of Law and Economics* 51, no. 1 (2008): 59–110.

398 John Haywood and Guy Brandon, 'Cohabitation: An Alternative to Marriage?', *Jubilee Centre*, June 2011, http://www.jubilee-centre.org/cohabitation-alternative-marriage-john-haywood-guy-brandon/.

399 Ellen C. Perrin, Benjamin S. Siegel, James G. Pawelski, Mary I. Dobbins, Arthur Lavin, Gerri Mattison, John Pascoe and Michael Yogman, 'Promoting the Well-Being of Children Whose Parents Are Gay or Lesbian', *Pediatrics* 131, no. 4 (2013): e1374-e1383.

400 Dan Gilbert, quoted in Devlin, 'Marriage Without Children'.

401 Shawn Grover and John F. Helliwell, *How's Life at Home? New Evidence on Marriage and the Set Point for Happiness*, No. w20794 (National Bureau of Economic Research, 2014).

402 Shawn Grover, quoted in Claire Cain Miller, 'Study Finds More Reasons to Get and Stay Married', *New York Times*, 8 January 2015.

403 John F. Helliwell, quoted in Miller, 'Study Finds More Reasons'.

404 Anne-Marie Slaughter, 'Why Women Still Can't Have It All', *The Atlantic*, 13 June 2012.

405 Liza Mundy, 'Daddy Track: The Case for Paternity Leave', *Atlantic*, January/February 2014.

406 Heather Boushey and Sarah Jane Glynn, *The Effects of Paid Family Medical Leave on Employment Stability and Economic Stability*, (Washington, DC: Center for American Progress, April 2012), 3.

407 According to the OECD, children whose families the eat their main meal together are less likely to be truant in school. See: 'Who Are the School Truants?', *PSIA in Focus*, January 2014, http://www.oecd.org/pisa/pisaproducts/pisainfocus/PISA-in-Focus-n35-(eng)-FINAL.pdf.

408 Eileen Appelbaum, and Ruth Milkman, *Leaves That Pay: Employer and Worker Experiences with Paid Family Leave in California* (Washington, DC: Center for Economic and Policy Research, 2011).

409 Mundy, 'The Daddy Track', 16.

410 Indeed, feeling overwhelmed and unprepared is common for parents. See: Susanne N. Biehle and Kristin D. Mickelson, 'Preparing for Parenthood: How Feelings of Responsibility and Efficacy Impact Expectant Parents', *Journal of Social and Personal Relationships* 28, No. 5, (2011): 668–683.

411 Octavius Black, quoted in Amelia Gentleman, 'Do We Need Parenting Classes?', *Guardian*, 31 March 2012.

412 Geoff Lindsay, Mairi Ann Cullen, Stephen Cullen, Vaso Totsika, Ioanna Bakopoulou, Susan Goodlad, Richard Brind et al., *CANparent Trial Evaluation: Final Report Research Report*, Department for Education (University of Warwick, 2014).

Chapter 8. Childhood

413 Hanna Rosin, 'Hey! Parents, Leave Those Kids Alone', *Atlantic*, April 2014, 77.

414 Lenore Skenazy, 'Free Range Kids: FAQ', *Free Range Kids*, https://freerangekids.wordpress.com/faq/.

415 David Ball in Tim Gill, *No Fear: Growing Up in A Risk Averse Society* (London: Calouste Gulbenkian Foundation, 2007), 26–27.

416 Gill, *No Fear*, 37–38.

417 David Yearley in ibid., 25–26.

418 David Ball in Gill, 29; and Department for Transport, 'Reported Casualties by Road User Type, Age and Severity, Great Britain, 2011 (TableRAS300002) in *Transport Studies* (2012), https://www.gov.uk/government/statistics/reported-road-casualties-great-britain-main-results-2011. See also: David J., 'Policy issues and Risk–Benefit Trade-offs of "Safer Surfacing" for Children's Playgrounds', *Accident Analysis & Prevention* 36, no. 4 (2004).

419 'Cancel That Violin Class: Helicopter Moms and Dads Will Not Harm Their Kids If They Relax a Bit', *The Economist*, 26 July 2014.

420 A Home Office report found that only 7 per cent of murdered children were killed by a stranger. See Research, Development and Statistics Directorate, *Reducing Homicide: A Review of the Possibilities*, by Fiona Brookman and Mike Maguire (London, Home Office, 2003), 16.

421 Jay Griffiths, *A Country Called Childhood* (Berkeley: Counterpoint, 2014), 57.

422 Ibid., 54 and 57.

423 Ellen B. H. Sandseter, 'Children's Risky Play from an Evolutionary Perspective: The Anti-Phobic Effects of Thrilling Experiences', *Evolutionary Psychology* 9(2), (2001): 257–84.

424 Paul Hocker, interview by authors, London, 26 September 2014.

425 Annie Murphy Paul, 'School of Hard Knocks: "How Children Succeed", by Paul Tough', *New York Times Sunday Book Review*, 26 August 2012.

426 Before the May 2015 General Election. See: 'Frequenty Asked Questions: MPs', Parliament, http://www.parliament.uk/about/faqs/house-of-commons-faqs/members-faq-page2/.

427 Jennifer Rankin, 'Fewer Women Leading FTSE Firms Than Men Called John'. *Guardian*, 6 March 2015.

428 Emma Rush and Andrea La Nauze, *Corporate Paedophilia: Sexualisation of Children in Australia*, (Canberra, Australia: Australia Institute, 2006).

429 Samantha M. Goodin, Alyssa Van Denburg, Sarah K. Murnen, and Linda Smolak, '"Putting on" Sexiness: A Content Analysis of the Presence of Sexualizing Characteristics in Girls' Clothing', *Sex Roles* 65, no. 1–2 (2011): 1–12.

430 APA Task Force on the Sexualization of Girls, *Report of the APA Task Force on the Sexualization of Girls*, American Psychological Association, Washington, DC, 2010.

431 Barbara L. Fredrickson, Tomi-Ann Roberts, Stephanie M. Noll, Diane M. Quinn and Jean M. Twenge, 'That Swimsuit Becomes You: Sex Differences in Self-Objectification, Restrained Eating, and Math Performance', *Journal of Personality and Social Psychology*, Vol. 75, no. 1 (July 1998), 269–284.

432 Kathrine D. Gapinski, Kelly D. Brownell, and Marianne LaFrance, 'Body Objectification and "Fat Talk": Effects on Emotion, Motivation, and Cognitive Performance', *Sex Roles* 48, no. 9–10 (2003): 377–388.

433 Ibid.

434 Beverley Turner, 'Pubic Hair Is Back Ladies. The Men Don't Care and the Women Can't Be Bothered', *Telegraph*, 15 November 2013. Heidi Stevens, 'Your 11-Year-Old Daughter Wants to Share. Everywhere, *Chicago Tribune*, 10 July 2012.

435 'One in Ten British Kids Own A Mobile Phone by the Age of Five', *uSwitch*, August 2013, http://www.uswitch.com/mobiles/news/2013/08/one_in_ten_british_kids_own_mobile_phone_by_the_age_of_five/.

436 Ofcom, *Children and Parents: Media Use and Attitudes Report*, 2014. 29.

437 Ibid., 32.

438 Ibid., 4.

439 Ibid., 163.

440 Ibid., 199.

441 Jane D. Brown, and Kelly L. L'Engle, 'X-rated Sexual Attitudes and Behaviors Associated with US Early Adolescents' Exposure to Sexually Explicit Media', *Communication Research* 36, no. 1 (2009): 129–151.

442 Patricia Romito and Lucia Beltramini, 'Watching Pornography: Gender Differences, Violence and Victimization: An Exploratory Study in Italy', *Violence Against Women* (2011): 1077801211424555.

443 'Young People Sexual Relationships', *IPPR*, http://www.ippr.org/assets/media/publications/attachments/youngpeoplesexrelationships.jpg.

444 Michael Flood, 'The Harms of Pornography Exposure Among Children and Young People', *Child Abuse Review* 18, no. 6 (2009): 384–400.

445 Tori DeAngelis, 'Web Pornography's Effect on Children', *American Psychological Association Monitor*, 38, no. 10 (November 2007): 50.

446 *People Who Abuse Children (An NSPCC Research Briefing)* NSPCC, 2014, http://www.nspcc.org.uk/global/assets/documents/information-service/research-briefing-people-who-abuse-children.pdf

447 Wesley Johnson, 'Children, Some Age Five, Commit Thousands of Child Sex Offences', *Telegraph*, 4 March 2013.

448 Gail Dines, quoted in Martin Daubney, 'Experiment That Convinced Me Online Porn is the Most Pernicious Threat Facing Children Today: By Ex Lads' Mag Editor Martin Daubney', *Daily Mail*, 25 September 2013.

449 Todd G. Morrison, Shannon R. Ellis Melanie A. Morrison, Anomi Bearden, and Rebecca L. Harriman, 'Exposure to Sexually Explicit Material and Variations in Body Esteem, Genital Attitudes, and Sexual Esteem Among a Sample of Canadian Men', *The Journal of Men's Studies*, 14, No. 2 (Spring 2006): 209–222.

450 Daubney, 'Experiment That Convinced Me'.

451 Ofcom, Media Use and Attitudes.

452 Linda Papadopoulos, 'Sexualisation of Young People Review', (2010), 9.

453 Daubney, 'Experiment That Convinced Me'.
454 Sally Kalson, 'Sexting ... and Other Stupid Teen Tricks', *Pittsburgh Post-Gazette*, 29 March 2009.
455 Hanna Rosin, 'Why Kids Sext', *The Atlantic*, November 2014, 65–77.
456 Donald Lowe, quoted in Rosin, 'Why Kids Sext', 67.
457 Rosin, 'Why Kids Sext', 68.
458 'Lean In Collection', *Getty Images*, http://www.gettyimages.com/creative/frontdoor/leanin.
459 'Physical Activity Guidelines for Children and Young People' *NHS Choices*, http://www.nhs.uk/Livewell/fitness/Pages/physical-activity-guidelines-for-young-people.aspx.
460 Susan Strife and Liam Downey, 'Childhood Development and Access to Nature: A new Direction for Environmental Research', *Organ Environment*, 22, no. 1 (March 2009): 99–122.
461 Brian Verdine, quoted in Allison Bond, 'Blocks, Puzzles Help Kids Prep for School', *Reuters*, 20 March 2014.
462 Ofcom.
463 Marsha Gerdes, quoted in Bond, 'Blocks, Puzzles Help Kids Prep for School'.
464 Brian N. Verdine, Roberta M. Golinkoff, Kathryn Hirsh Pasek, Nora S. Newcombe, Andrew T. Filipowicz and Alicia Chang, 'Deconstructing Building Blocks: Preschoolers' Spatial Assembly Performance Relates to Early Mathematical Skills', *Child Development* 85, no. 3 (2014): 1062–1076.
465 Pooja S. Tandon, Chuan Zhou, Paula Lozano, and Dimitri A. Christakis, 'Preschoolers' Total Daily Screen Time at Home and by Type of Child Care', *Journal of Pediatrics* 158, no. 2 (2011): 297–300. See also 'Zero to Eight': Children's Media Use in America 2013', *Common Sense Media*, Fall 2013.
466 'Touch Screens', *Michael Cohen Group LLC*, 17 February 2014.
467 Sherry Turkle, 'Connected, But Alone?' (presentation, TED, April 2012).
468 Ofcom, 81.
469 Sherry Turkle, *Alone Together: Why We Expect More from Technology and Less From Each Other* (New York: Basic Books, 2011), 268.
470 'The Dos and Don'ts of Using Your Phone at a Party', *Huffington Post*, 26 September 2014.
471 Sherry Turkle, quoted in Catherine de Lange, 'Sherry Turkle: "We're Losing the Raw, Human Part of Being with Each Other"', *Guardian*, 5 May 2013.
472 Justin Higginbottom, 'Growing Number of Children with Cellphones Adds Pressure to Purchase', *Desert News*, 22 April 2012.

Chapter 9. Spaces
473 Will Hunter, 'The Best Office in the World? Selgas Cano's New Work Space in London', *The Architectural Review*, 29 January 2015.
474 José Selgas and Lucia Cano, quoted in 'Future of Work', *Courier* 5 (August 2014), 5.
475 Interview with Rohan Silva.
476 Winston Churchill, Hansard HC Deb 28 October 1943, vol. 393, cols. 403–73.
477 Yuichi Shoda, 'Individual Differences in Social Psychology: Understanding Situations to Understand People, Understanding People to Understand Situations', in Carol Sansone, Carolyn C. Morf, and Abigail T. Panter, eds., *The Sage Handbook of Methods in Social Psychology* (Thousand Oaks, CA: Sage Publications, 2004), 119–121.
478 John Banham, Kate Faulkner, Roger Graef and Mavis McDonald, *Building the Homes and Communities Britain Needs*, (Future Homes Commission, Royal Institute of British Architects, 2012), 6.
479 *Building in a Small Island – Why We Still Need the Brownfield First Approach*, (Kemsing, Kent: Green Balance (for the Campaign to Protect Rural England), 2011), 4.
480 Pete Jeffrys, Toby Lloyd, et al., *Building the Homes We Need: A Programme for the 2015 Government*, KPMG and Shelter, 2014, 4 and 25.
481 Office for National Statistics, *Trends in the United Kingdom Housing Market, 2014* (calculated from Table 6) (London: Office for National Statistics, 22 September

2014), http://www.ons.gov.uk/ons/rel/hpi/house-price-index-guidance/trends-in-the-uk-housing-market-2014/housing-trends-article.html?format=print.
482 'Building Blocks', *The Economist*, 22 December 2014.
483 Jeffrys and Lloyd, 'Building the Homes We Need', 18.
484 Department for Communities and Local Government, *Live Tables on Housing Building*, https://www.gov.uk/government/statistical-data-sets/live-tables-on-house-building#discontinued-tables.
485 Robert Watson, Steve Albon, et al., *UK National Ecosystem Assessment: Synthesis of the Key Findings* (Cambridge, England: UNFP-WCMC, 2011), 60.
486 Rebecca Roberts-Hughes, *The Case for Space: The Size of England's New Homes*, Will Fox and Anna Scott-Marshall, eds. (RIBA, 2011), 8.
487 'Future Homes Commission Report', 33.
488 Jeffrys and Lloyd, 19.
489 Roberts-Hughes, 8.
490 Jeffrys and Lloyd, 43.
491 Tom Archer and Ian Cole, 'Over-Reliance on Private House Builders is Fuelling UK's Housing Crisis', *Guardian*, 12 September 2014.
492 Jeffrys and Lloyd, 22.
493 Stephen Finlay, Isabella Pereiva, Ella Fryer-Smith, Anne Charlton and Rebecca Roberts-Hughes, *The Way We Live Now: What People Need and Expect From Their Homes* (London: Ipsos MORI and RIBA, 2012), 11.
494 Bruce Bell, interview and correspondence by authors, October/November 2014.
495 Jeffrys and Lloyd, 42.
496 'Bevolkingsontwikkeling; regio per maand', CBS Statline (in Dutch), 26 June 2014.
497 Patrick Collinson, 'Self-Build: It's Time to Go Dutch', *Guardian*, 25 November 2011.
498 Elizabeth Hopkirk, 'The Netherlands' Almere Leads the Way on Self-Build Communities', *bdonline*, 6 June 2011.
499 'Almere, Holland', *The Self-Build Portal*, 2015 http://www.selfbuildportal.org.uk/homeruskwartier-district-almere, 2015.
500 Jacqueline Tellinga, quoted in Collinson.
501 Jacqueline Tellinga, quoted in Hopkirk.
502 Ian Steadman, 'Dutch City Gives Residents a Self-Build Affordable Housing Catalogue', *Wired*, 18 April 2013.
503 Ed Monk, 'The Ultimate DIY Investment', *This Is Money.co.uk*, 8 November 2013.
504 'Survey of Self-Build Intentions', *Ipsos-Mori*, 12 March 2013.
505 Angela Monaghan, 'UK Housebuilders Counter Ed Miliband's Land-Hoarding Claim', *Guardian*, 16 December 2013.
506 Jeffrys and Lloyd, 57.
507 Tim Craine, *Barriers to Housing Delivery: What Are the Market-Perceived Barriers to Residential Development in London?* (London: Greater London Authority and Molior London Ltd, December 2012), http://www.london.gov.uk/sites/default/files/Barriers%20to%20Housing%20Delivery.pdf.
508 Robert Fulford, *Accidental City: The Transformation of Toronto* (Canada: MacFarlane, Walter & Ross, 1995), 77
509 Jacobs, *The Death and Life of Great American Cities*, 4.
510 As characterised by the author; Napoleon III, quoted in Colin Jones, *Paris: A History* (New York: Penguin Books, 2004), 301.
511 David Pinkney, *Napoleon III and the Rebuilding of Paris* (Princeton, NJ: Princeton University Press, 1972), 18.
512 Maxime Du Camp, quoted in Jones, *Paris: A History*, 304.
513 Jones, *Paris*, 301.
514 Georges-Eugène Haussmann, quoted in Friedrich Lenger, *European Cities in the Modern Era, 1850–1914*, trans. Joel Golb (Leiden, Netherlands: Koninklijke Brill NV, 2012), 22.
515 Christopher Caldwell, 'Revolting High Rises', *New York Times Magazine*, 27 November 2005.
516 Fulford, *Accidental City*, 85.

517 Nadine Kalinauskas, 'St. Lawrence Market in Toronto Named Worldl's Best Food Market by National Geogrpahic', *Shine On*, 5 April 2012.

518 Jacobs, *Death and Life*, 50.

519 Dave LeBlanc, '35 Years on, St. Lawrence Is A Template for Urban Housing', *Globe and Mail*, 6 February 2013.

520 David Crombie, interview by authors, 17 September 2014.

521 'Why Plants in the Office Make Us More Productive', *ScienceDaily*, 1 September 2014..

522 Mohamed Boubekri, Ivy N. Cheung, Kathryn J. Reid, Chia-Hui Wang, and Phyllis C. Zee, 'Impact of Windows and Daylight Exposure on Overall Health and Sleep Quality of Office Workers: A Case-Control Pilot Study', *Journal of Clinical Sleep Medicine: JCSM: Official Publication of the American Academy of Sleep Medicine* 10, no. 6 (2014), 603.

523 Carlo Ratti, interview by authors, 13 October 2014.

524 Judith Heerwagen, 'Green Buildings, Organizational Success and Occupant Productivity', *Building Research & Information* 28, no. 5–6 (2000): 353–367.

525 Kimberly Bradley, 'Model Factories: Fagus-GreCon', *Monocle*, 69, No. 7 (December 2013–January 2014): 133–4.

526 Christine Congdon, Donna Flynn, and Melanie Redman, 'Balancing "We" and "Me": The Best Collaborative Spaces Also Support Solitude', *Harvard Business Review*, October 2014.

527 'Power of Place', *Steelcase 360º*, No. 68 (2014), 17.

528 Kaisa Nuikkinen, 'Vision of the Helsinki City School Building Program: Healthy and Safe School Building', (presentation at the American Institute for Architects' 'Schools in a Flat World' conference, Helsinki, Finland, 11 September 2008).

529 Unfortunately, misinterpretation of the theory has been used to support other, only partially related policies. Critics use (far too-frequent) occasions of abusive police overreaction as an indictment of 'broken-windows' policing writ large. Such criticism is an inaccurate conflation of two completely different phenomena. Yes, broken-windows theory suggests it's important to police petty crime. But it also suggests that community policing – more human policing, whereby officers walk the beat and actively foster relationships – is the answer. A proper application of broken-windows policing is community engagement, not creating an authoritarian police state.

530 Kees Keizer, Siegwart Lindenberg, and Linda Steg, 'The Spreading of Disorder', *Science* 322, no. 5908 (2008): 1681–1685.

531 Anthony A. Braga, and Brenda J. Bond, 'Policing Crime and Disorder Hot Spots: A Randomized Controlled Trial', *Criminology* 46, no. 3 (2008): 577–607.

532 Keizer, Lindberg and Steg.

533 OECD, *Road Safety Annual Report 2014* (OECD Publishing, 2014), DOI: 10.1787/irtad-2014-en.

534 'Why Sweden Has So Few Road Deaths', *The Economist*, 26 February 2014.

535 'Vision Zero Initiative: Traffic Safety by Sweden', Swedish Government and Business Sweden, http://www.visionzeroinitiative.com/en/.

536 'Why Sweden Has So Few Road Deaths'.

537 'Cycling Facts and Figures', *IAmsterdam, 2015*, http://www.iamsterdam.com/en/media-centre/city-hall/dossier-cycling/cycling-facts-and-figures; Amanda Buck, 'Transparency: The Most Dangerous Cities for Walking', *GOOD Magazine*, 3 September 2010.

538 Statistics Netherlands, *Traffic Deaths Down Again*, 18 April 2011, http://www.cbs.nl/en-GB/menu/themas/gezondheid-welzijn/publicaties/artikelen/archief/2011/2011-029-pb.htm; Ben Fried, 'The Origins of Holland's "Stop Murdering Children" Street Safety Movement', StreetsBlog Network, 20 February 2013, http://streetsblog.net/2013/02/20/the-origins-of-hollands-stop-murdering-children-street-safety-movement/.

539 'Amsterdam Children Fighting Cars in 1972', *Bicycle Dutch*, https://bicycledutch.wordpress.com/2013/12/12/amsterdam-children-fighting-cars-in-1972/.

540 Department of Energy & Climate Change, *Delivering UK Energy Investment* (London: Department of Energy & Climate Change, July 2014) https://www.

gov.uk/government/uploads/system/uploads/attachment_data/file/331071/DECC_Energy_Investment_Report.pdf.

541 Lucy Woods, 'Friday Focus: Solar's Future Fantasies', *PV Tech*, 13 December 2013.

542 Francie Diep, 'Watch a Spray-On Solar Getting Made', *Popular Science*, 9 December 2014.

543 'Jan Gehl: Biography', Project for Public Spaces, http://www.pps.org/reference/jgehl/.

544 Rogers, Richards, 'Forward', in Jan Gehl, *Cities for People* (Washington, DC: Island Press, 2010), ix.

545 Jan Gehl, quoted in Ellie Violet Bramley, 'Is Jan Gehl Winning His Battle to Make Our Cities Liveable?', *Guardian*, 8 December 2014.

546 Jan Gehl, quoted in 'Interview with Jan Gehl', *American Society for Landscape Architects*, http://www.asla.org/ContentDetail.aspx?id=31346.

547 Bramley, 'Is Jan Gehl Winning His Battle?'

548 'Towards a Fine City for People' (Copenhagen, Denmark: Gehl Architects, June 2004), http://issuu.com/gehlarchitects/docs/issuu_270_london_pspl_2004/0.

Chapter 10. Nature

549 Matthew Browning, quoted in Emma Marris, 'Let Kids Run Wild in the Woods', *Slate*, 25 May 2014.

550 Edward O. Wilson, *Biophilia* (Cambridge, MA: Harvard University Press, 1984), 85.

551 David Hancocks, 'Bringing Nature Into the Zoo: Inexpensive Solutions for Zoo Environments', *International Journal for the Study of Animal Problems* 1, No. 3 (1980): 170–177.

552 Roger S.Ulrich, et al. 'Stress recovery during exposure to natural and urban environments', *Journal of Environmental Psychology* 11, No. 3 (1991): 201–230; Chen-Yen Chang and Ping-Kun Chen, 'Human Response to Window Views and Indoor Plants in the Workplace', *HortScience*, 40, no. 5 (2005): 1354–1359; Terry Hartig et al., 'Tracking Restoration in Natural and Urban Field Settings', *Journal of Environmental Psychology* 23, No. 2 (2003): 109–123.

553 Maria Bodin and Terry Hartig, 'Does the Outdoor Environment Matter for Psychological Restoration Gained Through Running?', *Psychology of Sport and Exercise* 4, no. 2 (2003): 141–153.

554 Roger S. Ulrich, 'View Through a Window May Influence Recovery Surgery', *Science*, New Series 224, no.4647 (27 April 1984): 420–421.

555 'The Great Smog of 1952', *Met Office*, 10 June 2014, http://www.metoffice.gov.uk/education/teens/case-studies/great-smog.

556 Louis Bainbridge to James T. Duff, 31 October 1948, in 'The Denora Smog Disaster October 30–31, 1948', *Pennsylvania Historical & Museum Commission*, http://www.portal.state.pa.us/portal/server.pt/community/documents_from_1946_-_present/20426/donora_smog_disaster/999079.

557 'Theodore Roosevelt' in 'The National Parks: America's Best Idea', *PBS*, 2009, http://www.pbs.org/nationalparks/people/historical/roosevelt/.

558 E. F. Schumacher, *Small Is Beautiful: A Study of People As If People Mattered* (New York: Harper Perennial, 2010), 14.

559 Rhett Butler, 'Brazil', *Mongabay.com*, 13 July 2014, http://rainforests.mongabay.com/20brazil.wtm; 'Coordenaçã-Geral de Observção da Terra – OBT: Projecto Prodes: Monitoramenot da Floresta Amazônica Brasileira por Satélite,' (in Portuguese) *Ministério da Ciêcia e Tecnologia e Inovação e Minstério do Melo Ambiente*, 2014, http://www.obt.inpe.br/prodes/index.php.

560 'Measuring the Daily Destruction of the World's Rainforests', *Scientific American*, 19 November 2009.

561 Marcus Erikson et al., 'Plastic Pollution in the World's Oceans: More than 5 Trillion Plastic Pieces Weighing over 250,000 Tons Afloat at Sea', *PloS One 9*, no.12 (2014).

562 'Coral Reefs: Facts and Figures,' *IUCN*, 20 March 2013, http://www.iucn.org/media/facts_and_figures/?12680/Coral-reefs---Facts-and-figures.

563 Richard Monastersky, 'Life: A Status Report', *Nature* 516 (11 December 2014): 159–161.

564 Edward O. Wilson, quoted in 'Edward O. Wilson: "The Loss of Biodiversity Is a Tragedy",' *UNESCO Media Services*, 2 September 2010.

565 David J. Newman and Gordon M Cragg, 'Natural Products As Sources of New Drugs over the 30 Years from 1981 to 2010', *Journal of Natural Products* 75, no. 3 (2012): 311–335.

566 Edward O. Wilson, 'My Wish: Build the Encyclopedia of Life' (presentation, TED 2007, 2007).

567 Monastersky, 'Life'.

568 Tony Hiss, 'Can the World Really Set Aside Half of the Planet for Wildlife?', *Smithsonian Magazine*, September 2014.

569 I encourage you to learn more about their amazing work at www.whitehawkproject.org.

570 Patrick ten Brink, Daniela Russi, Andrew Farmer, Tomas Badura, David Coates, Johannes Förster, Ritesh Kumar and Nick Davidson, *The Economics of Ecosystems and Biodiversity for Water and Wetlands: Executive Summary* (Institute for European Environmental Policy & Ramsar Secretariat, 2013), 50.

571 Environmental Protection Agency, Office of Water, *Wetlands: Protection Life and Property from Flooding*, May 2006, http://water.epa.gov/type/wetlands/outreach/upload/Flooding.pdf.

572 There has been debate in the scientific community about the validity of this number, as there have been some instances in which the presence of intact wetlands do not reduce storm surge. (For a thoughtful analysis, see: Jeffrey Masters, 'Storm Surge Reduction by Wetlands,' *Weather Underground*, http://www.wunderground.com/hurricane/surge_wetlands.asp?MR=1.) We acknowledge that the impact wetlands can have on reducing storm surges can't be generalised to all scenarios, but the benefit they have and can have in many others is undeniable. See also: Corps of Engineers, US Army Engineer District, New Orleans, *Interim Survey Report, Morgan City, Louisiana and Vicinity*, no. 63 (New Orleans, LA: US Army Engineer District, November 1963).

573 Robert G. Dean, 'New Orleans and the Wetlands of Southern Louisiana', *Bridge* 36, no. 1 (2006): 35–42.

574 Donald F. Boesch, Leonard Shabman, et al., 'A New Framework for Planning the Future of Coastal Louisiana After the Hurricanes of 2005' (Cambridge, MD: University of Maryland Center for Environmental Science, 2006), 16.

575 Edward B. Barbier, 'Valuing Ecosystem Services As Productive Inputs', *Economic Policy* 22, no. 49 (2007): 178–229.

576 'Sebago Lake,' *Portland Water District*, http://www.pwd.org/environment/sebago/sebago.php.

577 John Talberth, Erin Gray, Evan Branosky, and Todd Gartner, *Insights from the Field: Forests for Water* (Washington, DC: Water Resources Institute, 2012).

578 Caryn Ernst, *Protecting the Source: Land Conservation and the Future of America's Drinking Water* (San Francisco: The Trust for Public Land, 2004).

579 Robert Costanza, Rudolf de Groot, Paul Sutton, Sander van der Ploeg, Sharolyn J. Anderson, Ida Kubiszewski, Stephen Farber and R. Kerry Turner, 'Changes in the Global Value of Ecosystem Services', *Global Environmental Change* 26 (2014): 152–158.

580 United Nations, Department of Economic and Social Affairs, Population Division, *World Urbanization Prospects: The 2014 Revision, Highlights* (ST/ESA/SER.A/352) 1.

581 The term was coined by the writer Richard Louv in his book *Last Child in the Woods: Saving Our Children From Nature-Deficit Disorder* (Chapel Hill: Algonquin Books, 2005).

582 *Reconnecting Children with Nature: Findings of the Natural Childhood Inquiry* (The National Trust, 2012), http://www.nationaltrust.org.uk/document-1355773744553/.

583 Christiane Dorion, interview by authors, London, 26 September 2014.

584 Jeremy Bailenson, 'Virtual Reality Could make a Real Difference in Environment', *San Francisco Chronicle*, 15 August 2014.

585   Sun Joo Grace Ahn, Jeremy N. Bailenson and Dooyeon Park, 'Short- and Long-term Effects of Embodied Experiences in Immersive Virtual Environments on Environmental Locus of Control and Behavior', *Computers in Human Behavior* 39 (2014): 235–245.

586   Jeremy Bailenson, quoted in Amy Westervelt, 'Can't Picture a World Devastated By Climate Change? These Games Will Do It for You', *Smithsonian.com*, 21 July 2014.

587   Henry W. Randle, 'Suntanning: Differences in Perceptions Throughout History', in *Mayo Clinic Proceedings* 72, no. 5, 1997: 461–466.

588   'Ballona Wetlands Restoration Project', 2014, http://ballonarestoration.org.

589   'Grunewald', *Visit Berlin*, http://www.visitberlin.de/en/spot/grunewald.

590   'Outdoor Knoxville,' *Legacy Parks Foundation*, 2014, http://www.outdoorknoxville.com/urban-wilderness.

591   Outdoor play, studies show, is pivotal for a child's development and well-being. See: Peter Gray, 'The Decline of Play and the Rise of Psychopathology in Children and Adolescents', *American Journal of Play* 3, no. 4 (2011): 443–463.

Conclusion

592   Christian Dustmann and Tommaso Frattini. 'The Fiscal Effects of Immigration to the UK', *Economic Journal* 124, no. 580 (2014): F593–F643.

593   'What Have the Immigrants Ever Done for Us?', *The Economist*, 8 November 2014, 59.

594   Rob Portman, 'Gay Couples Also Deserve Chance to Get Married', *Columbus Dispatch*, 15 March 2013.

595   Ray Kurzweil, 'The Singularity is Near', http://www.singularity.com/aboutthebook.html.

596   Michael Howard, 'The Movie That Accurately Predicted the Future of Technology', *Esquire.com*, 23 September 2014.

597   Stephen Hawking, quoted in Rory Cellan-Jones, 'Stephen Hawking Warns Artificial Intelligence Could End Mankind', *BBC News*, 2 December 20.

598   'She, Robot: A Conversation with Helen Greiner', *Foreign Affairs* 94, no. 1 (Jan/Feb 2015) 21.

599   Diane Ackerman, *The Human Age: The World Shaped By Us* (New York: W. W. Norton & Company, 2014), 225.

600   Ackerman, *The Human Age*, 221–2.

601   Elon Musk, quoted in Miriam Kramer, 'Elon Musk: Artificial Intelligence is Humanity's Biggest Existential Threat', *Live Science*, 27 October 2014.

602   Susannah F. Locke, 'Robots That Eat Bugs and Plants for Power', *Popular Science*, 9 October 2009.

603   Stephen Hawking, quoted Cellan-Jones, 'Stephen Hawking Warns Artificial Intelligence Could End Mankind'.

604   Sherry Turkle, 'Authenticity in the Age of Digital Companions', *Interaction Studies* 8, no. 3 (2007), 514.

605   Steve Jobs, 'Stanford Commencement Address' (speech, Stanford University, Stanford, CA, 14 June 2005).

606   Hawking, quoted in Cellan-Jones.

607   Hugh Herr, 'The New Bionics That Let Us Run, Climb, and Dance' (presentation, TED 2014: The Next Chapter, Vancouver, Canada, March 2014).

608   Chris Cesare, 'Stanford to Host 100-year Study on Artificial Intelligence', *Stanford Report*, 16 December 2014, http://news.stanford.edu/news/2014/december/ai-century-study-121614.html; John Markoff, 'Study to Examine Effects of Artificial Intelligence', *New York Times*, 16 December 2014.

609   Cesare, 'Stanford to Host 100-year Study on Artificial Intelligence'.

610   Mary Warnock, *A Question of Life: The Warnock Report on Human Fertilisation and Embryology* (London: Her Majesty's Stationery Office, 1984).

611   *Fertilisation, Human, and Embryology Act*, 'Chapter 37' (London: Her Majesty's Stationery Office, London, 1990).

Postscript: The First Step

612   Fukuyama, 455–548.

613   Lawrence Lessig, 'We the People, and the Republic We Must Reclaim' (presentation, TED 2013, Long Beach, CA, February 2013).

BIBLIOGRAPHY

Abel, Jaison R., Richard Deitz and Yaqin Su. 'Are Recent College Graduates Finding Good Jobs?'. *Current Issues in Economics and Finance* 20, no. 1 (2014).

'About: Secretary of the Treasury Jacob J. Lew'. *US Department of the Treasury*, 5 June 2014. http://www.treasury.gov/about/Pages/Secretary.aspx.

Ackerman, Diane. *The Human Age: The World Shaped By Us*. New York: W.W. Norton & Company, 2014.

'Advance Care Planning: National Guidelines'. *Concise Guidance to Good Practice* 12. Royal College of Physicians, 2009.

'Agenda Materials: College Board Forum 2014'. *The College Board*. 27–29 October 2013.

Ahn, Sun Joo Grace, Jeremy N. Bailenson and Dooyeon Park. 'Short-and Long-term Effects of Embodied Experiences in Immersive Virtual Environments on Environmental Locus of Control and Behavior'. *Computers in Human Behavior* 39 (2014): 235–245.

'Alan Greenspan to Consult for Deutsche Bank Corporate and Investment Bank'. *Deutsche Bank*, 13 August 2007. https://www.db.com/presse/en/content/press_releases_2007_3606.htm.

'Almere, Holland'. *The Self-Build Portal*, 2015. http://www.selfbuildportal.org.uk/homeruskwartier-district-almere.

'America's Elite: An Hereditary Meritocracy'. *The Economist*. 24 January 2015.

'America's New Aristocracy'. *The Economist*. 24 January 2015.

Amos, Nicky and Rory Sullivan. 'The Business Benchmark on Farm Animal Welfare: 2014 Report.' *Business Benchmark on Farm Animal Welfare*. 2014.

'Amsterdam Children Fighting Cars in 1972'. *Bicycle Dutch*. https://bicycledutch.wordpress.com/2013/12/12/amsterdam-children-fighting-cars-in-1972/.

'An Unhealthy Dose of Stress: The Impact of Adverse Childhood

Experiences and Toxic Stress on Childhood Health and Development'. Center for Youth Wellness.

'Animal Welfare'. Jeremy Coller Foundation. http://www.jeremycollerfoundation.org/programmes/animal-welfare.

'Antimicrobial Resistance – Why the Irresponsible Use of Antibiotics in Agriculture Must Stop'. *Alliance to Save Our Antibiotics*, June 2014.

APA Task Force on the Sexualization of Girls. *Report of the APA Task Force on the Sexualization of Girls*. Washington, DC: American Psychological Association, 2010.

Appelbaum, Eileen and Ruth Milkman. 'Leaves That Pay: Employer and Worker Experiences with Paid Family Leave in California'. Washington, DC: Center for Economic and Policy Research, 2011.

Archer, Tom and Ian Cole. 'Still Not Plannable? Housing Supply and the Changing Structure of the Housebuilding Industry in the UK in "Austere" Times'. *People, Place and Policy* 8, no. 2 (2014): 93–108.

Aubry, Allison. 'Antibiotic-Free Meat Business Is Booming, Thanks to Chipotle'. *NPR*, 31 May 2012.

Bailenson, Jeremy. 'Virtual Reality Could Make a Real Difference in Environment'. *San Francisco Chronicle*, 15 August 2014.

Bainbridge, Louis. Louis Bainbridge to James T Duff, 31 October 1948. In 'The Denora Smog Disaster October 30–31, 1948'. Pennsylvania Historical & Museum Commission. http://www.portal.state.pa.us/portal/server.pt/community/documents_from_1946_-_present/20426/donora_smog_disaster/999079.

Ball, David J. 'Policy Issues and Risk–Benefit Trade-offs of "Safer Surfacing" for Children's Playgrounds'. *Accident Analysis & Prevention* 36, no. 4 (2004): 661–670.

'Ballona Wetlands Restoration Project'. 2014. http://ballonarestoration.org.

Banham, John, Kate Faulkner, Roger Graef and Mavis McDonald. *Building the Homes and Communities Britain Needs*. Future Homes Commission, Royal Institute of British Architects, 2012.

Barbier, Edward B. 'Valuing Ecosystem Services As Productive Inputs. *Economic Policy* 22, no. 49 (2007): 178–229.

'Barclays Appoints Hector Sants'. *Barclays*, 12 December 2012. http://www.barclays.com/news/2012/12/barclays-appoints-hector-sants.html.

Barnett, Alina, Sandra Batten, Adrian Chiu, Jeremy Franklin, and Maria Sebastia-Barriel. 'The UK Productivity Puzzle'. *Bank of England Quarterly Bulletin* Q2 (2014): 114–128.

'BBC Poll: One in Five 'Disillusioned' with Westminster'. *BBC News*, 31 October 2014.

Bennett, Drake. 'The Dunbar Number, From the Guru of Social Networks'. *BloombergBusinesseweek*, 10 January 2013.

Bentham, Jeremy. *An Introduction to the Principles of Morals and Legislation*. 1789.

Berman, Rick. 'Commentary: Playing Chicken with Pork'. *PORK Network*, 28 February 2013. http://www.porknetwork.com/pork-news/Commentary-Playing-chicken-with-pork-193903501.html?view=all.

'Bevolkingsontwikkeling; regio per maand' (in Dutch). CBS Statline, 26 June 2014.

Biehle, Susanne N. and Kristin D. Mickelson. 'Preparing for Parenthood: How Feelings of Responsibility and Efficacy Impact Expectant Parents'. *Journal of Social and Personal Relationships* 28, No. 5, (2011): 668–683.

Blundell, Richard, Alan Duncan, Julian McCrae and Costas Meghir. 'The Labour Market Impact of the Working Families' Tax Credit'. *Fiscal Studies* 21, no. 1 (2000): 75–104

Boesch, Donald F., Leonard Shabman, et al. 'A New Framework for Planning the Future of Coastal Louisiana After the Hurricanes of 2005'. Cambridge, MD: University of Maryland Center for Environmental Science, 2006.

Bond, Allison. 'Blocks, Puzzles Help Kids Prep for School'. *Reuters*, 20 March 2014.

Bornstein, David. 'Out of Poverty, Family-Style'. *New York Times*, 14 July 2011.

Borowtiz, Andy. 'Citigroup to Move Headquarters to US Capitol Building'. *The New Yorker*, 13 December 2013.

Boseley, Sarah. 'Mid Staffordshire NHS Trust Fined for "Avoidable and Tragic Death"'. *Guardian*, 28 April 2014.

Boubekri, Mohamed, Ivy N. Cheung, Kathryn J. Reid, Chia-Hui Wang and Phyllis C. Zee. 'Impact of Windows and Daylight Exposure on Overall Health and Sleep Quality of Office Workers: A Case-Control Pilot Study'. *Journal of Clinical Sleep Medicine: JCSM: Official Publication of the American Academy of Sleep Medicine* 10, no. 6 (2014): 603.

Boushey, Heather and Sarah Jane Glynn. *The Effects of Paid Family Medical Leave on Employment Stability and Economic Stability*. Washington, DC: Center for American Progress, 2012.

Bowers, Becky. 'Rep. Louise Slaughter Says 80% of Antibiotics Are Fed to Livestock'. *Tampa Bay Times' PolitiFact.com*, 15 October 2013.

Bradley, Kimberly. 'Model Factories: Fagus-GreCon.' *Monocle*, 69, no. 7 (December 2013–January 2014): 133–4.

Bradshaw, Tim. 'Airbnb Valued at $13 B Ahead of Staff Stock Sale'. *Financial Times*, 23 October 2014.

Braga, Anthony A. and Brenda J. Bond. 'Policing Crime and Disorder Hot Spots: A Randomized Controlled Trial'. *Criminology* 46, no. 3 (2008): 577–607.

Bramley, Ellie Violet. 'Is Jan Gehl Winning His Battle to Make Our Cities Liveable?'. *Guardian*, 8 December 2014.

Brat, Illan and Sarah Nassauer. 'Chipotle Suspends Pork Sales at a Third of Its Restaurants'. *Wall Street Journal*, 13 January 2015.

Bredgaard, Thomas and Arthur Daemmrich. 'The Welfare State as an Investment Strategy: Denmark's Flexicurity Policies'. July 2012. http://ilera2012.wharton.upenn.edu/RefereedPapers/BredgaardThomas%20ArthurDaemmrich.pdf.

Brooks, David. 'The Character Factory'. *New York Times*, 1 August 2014.

—— . 'Out of Poverty, Family-Style'. *New York Times*, 14 July 2011.

Brown, Jane D., and Kelly L. L'Engle. 'X-rated Sexual Attitudes and Behaviors Associated with US Early Adolescents' Exposure to Sexually Explicit Media'. *Communication Research* 36, no. 1 (2009): 129–151.

British Government. *Number of Individual Income Taxpayers by Marginal Rate, Gender and Age, 1990–91 to 2014–15*. https://www.gov.uk/government/uploads/system/uploads/attachment_data/file/404149/Table_2.1.pdf.

Brown, S. L. 'Family Structure and Child Well-Being: The Significance of Parental Cohabitation'. *Journal of Marriage and Family* 66 (2004): 351–367.

Buck, Amanda. 'Transparency: The Most Dangerous Cities for Walking'. *GOOD Magazine*, 3 September 2010.

'Building Blocks'. *The Economist*, 22 December 2014.

Building in a Small Island? Why We Still Need the Brownfield First Approach. Kemsing, Kent: Green Balance (for the Campaign to Protect Rural England), 2011.

Butler, Rhett. 'Brazil'. *Mongabay.com*, 13 July 2014. http://rainforests.mongabay.com/20brazil.htm.

Cadwalladr, Carole. 'My Week as an Amazon Insider'. *Observer*, 1 December 2013.

Caldwell, Christopher. 'Revolting High Rises'. *New York Times Magazine*, 27 November 2005.

'Campylobacter". *Food Standards Agency*. https://www.food.gov.uk/science/microbiology/campylobacterevidenceprogramme.

'Cancel That Violin Class: Helicopter Moms and Dads Will Not Harm Their Kids If They Relax a Bit'. *The Economist*, 26 July 2014.

Card, David and Alan B. Krueger. 'Minimum Wages and Employment: A Case Study of the Fast Food Industry in New Jersey and Pennsylvania'. *National Bureau of Economic Research*, no. w4509, 1993.

Caro, Robert. *The Path to Power, vol. 1 of The Years of Lyndon Johnson*. 1981. Reprint: London: Pimlico, 2003.

Carr, Nicholas. *The Shallows: What the Internet Is Doing to Our Brains*. New York: W. W. Norton & Company, 2010.

Casciani, Dominic. 'Secret Life of the Office Cleaner'. *BBC News*, 19 September 2005.

Cavendish, Camilla. *The Cavendish Review: An Independent Review Into Healthcare Assistants and Support Workers in the NHS and Social Care Settings*. London: Department of Health, 2013.

Cellan-Jones, Rory. 'Stephen Hawking Warns Artificial Intelligence Could End Mankind'. *BBC News*, 2 December 2014.

'Census Shows Rise in Foreign-Born'. *BBC News*, 11 December 2012.

Cesare, Chris. 'Stanford to Host 100–year Study on Artificial Intelligence'. *Stanford Report*, 16 December 2014. http://news.stanford.edu/news/2014/december/ai-century-study-121614.html.

Chandler, Jr., Alfred D. *The Visible Hand: The Managerial Revolution in American Business*. Cambridge, MA: Harvard University Press, 1977.

Chandy, Laurence and Geoffrey Gertz. *Poverty in Numbers: The Changing State of Global Poverty from 2005 to 2015*. Brookings Institution, 2011.

Chang, Chen-Yen and Ping-Kun Chen. 'Human Response to Window Views and Indoor Plants in the Workplace'. *HortScience* 40, no. 5 (2005): 1354–1359.

Chang, Emily. 'China's Famed Pearl River Under Denim Threat'. *CNN*, 27 April 2010.

Cherlin, Andrew J., Elizabeth Talbert and Suzumi Yasutake. 'Changing Fertility Regimes and the Transition to Adulthood: Evidence from a Recent Cohort'. In *Annual Meeting of the Population Association of America, Boston, MA*, May 3, 2014.

Chew, Jesslyn. 'Marriages Benefits When Fathers Share Household Parenting Responsibilities, MU Researchers Say'. *University of Missouri News Bureau*, 8 April 2013. http://munews.missouri.edu/news-releases/2013/0408–marriages-benefit-when-fathers-share-household-parenting-responsibilities-mu-researcher-says/.

Chingos, Matthew M. *Strength in Numbers: State Spending on K-12 Assessment Systems*. Washington, DC: Brown Center for Education at the Brookings Institution, 2012.

Cho, Illseung, Shingo Yamanishi, Laura Cox, Barbara A. Methé, Jiri Zavadil, Kelvin Li, Zhan Gao et al. 'Antibiotics in Early Life Alter the Murine Colonic Microbiome and Adiposity'. *Nature* 488, no. 7413 (2012): 621–626.

Christensen, Clayton. 'The Capitalist's Dilemma'. Lecture, RSA, London, 23 September 2013.

Chu, Jenny, Jonathan Faasse and P. Raghavendra Rau. 'Do Compensation Consultants Enable Higher CEO Pay?'. *New Evidence from Recent Disclosure Rule Changes*, September 23, 2014.

Churchill, Winston. Hansard HC Deb 28 April 1909, vol. 4, cols. 342–411.

—. Hansard HC Deb 28 October 1943, vol. 393, cols. 403–73.

Cialdini, Robert B., Linda J. Demaine, Brad J. Sagarin, Daniel W. Barrett, Kelton Rhoads and Patricia L. Winter. 'Managing Social Norms for Persuasive Impact', *Social Influence* 1, no. 1 (2006): 3–15.

Citizens UK. 'Living Wage Week 2013'. *YouTube* video, 3:48. 3 November 2013. https://www.youtube.com/watch?v=7Xz0ylCLBgE.

Cohen, Nick. 'A Tale of Two Cities'. *Observer*, 19 October 2013.

Collins, James C. and Jerry I. Porras. 'Building Your Company's Vision'. *Harvard Business Review*, September 1996.

Collins Atlas of World History. Edited by Geoffrey Barraclough. Ann Arbor, MI: Arbor Press, 2003.

Collinson, Patrick. 'Self-Build: It's Time to Go Dutch'. Guardian, 25 November 2011.

Colvile, Robert. 'Yes, CEOs Are Ludicrously Overpaid. And Yes, It's Getting Worse'. *Telegraph*, 13 October 2014.

Competition Commission. *Market Investigation into the Supply of Groceries in the UK*. London: UK Competition Commission, 2008.

Comptroller and Auditor General. *The Criminal Justice System: Landscape Review*. National Audit Office, 2014.

Congdon, Christine, Donna Flynn and Melanie Redman. 'Balancing "We" and "Me": The Best Collaborative Spaces Also Support Solitude'. *Harvard Business Review*, October 2014.

'Consumers Face "Lost Decade" as Spending Squeeze Bites'. *BBC News*, 29 September 2014.

'Coordenaçã-Geral de Observção da Terra – OBT: Projecto Prodes: Monitoramenot da Floresta Amazônica Brasileira por Satélite' (in Portuguese). *Ministério da Ciêcia e Technologia e Inovação e Minstério do Melo Ambiente*, 2014. http://www.obt.inpe.br/prodes/index.php.

'Coral Reefs: Facts and Figures'. *IUCN*, 20 March 2013. http://www.iucn.org/media/facts_and_figures/?12680/Coral-reefs---Facts-and-figures.

Corlett, Adam and Matthew Whittaker. *Low Pay Britain 2014*. London: Resolution Foundation, 2014.

Corps of Engineers, US Army Engineer District, New Orleans.

Interim Survey Report, Morgan City, Louisiana and Vicinity, no. 63. New Orleans, LA: US Army Engineer District, 1963.

'Cost of Outcomes Associated with Low Levels of Adult Numeracy in the UK'. *National Numeracy* and *Pro Bono Economics*. 2014.

Costco Wholesale Corp.'. *Marketwatch*, 29 March 2015. http://www.marketwatch.com/investing/stock/cost/financials.

Costanza, Robert, Rudolf de Groot, Paul Sutton, Sander van der Ploeg, Sharolyn J. Anderson, Ida Kubiszewski, Stephen Farber and R. Kerry Turner. 'Changes in the Global Value of Ecosystem Services'. *Global Environmental Change* 26 (2014): 152–158.

Coughlan, Sean. 'Is Five Too Soon to Start School?'. *BBC News*, 8 February 2008.

Council Regulation (EC) 1999/74 of 19 July 1999 laying down minimum standards for the protection of laying hens [1999] OJ L203/53.

Couzigou, Irène. 'France: Territorial Decentralisation in France: Towards Autonomy and Democracy'. In *Local Government in Europe: The 'Fourth Level' in the EU Multi-Layered System of Governance*. Edited by Carlo Panara and Michael R. Varney, 73–96. New York: Routledge, 2013.

Cowen, Tyler. 'Automation Alone Isn't Killing Jobs'. *New York Times*, 6 April 2014.

Coyle, Diane. *GDP: A Brief but Affectionate History*. Princeton, NJ: Princeton University Press, 2014.

— . 'GDP Is A Mirror on the Markets. It Must Not Rule Our Lives'. *Guardian*, 20 November 2014.

Cragg, Gordon M. 'Natural Products as Sources of New Drugs Over the 30 Years from 1981 to 2010'. *Journal of Natural Products* 75, no. 3 (2012): 311–335.

Craigie, Terry-Ann, Jeanne Brooks-Gunn and Jane Waldfogel. 'Family Structure, Family Stability and Early Child Wellbeing', No. 1275 (2010). http://crcw.princeton.edu/workingpapers/WP10–14–FF.pdf.

Craine, Tim. *Barriers to Housing Delivery: What Are the Market-Perceived Barriers to Residential Development in London?*. London: Greater London Authority and Molior London Ltd, December 2012.

Curtis, Polly. 'French Civil Servant's Confession Strikes a Chord in Drive to Shrink State'. *Guardian*, 23 March 2011.

'Cycling Facts and Figures'. *IAmsterdam*, 2015. http://www.iamsterdam.com/en/media-centre/city-hall/dossier-cycling/cycling-facts-and-figures.

Darzi, Ara. *High Quality Care For All: NHS Next Stage Review Final Report (The Darzi Report)*. London: The Stationery Office, 2008.

Daubney, Martin. 'Experiment That Convinced Me Online Porn

in the Most Pernicious Threat Facing Children Today: By Ex Lads' Mag Editor Martin Daubney'. *Daily Mail*, 25 September 2013.

Davis, Joshua. 'How a Radical New Teaching Method Could Unleash A Generation of Geniuses'. *Wired*, 15 October 2013.

de Lange, Catherine. 'Sherry Turkle: "We're Losing the Raw, Human Part of Being with Each Other'. *Guardian*, 5 May 2013.

de Ruiter, Jan, Gavin Weston and Stephen M. Lyon. 'Dunbar's Number: Group Size and Brain Physiology in Humans Reexamined'. *American Anthropologist* 113, no. 4 (2011): 557–568.

Dean, Robert G. 'New Orleans and the Wetlands of Southern Louisiana'. *Bridge* 36, no. 1 (2006): 35–42.

DeAngelis, Tori. 'Web Pornography's Effect on Children'. *American Psychological Association Monitor*, 38, no. 10 (November 2007): 50.

Deloitte and Department for Employment and Learning. *Removing the Barriers to Learning: Exploring Adult Perceptions and Attitudes to Participation in Further Education, Part One: Research Report*. 2012.

Department for Business Innovation & Skills. *Motivation and Barriers to Learning for Young People Not in Education, Employment or Training*. BIS Research Paper Number 87, 2013.

Department for Communities and Local Government. *Troubled Families: Progress Information at December 2014 and Families Turned Around at February 2015*. British Government. 10 March 2015.

— . *Tackling Troubled Families* (British Government: 15 December 2011), https://www.gov.uk/government/news/tackling-troubled-families.

—. Live Tables on Housing Building. https://www.gov.uk/government/statistical-data-sets/live-tables-on-house-building#discontinued-tables.

Department for Education. *Barriers to Participation in Education and Training*. By Thomas Spielhofer, Sarah Golden, Kelly Evans, Helen Marshall, Ellie Mundy, Marco Pomati and Ben Styles. National Foundation for Education Research, 2010.

— . *CANparent Trial Evaluation: Final Report Research*. By Geoff Lindsay, Mairi Ann Cullen, Stephen Cullen, Vaso Totsika, Ioanna Bakopoulou, Susan Goodlad, Richard Brind et al. University of Warwick, 2014.

Department of Energy & Climate Change. *Delivering UK Energy Investment*. London: Department of Energy & Climate Change, 2014.

Department for Environment, Food and Rural Affairs, Department of Agriculture and Rural Development (Northern Ireland), The Scottish Government, Rural and Environment Research and Analysis Directorate, Welsh Assembly Goverment, The

Department for Rural Affairs and Heritage. *Agriculture in the United Kingdom, 2012*. National Statistics, 2013.

Department of Health. National Audit Office. The National Programme for IT in the NHS: An Update on the Delivery of Detailed Care Records Systems. London: The Stationery Office, 2011.

Department of Health and Human Services (US). Office of the Inspector General. *Medicare Atypical Antipsychotic Drug Claims for Elderly Nursing Home Residents*. Office of the Inspector General, May 2011.

Department of State (US). Department of Commerce (US). *Action Plan for Implementing the Task Force Recommendations*. Presidential Task Force on Combatting IUU Fishing and Seafood Fraud, 2015.

Department for Transport. 'Reported Casualties by Road User Type, Age and Severity, Great Britain, 2011 (TableRAS30002)'. In *Transport Statistics*. 2012. https://www.gov.uk/government/statistics/reported-road-casualties-great-britain-main-results-2011.

Devereaux, Jennifer. NewsNation with Tamron Hall, MSNBC, 19 June 2014. Devlin, Kate. 'Marriage Without Children the Key to Bliss'. *Telegraph*, 9 May 2008

Devlin, Stephen, Thomas Dosch, Aniol Esteban and Griffin Carpenter. *Urgent Recall: Our Food System Under Review*. New Economics Foundation, 2014.

Diep, Francie. 'Watch a Spray-On Solar Getting Made'. *Popular Science*, 9 December 2014.

Donaldson, Liam. *150 Years of the Annual Report of the Chief Medical Officer: On the State of Public Health 2008*. London: Department of Health, 2009.

'The Dos and Don'ts of Using Your Phone at a Party'. *Huffington Post*, 26 September 2014.

Duckworth, Angela L. and Martin E. P. Seligman. 'Self-Discipline Outdoes IQ in Predicting Academic Performance of Adolescents', *Psychological Science* 16, no. 12 (2005): 939–944.

Dunbar, Robin I. M. 'Neocortex Size as a Constraint on Group Size in Primates'. *Journal of Human Evolution* 22, No. 6 (1992): 469–493.

Dustmann, Christian and Tommaso Frattini. 'The Fiscal Effects of Immigration to the UK'. *The Economic Journal* 124, no. 580 (2014): F593–F643.

'Dye Industry: Fact Sheet'. *Green Cross Switzerland*, 2012. http://www.greencross.ch/nc/en/print/news-info-en/case-studies/environmental-reports/ten-most-dangerous-sources-of-environmental-toxins-2012/2012/dye-industry.html.

Editorial Board. 'Mr. Bratton Reverses to Go Forward'. *New York Times*, 13 September 2014.

Editors. 'Why Should Taxpayers Give Big Banks $83 Billion a Year?'. *Bloomberg View*, 20 February 2013.

— . 'Small Schools Work in New York'. *New York Times*, 18 October 2014.

'Edward O. Wilson: "The Loss of Biodiversity Is a Tragedy"'. *UNESCO Media Services*, 2 September 2010. http://www.unesco. org/new/en/media-services/single-view/news/edward_o_wilson_ the_loss_of_biodiversity_is_a_tragedy/#.U7x4hxZbuuc.

Elkin, David. Interview with Neal Conan. 'Can You Make Your Baby Smarter, Sooner?'. *Talk of the Nation*. NPR, 28 October 2009.

Ellicott, Claire. 'NHS Hospital Scandal Which Left 1,200 Dead Could Happen Again, Warn Campaigners'. *Daily Mail*, 9 November 2010.

Ellis, Aleksander P. J., Bradford S. Bell, Robert E. Ployhart, John R. Hollenbeck and D. R. Ilgen. 'An Evaluation of Generic Teamwork Skill Training with Action Teams: Effects on Cognitive and Skill-Based Outcomes', *Personnel Psychology* 58, no. 3 (2005): 641–672.

Ellyatt, Wendy, Al Aynsley-Green, Richard Layrd, et al. 'The Government Should Stop Intervening in Early Education' (signed letter to the editor), *Telegraph*, 11 September 2013.

Engert, Veronica, Franziska Plessow, Robert Miller, Clemens Kirschbaum and Tania Singer. 'Cortisol Increase in Empathic Stress Is Modulated by Emotional Closeness and Observation Modality'. *Psychoneuroendocrinology* 45 (2014): 192–201.

Environmental Protection Agency. Office of Water. *Wetlands: Protection Life and Property from Flooding*, 2006. http://water.epa. gov/type/wetlands/outreach/upload/Flooding.pdf.

'English Mayoral Elections and Referendums'. *BBC News*, 4 May 2012.

Erikson, Marcus, et al. 'Plastic Pollution in the World's Oceans: More than 5 Trillion Plastic Pieces Weighing Over 250,000 Tons Afloat at Sea'. *PloS One* 9, no.12 (2014).

Ernst, Caryn. *Protecting the Source: Land Conservation and the Future of America's Drinking Water*. San Francisco, CA: The Trust for Public Land, 2004.

Evans, Stephen. 'Mislabelled Fish Slip Into Europe's Menus'. *BBC News*, 2 April 2013.

Fackler, Martin. 'District in Tokyo Plans to Extend Rights of Gay Couples'. *New York Times*, 13 February 2015.

Farm Assurance Schemes & Animal Welfare: How the Standards Compare: 2012. Edinburgh and Surrey: *OneKind* and *Compassion in World Farming*, 2012.

Feinstein, Leon. 'Very Early'. *CentrePiece*, Summer 2003.

Felitti, Vincent J., Robert F. Anda, Dale Nordenberg, David F. Williamson, Alison M. Spitz, Valerie Edwards, Mary P. Koss, et al. 'The Relationship of Adult Health Status to Childhood Abuse and Household Dysfunction'. *American Journal of Preventive Medicine* 14 (1998): 245–258.

Fernandez, Manny. 'Cheese Whatevers, City Has Them by the Handful'. *New York Times*, 4 August 2010.

Fernández-Armesto, Felipe. *The World: A History, 2nd ed.* London: Prentice Hall, 2010.

Fertilisation, Human, and Embryology Act, 'Chapter 37'. Her Majesty's Stationery Office: London, 1990.

Finlay, Stephen, Isabella Pereira, Ella Fryer-Smith, Anne Charlton and Rebecca Roberts-Hughes. *The Way We Live Now: What People Need and Expect From Their Homes*. London: Ipsos MORI and the Royal Institute of British Architects, 2012.

'Fight Cruelty: Chicken FAQ', *ASPCA*, 2015, http://www.aspca.org/fight-cruelty/farm-animal-cruelty/chicken-faq.

Fitzgerald, Alison. 'Koch, Exxon Mobil Among Corporations Helping Write State Laws'. *Bloomberg*, 21 July 2011.

'Flexicurity'. *Denmark: The Official Website of Denmark*. http://denmark.dk/en/society/welfare/flexicurity/.

Flood, Michael. 'The Harms of Pornography Exposure Among Children and Young People'. *Child Abuse Review* 18, no. 6 (2009): 384–400.

Foer, Jonathan Safran. *Eating Animals*. New York: Back Bay Books, 2009.

Ford, Henry and Samuel Crowther. *Great Today and Greater Future*. 1926. Reprint: Kessinger Publishing, LLC, 2003.

Forgacs, Ian, and Aathavan Loganayagam. 'Overprescribing Proton Pump Inhibitors'. *BMJ* 336, no. 7634 (2008): 2–3.

Fractured Families: Why Stability Matters. London: Centre for Social Justice, 2013.

Francis, *Evangelli Gaudium: Apolistic Exhortation on the Proclamation of the Gospel in Today's World*. Vatican City: Libreria Editrice Vaticana, 2013.

Francis, Robert. *The Mid Staffordshire NHS Foundation Trust Inquiry: Independent Inquiry Into Care Provided by Mid Staffordshire Foundation Trust, January 2005–March 2009*, Vol. 1. London: The Stationery Office, 2010.

Frank, Thomas. 'David Graeber: "Spotlight on the Financial Sector Did Make Apparent Just How Bizarrely Skewed Our Economy Is In Terms of Who Gets Rewards"'. *Salon*, 1 June 2014.

Fredrickson, Barbara L., Tomi-Ann Roberts, Stephanie M. Noll, Diane M. Quinn and Jean M .Twenge. 'That Swimsuit Becomes You: Sex Differences in Self-Objectification, Restrained Eating, and Math Performance. *Journal of Personality and Social Psychology* 75, no. 1, (July 1998): 269–284.

'Frequently Asked Questions: MPs'. *Parliament*. http://www.parliament.uk/about/faqs/house-of-commons-faqs/members-faq-page2/.

Frey, Carl Benedikt and Michael A. Osborne. 'The Future of Employment: How Susceptible Are Jobs to Computerisation?'. 2013.

Fried, Ben. 'The Origins of Holland's "Stop Murdering Children" Street Safety Movement'. *StreetsBlog Network*, 20 February 2013. http://streetsblog.net/2013/02/20/the-origins-of-hollands-stop-murdering-children-street-safety-movement/.

Fryer Jr., Ronald G., Steven D. Levitt, John List and Sally Sadoff. 'Enhancing the Efficacy of Teacher Incentives Through Loss Aversion: A Field Experiment'. *National Bureau of Economic Research*, No. w18237 (2012).

'FTSE 100 Directors' Total Earnings Jump By 21% in a Year'. *Thomson Reuters* and *IDS*. 13 October 2014.

Fukuyama, Francis. *Political Order and Political Decay*. New York: Farrar, Straus and Giroux, 2014.

Fuller, Matt. 'Republican Champion of Dodd-Frank Changes Goes After Elizabeth Warren'. *Roll Call*, 28 January 2015.

Fulford, Robet. *Accidental City: The Transformation of Toronto*. Canada: MacFarlane, Walter & Ross, 1995.

'The Future of Jobs'. *The Economist*, 18 January 2014.

'Future of Work'. *Courier*, August 2014.

Gamerman, Ellen. 'What Makes Finnish Kids So Smart?'. *Wall Street Journal*, 28 February 2008.

Gapinski, Kathrine D., Kelly D. Brownell and Marianne LaFrance. 'Body Objectification and "'Fat Talk'": Effects on Emotion, Motivation, and Cognitive Performance'. *Sex Roles* 48, no. 9–10 (2003): 377–388.

Geico Insurance. 'Free Range Chicken: It's What You Do', 0:30. 8 March 2015. https://www.youtube.com/watch?v=3v1wFKKWMCA.

Gentleman, Amelia. 'Do We Need Parenting Classes?'. *Guardian*, 31 March 2012.

'George Osborne: Greater Manchester to Have Elected Mayor'. *BBC News*, 3 November 2014.

Gilbert, Mark. 'British Pubs Cry in Their Beer'. *BloombergView*, 12 December 2014.

Gill, Tim. *No Fear: Growing Up in A Risk Averse Society*. London: Calouste Gulbenkian Foundation, 2007.

Global Powers of Retailing 2015: Embracing Innovation. Deloitte, 2015.

'Global Wealth Databook 2014'. *Credit Suisse Research Institute*, 2014. https://publications.credit-suisse.com/tasks/render/file/?fileID=5521F296–D460–2B88–081889DB12817E02.

Glotz, Julia. 'Sainsbury's and Co-op Follow Tesco with Milk Price Cuts'. *The Grocer*, 5 March 2014.

Gomes, Barbara, Natalia Calanzani and Irene J. Higginson. *Local Preferences and Place of Death in Regions within England 2010*. London: Cicely Saunders International, 2011.

Goodin, Samantha M., Alyssa Van Denburg, Sarah K. Murnen and Linda Smolak. '"Putting On" Sexiness: A Content Analysis of the Presence of Sexualizing Characteristics in Girls' Clothing'. *Sex Roles* 65, no. 1–2 (2011): 1–12.

Goodley, Simon and Leila Haddou. 'Revealed: Tesco Hoarding Land That Could Build 15,000 Homes'. *Guardian*, 26 June 2014.

Goodrich, Joanna and Jocelyn Cornwell. *Seeing the Person in the Patient*. London: The King's Fund, 2008.

Government Office for Science. *Foresight: Tackling Obesities: Future Choices, Project Report*. By Bryony Butland, Susan Jebb, Peter Kopelman, K. McPherson, S. Thomas, J. Mardell and V. Parry. Department of Innovation, Universities and Skills, 2007.

Gray, Peter. 'The Decline of Play and the Rise of Psychopathology in Children and Adolescents'. *American Journal of Play* 3, no. 4 (2011): 443–463.

'The Great Smog of 1952'. *Met Office*, 10 June 2014. http://www.metoffice.gov.uk/education/teens/case-studies/great-smog.

Green, Duncan. 'Robert Chambers: Why Don't All Developments Do Immersions?'. *People, Spaces, Deliberation (The World Bank)*, 6 September 2012. http://blogs.worldbank.org/publicsphere/node/6091.

Griffiths, Jay. *A Country Called Childhood*. Berkeley, CA: Counterpoint, 2014.

Groceries Code Adjudicator. *Notice of Investigation*. 5 February 2015. https://www.gov.uk/government/uploads/system/uploads/attachment_data/file/401349/Notice_of_Investigation_final.pdf.

'Grocery Market Share'. *Kanter World Panel*. http://www.kantarworldpanel.com/en/grocery-market-share/great-britain.

Grover, Shawn and John F. Helliwell. *How's Life at Home? New Evidence on Marriage and the Set Point for Happiness*. No. w20794. National Bureau of Economic Research, 2014.

'Grunewald'. Visit Berlin. http://www.visitberlin.de/en/spot/grunewald.

Guerrera, Francesco. 'Welch Condemns Share Price Focus'. *Financial Times*, 12 March 2009.

HM Revenue & Customs. *Child and Working Tax Credits Statistics: Finalised Annual Awards in 2012–13*. London: National Statistics, 2014.

HM Revenue & Customs. *National Insurance Fund Account, For the Year Ended 31 March 2013*. London: The Stationery Office, 2013.

Hakim, Danny. 'Saving an Endangered British Species: The Pub'. *New York Times*, 17 February 2014.

Hamlin, J. Kiley. 'Moral Judgment and Action in Preverbal Infants and Toddlers Evidence for an Innate Moral Core'. *Current Directions in Psychological Science* 22, no. 3 (2013): 186–193.

Hancocks, David. 'Bringing Nature Into the Zoo: Inexpensive Solutions for Zoo Environments'. *International Journal for the Study of Animal Problems* 1, No. 3 (1980): 170–177.

Hand, Larry and Madeline Drexler. 'Public Health Takes Aim at Sugar and Salt'. *Harvard School of Public Health Review*, Fall 2009.

Harmon, Katherine. 'How Important Is Physical Contact with Your Infant?'. *Scientific American*, 6 May 2010.

Harris, Nadine Burke. 'The Chronic Stress of Poverty: Toxic Stress to Children'. *Shriver Report*, 12 January 2014.

Harris, William T. 'Elementary Education'. *The North American Review* (1895): 538–546.

Hart, Betty and Todd R. Risley. 'The Early Catastrophe: The 30 Million Word Gap By Age 3'. *American Educator* 27, no. 1 (2003): 4–9.

Hartig, Terry, et al. 'Tracking Restoration in Natural and Urban Field Settings'. *Journal of Environmental Psychology* 23, No. 2 (2003): 109–123.

Haywood, John and Guy Brandon. 'Cohabitation: An Alternative to Marriage?'. *Jubilee Centre*, 2011. http://www.jubilee-centre.org/cohabitation-alternative-marriage-john-haywood-guy-brandon/.

Head, Simon. 'Amazon's Sick Brutality and Secret History of Ruthlessly Intimidating Workers (Excerpt of *Mindless: Why Smarter Machines Are Making Dumber Humans*)'. *Salon*, 23 February 2014.

Health and Social Care Information Centre. Prescription Cost Analysis: England 2008. National Statistics, 2009.

— . Prescription Cost Analysis: England 2013. National Statistics, 2014.

— . Prescriptions Dispensed in the Community: England 2002–12. National Statistics, 2013.

Heckman, James J. 'Skill Formation and the Economics of Investing in Disadvantaged Children', *Science* 312, no. 5782 (2006): 1900–1902.

Heerwagen, Judith. 'Green Buildings, Organizational Success and Occupant Productivity'. *Building Research & Information* 28, no. 5–6 (2000): 353–367.

'Helping New Families: Support in the Early Years Through Universal Health Visiting'. *Conservative Research Department*.

https://www.conservatives.com/~/media/Files/Downloadable%20
Files/Helping%20new%20families.ashx.

Henley, Jon. 'Why Are Homes in Britain So Small?'. *Guardian*, 16
May 2012.

Herr, Hugh. 'The New Bionics That Let Us Run, Climb, and
Dance'. Presentation, TED 2014: The Next Chapter, Vancouver,
Canada, March 2014.

Higginbottom, Justin. 'Growing Number of Children with
Cellphones Adds Pressure to Purchase'. *Deseret News* (Salt Lake
City, UT), 22 April 2012.

Higginson, Irene J., Ilora G. Finlay, Danielle M. Goodwin, Kerry
Hood, Adrian G. K. Edwards, Alison Cook, Hannah-Rose
Douglas and Charles E. Normand. 'Is There Evidence that
Palliative Care Teams Alter End-of-Life Experiences of Patients
and Their Caregivers?', *Journal of Pain and Symptom Management*
25, no. 2 (2003): 150–168.

Hill, Peter and Michael Barber. *Preparing for a Renaissance in
Assessment*. London: Pearson PLC, 2014.

Hirsch, Donald. *An Estimate of the Cost of Child Poverty in 2013*.
Child Poverty Action Group, 5 June, 2013.

Hiss, Tony. 'Can the World Really Set Aside Half of the Planet for
Wildlife?'. *Smithsonian Magazine*, September 2014.

Hitt, Michael A., David King, Menna Krishnan, Marianna Makri,
Mario Schijven, Katsuhiko Shimizu, and Hong Zhu. 'Creating
Value Through Mergers and Acquisitions: Challenges and
Opportunities'. In The Handbook of Mergers and Acquisitions.
Edited by David Faulkner, Satu Teerikangas and Richard J.
Joseph, Oxford, England: Oxford University Press, 2012.

Holden, Patrick. 'The Price of Milk'. *Sustainable Food Trust*, 16
January 2015. http://sustainablefoodtrust.org/articles/price-
milk/.

'Hospitals "Are Medical Factories"'. *BBC News*, 3 December 2008.

House of Commons Library. *Supermarkets: Competition Inquiries Into
the Groceries Market*. By Antony Seely. SN03653. London: House
of Commons Library, 2012.

—— . *Directly-Elected Mayors*. By Mark Sandford. SN/PC/5000.
London: House of Commons Library, 2014.

Holan, Angei Drobnic and Nai Issa. 'In Context: Hillary Clinton
and Don't Let Anybody Tell You That Corporations Create
Jobs'. *Tampa Bay Times' Politifact*, 30 October 2014. http://www.
politifact.com/truth-o-meter/article/2014/oct/30/context-hillary-
clinton-and-dont-let-anybody-tell-/.

Holden, Patrick. 'The Price of Milk.' Sustainable Food Trust, 16
January 2015. http://sustainablefoodtrust.org/articles/price-milk.

Hood, Andrew and Paul Johnson. 'What Is Welfare Spending?'

Institute for Fiscal Studies, 4 November 2014. http://www.ifs.org.uk/publications/7424.

'Hospitals "Are Medical Factories"'. *BBC News*, 3 December 2008.

House of Commons Committee of Public Accounts. *Department of Health: The National Programme for IT: – the NHS*. Twentieth Report of Session 2006–07, HC 390. London: The Stationery Office, 2007.

— . Department of Health. *Review of the Final Benefits Statement for Programmes Previously Managed Under the National Programme for IT: – the NHS*. London: National Audit Office, 2015.

Hopkirk, Elizabeth. 'The Netherlands' Almere Leads the Way on Self-Build Communities'. *bdonline*, 6 June 2011. http://www.bdonline.co.uk/the-netherlands-almere-leads-the-way-on-self-build-communities/5019196.article.

Howard, Michael. 'The Movie That Accurately Predicted the Future of Technology'. *Esquire.com*, 23 September 2014.

Hunter, Will, 'The Best Office in the World? Selgas Cano's New Work Space in London', *Architectural Review*, 29 January 2015.

'IBM 2010 Global CEO Study: Creativity Selected as Most Crucial Factor for Future Success', *IBM*, 18 May 2010, https://www-03.ibm.com/press/us/en/pressrelease/31670.wss.

Ilves, Toomas. 'Evolving Into a Genuinely Digital Society'. Speech at Green Library, Stanford University, Stanford, CA, 23 May 2014.

'Interview with Jan Gehl'. *American Society for Landscape Architects*. http://www.asla.org/ContentDetail.aspx?id=31346.

'Introducing the Vscan Family'. *GE Healthcare*, 2015. https://vscan.gehealthcare.com/introducing-vscan-family.

Jacobs, Jane. *The Death and Life of Great American Cities*. New York: Vintage Books, 1961.

Jaffe, Ina and Robert Benincasa. 'Nursing Homes Rarely Penalized for Oversedating Patients'. *NPR*, 9 December 2014.

— . 'Old and Over Medicated: The Real Drug Problem in Nursing Homes'. *NPR*, 8 December 2014.

— . 'This Nursing Home Calms Troubling Behavior Without Risky Drugs'. *NPR*, 9 December 2014.

'Jan Gehl: Biography'. *Project for Public Spaces*. http://www.pps.org/reference/jgehl/.

Jeffrys, Pete, Toby Lloyd, et al. *Building the Homes We Need: A Programme for the 2015 Government*. KPMG and Shelter, 2014.

Jobs, Steve. 'Stanford Commencement Address'. Speech, Stanford University, Stanford, CA, 14 June 2005.

Joffe-Walt, Chana. 'The Town Where Everyone Talks About Death'. *NPR*, 5 March 2014.

Johnson, James R., Michael A. Kuskowski, Kirk Smith, Timothy T. O'Bryan and Sita Tatini. 'Antimicrobial-Resistant and

Extraintestinal Pathogenic Escherichia coli in Retail Foods'. *Journal of Infectious Diseases* 191, no. 7 (2005): 1040–1049.

Johnson, Nathanael J. 'Swine of the Times'. *Harper's Magazine*, May 2006.

Johnson, Sara B., Anne W. Riley, Douglas A. Granger and Jenna Riis. 'The Science of Early Life Toxic Stress for Pediatric Practice and Advocacy'. *Pediatrics* 131, no. 2 (2013): 319–327.

Johnson, Susan R. 'A Developmental Approach Looking at the Relationship of Children's Foundational Neurological Pathways to Their Higher Capacities for Learning'. 7 May 2007.

Johnson, Wesley. 'Children, Some Age Five, Commit Thousands of Child Sex Offenses'. *Telegraph*. 4 March 2013.

Jones, Colin. *Paris: A History*. New York: Penguin Books, 2004.

Jones, Nicholas R.V., Annalijn I. Conklin, Marc Suhrcke and Pablo Monsivais. 'The Growing Price Gap between More and Less Healthy Foods: Analysis of a Novel Longitudinal UK Dataset'. *PloS one* 9, no. 10 (2014): e109343.

Kahneman, Daniel and Amos Tversky. 'Choices, Values, and Frames' *American Psychologist* 39, no. 4 (1984): 341.

Kalinauskas, Nadine. 'St. Lawrence Market in Toronto Named World's Best Food Market by National Geographic'. *Shine On*, 5 April 2012. https://ca.shine.yahoo.com/blogs/shine-on/st-lawrence-market-toronto-named-world-best-food-145127435.html.

Kalson, Sally. 'Sexting...and Other Stupid Teen Tricks'. *Pittsburgh Post-Gazette*, 29 March 2009.

Kang, Yewon. 'Poll Shows Half of Korean Teenagers Have Suicidal Thoughts.' *Wall Street Journal*, 20 March 2014.

Karabell, Zachary. *The Leading Indicators: A Short History of the Number That Rule Our World*. New York: Simon & Schuster, 2014.

Keizer, Kees, Siegwart Lindenberg and Linda Steg. 'The Spreading of Disorder'. *Science* 322, no. 5908 (2008): 1681–1685.

Kennedy, Jack, Tim Moore and Annabel Fiddes. *Living Wage Research for KPMG: Structural Analysis of Hourly Wages and Current Trends in Household Finances, 2014 Report*. Henley on Thames, England: Markit, 2014.

Kennedy, Robert F. 'Speech at the University of Kansas'. Speech, University of Kansas, Lawrence, KS, 18 March 1968.

Khazan, Olga. 'The Luxury of Waiting for Marriage to Have Kids'. *The Atlantic*, 17 June 2014.

Khimm, Suzy. 'How Paying No Federal Income Tax Helps the Poor Get Off Welfare and Into Work'. *Washington Post*, 18 September 2012.

King, Anthony and Ivor Crewe. *The Blunders of Our Governments*. London: Oneworld Publications, 2013.

'KitKat Collection: 4 Finger Milk Nutritional Information'. *Société des Produits Nestlé S.A*, 2015. http://www.kitkat.co.uk/content/kitkatcollection/FourFinger.

Klein, Ezra. 'Big Food: Michael Pollan Thinks Wall Street Has Way Too Much Influence Over What We Eat'. *Vox*, 23 April 2014.

Kleiner, Morris. *Reforming Occupational Licensing Practices*. Washington, DC: Brookings Institute: Hamilton Project, 2015.

Koepp, Matthias J., Roger N. Gunn, Andrew D. Lawrence, Vincent J. Cunningham, Alain Dagher, Tasmin Jones, David J. Brooks, C. J. Bench and P. M. Grasby. 'Evidence for Striatal Dopamine Release During a Video Game'. *Nature* 393, no. 6682 (1998): 266–268.

Konnikova, Maria. 'No Money, No Time'. *New York Times*, 15 June 2014.

Koo, Se-Woong. 'An Assault Upon Our Children', *New York Times*, 3 August 2014.

Kramer, Miriam. 'Elon Musk: Artificial Intelligence Is Humanity's Biggest Existential Threat'. *Live Science*, 27 October 2014.

Kristof, Nick. 'Is That Sausage Worth This?,' *New York Times*, 20 February 2014.

—-. 'Oklahoma! Where the Kids Learn Early'. *New York Times*. 10 November 2013.

— . 'The Way to Beat Poverty'. *New York Times*, 12 September 2014.

Krueger, Alan B, Judd Cramer, and David Cho. 'Are the Long-Term Unemployed on the Margins of the Labor Market?'. *Brookings Papers on Economic Activity* (2014): 229–280.

Kruus, Priit, Peeter Ross, Riina Hallik, Reelika Ermel and Ain Aaviksoo. 'Wider Implementation of Telemedicine in Estonia' (English Summary of the Study's Results). Tallinn, Estonia: Praxis / Center for Policy Studies, 2014.

Kuyken, Willem, Katherine Weare, Obioha C. Ukoumunne, Rachael Vicary, Nicola Motton, Richard Burnett, Chris Cullen, Sarah Hennelly and Felicia Huppert. 'Effectiveness of the Mindfulness in Schools Programme: Non-Randomised Controlled Feasibility Study'. *The British Journal of Psychiatry* 203, no. 2 (2013): 126–131.

Lake, Marilyn. 'Minimum Wage Is More Than a Safety Net, It's a Symbol of Australian Values'. *The Age* (Melbourne, Australia), 10 April 2014.

Larsson, Stefan. 'What Doctors Can Learn from Each Other'. Presentation at TED@BCG Singapore, Singapore, October 2013.

Lawrence, Felicity, Andrew Wasley and Radu Ciorniciuc. 'Revealed: The Dirty Secret of the UK's Poultry Industry'. *Guardian*, 23 July 2014.

Lawton, Kayte and Matthew Pennycook. *Beyond the Bottom Line:*

The Challenges and Opportunities of a Living Wage. London: IPPR and Resolution Foundation, 2013.

Lazonick, William. 'Profits Without Prosperity'. *Harvard Business Review*, September 2014.

Leadbeater, Charles and Jake Garber. *Dying for Change*. London: Demos, 2010.

'Lean In Collection'. *Getty Images*. http://www.gettyimages.com/creative/frontdoor/leanin.

LeBlanc, Dave. '35 Years On, St. Lawrence is a Template for Urban Housing'. *Globe and Mail* (Canada), 6 February 2013.

Lenger, Friedrich. *European Cities in the Modern Era, 1850–1914*. Translated by Joel Golb. Leiden, Netherlands: Koninklijke Brill NV, 2012.

Leicester City Council. 'Council Meat Tests Highlight Labelling Concerns'. 3 November 2014. http://news.leicester.gov.uk/newsArchiveDetail.aspx?Id=f2792.

Lessig, Lawrence. 'We the People, and the Republic We Must Reclaim'. Presentation, TED 2013, Long Beach, CA, February 2013.

Liebenwein, Sylva, Heiner Barz, and Dirk Randoll. 'Zusammenfassung zentraler Befunde: Waldorfschule aus Schülersicht' (in German). In *Bildungserfahrungen an Waldorfschulen*. Edited by Sylva Liebenwein, Heiner Barz and Dirk Randoll, 5–12. Wiesbaden, Germany: VS Verlag für Sozialwissenschaften, 2012.

Lim Miller, Mauricio. 'When Helping Doesn't Help'. *Huffington Post*, 7 May 2012..

Liiten, Marjukka. 'Top Favorite: Teaching Profession' (in Finnish). *Helsingin Sanomat*, 11 February 2004. Cited in Sahlberg, Pasi. *Finnish Lessons: What Can the World Learn from Educational Change in Finland?*. New York: Teachers College Press, 2010.

Light, John. 'Frequently Asked Questions About ALEC'. *Moyers & Company*, 28 September 2012. http://billmoyers.com/content/frequently-asked-questions-about-alec/.

Lipton, Eric and Ben Protess. 'Banks' Lobbyists Help in Drafting Financial Bills'. *New York Times*, 24 May 2013.

'Living Wage Employers'. *Living Wage Foundation*. March 2015. http://www.livingwage.org.uk/employers.

The Local Goverment Boundary Commission for England. *Counties Pivot Data*. 2014. https://www.lgbce.org.uk/__data/assets/excel_doc/0006/22839/NEW-Copy-of-Counties-Pivot-Table-2014.xlsx.

'Local Elections'. *France in the United States, Embassy of France in the United States*. 20 December 2013. http://www.ambafrance-us.org/spip.php?article518.

Locke, Susannah F. 'Robots That Eat Bugs and Plants for Power'. *Popular Science*, 9 October 2009.

Lorber, Janie. 'Former IRS Official Demands Investigation of ALEC'. *Roll Call*, 1 July 2012.

Louy, Richard. *Last Child in the Woods: Saving Our Children From Nature-Deficit Disorder*. Chapel Hill, NC: Algonquin Books, 2005.

Lowe, Simon. 'Plotting A New Course to Improved Governance' in *Corporate Governance Review 2014*. Grant Thornton UK LLP, 2014.

MacInnes, Tom, Hannah Aldridge, Sabrina Bushe, Peter Kenway and Adam Tinson. *Monitoring Poverty and Social Exclusion, 2013*. York, England: Joseph Rowntree Foundation, 2013.

Mafi, John N., Ellen P. McCarthy, Roger B. Davis and Bruce E. Landon. 'Worsening Trends in the Management and Treatment of Back Pain', *JAMA Internal Medicine* 173, no. 17 (2013): 1573–1581.

Manchin, Stephen. *Real Wages and Living Standards*. London: London School of Economics and Political Science Centre for Economic Performance, 2015. http://cep.lse.ac.uk/pubs/download/EA024.pdf.

Manjoo, Farhad. 'Amazon Not As Unstoppable as It Might Appear'. *New York Times*, 18 December 2014.

Manning, Alan. 'The UK's National Minimum Wage'. *CentrePiece*, Autumn 2009.

Marris, Emma. 'Let Kids Run Wild in the Woods'. *Slate*, 25 May 2014.

Massad, Timothy G . 'Overall $182 Billion Committed to Stabilize AIG During the Financial Crisis Is Now Fully Recovered'. *Treasury Notes (U.S. Department of the Treasury)*, 11 September 2012. http://www.treasury.gov/connect/blog/Pages/aig-182–billion.aspx.

Masters, Jeffrey. 'Storm Surge Reduction by Wetlands'. *Weather Underground*. http://www.wunderground.com/hurricane/surge_wetlands.asp?MR=1.

Matouschek, Niko and Imran Rasul. 'The Economics of the Marriage Contract Theories and Evidence'. Journal of Law and Economics 51, no. 1 (2008): 59–110.

McCullough, Dennis. *My Mother, Your Mother: Embracing 'Slow Medicine", the Compassionate Approach to Caring for Your Aging Loved Ones*. New York: Harper, 2008.

McKenna, Maryn. 'How Your Chicken Dinner Is Creating a Drug-Resistant Superbug'. *The Atlantic*, 11 July 2012.

McVeigh, Tracy McVeigh. 'Scandal of NHS "Death Factories"'. *Observer*, 11 August 2002.

'Measure for Measure'. *The Economist*, 30 November 2013.

'Measuring the Daily Destruction of the World's Rainforests', *Scientific American*, 19 November 2009.

Mele, Nicco. *The End of Big: How the Internet Makes David the New Goliath.* New York: St. Martin's Press, 2013.

Meyerson, Harold. 'How Workers Lost the Power Struggle – and Their Pay Raises'. *Washington Post*, 8 October 2014.

'Michigan Becomes 5th US State to Thwart Direct Tesla Car Sales'. *Reuters*, 22 October 2014.

Miller, Claire Cain. 'Study Finds More Reasons to Get and Stay Married'. *New York Times*, 8 January 2015.

Miller, Dana D. and Stefano Mariani. 'Smoke, Mirrors, and Mislabeled Cod: Poor Transparency in the European Seafood Industry'. *Frontiers in Ecology and the Environment* 8, no. 10 (2010): 517–521.

Mirani, Leo. 'The Secret to the Uber Economy: Wealth Inequality'. *Quartz*, 16 December 2014.

Monaghan, Angela. 'UK Housebuilders Counter Ed Miliband's Land-Hoarding Claim'. *Guardian*, 16 December 2013.

Monastersky, Richard. 'Life: A Status Report'. *Nature* 516 (11 December 2014): 159–161.

Monk, Ed. 'The Ultimate DIY Investment'. This Is M*oney.co.uk*, 8 November 2013. http://www.thisismoney.co.uk/money/mortgageshome/article-2491020/The-ultimate-DIY-investment-Novices-urged-self-build-solve-housing-shortage--make-30-cent-profit-bargain.html.

Morozov, Evgeny. *To Save Everything, Click Here: The Folly of Technological Solutionism.* New York: Public Affairs, 2013.

Morrison, Todd G., Shannon R. Ellis, Melanie A. Morrison, Anomi Bearden and Rebecca L. Harriman. 'Exposure to Sexually Explicit Material and Variations in Body Esteem, Genital Attitudes, and Sexual Esteem Among a Sample of Canadian Men'. *The Journal of Men's Studies* 14, No. 2 (Spring 2006): 209–222.

Moss, Michael. 'The Extraordinary Science of Addictive Junk Food'. *New York Times Magazine*, 24 February 2013.

Moyer, Virginia A. 'Vitamin, Mineral, and Multivitamin Supplements for the Primary Prevention of Cardiovascular Disease and Cancer: US Preventive Services Task Force Recommendation Statement', *Annals of Internal Medicine* 160, no. 8 (2014): 558–564.

Mufson, Steven and Tom Hamburger. 'Jamie Dion Himself Called to Urge Support for the Derivatives Rule in the Spending Bill'. *Washington Post*, 11 December 2014.

Mullainathan, Sendhil and Eldar Shafir. *Scarcity: Why Having Too Little Means So Much.* New York: Time Books, 2013.

'Müller Fruit Corner Strawberry'. *Müller Dairy.* 2012. http://www.mullerdairy.co.uk/nutrition-information/fruit-corner.

Mundy, Liza. 'Daddy Track: The Case for Paternity Leave'. *The Atlantic*, January/February 2014.

National Audit Office. *End of Life Care*. London: The Stationery Office, 2008.

Nelson, Fraser. 'Milburn: How I Can Help Gordon Brown', *Spectator*, 19 May 2007.

Neumark, David and William Wascher. 'Minimum Wages, the Earned Income Tax Credit, and Employment: Evidence from the Post-Welfare Reform Era'. *IZA Discussion Papers*, No. 26100, 2007.

Nicholls, Dana and Peggy Syvertson. 'Sensory Integration'. *New Horizons for Learning, Johns Hopkins School of Education*, 2012.

'No Quick Fix: Exposing the Depth of Britain's Drug and Alcohol Problem,' part of *Breakdown Britain II*. London: Centre for Social Justice, 2013.

Nuikkinen, Kaisa. 'Vision of the Helsinki City School Building Program: Healthy and Safe School Building'. Presentation at the American Institute for Architects' 'Schools in a Flat World' conference, Helsinki, Finland, 11 September 2008.

Nunan, Cólín and Richard Young. 'E.coli Superbugs on Farms and Food'. *The Use and Misuse of Antibiotics in UK Agriculture*, 6. Bristol, England: Soil Association, 2012.

Nutting, Rex. 'Transcript of Holder's Admission on Too-Big-To-Jail Banks'. *Market Watch*, 7 March 2013.

OECD. *Consumer Prices*. OECD, 30 March 2015. https://stats.oecd.org/index.aspx?queryid=221.

—. *Education At a Glance 2014: OECD Indicators*. OECD Publishing, 2014.

—. *OECD Income Distribution Database: Gini, Poverty, Income, Methods, and Concept*. OECD, 2014. http://www.oecd.org/social/income-distribution-database.htm.

—. *PISA 2012 Database Tables*. OECD, 2012. http://www.oecd.org/pisa/keyfindings/PISA-2012–results-snapshot-Volume-I-ENG.pdf

—. *Road Safety Annual Report 2014*. OECD Publishing, 2014.

Office for National Statistics. *Annual Survey of Hours and Earnings, 2014 Provisional Results*. 2014. http://www.ons.gov.uk/ons/rel/ashe/annual-survey-of-hours-and-earnings/2014–provisional-results/stb-ashe-statistical-bulletin-2014.html.

—. *Divorces in England and Wales, 2012: Number of Divorces, Age at Divorce and Marital Status Before Marriage, Table 3a*. Office of National Statistics, 2012. http://www.ons.gov.uk/ons/rel/vsob1/divorces-in-england-and-wales/2012/stb-divorces-2012.html.

—. Underemployed and Overemployed: – the UK, 2014. http://www.ons.gov.uk/ons/dcp171776_387087.pdf.

—. Labour Market Statistics, March 2015: Unemployment by Age and Duration. 2015. http://www.ons.gov.uk/ons/publications/

re-reference-tables.html?edition=icm%3A77-35368#tab-Unemployment-economic-inactivity-tables.

— . *Marriages in England and Wales (Provisional), 2012*. Office for National Statistics, 2014.

— . *UK National Population Projections – Principals and Variants, 2012–2087*. http://www.ons.gov.uk/ons/interactive/uk-national-population-projections---dvc3/index.html.

— . *2011 Census: Key Statistics for England and Wales, March 2011*. 2012. http://www.ons.gov.uk/ons/rel/census/2011–census/key-statistics-for-local-authorities-in-england-and-wales/stb-2011–census-key-statistics-for-england-and-wales.html#tab---Religion.

— . Trends in the United Kingdom Housing Market, 2014 (calculated from Table 6). London: Office for National Statistics, 2014. http://www.ons.gov.uk/ons/rel/hpi/house-price-index-guidance/trends-in-the-uk-housing-market-2014/housing-trends-article.html?format=print.

Ofcom. *Children and Parents: Media Use and Attitudes Report*. 2014.

Ofgem. *The Revenues, Costs and Profits of the Energy Companies in 2013*. 2013.

— . *Supply Market Indicator for January 2015*. 29 January 2015.

Olesund, Erik. 'How the Tractor Ruined Farming'. *Green Grid Radio*, 28 June 2014.

Oliver, John. *Last Week Tonight with John Oliver*. Television. HBO, 2014.

'One in Ten British Kids Own A Mobile Phone by the Age of Five'. *uSwtich*, August 2013. http://www.uswitch.com/mobiles/news/2013/08/one_in_ten_british_kids_own_mobile_phone_by_the_age_of_five/.

'Outdoor Knoxville'. *Legacy Parks Foundation*, 2014. http://www.outdoorknoxville.com/urban-wilderness.

Overby, Peter. 'Conservative Group's Charity Status Draws Questions'. *NPR*, 19 April 2012.

Panorama. Television. BBC, 2013.

Papadopoulos, Linda. 'Sexualisation of Young People Review.' (2010).

Parliament of the United Kingdom. *Agricultural Incomes and Subsidies* (2012 Data).

Paul, Annie Murphy. 'School of Hard Knocks: "How Children Succeed', by Paul Touch'. *New York Times Sunday Book Review*. 26 August 2012.

Peabody, Francis W. 'The Care of the Patient'. *Journal of the American Medical Association* 88 (1927): 876–82.

People Who Abuse Children (An NSPCC Research Briefing). NSPCC, 2014. http://www.nspcc.org.uk/globalassets/documents/information-service/research-briefing-people-who-abuse-children.pdf.

Perrin, Ellen C., Benjamin S. Siegel, James G. Pawelski, Mary I. Dobbins, Arthur Levin, Gerri Mattson, John Pascoe and Michael

Yogman, 'Promoting the Well-Being of Children Whose Parents Are Gay or Lesbian', *Pediatrics 131*, no. 4 (2013); e1374-31383.

'Philip Lymbery: Chief Executive'. *Compassion in World Farming*, 2014. http://www.ciwf.org.uk/about-us/our-staff/philip-lymbery/.

'Physical Activity Guidelines for Children and Young People'. *NHS Choices*. http://www.nhs.uk/Livewell/fitness/Pages/physical-activity-guidelines-for-young-people.aspx.

Pilgrim, Tanya. 'The End of the Supermarket Sweep?'. *Pennington Manches*, 8 October 2012. http://www.penningtons.co.uk/news-publications/archive-news/2012/the-end-of-the-supermarket-sweep/.

Pinkney, David. *Napoleon III and the Rebuilding of Paris*. Princeton, NJ: Princeton University Press, 1972.

'PISA Interactive Data Selection – Variable ST42Q03 ("Math Anxiety – Get Very Tense")'. *OECD*, 2012. http://pisa2012.acer.edu.au/interactive.php.

Pollack, Keshia M., Dan Morhaim and Michael A. Williams. 'The Public's Perspectives on Advance Directives in Maryland: Implications for State Legislative and Regulatory Policy'. *Health Policy* 96, no. 1 (2010): 57–63.

Pollan, Michael. *In Defense of Food: An Eater's Manifesto*. New York: Penguin Press, 2008.

Porter, Eduardo. 'A Relentless Widening of Disparity in Wealth'. *New York Times*, 12 March 2014.

Portman, Rob. 'Gay Couples Also Deserve Chance to Get Married'. *Columbus Dispatch*, 15 March 2013.

'Poultry Processors and Retailers Respond to the Campylobacter Claims'. *Guardian*. 23 July 2014.

'Power of Place'. *Steelcase 360º*, No. 68 (2014).

'Press Release'. *Resolution Foundation*, 1 October 2014. http://www.resolutionfoundation.org/media/press-releases/a-record-1–2–million-workers-to-benefit-from-first-real-terms-minimum-wage-rise-for-six-years-today/.

'Preterm Birth (Fact Sheet 363)'. *World Health Organization*, November 2014. http://www.who.int/mediacentre/factsheets/fs363/en/

Price, Catherine. 'Vitamins Hide the Low Quality of Our Food'. *New York Times*, 15 February 2015.

Priorities USA Action. 'Stage'. *YouTube* video, 1:02. 23 June 2012. https://www.youtube.com/watch?v=oLo0Jwj03JU.

Purvis, Andrew. 'Running on Empty Carbs'. *Guardian*, 22 March 2009.

Ramesh, Randeep. 'Give Each NHS Hospital Patient A Single Consultant, Says Jeremy Hunt'. *Guardian*, 23 January 2014.

Randle, Henry W. 'Suntanning: Differences in Perceptions Throughout History'. In Mayo Clinic Proceedings 72, no. 5 (1997): 461–466.

Rankin, Jennifer. 'Fewer Women Leading FTSE Firms Than Men Called John'. *Guardian*. 6 March 2015.

Rayner, Jay. 'Booths: The Honest Supermarket'. *Observer*, 13 November 2011.

Reconnecting Children with Nature: Findings of the Natural Childhood Inquiry. The National Trust, 2012.

'Red Dress Boutique'. *SharkTank Blog*. http://sharktankblog.com/business/red-dress-boutique/.

Redlawsk, David P., Caroline J. Tolbert and Todd Donovan. *Why Iowa?: How Caucuses and Sequential Elections Improve the Presidential Nominating Process*. Chicago: University of Chicago Press, 2011.

Reeves, Richard. 'Bringing Up Baby'. *New Statesman*, 29 January 2009.

Reguly, Eric. 'Time to Put An End to the Cult of Shareholder Value'. *Globe and Mail* (Toronto, Canada). 26 September 2013.

Reilly, Brendan M. 'Physical Examination in the Care of Medical Inpatients: An Observational Study', *Lancet* 362, no. 9390 (2003): 1,103.

'Rep. Kevin Yoder: Top 20 Industries Contributing to Campaign Committee'. *OpenSecrets.org*, 2 February 2015. https://www.opensecrets.org/politicians/industries.php?cycle=2014&cid=N00031502&type=I&newmem=N.

Research, Development and Statistics Directorate. *Reducing Homicide: A Review of the Possibilities*. By Fiona Brookman and Mike Maguire. London: Home Office, 2003.

Reuters. 'A.I.G. Pays Its Ex-Chief $47 Million'. *New York Times*, 2 July 2008.

Ridley, Matt. *The Rational Optimist: How Prosperity Evolves*. New York: Harper Perennial, 2010.

—— . 'When Ideas Have Sex'. Presentation at TEDGlobal 2010, Oxford, England, July 2010.

Rifkin, Jeremy. *The Empathetic Civilization: The Race to Global Consciousness in a World in Crisis*. New York: Jeremy P Tarcher / Penguin, 2009.

'Robert Rubin'. *Council on Foreign Relations*. http://www.cfr.org/staff/b292.

Robert-Hughes, Rebecca. *The Case for Space: The Size of England's New Homes*. Edited by Will Fox and Anna Scott-Marshall. Royal Institute of British Architects, 2011.

Robinson, David. *Out of the Ordinary: Learning from the Community Links Approach to Social Regeneration*. London: Community Links, 2010.

Rogers, Richards. Forward to Jan Gehl, *Cities for People*. Washington, DC: Island Press, 2010.

Rogowsky, Mark. 'After the New Jersey Ban, Here's Where Tesla Can (And Cannot) Sell Its Cars'. *Forbes*, 15 March 2014

Romito, Patricia and Lucia Beltramini. 'Watching Pornography: Gender Differences, Violence and Victimization: An Exploratory Study in Italy'. *Violence Against Women* (2011): 1077801211424555.

Rosin, Hanna. 'Hey! Parents, Leave Those Kids Alone'. *The Atlantic*, April 2014.

— . 'Why Kids Sext'. *The Atlantic*, November 2014.

Rothstein, Jesse. 'The Unintended Consequences of Encouraging Work: Tax Incidence and the EITC'. *Center for Economic Policy Studies*. Princeton, NJ: Princeton University, 2008.

Russell, Jenni. 'Let's Put Character Above Exam Results'. *The Sunday Times*, 5 June 2011.

Rush, Emma and Andrea La Nauze. *Corporate Paedophilia: Sexualisation of Children in Australia*. Australia Institute, 2006.

Ryan, Richard M. and Edward L. Deci. 'Self-Determination Theory and the Facilitation of Intrinsic Motivation, Social Development, and Well-Being'. *American Psychologist* 55, no. 1 (2000): 68.

Sacks, Jonathan. 'The Dignity of Difference: Avoiding the Clash of Civilizations'. *Foreign Policy Research Institute*, July 2002.

Sagi, Abraham and Martin L Hoffman. 'Empathic Distress in the Newborn'. *Developmental Psychology* 12, no. 2 (1976): 175.

Sahlberg, Pasi. *Finnish Lessons: What Can the World Learn from Educational Change in Finland?*. New York: Teachers College Press, 2010.

Said, Carolyn. 'Peers Helps Uber, Lyft Drivers Get Back On Road After Accidents'. *San Francisco Chronicle*, 4 December 2014.

Salazar, Angela. 'BeGood Clothing's New Line – Organic Cotton and Silk Basics'. *SF Gate*, 12 September 2014.

Salam, Reihan. 'The Upper Middle Class is Ruining America'. *Slate*, 30 January 2015.

Sanders, Michael and Elspeth Kirkman. *I've Booked You a Place. Good Luck: A Field Experiment Applying Behavioural Science to Improve Attendance at High-Impact Recruitment Events*. No. 13/334 Bristol, England: Department of Economics, University of Bristol, 2014.

Sandseter, Ellen B. H. 'Children's Risky Play from an Evolutionary Perspective: The Anti-Phobic Effects of Thrilling Experiences'. *Evolutionary Psychology* 9, no. 2 (2001): 257–84.

Schuck, Peter. *Why Government Fails So Often: And How It Can Do Better*. Princeton, NJ: Princeton Univeristy Press, 2014.

Schumacher, E. F. *Small Is Beautiful: A Study of People As If People Mattered*. New York: Harper Perennial, 2010.

Schroeder, Peter and Kevin Cirilli. 'Warren, Left Fume Over Deal'. *The Hill*, 10 December 2014.

Schwarz, Alan. 'Attention Disorder or Not, Pills to Help in School', *New York Times*, 9 October 2012.

'Seafood Fraud'. *Oceana*. http://oceana.org/sites/default/files/euo/OCEANA_fish_label_english.pdf.

'Sebago Lake'. *Portland Water District*. http://www.pwd.org/environment/sebago/sebago.php.

Seldon, Anthony. *An End to Factory Schools: An Education Manifesto 2010–2020*. Surrey, England: Centre for Policy Studies, 2010.

Service, Owain, Michael Hallsworth, David Halpern, et al. *EAST: Four Simple Ways to Apply Behavioural Insights*. London: The Behavioural Insights Team, 2014.

Seymour, Philip H. K., Mikko Aro, and Jane M. Erskine. 'Foundation Literacy Acquisition in European Orthographies'. *British Journal of Psychology* 94, no. 2 (2003): 143–174.

'She, Robot: A Conversation with Helen Greiner'. *Foreign Affairs* 94, No. 1 (Jan/Feb 2015): 16–22.

Shenk, Joshua Wolf. *Powers of Two: How Relationships Drive Creativity*. Boston, MA: Eamon Dolan, 2014.

Shoda, Yuichi. 'Individual Differences in Social Psychology: Understanding Situations to Understand People, Understanding People to Understand Situations'. In *The Sage Handbook of Methods in Social Psychology*. Edited by Carol Sansone, Carolyn C. Morf and Abigail T. Panter, 119–121. Thousand Oaks, CA: Sage Publications, 2004.

Singleton, Alex. 'Obituary: Sir John Cowperthwaite'. *Guardian*, 8 February 2006.

'Sir James Crosby Resigns from FSA'. *BBC News*, 11 February 2009.

'Sir Jeremy Heywood, Cabinet Secretary and Head of the Civil Service: Biography'. *British Goverment*. https://www.gov.uk/government/people/jeremy-heywood.

Skenazy, Lenore. 'Free Range Kids: FAQ'. *Free Range Kids*. https://freerangekids.wordpress.com/faq/.

Slaughter, Anne-Marie. 'Why Women Still Can't Have It All'. *The Atlantic*, 13 June 2012.

Snowdon, Christopher. *Who's Killing the British Pub? Institute for Economic Affairs*. London: The Institute for Economic Affairs, 2014.

'Soil Association 2014 Organic Market Report Reveals Growth in Organic Sales for the First Time in Four Years'. *Soil Association*, 13 March 2014. http://www.soilassociation.org/news/newsstory/articleid/6650/soil-association-2014–organic-market-report-reveals-growth-in-organic-sales-for-the-first-time-in-fo.

'Soil: Protect European Soil From Environmental Damage'. *European Environmental Bureau*, 2015. http://www.eeb.org/index.cfm/activities/biodiversity-nature/soil/.

'Spare5 – Preview Addition'. *CNET*. http://download.cnet.com/Spare5–Preview-Edition/3000–31709_4–76156057.html.

'Stafford Hospital: Q&A'. *BBC News*, 25 March 2013.

'Stafford Hospital: The Victims of the Hospital Scandal'. *BBC News*, 6 February 2013.

Statistics Netherlands. *Traffic Deaths Down Again*. 18 April 2011. http://www.cbs.nl/en-GB/menu/themas/gezondheid-welzijn/publicaties/artikelen/archief/2011/2011–029–pb.htm

Steadman, Ian. 'Dutch City Gives Residents a Self-Build Affordable Housing Catalogue'. *Wired*, 18 April 2013.

Steenhuysen, Julie. 'Overuse of Heartburn Drugs is Risky: Study'. *Reuters*, 10 May 2010.

Sternin, Jerry. 'The Viet Nam Story'. http://www.positivedeviance.org/about_pd/Monique%20VIET%20NAM%20CHAPTER%20Oct%2017.pdf.

Stevens, Heidi. 'Your 11–Year-Old Daughter Wants to Shave. Everywhere'. *Chicago Tribune*. 10 July 2012.

Stevens, Jane Ellen Stevens. 'The Adverse Childhood Experiences Study – The Largest, Most Important Public Health Study You Never Heard of Began in an Obesity Clinic'. *ACES Too High News*, 3 October 2012. http://acestoohigh.com/2012/10/03/the-adverse-childhood-experiences-study-the-largest-most-important-public-health-study-you-never-heard-of-began-in-an-obesity-clinic/.

Stewart, William. 'Is Pisa Fundamentally Flawed?'. *TES Connect*, 27 September 2014. https://www.tes.co.uk/article.aspx?storycode=6344672.

Stone, Brad. 'Costco CEO Craig Jelinek Leads the Cheapest, Happiest Company in the World'. *BloombergBusiness*, 6 June 2013.

Strife, Susan and Liam Downey. 'Childhood Development and Access to Nature: A New Direction for Environmental Research'. *Organ Environment* 22, no. 1 (March 2009): 99–122.

Stuhldreher, Anne and Rourke O'Brien. *The Family Independence Initiative: A New Approach to Help Families Exit Poverty*. Washington, DC: New America Foundation, 2011.

Suggate, Sebastian P., Elizabeth A. Schaughency and Elaine Reese. 'Children Learning to Read Later Catch Up to Children Reading Earlier', *Early Childhood Research Quarterly* 28, no. 1 (2013): 33–48.

'Survey of Self-Build Intentions.' *Ipsos-Mori*, 12 March 2013. https://www.ipsos-mori.com/researchpublications/researcharchive/3171/Survey-of-selfbuild-intentions.aspx.

Sweet, Victoria. *God's Hotel: A Doctor, a Pilgrimage, and a Journey to the Heart of Medicine*. New York: Penguin, 2013.

— . 'The Efficiency of Inefficiency'. Presentation at TEDxMiddlebury, Middlebury, VT, 9 March 2013.

Tait, Cameron. *Work That Pays: The Final Report of the Living Wage Commission*. London: Living Wage Commission, 2014.

Talberth, John, Erin Gray, Evan Branosky and Todd Gartner. *Insights from the Field: Forests for Water*. Washington, DC: Water Resources Institute, 2012.

Taleb, Nassim Nicholas. *Antifragile: Things That Gain From Disorder*. New York: Random House Trade Paperbacks, 2014.

— . *Black Swan: The Impact of the Highly Improbable Fragility*. New York: Random House, 2010.

Tandon, Pooja S., Chuan Zhou, Paula Lozano and Dimitri A. Christakis. 'Preschoolers' Total Daily Screen Time at Home and by Type of Child Care'. *The Journal of Pediatrics* 158, no. 2 (2011): 297–300.

ten Brink, Patrick, Daniela Russi, Andrew Farmer, Tomas Badura, David Coates, Johannes Förster, Ritesh Kumar and Nick Davidson. *The Economics of Ecosystems and Biodiversity for Water and Wetlands: Executive Summary*. Institute for European Environmental Policy & Ramsar Secretariat, 2013.

'Tesco's Travails: Supermarket Sweep'. *The Economist*, 21 April 2012.

Thaler, Richard H. and Cass R. Sunstein. *Nudge: Improving Decisions About Health, Wealth, and Happiness: Revised and Expanded Edition*. New York: Penguin Books, 2009.

— , and Shlomo Benartzi. *The Behavioral Economics of Retirement Savings Behavior*. Washington DC: AARP Public Policy Institute, 2007.

Theodore Roosevelt'. In 'The National Parks: America's Best Idea'. *PBS*, 2009. http://www.pbs.org/nationalparks/people/historical/roosevelt/.

Timmins, Nicholas. 'NHS Electronic Records Are Two Years Late'. *Financial Times*, 29 May 2006.

'Touch Screens'. *Michael Cohen Group LLC*, 17 February 2014.

Tough, Paul. 'The Poverty Clinic'. *The New Yorker*, March 21, 2008.

Towards a Fine City for People. Copenhagen, Denmark: Gehl Architects, 2004. http://issuu.com/gehlarchitects/docs/issuu_270_london_pspl_2004/0.

Trasande, L., J. Blustein, M. Liu, E. Corwin, L. M. Cox and M. J. Blaser. 'Infant Antibiotic Exposures and Early-Life Body Mass', *International Journal of Obesity* 37, no. 1 (2013): 16–23.

'Troubled Families'. *Local Government Association*, 29 January 2015. http://www.local.gov.uk/community-budgets/-/journal_content/56/10180/3691966/ARTICLE.

Turkle, Sherry. *Alone Together: Why We Expect More from Technology and Less From Each Other*. New York: Basic Books, 2011.

— . 'Authenticity in the Age of Digital Companions'. *Interaction Studies* 8, no. 3 (2007): 501–517.

— . 'Connected, But Alone?. Presentation at TED. April 2012.

Turner, Beverley. 'Pubic Hair Is Back Ladies. The Men Don't Care and the Women Can't Be Bothered'. *Telegraph*, 15 November 2013.

Twenge, Jean M., Keith W. Campbell and Craig A. Foster. 'Parenthood and Marital Satisfaction: A Meta-Analytic Review'. *Journal of Marriage and the Family* 65, (2003), 574–583.

Twentyman, Jessica. 'Tesco CIO Sharpens Focus on the Digital Customer Experience'. *I-CIO*, October 2013. http://www.i-cio.com/strategy/big-data/item/tesco-cio-sharpens-focus-on-the-digital-customer-experience.

Ueda, Kenichi and Beatrice Weder di Mauro. 'Quantifying Structural Subsidy Values for Systemically Important Financial Institutions'. *Journal of Banking & Finance* 37, no. 10 (2013): 3830–3842

Ulrich, Roger S., et al. 'Stress Recovery During Exposure to Natural and Urban Environments'. *Journal of Environmental Psychology* 11, No. 3 (1991): 201–230.

—— . 'View Through a Window May Influence Recovery Surgery'. *Science*, New Series 224, no. 4647 (27 April 1984): 420–421.

UNICEF. 'Child Poverty in Perspective: An Overview of Child Well-Being in Rich Countries'. *Innocenti Report Card* 7. Florence, Italy: UNICEF Innocenti Research Centre, 2007.

United Nations. Department of Economic and Social Affairs. Population Division. *World Urbanization Prospects: The 2014 Revision, Highlights*. (ST/ESA/SER.A/352).

Unterman, Rebecca. *Headed to College: The Effects of New York City's Small High Schools of Choice on Postsecondary Enrollment*. New York: MDRC, 2014.

The Use of Medicines in the United States: Review of 2011. Parsippany, NJ: IMS Institute for Healthcare Informatics, 2011.

Vangelova, Luba. 'How the English Language Is Holding Kids Back'. *The Atlantic*, 9 February 2015.

Verdine, Brian N., Roberta M. Golinkoff, Kathryn Hirsh Pasek, Nora S. Newcombe, Andrew T. Filipowicz and Alicia Chang. 'Deconstructing Building Blocks: Preschoolers' Spatial Assembly Performance Relates to Early Mathematical Skills'. *Child Development* 85, no. 3 (2014): 1062–1076.

Verghese, Abraham. 'A Doctor's Touch'. Presentation at TEDGlobal 2011: The Stuff of Life, Edinburgh, Scotland, September 2011.

'Vision Zero Initiative: Traffic Safety by Sweden'. *Swedish Government* and *Business Sweden*. http://www.visionzeroinitiative.com/en/.

von Grebmer, Klaus, Amy Saltzman, Ekin Birol, Doris Weismann, et. al. *Global Hunger Index: The Challenge of Hidden Hunger, Synopsis*. Bonn, Germany, Washington, DC, Dublin, Ireland: International Food Policy Research Institute, October 2014.

Wainwright, Oliver. 'Right to Build: Nick Boles Tells Councils to Offer Land for Self-Builds "Or Be Sued"'. *Guardian*, 7 May 2014.

Walker, Tim. 'How Finland Keeps Kids Focused Through Free Play'. *The Atlantic*, 30 June 2014.

Walton, Alice G. 'Steve Jobs' Cancer Treatment Regrets'. *Forbes*, 24 October 2011.

Warner, Kimberley, Walker Timme, Beth Lowell and Michael Hirshfield. 'Oceana Study Reveals Seafood Fraud Nationwide'. *Oceana*, 2013.

Warnock, Mary. *A Question of Life: The Warnock Report on Human Fertilisation and Embryology*. London: Her Majesty's Stationery Office, 1984.

Warren, Elizabeth. *Forum*. By Michael Krasny. *Forum*, 88.5 KQED FM, 7 May 2014.

Watson, Peter. *Ideas: A History of Thought and Invention, From Fire to Freud*. New York: Harper Perennial, 2005.

Watson Robert, Steve Albon, et al. *UK National Ecosystem Assessment: Synthesis of the Key Findings*. Cambridge, England: UNEP-WCMC, 2011.

'Welfare Issues for Meat Chickens'. *Compassion in World Farming*, 2014. http://www.ciwf.org.uk/farm-animals/chickens/meat-chickens/welfare-issues/.

Westervelt, Amy. 'Can't Picture a World Devastated By Climate Change? These Games Will Do It for You'. *Smithsonian.com*, 21 July 2014.

Whalen, Jeanne. 'How Glaxo Marketed a Malady to Sell a Drug'. *Wall Street Journal*, 25 October 2006.

'What Have the Immigrants Ever Done for Us?'. *The Economist*, 8 November 2014.

'What Is the Living Wage?'. *BBC News* 2 November 2014.

'Who Are We?'. *Embrace*. 2015. http://embraceglobal.org/who-we-are/our-story/.

'Who Are the School Truants?'. *PSIA in Focus*, January 2014.

'Why Plants in the Office Make Us More Productive'. *ScienceDaily*, 1 September 2014.

'Why Sweden Has So Few Road Deaths'. *The Economist*, 26 February 2014. http://www.economist.com/blogs/economist-explains/2014/02/economist-explains-16.

'Why Waldorf Works: Frequently Asked Questions'. *Association of Waldorf Schools of North America*. http://www.whywaldorfworks.org/02_W_Education/faq_about.asp.

Wildman, Charlotte. 'The "Chicago of Great Britain": Growth and Urban Regeneration in Liverpool'. In *The History Boys: Lessons from Local Government's Past*. Edited by Simon Parker and Joe Manning, 29–38. London: New Local Government Network, 2013.

Wilson, Edward O. *Biophilia: The Human Bond With Other Species*. Cambridge, MA: Harvard University Press, 1984.

—— . 'My Wish: Build the Encyclopedia of Life'. Presentation at TED 2007, 2007.

Wintour, Patrick. 'Government "Is Starting to Help 120,000 Troubled Families"'. *Guardian*, 29 October 2014.

Woloshin, Steven and Lisa M. Schwartz. 'Giving Legs to Restless Legs: A Case Study of How the Media Helps Make People Sick', *PLoS Medicine* 3, no. 4 (2006): e170.

'Woman Dies After Farewell to Horse at Wigan Hospital', *BBC News*, 7 November 2014.

Woods, Lucy. 'Friday Focus: Solar's Future Fantasies'. *PV Tech*, 13 December 2013. http://www.pv-tech.org/friday_focus/friday_focus_solars_future_fantasies.

'Working Paper: Uprating the UK Living Wage in 2014'. *Centre for Research in Social Policy, Loughborough University*. 2014.

Wuttke, Joachim. 'Uncertainty and Bias in PISA' In *Pisa According to Pisa: Does Pisa Keep What It Promise?*. Edited by Stefan Thomas Hopmann, Gertrude Brinek and Martin Retzl, 241–263. Vienna, Austria: Lit Verlag, 2007.

Yardley, Jim. 'Bangladesh Pollution, Told in Colors and Smells'. *New York Times*, 15 July 2013.

'Young People Sexual Relationships'. *IPPR*. http://www.ippr.org/assets/media/publications/attachments/youngpeoplesexrelationships.jpg.

World Bank. Long-Term Unemployment (% of Total Unemployment). 2015. http://data.worldbank.org/indicatorSL.UEM.LTRM.2S?order=wbapi-data-value-last&sort-asc.

'Zero to Eight: Children's Media Use in America 2013'. *Common Sense Media*, Fall 2013.

'6–inch Low Fat Subs: Nutritional Information'. *Subway*, http://www.subway.co.uk/assets/pdf/subway-nutritional-values-uk.pdf.

List of Interviews and Correspondence:

Bonbright, David. Interview by authors. Palo Alto, CA, 24 October 2014.

Casey, Louise. Interview by authors. 7 November 2014.

—— . Interview by authors. 28 November 2014.

Cavendish, Camilla. Interview by authors. 8 September 2014.

——. Interview by authors. London. 25 September 2014.

Crombie, David. Interview by authors. 17 September 2014.

Dorion, Christiane. Interview by authors. London. 26 September 2014.

Frenald, Anya. Interview by authors. 20 October 2014.

Harris, Nadine Burke. Interview by authors. San Francisco, CA, 6 October 2014.

Heller, Lucy. Interview by authors. 15 October 2014.

Helm, Dieter. Interview by authors. 21 November 2014.

Heywood, James. Interview by authors. 9 October 2014.

Hocker, Paul. Interview by authors. London. 26 September 2014.

Holden, Patrick. Interview by authors. Belvedere, CA. 3 October 2014.

Jacobson, Niclas. Interview by authors. 6 November 2014.

Jameson, Neil. Interview by authors. London. 25 September 2014.

Kelly, Mike. Interview by authors, London. 25 September 2014.

Lymbery, Philip. Email to authors. 29 March 2015.

Letwin, Oliver. Interview by authors. London. 26 September 2014.

Manzoni, Niccolo and Rosie Wardle. Interview by authors. 5 February 2015.

Mayfield, Charlie. Interview by authors. 22 October 2014.

Melchett, Peter. Interview by authors. 15 October 2014.

Oakeshott, Isabel. Email to authors. 14 March 2015.

Oberfest, Jason. Interview by authors. San Francisco, CA. 27 August 2014.

O'Shaughnessy, James. Interview by authors. 19 November 2014.

Parsa, Ali. Interview by authors. 28 October 2014.

Pittman, Jason. Interview by authors. Mountain View, CA. 5 November 5, 2014.

Ratti, Carlo. Interview by authors. 13 October 2014.

Ricks, Alan. Interview by authors. 8 October 2014.

Robinson, David. Interview by authors. London. 24 September 2014.

Rothe, Matt. Interview by authors. Stanford, CA. 24 October 2014.

Sandefer, Jeff. Email to authors. 3 September 2014

Schwegler, Ben. Interview by authors. 20 August 2014.

Seldon, Anthony. Interview by authors. 17 October 2014.

Silva, Rohan. Interview by authors. London. 17 September 2014.

Stein-Greenberg, Sarah. Interview by authors. 23 October 2014.

Stockton, Paul. Interview by authors. 1 October 2014.

Tamkivi, Sten. Interview by authors. Palo Alto, CA. 28 August 2014.

Tatham, Ken. Interview by authors. 16 December 2014.

Thomas, Jeff and Rachael. Interview by authors. 9 October 2014.

Thrun, Sebastian. Interview by authors. Mountain View, CA. 11 November 2014.

Vaarik, Daniel. Interview by authors. Menlo Park, CA. 2 December 2014.

Willis, Paul. Interview by authors. 12 November 2014.

INDEX